WOMEN'S WRITING IN CANADA

Spanning the period from the Massey Commission to the present and reflecting on the media of print, film, and song, this study attends to the burgeoning energy of women writers across genres and explores how their work interprets our national story. The questioning, disruptive feminist practice of their fiction, filmmaking, poetry, song-writing, drama, and non-fiction reveals the tensions of colonial society at the same time as it transforms cultural life in Canada.

Women's Writing in Canada pays tribute to foremothers who were active before and after the mid-century – Ethel Wilson, Gabrielle Roy, Gwen Pharis Ringwood, Dorothy Livesay, and P.K. Page – as well as such forgotten writers as Grace Irwin, Patricia Blondal, and Edna Jaques. Its breadth extends to the contemporary voices and influences of novelists Tracey Lindberg and Heather O'Neill, poets Marilyn Dumont and Leanne Betasamosake Simpson, playwrights Hannah Moscovitch and Anna Chatterton, and filmmakers Sarah Polley and Mina Shum. The rich and diverse works examined in this book illustrate the wide and impressive range of women's talents and the significant contributions they have made to Canadian culture.

PATRICIA DEMERS is a distinguished university professor in the Department of English and Film Studies at the University of Alberta.

WOMEN'S WRITING IN CANADA

Patricia Demers

UNIVERSITY OF TORONTO PRESS
Toronto Buffalo London

© University of Toronto Press 2019
Toronto Buffalo London
utorontopress.com

ISBN 978-0-8020-9339-4 (cloth)   ISBN 978-0-8020-9501-5 (paper)

Library and Archives Canada Cataloguing in Publication

Title: Women's writing in Canada / Patricia Demers.
Names: Demers, Patricia, 1946– author.
Description: Includes bibliographical references and index.
Identifiers: Canadiana 20190125977 | ISBN 9780802095015 (paper) | ISBN 9780802093394 (cloth)
Subjects: LCSH: Canadian literature – Women authors – History and criticism. | LCSH: Canadian literature – 20th century – History and criticism. | LCSH: Canadian literature – 21st century – History and criticism.
Classification: LCC PS8089.5.W6 D46 2019 | DDC C810.9/9287—dc23

This book has been published with the help of a grant from the Federation for the Humanities and Social Sciences, through the Awards to Scholarly Publications Program, using funds provided by the Social Sciences and Humanities Research Council of Canada.

University of Toronto Press acknowledges the financial assistance to its publishing program of the Canada Council for the Arts and the Ontario Arts Council, an agency of the Government of Ontario.

Contents

Preface ix

Acknowledgments xiii

Introduction: Imag(in)ing the National Terrain from the Mid-twentieth Century to the Sesquicentennial 3

    Approaching National Literature 4
    Women in the Linked Roles of Reading and Writing 7
    The Commissions: From Massey to Truth and Reconciliation 13
    From Total Refusal *and the Quiet Revolution to Cultural Accommodation* 20
    New Images of Movement and Diversity 27

1 Fiction 31

    Prospects at Mid-Century 32
    Wrestling with the Strictures of Marriage and Family 46
    Revolutionary Talents and Experiments 57
    Flowering Careers in the Sixties 62
    Trajectories of Celebrity: Munro and Atwood 65
    The Tangle of Domesticity and Independence 89
    Rhizomes of Sexuality, Nation, Race, and Ethnicity 98
    Extensions in 2017 115

2 Film   124

    Original Screenplays   125
    Adaptations of Women's Writing in Canada   131
    Documentaries   134

3 Poetry   138

    Jaques, Livesay, Waddington, and Page: "fired in the kiln of endurance"   139
    P.K. Page: Onlooker and Participant   146
    Wilkinson, Brewster, Avison, and Macpherson: "clearing the hurdles of sleep"   151
    MacEwen and Atwood: "the slow striptease of our concepts"   155
    Webb, Lowther, Marlatt, and Brossard: "the way any of us are tangled in the past"   158
    Tostevin, Brand, Halfe, and Dumont: "their fragile, fragile symmetries of gain and loss"   162
    Crozier, Moure, Zwicky, Carson, Michaels, Bolster, and Shraya: "the truth likes to hide / out in the open"   166
    Karen Solie: "poetic hipster"   172

4 Music   177

    Folk Singers Reclaiming Traditions   178
    Punk, Pop, and Country   181
    Adult Contemporary Styling   183

5 Drama   186

    Ringwood: Canadian Drama's Foremother   186
    Joudry, Henry, and Simons: Examining Emotions   190
    Pollock and Bolt: Re-viewing History and Power Politics   192
    Sharon Pollock: "meaning through the making of theatre"   194
    Ritter, Glass, Clark, and Lill: Enacting Vulnerabilities   200
    Thompson and MacDonald: Performing Marginalization and Shape Shifting   202
    Judith Thompson: "through the looking glass, darkly"   203
    Gale, Sears, Mojica, Cheechoo, Nolan, and Clements: Recording "Documemories"   209
    MacLeod, Moscovitch, and Chatterton: Exploring Impasses   215

6 Writing for Children   219

   Fiction about Children and Young Adults   220
   Other Times and Space of Fantasy   228
   Illustrated Narratives   231

7 Non-fiction   236

   Memoirists and Autobiographers   236
   Commentators on Our World   249
   Advisers and Observers   254

Conclusion   261

Timeline   265

Notes   275

Works Cited   281

Credits   319

Index   321

Preface

This project examines the major contributions of women writers in Canada to our cultural identity. It concentrates on the immensely productive sixty-seven-year period from the middle of the twentieth century to the present day, from the time of the Massey Commission to the explosion of global social media and the event of the sesquicentennial. Whether accessed in e-books or personal copies or collectors' first editions, the texts to be discussed affirm images of a changed and changing Canada.

It is a study addressed to readers interested in tracing the genealogy of the continuing tradition of women's writing in Canada during its most prolific, widely published, and acclaimed phase. With their work translated into many languages, these writers are recipients of prestigious honours and prizes. Aware of but not indebted to prior literature, they have set new and boldly subversive standards for exploring mental landscapes and creating unique inventories of the natural world. In every creative realm, they are acutely conscious of the subjectivity of our history as a nation and as distinct individuals. The genres of fiction, poetry, drama, and non-fiction are in the forefront for deliberate and practical reasons: breadth of content, availability in print and online formats, and the possibility of tracing idiosyncratic trajectories of development within genres and within individual careers. The freedom to pass beyond the production of a specific decade to follow the path of a writer's career is an invigorating element of this project. As well, the prospect of intermingling well-known and forgotten writers also makes the choice of these large and inherently multiform genres very appealing. Foremothers of the fifties, sixties, and seventies are too often neglected or eclipsed when we concentrate only on current work. Therefore, in an attempt to deal equitably with then and now, the examination of genres and the cultural topics they address underpin this study's consideration of the range of women writers' accomplishments in Canada.

The domain they share is the world of words, with all their nuances and emotional resonances, and their appearances in many textualities, from print and drawings to film and song. The texts are primarily in English with a few translations from French. While the coverage does not presume to be encyclopaedic or exhaustive, it strives to reflect the complexity and range of each genre. During the preparation of this book, dedicated research assistants over a few years have helped me to construct the website <canwwrfrom1950.org>, now migrated to the platform of the Canadian Writing Research Collaboratory (CWRC), founded and directed by Susan Brown. The bibliographical database for this project is searchable at cwrc.ca/canwwrfrom1950.

As an introduction for some readers and a revisitation for others, this study explores the ways in which women's writing continues to establish audiences for new forms of expression. It illustrates how critical studies enable and pursue a rethinking of the assumptions of Canadian literature. The introduction considers the social and imaginary elements of national space, in which the signposting narratives of commissions, reports, and legislation are interleaved with the counter-narratives of manifestos, inquiries, and confessions. It sets the scene for the consideration of specific genres.

The examination of fiction, organized around the concerns of decades and generations, looks back to the careers of women writers who were active and acknowledged in the pre-Massey era to weigh the influence of their work and, in some cases, its continuity. With the impetus of successive feminist waves, the strictures of marriage and family – so prevalent in the fiction of the fifties and early sixties – resulted in the explosive and often witty interrogation of patriarchal expectations of the next couple of decades in texts that unravel authority and work loose the constraints of power. Canada's changing demographics and the prominence of First Nations writers have created new networks for the understanding of sexuality, nationhood, race, and ethnicity. In fact, spirited interconnections of defence and support within communities of women writers remain a salient feature of this large corpus of work. Animating their own texts and adapting others, the art of women filmmakers, moreover, has enhanced and extended our capacity to be surprised by characters and follow their narrative development. Testifying to the amazing reverberation and prolongation of women's artistic excellence, the accounts of fiction, poetry, and drama pause periodically to note the extensive critical studies that the work of a writer has prompted.

With some notable and tragic exceptions, women poets have enjoyed long, productive careers. As well as helping to build and promote publishing outlets for their experimental writing, they have also written in other genres, particularly fiction and non-fiction. With moods ranging from a melancholic longing to reclaim what was lost to an ebullient proclamation of desire, their intuitive writing knits together several generations. Through removing veneers, exhuming histories, and weaving together disciplines and languages, poets continue to probe the expressive volatility of our passions. The addition of singer-songwriters enlarges the field of poetic emotions and attitudes.

Although fewer traditions for women playwrights existed before mid-century, their success in actualizing family, generational, and national histories, often tinged with a sardonic, tragic irony, has been remarkable. Appearing in the many specialty presses founded in this period, writers of fiction and poetry for children, exploring the slippery distances between fantasy and reality and welcoming young adults in their readership, have also flourished. Selections in non-fiction embrace the greatest degree of hybridity; including journalists, freelancers, politicians, novelists, historians, and urban theorists, they reflect the work of memoirists and autobiographers, social commentators, cookbook and comic-strip writers, and graphic novelists.

Rather than flattening or steamrolling through this metamorphosing literary terrain and its sociopolitical contexts, the project lingers over texts and comments on their varied features, complex materiality, and authoritative zest. These culturally formative documents mirror amazing images of ourselves.

Acknowledgments

This project emerges from real team work in which I feel privileged to have participated. I want to thank my colleague Gary Kelly for encouraging me initially to undertake the study. The journey from early modern England to contemporary Canada, where I've actually lived my life, has not been jarring but exhilarating and eventful. The students with whom I've discussed and planned portions of this work have fuelled the excitement, both in the seminar room and in the Digital Humanities Research Studio. It is a genuine delight to call the roll of the research assistants in humanities computing and literary studies who have helped to show me the way: Jocelyn Badley, Matt Bouchard, Ian Craig, Lindsay Doll, Amanda Daignault, Amy Dyrbye, Caitlin Elm, Carlos Fiorentino, Emily Hass, Calen Henry, Sarah Jefferies, Chloe Jones, Devorah Kobluk, Katie McConchie, Ashley Moroz, Claire Mulcahy, Khati Nagar, Jessica Ratcliffe, Scott Sharplin, Amy Stafford, Joyce Tam, and Wenjuan Xie. Working with students on their theses about women writers in Canada – Lindsay Doll on Anne Carson, Beth Gripping on Erin Moure, Katie McConchie on revised histories, Lidiane Cunha on Margaret Atwood, Jason Purcell on Anne Wilkinson and Elizabeth Smart, and Amy Stafford on Carol Shields – continues to lead to illuminating conversations. My Canadianist colleagues in English and Film Studies, in the Comparative Literature program, in Modern Languages and Cultural Studies, and at Campus Saint-Jean – particularly Bill Beard, Albert Braz, Marie Carrière, Cecily Devereux, Paul

Hjartarson, Sarah Krotz, Daniel Laforest, Julie Rak, Pamela Sing, Christine Stewart, Nora Stovel, Irene Sywenky, Christine Wiesenthal, and Janice Williamson – have generously dispensed information and example. Collaborating with Marie Carrière, director of the Canadian Literature Centre, on a conference dedicated to Canadian women writers enlarged the field of camaraderie and admiration. I have learned so much from the insightful studies and friendship of Carole Gerson, Sherrill Grace, Rosalind Kerr, Patricia Smart, and Christl Verduyn. Librarians throughout our system, especially at the Peel Special Collections Library, have been wonderfully accommodating; I thank Robert Desmarais, Jeff Papineau, and Linda Quirk. The assistance of Leah Brochu, Michael Brundin, Mihaela Ilovan, and Meredith Snyder has been critical in ingesting updates to the Women Writing and Reading in Canada site and migrating the contents to the Canadian Writing Research Collaboratory platform. At the University of Toronto Press, Mark Thompson has been supremely patient, and the constructive, generous comments of the anonymous reviewers have saved me from many gaffes. I am also grateful to the Social Sciences and Humanities Research Council of Canada for supporting this research, allowing me to study with research students and become acquainted with archives across the country.

WOMEN'S WRITING IN CANADA

Introduction: Imag(in)ing the National Terrain from the Mid-twentieth Century to the Sesquicentennial

Now the dark plunge of the year is done:
we make new prophecies
and stand, unhelmeted
facing remote certainties.
– Dorothy Livesay, "Prophet of the New World" (1945)

Perhaps the water was emerald, perhaps it was sapphire. It is both. It is neither. It is a brilliant river, blue-green with lacings of white foam and spray as the water hurls itself violently along in rapids against hidden or projecting rocks, a rapid, racing, calling river. The hills rise high and lost on each side of the banks ... Large and dark solitary pine trees give landmark and meaning.
– Ethel Wilson, *Hetty Dorval* (1947)

Notre pays est à l'âge des premiers jours du monde. La vie ici est à découvrir et à nommer; ce visage obscur que nous avons, ce cœur silencieux qui est le nôtre, tous ces paysages d'avant l'homme, qui attendent d'être habités et possédés par nous, et cette parole confuse qui s'ébauche dans la nuit, tout cela appelle le jour et la lumière.
– Anne Hébert, "Mystère de la Parole," *Poèmes* (1960)[1]

This study explores the changing cultural realities for women writers in Canada over more than six decades. Canadian by birth, location, or immigrant and refugee relocation, these authors write in the official national languages of English and French with a wide range of Native and first languages often inflecting their work. Such a large swath of territory – geographic, material, linguistic, demographic, theoretical, and gendered – calls for some preliminary explanations.

Approaching National Literature

Although the examples of this imaginative textuality I have chosen to include may not match every reader's favourites or expectations of representativeness, it is necessary at the outset to consider an understanding of national literature. When sesquicentennial popular histories, made-to-order documentaries, and glossy magazine inserts celebrate our transition from settler colony to nation state, an introspective and interrogatory attitude is a sobering counterpoint. Especially as nationalism, aligned with patriotism, is being moulded into a jingoistic reason to close doors, bar entry, and embolden racist arguments, the breadth of a national literature and the need to embrace its diverse bodies politic are necessary recognitions. Canada (derived from the Iroquoian for "land" or "village") is home to more than 600 First Nations. Within our diasporic reality, nation is not a monolithic concept. Justin D. Edwards's sketch of "Gothic Canada" notes how globalization pays "little attention to national borders" and concludes "that the nation no longer has a monopoly on conceptions of identity as tied to a particular place" (166). Paul Litt's study of the sixties zeitgeist, *Trudeaumania*, maintains that "nations are always aborning or coming of age because these [collective essences] are just metaphors for periodic identity tune-ups" (338).

Yet more transforming than tune-ups and global passageways are fundamental ideological shifts. The capaciousness and mutability of Nation as a concept are provocative. "We are sceptical, if not actively suspicious," Tony Judt observes, "of all-embracing political goals: The grand narratives of Nation and History and Progress that characterized the political families of the twentieth century seem discredited beyond recall" (11). Appeals to a single understanding of Nation carry their own set of blinkers. David

Damrosch's warning about "nativist public discourse [which] serve[s] as emblem and reinforcement of a unitary racial and cultural heritage" (122) is a caution worth keeping in mind. The global reality in which we participate involves "the disappearance of boundaries – cultural and economic boundaries, physical boundaries, linguistic boundaries – and the challenge of organizing our world in their absence" (Judt 407). The diversity and range of this survey, I trust, showcase a series of organizing perspectives – multivocal, contestatory, sociocultural, and interactive. In outlining a national literary ecology, Alexander Beecroft stresses the need to consider the variety and differing values of "environmental forces operating on that literature – the role that political, cultural, and educational institutions play in creating a demand for a literature to correspond to their own position, the economic forces that dictate the relative marketability of novels with explicitly Canadian themes, the desire of individual Canadians to read books about their nation" (19). Offering a useful definition, Beecroft sees a national literature as "one that reads and interprets texts through the lens of the nation-state, whether as that state's embodiment, as the dissent tolerated within its public sphere, as its legitimating precursors, or as its future aspirations" (197–8).

Adjusting their lens to fit different angles and subject positions, contemporary Canadian observers of the nation mirror the expansiveness Beecroft invokes. As they reflect on their experience of editing *Canadian Literature in English: Texts and Contexts*, Cynthia Sugars and Laura Moss highlight unlearning "what has been taken for granted as academic, social, and cultural inheritance" (170); with "renewed incredulity" (171), they debate the argument that "we are as post-racial as post-national" (187). Acknowledging the deep tensions and distortions of a colonial society, along with the ongoing legacy of colonialism, is a central theme. Len Findlay challenges the humanities to assume "a place in rebuilding the nation and its internationalism within and beyond its bodies politic" to include "the anti-Eurocentric Indigene, the Anglo-French colonizers, and participants in the immigrant-diaspora" (55). In surveying the place of Indigenous poetics in Canada, Neal McLeod attends to the "movement toward the edges" and imagines other possibilities for the "edgewalker" who punctures "holes in the expectations and understandings of contemporary life" (6). Daniel Heath Justice illustrates his argument in *Why Indigenous Literatures Matter* by moving beyond orthographic transcriptions, investigating the rich trove of syllabaries, and citing 366 Indigenous writers. As his commentary on the Truth and Reconciliation Commission procedures, David Garneau registers dissatisfaction with the "non-Indigenous narratives of healing and closure" (23) and its "public display of victims but not perpetrators" (24); arguing that "forced assimilation is the original sin that made Canada possible" (38), he promotes "perpetual conciliation [with] the potential to transform rather than contain" (24). Transformation is the salient impulse of Libe Garcia Zarranz's view of "the paradoxical nature of borders" in TransCanadian feminist fiction that "transform[s] normative conceptualizations of gender, time and space" (151). Since Kate Eichhorn and Heather Milne consider nation and gender "politically saturated concepts," their study of Canadian women's poetry and poetics not only "exists in tension with the nation" but "seeks to engage in the construction and interrogation of publics" (9, 12). Cheryl Suzack's examination of Indigenous women's writing focuses on another form of tension, "contrasting the privileged objectivity of law with the immediacy of personal experience" (53).

As for the concentration on women, Eichhorn and Milne explain that "Canadian women writers have always shaped the nation's literary avant-garde, often playing central roles in defining the contours of new movements and schools of new writing both as aesthetic innovators and cultural activists" (11). Numbers as well as accomplishments are on women's side. According to *A Statistical Profile of Artists and Cultural Workers in Canada*, released in 2014 and based on the 2011 National Household Survey and Labour Force Survey, women constitute over 51 per cent of artists in Canada (authors and writers, visual artists, musicians and singers, artisans and craftpersons, and dancers), with women authors and writers constituting 54 per cent.[2] Women writers produce and experiment in every conceivable medium and genre, from print to blogs, prose fiction to graphic novels, journals and diaries to film scripts, music scores and song lyrics, literary studies, and cookbooks. Connections between the writer and her audience or readership are a key element in this project, which intends to shine light on both the practical – in fact, commercial – link between writer and reader and the ways reading interprets and extends the life of texts. The growth of gigantic digital libraries today and access to them on hand-held devices or computer screens promise to usher in an abundance, perhaps a flood, of available texts and revisionary studies. As Dean Irvine and his co-editors argue in *Making Canada New*, new media and "globally articulated collaborative networks" (27) initiate new histories to call attention to omissions and distortions. Such "renovatory activity," Irvine remarks, invites and encourages overlapping, multiple positions as "historian, critic, bibliographer, archivist, librarian, and editor shift and shuffle" (5). This study aims to supply additional mapping devices and signposts.

Women in the Linked Roles of Reading and Writing

Because the project addresses readers, another preliminary explanation concerns the intricate bond shared by writing and reading. A writer's first and invaluable resource, reading is also one of the avenues through which social beings make sense of their own experience. "It comes as no surprise that reading matters to these writers – but it's good to be reminded that reading precedes writing" (R.M. Brown xi). Poet and novelist Anne Michaels admits, "I read to hold another human being close"; for crime writer Alison Gordon, "I am a writer because I was a reader first"; and for short-story writer, novelist, and playwright Mavis Gallant, "nobody has ever written who never read."[3] Poet, novelist, and essayist Nicole Brossard sees books as objects of desire and knowledge ("J'appartiens à une époque où les livres étaient des objets de désir et de connaissance"), while novelist, poet, and playwright Marie-Claire Blais views reading as a form of divine revelation, a sparkling light reflecting current, severe political and warring tensions ("Ce fut peut-être pour moi une sorte de révélation d'ordre divin. Il me semble encore ressentir l'éblouissement de la lecture envers et contre les tensions politiques et guerrières qui sévissaient à cette époque"). Poet and novelist Anne Hébert approached the reading of poetry, in particular, as an exercise in alertness and vulnerability, comparable to a child's learning of language ("le lecteur de poésie doit également demeurer attentif et démuni en face du poème, comme un tout petit enfant qui apprend sa langue maternelle"), and ultimately leading to a traveller's sudden discovery, after the blinding sun, of a forest glade ("tel un voyageur qui, après avoir marché longtemps sur des routes sèches, aveuglantes de soleil, tout à coup, entre en forêt").[4]

Since writers and readers live in interconnected worlds, reading selection and criteria help us to gauge the appeal and impact of women writers. However, sex differences in reading habits, as surveys confirm, continue to underestimate the work of women. Despite the international acclaim and awards of women's writing, men often avoid it, as Lisa Jardine and Annie Watkins of Queen Mary College, London, discovered, when they undertook research about reading practices to mark the tenth anniversary of the Orange Prize for Fiction (awarded annually to the best English-language novel written by a woman and won by Canadian writers Anne Michaels in 1997 and Carol Shields in 1998). Their report found that "fiction by women remains 'special interest,' while fiction by men still sets the standard for quality, narrative and style" (Smith 14).[5] As Jardine observed, "Men do not regard books as a constant companion to their life's journey, as consolers or guides, as women do. They read novels a bit like they read photography manuals" (Higgins 9). The readers' survey of undergraduate and graduate students, public library clients, and public sector employees conducted by my graduate research assistants corroborate the U.K. findings.[6] According to "The 2015 CWILA Count," the supportive network of Canadian Women in the Literary Arts, an inclusive organization committed to introducing relevant issues of gender, race, class, and sexuality into a national conversation and also tracking statistics of gender representation in book reviews, reports that women and men in that year published book reviews in nearly equal rates in Canadian publications.

Examining the immense range of Canadian women's writing is not an issue of exclusivity but of equitable, informed representation and treatment. Illuminating studies in which women's writing appears or is the main feature continue to point the way. William New's *A History of Canadian Literature* (2003) acknowledges the role of women writers as "narrators," "encoders," and, most recently, "reconstructors." While surveying women's contribution to canonical genres, Eva-Marie Kröller's edition of *The Cambridge Companion to Canadian Literature* (2004) also includes a chapter devoted to women's writing. Women's achievement in specific genres informs several studies; among them, work by Frank Davey (1993), Mickey Pearlman (1993), John Moss (1999), Gerald Lynch (2001), Sally Chivers (2003), Faye Hammill (2003), and Coral Ann Howells (2003) citing women's fiction; and David Bentley (1992) and Pauline Butling and Susan Rudy (2004) citing women poets. Linda Hutcheon (1988) values women writers' experiments with postmodernism, while Sneja Gunew (1998) and Smaro Kamboureli (2000) concentrate on multicultural and diasporic influences. Focusing on women writers, Dawn Thompson (2000) explores the role of memory; Helen Hoy, native writing (2001); Danielle Fuller, Atlantic Canadian women's textual communities (2004); Eleanor Ty, North American Asian narratives (2004; 2008); Tanis MacDonald, women's paternal elegies (2012); and Larissa Lai, Asian Canadian literary production (2014). Indigenous texts ground the work of Neal McLeod on poetics (2014), Dylan Robinson and Keavy Martin on artistic responses to the Truth and Reconciliation Commission (2016), Cheryl Suzack on the cultural study of law (2017), and Libe Garcia Zarranz on TransCanadian feminist fiction (2017). Women writers' grasp of large geographic and metaphoric concepts like the polyphony of nation concern Lynette Hunter (1996) and Jonathan Kertzer (1998). The north is a focus for Margaret Atwood (1995), Sherrill Grace (2002), and Renée Hulan (2002); the prairies, for Deborah Keahey (1998) and Alison Calder and Robert Wardaugh (2005). Anthologies edited by Marjorie Anderson, Sharon Cook, Elizabeth Dahab, Connie Fife, Agnes Grant, Heather Hodgson, Cynthia Sugars and Laura Moss, Jeanne Perreault, Rosemary Sullivan, and Penny Petrone make women's writing more readily accessible. The multidisciplinary challenges of editing in the digital age are the topic of Dean Irvine and Smaro Kamboureli's collection of essays (2016).

Penetrating biographies add depth and poignancy to our knowledge of these artists; consider the biographical studies of Elizabeth Smart and Gwendolyn MacEwen (by Rosemary Sullivan, 1991, 1995), Marian Engel (by Christl Verduyn, 1995), Gabrielle Roy (by François Ricard, 1996), the women artists of *Le refus global* (by Patricia Smart, 1998), Margaret Atwood (by Rosemary Sullivan, 1998; Nathalie Cooke, 1998), Margaret Laurence (by James King, 1997; Lyall Powers, 2003; Donez Xiquez, 2005; Nora Stovel, 2008), Ethel Wilson (by David Stouck, 2003), Sheila Watson (by Fred Flahiff, 2005), Alice Munro (by Robert Thacker, 2005/2011), Adele Wiseman (by Ruth Panofsky, 2006), Sharon Pollock (by Sherrill Grace, 2008), and Gwethalyn Graham (by Barbara Meadowcroft, 2008). Autobiographies are another revealing, at times intertextual, source, complicating our view of a writer's emotional and material circumstances, as in the re-created scenes of Gabrielle Roy's *La détresse et l'enchantement* (1984 [*Enchantment and Sorrow* 1987]), the rejoinder about an actual Saint-Henri upbringing in Lise Payette's *Des femmes d'honneur* (1997), and the confessions of Margaret Laurence's *Dance on the Earth* (1989). Memoirs demonstrate that public life and literary celebrity can bring their own upsets and challenges, as in singer-songwriter Shania Twain's *From This Moment On* (2011), filmmaker Sarah Polley's *Stories We Tell* (2012), and novelist Camilla Gibb's *This Is Happy* (2015). These reflexive examinations of particular times and places show how social forces shape individual lives. Building on the accomplishments of these scholarly inquiries and personal journeys, this project is a stock-taking: a wide-ranging, inclusive study of women's writing in Canada combining elite and popular work and assessing gains and losses for women along the way.

Alison Prentice and her historian colleagues ground their analyses in *Canadian Women: A History* in "women's work and material culture" (v). Recognizing "differing experiences of race, class, ethnicity, religion, bodily condition, and sexual orientation" (3), their robust account from early Indigenous and colonial cultures to the close of the twentieth century acknowledges both successes and failures, especially in the "long-hoped-for reforms to improve women's lives substantially" (357). An opportunity to consider a more compact path of celebrity and neglect accounts for the time frame of 1950 to 2017. The period from post-war prosperity to post-industrial late modernity has been one of unprecedented diversity and artistic productivity, reflecting transformations in demographic patterns, communications media, national and community expectations, and legislation. The marked shift from second- to third-wave feminism and, arguably, to post-feminism, has also been a prominent feature of cultural discourse, signalling the move from hetero-normative middle-class concerns for workforce and gender equity to pluralist concepts of race, class, and sexuality. These cultural currents, including the gradual shift from maternal to liberal feminism, shaped women's ambition and outlook in important but, as Catherine Gidney notes, "contradictory" ways. In "Feminist Ideals and Everyday Life" she argues that at the end of the first half of the twentieth century "the contradictions in professional women's beliefs and lived experience illuminate the transitional nature of a period in which the rhetoric of motherhood remained strong even as middle-class women had increasing opportunities to embark on careers" (109).

Of course poetry, fiction, drama, and essays are not primarily sociological documents but idiosyncratic, personally contoured reflections. The prismatic forces of human imagination, we realize, are most adept at translating the capital "H" of History into the emotive effects on an individual life. Because art satisfies our hunger and need "to create, contemplate, possess or repossess at least the shadow of what we do not have fully enough" (Scharfstein 3), it is understandable, and instructive, to turn to artists – including the 54 per cent who are women writers – to interpret, comment on, and, at times, refashion our national story. During this period of almost seven decades, Asian, Indian, and African immigration along with the prominence of Indigenous self-determination has altered the composition and attitude of the Canadian mosaic. The 2016 long-form census provides a revealing demographic overview: close to 22 per cent of Canadians are immigrants, with

7.7 million identifying as a visible minority; over 4 per cent (or 1.7 million) of Canadians claim Indigenous ancestry, with Cree as the most common Indigenous language spoken at home by almost 90,000 Canadians; and over 20 per cent (or 7.6 million) of the population are speakers of non-official languages. Further shifts can be noted in the sharp and often relocated divisions between affluence and deprivation and the passage or amendment of laws dealing with cultural identity, matrimonial and intellectual property, sexual abuse, and exploitation.[7] Using gender as a category of analysis, feminist historians in Canada "have maintained an ongoing interest in an empirical scholarship grounded in the rich details of people's daily lives" (Carstairs and Janovicek 7). In the second decade of the twenty-first century, Canada, as imagined, located, and perceived in the writing of women, is vastly different from the country it was in the middle of the previous century.

The exercise of conceptualizing this national terrain necessarily involves the social and imaginary elements of space along with the acknowledgment that postmodernity, from the late twentieth century on, has destabilized historical time and narrative. Pamela Gilbert explains: "As narrative, with its emphasis on an understandable causality, on the coherent and universal (usually white, Western male) subject, and on a historical teleology, came to seem increasingly suspect, many theorists turned away from time toward space – spatial relations would reveal to us a complexity and materiality which was being hidden away by narrative" (103). Barney Warf and Santa Arias identify the spatial turn as "a reworking of the very notion and significance of spatiality to offer a perspective in which space is every bit as important as time in the unfolding of human affairs, a view in which geography is not relegated to an afterthought of social relations, but is intimately involved in their construction" (1). Place *and* space remain suggestive principles for Ruth Panofsky and Kathleen Kellett in their consideration of the digital sphere and its "innovative practice to materials and subject matter that one appreciates deeply – and seeks to bring to a wider community of scholars, critics, and readers" (10). The movement from place, understood as "the particularities of a named space experienced as unified with clear boundaries, characteristics and a history" (Gilbert 103), to space, envisioned "not so much as bounded areas but as open and porous networks of social relations" (Massey 121), supplies one way of thinking about the calibrations in perspective during the period of this study.

We can cite a variety of signposts to map the timeline of the last sixty-seven years, with each indicating a predisposition to emphasize one of two paths – either an international coming of age or an eruptive questioning and overturning of stereotypes. Not only do they chart different routes: these markers themselves designate essentially different nation states. Such paths do not run along parallel lines but, like the writing produced in this period, are full of intersections and crossovers. Causes or irritants in one path often prompt developments or initiatives in the other. Because elements of both paths have influenced and continue to colour women's writing in Canada, I want to sketch briefly some of their signposts before investigating the ways women writers have participated in, challenged, and extended such developments.

The Commissions: From Massey to Truth and Reconciliation

The maturation line consists of many invariably contested markers, as well as its own setbacks and disappointed hopes. For the purposes of this project a revealing starting point is the vigorous assertion of Canadian cultural nationalism in the *Report of the Royal Commission on National Development in the Arts, Letters, and Sciences* (1951), commonly known as the Massey Commission, because of its chair, former high commissioner to London and chancellor of the University of Toronto, Vincent Massey.[8] The other commissioners were Georges-Henri Lévesque, a Dominican priest and founding dean of social sciences at Laval University; Norman MacKenzie, president of the University of British Columbia; Hilda Neatby, a bilingual historian of early Quebec from the University of Saskatchewan; and Arthur Surveyor, a civil engineer from Quebec.

Although the commission has come to be viewed as "a formative exercise in interest group politics" and "a creationist myth for Canadian cultural nationalists" with the limited appeal of its "liberal humanist formulation" (Litt 4, 5, 254), it is revealing to note the outsider status of at least two members of this so-called cultural elite. Along with the archbishop of Montreal and many members of the clergy espousing his social action principles, Lévesque had sided with the miners in the 1949 strike at Asbestos and Thetford Mines, Quebec, bringing him into direct conflict with the Union Nationale premier, Maurice Duplessis, who opted to ignore the commission's consultations in the province.[9] Later, Lévesque was also the mentor who championed the publication of Marie-Claire Blais's career-launching novel, *La belle bête* (1959). After scholarship study in Paris and a PhD from the University of Minnesota, Neatby only "found a permanent position at the University of Saskatchewan in 1946, a full twenty-one years after her first temporary appointment" (Corbett 174). Hence, the commissioner responsible for the bulk of the writing of the *Report* was the one who had struggled the most within a patriarchal academy. Neatby's bilingualism was an asset, as were her strong organizational skills, historical knowledge, intellectual acumen, and clear writing. Working "virtually full time on the commission from the summer of 1949 until January 1951," she was the person Massey depended on "heavily for critical aspects of the commission's work" (Litt 64, 116).[10]

The commission encapsulated the cultural norms of its authors and its time. With the epigraph drawn from Saint Augustine's *City of God* picturing a nation as "an association of reasonable beings ... sharing of the things they cherish" (1) and its defence of Bach over bombs in the assertion that "the things with which our inquiry deals are the elements which give civilization its character and its meaning" (274), the *Report* celebrated what the commissioners considered "a faithful adherence to a common set of beliefs" (4). It also pointed to absences: no national library and, despite its resistance to American influence, no Canadian equivalent to *The Atlantic* or *Harper's* or *The New Yorker*. It exposed the National Gallery's inadequate purchasing funds and limited staff. It recommended the foundation of a "Canada Council for the Encouragement of the Arts, Letters, Humanities, and Social Sciences" (377).

The *Report*'s treatment of literature is both significant and problematic. Agreeing "that today in Canada there exists no body of creative writing which reflects adequately the nature of the Canadian people" (222), and using masculine pronouns throughout to designate writers, the *Report* judges novels to be "too descriptive," poetry "rare," and theatre "almost non-existent" (226). Yet by mid-century, women writers had made forceful, acclaimed marks and were continuing to enlarge established reputations. In the novel *Shackles* (1926), Ottawa-based Madge Macbeth had explored the frustrations of a middle-class woman seeking to gain acceptance and respect as a writer. Starting with the blockbuster sales of her *Atlantic Monthly* prize-winning novel *Jalna* (1927), Mazo de la Roche had created more than half of her series of international bestsellers, sixteen novels about the southern Ontario house Jalna, the Whiteoak family, and their sexual appetites. With its gritty, dramatic realism, Irene Baird's novel *Waste Heritage* (1939) captured the violence and tragedy of the British Columbia labour disputes of 1938. Gwethalyn Graham had won two Governor General's Awards for Fiction, the second for *Earth and High Heaven* (1944), an exposé of anti-Semitism in Montreal's Westmount that was translated into eighteen languages and topped the *New York Times* bestseller list for almost a year. Winifred Bambrick's *Keller's Continental Revue* (1946), another Governor General's Award fiction winner, evoked the tensions of pre-World War II Europe from the perspective of a travelling theatrical troupe. Along with the first of her eventual three Governor General's Awards, Gabrielle Roy had been awarded France's prestigious Prix Femina for *Bonheur d'occasion* (1945), a poignant treatment of the struggles of poverty in Montreal's Saint-Henri district. Anne Hébert, another eventual recipient of three Governor General's Awards and the Prix Femina, had already published her inaugural volume of poetry, *Les songes en équilibre* (1942), which won the highest literary prize in Quebec, le Prix David, as did her first collection of stories, *Le torrent* (1950). By this point, too, the writing careers of Marie Le Franc, Constance Beresford Howe, Evelyn Eaton, and Mabel Dunham were immensely productive. Capping two decades of creative socialist activism, poet Dorothy Livesay had won two Governor

General's Awards in a row, for the social-revolutionary poetry of *Day and Night* (1944) and the empathetic humanism of *Poems for People* (1947). Innovations in narrative style and topographic location were also prominent in women's writing. Gwen Pharis Ringwood's theatrical experiments, with their intense regional and mythological resonances, had been produced at the Banff School of Fine Arts and on the University of Alberta radio station CKUA for more than a decade. Ethel Wilson's fiction, set largely in British Columbia, was gaining a dedicated following, and Elizabeth Smart's brilliant first novel, *By Grand Central Station I Sat Down and Wept* (1945), had already stirred a *succès de scandale*.

Its limited treatment of creative writing notwithstanding, the *Report* did strike a chord with Canadian readers. In 1951 "the King's Printer was expanding its first print run" (Litt 223) in response to anticipated general public interest, which was surprisingly high but also short-lived. While the Massey Commission made several prescient recommendations, its consultations also occurred at a time when Canadians were ready for a more integrated cultural outlook. The commission's attitudes, however, were unavoidably influenced by the well-established traditions of "cultural activism"; as Maria Tippett's detailed study of amateur and professional artists' groups, drama and music festivals, and commissioned work for memorials makes clear, "the idea that cultural education, broadly defined, could function as a vehicle for helping the nation mature was, then, much in evidence both before and after" the commission (37). Concluding glumly but honestly that many of the *Report*'s recommendations "almost never saw the light of day," Paul Litt does identify its key importance in ushering in "a new age in which a conscious and coordinated government cultural policy came to be expected" (247, 237). Plans for a National Library were approved in 1952 (the building came into existence in 1967); the Canada Council for the Arts was established in 1957; and the Social Sciences and Humanities Research Council (for university-based research) came into being in 1977.

Another development involving national identity emerged from *The Report of the Royal Commission on Bilingualism and Biculturalism* (1967), with its stress on "two dominant languages," "two principal cultures [whose] influence extends, in varying degrees, to the whole country," and its warning that "no artistic creation will take its place in the culture inherited by all Canadians unless its creator has become sufficiently integrated into the Canadian community to speak meaningfully to it" (I: xxxi, xxvi). A perceived element of integration was the Royal Commission on the Status of Women, the first commission to be headed by a woman, Ottawa journalist Florence Bayard Bird (who used the pen name Anne Francis). At a time when the earnings of men exceeded those of women by over 80 per cent, the commission's 488-page *Status of Women Report* (1970) recommended equal pay for work of equal value, maternity leave, day care provision, and women's access to managerial positions. Though criticized for "not admitting the complexities of the situation" and "avoid[ing] any argument about the basic biology of the human species" (Griffiths 219, 221), the *Report* did forecast other opportunities. In 1974 Kathleen Shannon founded Studio D of the National Film Board (NFB) to create films for, by, and about women. Located originally in the janitor's storeroom in the basement of the NFB building, Studio D was, in the words of its founding executive producer, "a maverick, minority division within an institution that, in many ways, represents the status quo you are trying to change" (Shannon 27). Despite having produced more than 150 documentaries creating "new knowledge about the politics of telling stories about women's lives" (Vanstone 189), winning three Academy Awards, and garnering more than 100 international prizes, this forum for women filmmakers was closed in 1996 with the slashing of the NFB budget by $20 million. Researchers and librarians at the University of Calgary are preserving the archives of Studio D. A second by-product of the *Bilingualism and Biculturalism Report* was the establishment of Status of Women Canada in 1976, a federal agency within the Heritage Ministry, which undertook to promote gender-based analysis and monitor progress on women's participation in all forms of public life. Status of Women Canada's 2005 report, *Equality for Women*, locates the "goal of equality ... at the heart of what it means to be Canadian" (Steinsky-Schwartz 3), but in light of a 40 per cent reduction of Status of Women Canada's administrative budget, continuing gender-based wage imbalances, cuts to adult literacy programs, and the alarming spike in rates of incarceration for First Nations people and particularly First Nations women, this goal might seem more shibboleth than reality.[11]

The national trajectory also notes the passage of the Canada Act (1982) patriating the Constitution (including the ability to amend it) and enacting the Charter of Rights and Freedoms, guaranteeing the "fundamental" freedom "of thought, belief, opinion, and expression, including freedom of the press and other media of communication."[12] Another signpost is the Multiculturalism Act (1988), providing all Canadians, "whether by birth or by choice ... equal status," proscribing "discrimination on the basis of race, national or ethnic origin, or colour," and promoting "the full and equitable participation of individuals and communities of all origins in the continuing evolution and shaping of all aspects of Canadian society."[13] Yet to some observers the purported equality is more rhetorical flourish than lived experience. In Neil Bissoondath's view, the "assigned role of multiculturalism" involves playing "the ethnic deracinated and costumed," which is ultimately an abdication of "one's full humanity" (223). He issues this challenge to multicultural Canada: "to cease erecting walls between the shards of the mosaic and to begin opening up doors between them so that as individuals make their way through territory previously unknown, distinctiveness will blur in the shards but take shape in the whole" (239). Pointing to the danger of "a new kind of ethnography rife with stereotypes" in Asian Canadian literary production, Larissa Lai is less sanguine; she cites the continued existence of "so many racial traumas" and "the romantic, exotic, Orientalized sign of something churning beneath the surface" to argue that "multicultural incorporation does not necessarily expiate the trauma" (59, 61).

The most stirring point in this path of development thus far has been the public, adult recognition of failure. The immediate focus of this admission was the system of residential schools, in effect from the 1870s until its final closure in the 1990s; the larger issue was the need to repeal the Indian Act (1876) that gave the federal government legislative authority over First Nations and their reserved lands. "Section 91 (24) of the Constitution Act, 1867, g[ave] exclusive legislative jurisdiction over 'Indians and Lands reserved for the Indians' to the federal government," with the Indian Act allowing provincial laws of general application to apply to First Nations "unless the laws are inconsistent with the Indian Act" (Ursel 217). As survivor testimonials, historical studies, plays, poems, and novels bear witness, the "assimilative policies" of residential schools constitute "the lethal legacy Canadians face in the twenty-first century" (Miller 264). Prime Minister Stephen Harper acknowledged as much in his national apology in the House of Commons: "The government now recognizes that the consequences of the Indian Residential Schools policy were profoundly negative and that this policy has had a lasting and damaging impact on aboriginal culture, heritage, and language ... We are sorry" (11 June 2008).[14] The promised Residential Schools Truth and Reconciliation Commission was reconstituted under the chairmanship of Justice Murray Sinclair, Manitoba's first Indigenous judge and now a member of the Canadian Senate, with commissioners Chief Wilton Littlechild, a lawyer from Maskawacis Cree Territory of Treaty 6, and Marie Wilson, a senior Canadian Broadcasting Corporation (CBC) executive producer from Yellowknife, Northwest Territories, with strong family and community ties to residential schools. A victim-centred and forward-looking enquiry, it began its five-year mandate in June 2009, to acknowledge intergenerational consequences and promote awareness of the schools' ongoing legacy. The commission's report, *Honouring the Truth, Reconciling for the Future*, including ninety-four calls to action, was released in 2015. With the British Columbia Court of Appeal's determination that the Indian Act violates the equality provisions of the Charter of Rights and Freedoms, the Ministry of Indian and Northern Affairs, now called Indigenous and Northern Affairs Canada, is undertaking consultations to reform the legislation, which has been amended throughout virtually every decade of its existence. By the amendment of 1951 the act allowed previously banned religious ceremonies, including "Give Away Dances," which were essential opportunities for passing on insights within the community and resisting assimilation (Backhouse 64). Only in 1960 was the amendment passed disallowing Indian enfranchisement, by which voting in a federal election meant renouncing Indian status; it took until 1985 for the amendment that allowed First Nations women who had "married out" (married a non-Native) to keep or regain their status.

From *Total Refusal* and the Quiet Revolution to Cultural Accommodation

The contemporaneous but interrogating route, the counter-narrative, relies less on commissions and more on manifestos and enquiries, questions and confessions. It regularly challenges the upbeat rhetoric of royal commissions. The starting point here is *Le refus global* (1948) or *Total Refusal*, a manifesto-like pamphlet composed by Paul-Émile Borduas and signed by fifteen of his artist friends in the Montreal Automatist Movement. Significantly, seven of the signatories were women: designer Madeleine Arbour, theatre and radio actor Muriel Guilbault, glass artist and painter Marcelle Ferron, dancer Jeanne Renaud, autobiographer Thérèse Renaud, dancer Françoise Riopelle, and dancer, painter, and essayist Françoise Sullivan. The fact that seven women artists were signatories in August 1948, rebels *with* causes, signified a challenging, egalitarian move, especially in the midst of the stifling and deeply conservative Quebec regime (1944–59) of Premier Maurice Duplessis, leader of the Union Nationale party. As Patricia Smart's richly detailed biography of these seven artists affirms, the women of *Le refus global* remain an inspiration – in their energy, creative spirit, embrace of life, wisdom, and friendship maintained over fifty years; they are for Smart models for future generations and beacons in today's foggy cultural landscape (Smart 296).[15]

Instead of affirming a belief in rationality, as the Massey Commission did, *Le refus global* questioned it. Although not as well known outside Quebec as the commission's *Report*, the pamphlet's small print run (400 copies sold out in three weeks) did not lessen its impact. Borduas himself, who had begun his career as a church decorator and a teacher of drawing, lost his teaching position at l'École du Meuble; Dominican, Jesuit, and Oblate clergy denounced it; and as early as 1950 Simon Wilson Taylor translated the document into English. Reflecting the tenets of surrealist-inspired automatist artists, whose style has been labelled variously "abstract expressionist," "non-figurative," and "lyrical abstractionist" (Ellenwood xiv), *Le refus global* was a radical call for modernism in Quebec and, arguably, Canada; it called for a little people – "isolated, colonized, Jansenized" (Ellenwood 134) – to liberate itself by breaking through self-imposed walls ("Petit peuple issu d'une colonie janséniste, isolé, vaincu").[16] The description "petit peuple" deliberately invoked the words of University of Montreal historian and ardent Québécois nationalist of an earlier generation l'Abbé Lionel Groulx. A galvanizing leader of the nationalist movement in Montreal in the 1920s, l'Action française, "an organization for the preservation of French Canada," Groulx had pictured his "petit peuple" as "charmed by providence but doomed by history to the status of an ever-vigilant minority" (Trofimenkoff 221). With its forceful language directed against "la décadence chrétienne" and "son exécrable exploitation," *Le refus global* announced a definitive break with the conventions of a utilitarian society ("Rompre définitivement avec toutes les habitudes de la société, se désolidariser de son esprit utilitaire") and with the easy refuge of academicism ("Refus d'un cantonnement la seule bourgade plastique"), supplanting reason and intention with magic ("place à la magie!"), objective mysteries ("mystères objectifs"), love ("place à l'amour!"), passionate acts ("les actes passionnels"), and cynical spontaneity ("nous préférons être cyniques spontanément sans malice"). Not the result of national consultation like the Massey Commission, the coterie-derived *Total Refusal* along with its appended documents[17] was flamboyant and incendiary.

Despite the localized origin of *Le refus global*, its resonances for an alternative understanding of nationhood are important. The fact that the signatories aligned themselves with the striking miners at Asbestos set up a fractious division with the paternalistic, authoritarian regime of Premier Duplessis. Stirring Quebec's awakening from *le grande noirceur* (the great gloom) and emergence "from the bucolic dreams of a peasant people" (Pelletier 116),[18] *Total Refusal* not only provided an impetus for the Quiet Revolution, which gained momentum in the early sixties, but also captured the sense that traditionalist self-images – pious and obedient or "raw, rural and undeveloped" (Bothwell 364) – needed to be brought into accord with urban, industrial realities.

The key concept in la Revolution Tranquille was *"rattrapage –* catching up" (Linteau et al. 308). Major economic, social, and demographic transformations marked the early sixties – in Quebec as elsewhere in Canada. The newly formed Liberal government (1960–6) of Jean Lesage established a cultural affairs ministry and a federal-provincial hospital insurance plan in 1961 and, in 1964, a ministry of education, which set up junior colleges (CEGEPs) and which was officially secularized in 1997. Although schools initially maintained their confessional character, the role of the church – no longer a major employer – was much less prominent. "Montreal's churches attracted only 50% of declared Catholics throughout the 1960s" and because of the "cultural effervescence of the time ... poets and politicians had taken on the role of definers of the people" (Trofimenkoff 303). Illustrating the slogan *"maîtres chez nous,"* another borrowing from Groulx, a unified hydro-electric system, the new Hydro-Québec, was the engine of industrialization in all regions. Other features of the Quiet Revolution were the "accession of members of the French majority to leading positions" (Linteau et al. 308), largely helped by the Laurendeau-Dunton Bilingualism and Biculturalism Commission and the 1969 Official Languages Act, and a dramatic fall in the birth rate, which eventually became the lowest in Canada. Violent interruptions in public life shocked Canadians in 1970. The October Crisis and implementation of the War Measures Act were precipitated by the kidnappings of two public figures by members of the Front de Libération du Québec (FLQ); Pierre Laporte, the Quebec minister of labour, was murdered, while diplomat James Cross, the British trade commissioner in Montreal, was released. Within a year, one of the FLQ's most influential figures, Pierre Vallières, author of *Nègres blancs d'Amérique* (*White Niggers of America*), "publicly denounced terrorism as an effective means of bringing about social change"

(Trofimenkoff 324) and threw his support behind the separatist Parti Québécois.

Unlike the unifying, homogenizing impulses characteristic of the maturation trajectory, the contestatory narrative emphasizes divisions – both perennial and newly inflamed – between north and south within the country and the continent, between anglophone and francophone, between east and west, between centre and regions, and between First Nations and colonizers. In 1974, the appointment of Justice Thomas Berger of the British Columbia Supreme Court as head of an enquiry into the feasibility of oil and gas development in the western Canadian Arctic and a pipeline from the Mackenzie Valley south launched a documented, video-recorded, three-year consultation across the Arctic that prompted Canadians to consider what the north means to the nation. Recommending against any development until land claims were settled, Berger's 240-page report, *Northern Frontier, Northern Homeland* (1977), still a best-selling government publication, outlined the differences between viewing the north as a frontier to be developed for the expansion of our "industrial machine" (1) or as the homeland for generations and centuries of First Peoples. The enquiry, which is entwined in the development of Elizabeth Hay's Giller Prize-winning novel *Late Nights on Air* (2007), "was making so much visible and noteworthy," creating "a remarkable time of hope ... for anyone in favour of the present learning from the past" (Hay 162, 163).

While widespread consultation with Indigenous peoples contributed to the drama and depth of the Berger Report, the lack of consultation, particularly with First Nations, spelled defeat for the Meech Lake Accord in the 1980s. The accord, named after the lake in the Gatineau Hills where all premiers initially signed the document in 1987, was an attempt to include Quebec in the patriation of the Constitution; Quebec had not signed the accord on amendments to the Constitution Act in 1982. The promised recognition of Quebec as a "distinct society" and the need to secure unanimous provincial consent for the amending formula proved to be flashpoints of bitter disagreement. "The fact that the two territories, where the population is mainly Native, were not invited to the retreat" (Bowering, *Stone Country* 316) at Meech Lake was a mortal blow. The refusal of a Cree member of the Manitoba Legislative Assembly to approve and the refusal of Newfoundland to hold a provincial vote meant that the accord died in 1990. Elijah Harper's eagle feather was the iconic representation that no notice had been taken of the *several* distinct societies formed by Indigenous people. The confrontation at Oka, Quebec, in the same year, was more violent. The Mercier Bridge, used by Chateaugai residents to commute to Montreal and originally built and enlarged by a sizeable contingent of Mohawk ironworkers, had been blocked by the Mohawks of Kahnawake in resistance to the destruction of sacred land for the proposed building of a golf course and in support of the Mohawks of Kahnesatake. The Canadian army planned to enter Kahnawake as an approach to Kahnesatake. In late August, when a convoy of seventy-five cars carrying women, children, and elders left Kahnawake to cross the Mercier Bridge, the enraged residents of Chateaugai pelted the convoy with rocks as it passed through the narrow access route, called Whiskey Trench because of the Seagrams distilleries on either side. The avalanche of rocks shattered windshields, terrorized drivers and passengers, and injured babies and eighty-year-old grandparents huddled under blankets and mattresses in the back seats. The remarkable footage of celebrated Abenaki filmmaker Alanis Obomsawin, in the NFB documentary *Rocks at Whiskey Trench* (2000), the fourth instalment of her quartet about the Oka crisis, contains on-the-spot coverage, no re-enactment, from inside the Mohawk community before, during, and after the event. Combining historical accounts of the Jesuit seigneury and the Longhouse traditions of the Mohawk, *Rocks at Whiskey Trench* creates and circulates empathy through a series of continuous contrasts between attitudes inside and outside Kahnawake. While tabloids flash announcements of "Le Pont Mercier – un champ de bataille" and "des heures sombres," the filmmaker's narratorial voice informs us of Mohawk ways of the Wolf (pathfinder), Bear (keeper of medicine), and Turtle (wisdom), of the determination to stop the desecration of the area called The Pines, and of the decision to support the community at Kahnesatake. On the other side we see the angry lobs from Chateaugai residents, learn that only thirty were arrested (many with conditional discharges, others with weekend detentions or fines), and hear a proud Chateaugai merchant declare belligerently to the camera, "Ça n'a changé rien de ma vie" ("it didn't change anything in my life"). The Kahnawake residents pelt the army with stones as they attempt to cross the bridge and occupy the Longhouse. After the seventy-eight-day siege, Mohawk warriors face criminal charges; a Healing Circle is established; but only a thin layer of tolerance for Chateaugai remains. The unease of suspicion hangs in the air.

Unease is another appropriate description for the relationship of Quebec with Canada. The 1980 Quebec Referendum on Sovereignty, which almost 60 per cent of the votes cast rejected, was a federalist victory of sorts. It spurred the move to patriate the Constitution in 1982. However, the second referendum, held in 1995, testing Québécois attitudes towards sovereignty-association, was not nearly so decisive. Slightly more than 1 per cent separated the minority "yes" side (for sovereignty) from the prevailing "no" side (for remaining within Canadian federalism).

Although this route acknowledges disconnections, it also includes instances when failure can be moving and instructive. Two distinct examples share the feature of attracting international attention. When Canadian Lieutenant General Roméo Dallaire was appointed commander of the United Nations Peacekeeping Force in Rwanda, he encountered a situation of stockpiled weapons and escalating violence that exploded into genocide. As Hutu extremists attacked and slaughtered Tutsis and Hutu moderates, the UN Security Council refused Dallaire's urgent request for additional and armed troops. The world's deaf ear and blind eye meant that in 100 days in 1994 more than 800,000 (possibly more than a million) people were killed. Dallaire's actions saved more than 35,000 Tutsis. Yet the effects of this sordid campaign, which his troops were initially so ill-equipped to halt, haunted – and continue to haunt – Dallaire. His bravery in recounting the abortive mission and his own subsequent battles with suicidal depression in his Governor General's Award-winning *Shake Hands with the Devil* (2003) made this senior soldier, now a retired member of the Senate of Canada, a compassionate figure of nobility and humanity. His wake-up call about the dangers of isolationism, his insistent plea for engaging in global affairs, and his stirring admission of helplessness and guilt constitute both a mature personal assessment and a ringing challenge to any sense of self-satisfaction or smugness.

The second example in this admittedly idiosyncratic routing focuses on the recognition that a truly intercultural society understands and promotes openness. The Consultation Commission on Accommodation Practices Related to Cultural Differences, called in 2007 by the government of Quebec and headed by sociologist Gérard Bouchard and philosopher Charles Taylor, addressed the realities that the percentage of immigrants opting to stay in the province was falling and that accommodation practices needed to conform to the values of a pluralistic, democratic, egalitarian Quebec. Though accused of pre-formed ideas and conflicting loyalties, Bouchard and Taylor reviewed 900 briefs, heard 241 testimonies, and convened more than fifty regional forums and focus groups before they released their report in May 2008. Diagnosing that the perceived identity crisis was not critical, their report includes practical, though still contentious, recommendations about religious and cultural accommodation concerning the wearing of headgear and the observance of holy days. It is another mature acknowledgment of a society vastly changed from the time of the dawning of the Quiet Revolution.

Whether viewed from an international perspective as a highly desired country of residence with a necklace of smart cities and intelligent communities from coast to coast to coast or considered as a work in progress energized by creative tensions, Canada as a nation is a complex, diverse, often contradictory reality. Within the thirty-four democracies of the Organization for Economic Co-operation and Development (OECD), Canada, with the fifth-largest net national income, is secure in the upper quadrant measuring the population that has attained at least upper secondary education: "Canadians are the most educated of the OECD countries," and women's education attainment at the tertiary level is the highest in OECD countries, yet provincial funding for postsecondary education is falling behind that of other countries (Buchanan n.p.).

New Images of Movement and Diversity

The creative tensions constituting a national work in progress or a transfiguration of disciplinary and institutional frameworks have definitely changed throughout this sixty-seven-year period. American critic Edmund Wilson's assessment of Canadian criticism as "provincial" and "predisposed to be spiteful to talent" (105) seems peculiarly dated. When the *Atlantic Monthly* solicited commentary from Canadians for its Supplement on Canada in 1964, a mixture of trenchant and dyspeptic observations emerged. Few readers today would agree with transplanted English professor Brian Stock's view of his Canadian heritage as "schizophrenic" and spiritually malnourished, since in "the battle for culture and art in Canada ... the country does not have the spiritual resources to support them" (114). Other insights have proved to be more durable and prescient. Among them are the observations of historian John Conway that "we are traditionalists" living in a "state of psychological and emotional dependence" (105) on European models. Poet Douglas LePan summed up our "bourgeois and voyageur" history in the figure of Louis Riel receiving visitors at Fort Garry "wearing leather moccasins and a frock coat" (161), and novelist Robertson Davies called for a dose of "Scottish pragmatism and Scottish dourness ... in demanding a new approach to the study of language" (144). The present-day equivalent of such an external assessment by citizens in the public eye is the scholarly TransCanLit project, headed by Smaro Kamboureli and Roy Miki, with the task to "undertake a major rethinking of the assumptions that ha[ve] governed the field of CanLit studies and to rejuvenate the field through a renewed sense of collective purpose" (xiii). Keenly aware of "how history, ideology, method, pedagogy, capital economies, cultural capital, institutional and social structures, community, citizenship, advocacy, racialization, indigeneity, diaspora, and globalization are all intricately related to CanLit and its complex, often torturous, trajectories," this collaborative research network aims to "split open" and "'unmake' CanLit" (xv).

A sense of purposive accommodation – introspective and pragmatic – continues to characterize Canadians' ideas of their country. Picturing the nation as "both fact (historical reality) and fiction (imagined community)," Jonathan Kertzer sees a national literature as swerving "back and forth by marshalling communities, which it shows to be divisive" (*Worrying the Nation* 18, 193). As either geographic place or social space, the nation is never fully realized or imagined. Poet and critic E.D. Blodgett argues that since nationhood embodies conditions of "unresolved tension," its "literary history emphasizes struggle" (290, 293). Historian Vivian Nelles resorts to the image of the Pacific Coast Transformation Mask; its strings, pulled to display different motifs (raven or sun or killer whale), signal that the era of globalization, when "Canada is better known for novelists, singers, actors, filmmakers, artists, athletes, academics, engineers, and business leaders than natural resources," is a time when "the Transformation Mask is opening again" (256–7). Although it can prompt us to "imagine ourselves anew," "the question of who we are," writer, academic, and past political leader Michael Ignatieff declares, "is never settled" (177).

Other recent images of Canada forcefully capture the essence of potentiality. Philosopher John Ralston Saul looks back over the "Métis civilization" of Canada and its values of welcome, adaptation, and inclusion to propose that "the long Canadian experiment with complexity and fairness has never appeared more modern" (323). In *The Promise of Canada*, biographer and historian Charlotte Gray maintains that the images of today's Canada are "unrelated to stalwart Mounties, maple syrup, or snow-capped mountains"; instead she cites the Tam-Tams weekly festival in Mount Royal Park in downtown Montreal, where the bronze figure of Sir George-Étienne Cartier, "the Father of Confederation who ensured that different peoples could live alongside each other," presides "over a montage of urban Canada in the twenty-first century" (324, 325). For former Governor General David Johnston and National Research Council chair Tom Jenkins, the Truth and Reconciliation Commission "managed in 2015 to finesse what will likely prove a dramatic turning point in the country's capacity to tap the ingenuity made possible by its Indigenous inheritance" (88). Historian Jocelyn Létourneau envisions Canada as a postmodern mobile, flexibly in orbit with other mobiles, shunning equilibrium in favour of the principle of movement, combining diversity and unity, disaccord and cohesion.[19]

As these examples show, analogy is the realism of metaphor, which can refresh our understanding. Metaphor deploys "a circle of linguistic forms that no longer need to be taken literally," making possible "a free control over what is not present" (Blumenberg 94, 97). Let me offer my own metaphor for Canada from 1950. I happened to be mentally shuffling the pack of metaphors about Canada, Canadian history, and Can Lit while on a trip to Chile. The irony of thinking about the immensity of one country while visiting a narrow slip of another, its thinness bounded by the Pacific and the cordillera of the Andes, fascinated me. Outside La Serena, en route to Vicuña, birthplace of poet Gabriela Mistral, the first South American to win the Nobel Prize for Literature, I travelled through the Elqui Valley, its sloping vineyards, the centre of Chilean pisco production, irrigated by the Puclaro Dam. Here in the valley so far away from Canada, I encountered many reminders of home and this project. Certainly the Mistral pilgrimage was important because of the spare beauty of her work and the wonderful pride of Chileans in memorializing this strict, ascetic native daughter.

As the sun glinted on the confluence of the Claro and Turbio Rivers (Clear and Muddy), I was carried back with a surprising rush to Ethel Wilson's depictions of the meeting of the Fraser and the Thompson. But standing on the bridge overlooking the huge reservoir of the Puclaro Dam on one side and the stream radiating to valleys on the other, with a metallic installation of an eolian harp, titled "arpa aeolica," capturing different rhythms on this wind-swept height, made me think more and more of Canada over the past sixty-seven years. The music of these vibrating wires stretched across two towering poles did prompt an almost Coleridgean "trembl[ing] into thought." Almost Coleridgean. Unlike Coleridge's romantic composition in Somersetshire, the moment in the Elqui Valley was not "plastic and vast, one intellectual breeze" ("The Aeolian Harp," lines 46–7), but rather consisted of continuous chords of sound, at times euphonious then cacophonous. It struck me that here, many thousands of kilometres away, an understanding of Canada was taking shape. However jarring the adjustment, the additional element of agency was essential to see this parliamentary democracy of provinces and territories as not merely a reactive, uncontrolled instrument played on by the winds of change but an alert configuration responding to forces within and around, allowing harmony and discord to co-exist, creating distinctive sounds from the angles, breadth, and differences of its position.

chapter one

Fiction

A mainstream feature of writing in Canada, fiction reveals the contours of the tradition and its range of experimentation. Illustrating "an unwillingness to jettison realism" (Hutcheon, "The Novel" 87), the stories women write continue to intensify and thicken our understanding of realities – psychological and social, domestic and political, regional and international. From divergent perspectives both within and on the periphery of cultural commerce, they detect changing societal premises, document unpredictable events punctuating a life or an era, explore the role of chance in everyday life, and remind us of the contradictions and uncertainties of relationships and existence.

If we see Canadian fiction as essentially "the novel of the puritan conscience in action," narratives in which "the repressive forces of family and society become forms of the trap that a ... Calvinist society sets for the individual" (MacLulich 199, 203), then it is appropriate to consider the ways women writers characterize protagonists who are challenging and attempting to snap these bonds. If we see the Canadian procedure as "pragmatic, compromising, ad hoc, ramshackle" (Frye, "Conclusion" 321), it is worth exploring how women's writing creates a certain continuity and confidence in such a tradition. If we see the Canadian practice as "anglo-saxon small-town protestant conservative," obsessing about "the most hidden secret ... [of] sexuality," "the bond to the land," and the disastrous "sacrifice of desire to duty" (Cohen 67), it is important to interleave views of the urban, heterosexual, and homoerotic joys and dilemmas vivified in women's writing.

The sixty-seven years this study surveys have introduced modern and postmodern experiments, riffs on various traditions, and classical influences. They include radical challenges to "literary 'universals,'" parody as "an ironic form of intertextuality" (Hutcheon, *The Canadian Postmodern* 109), and the deliberate pastiche of hybridized genres. Multilingual interventions – beyond English and French and outside European borders – have complicated and troubled concepts of a "monocultural" reality (Marlatt, "Entering In" 220). In fact, generic boundaries have been intermixed and redrawn, from prose poetry and ficto-criticism to autobiografiction and geografictione. Within the polyphony of multicultural cross-currents and metafictional innovations, the idea of the fragility of the self, specifically the female self, remains salient. Whether exposing the invisibility of domestic life or animating the sense of being on the brink, the images of female existence realized by women writers in Canada underscore the importance of the role of a moral witness, even as conventional expectations are upended, in their willingness to judge others and themselves.

Prospects at Mid-Century

This zesty and acclaimed fiction did not simply sprout in the 1950s or blossom later. In the preceding decades, a sizeable contingent of women had been winning recognition. In addition to the celebrated blockbusters of Mazo de la Roche's (1870–1961) instalments to the Whiteoaks saga, with their associations of land ownership and eroticism, women's fiction had expanded the range of the historical romance, the roman de la terre, and the psychological thriller.

Declaring her independence of her family's British loyalties, Evelyn Eaton (1902–83) produced a series of historical romances (*Quietly My Captain Waits*, 1940; *Restless Are the Sails*, 1942; *The Sea Is Wide*, 1943; *In What Torn Ship*, 1945; *Every Month Was May*, 1946; *The North Star Is Nearer*, 1949) set in Acadia and New France; they feature women at the heart of the stories, where the narrator's sympathies are with the Acadians. An admiration for the writing of the immigrant Frenchman Louis Hémon and his evocation of rural traditions inspired the work of Marie le Franc (1879–1965) in its preoccupation with simple folk, as in *Hélier, fils des bois* (1930) and *Le fils de la forêt* (1952). Germaine Guèvremont (1893–1968) was another Hémon enthusiast; set in the small parish of Chenal du Moine in the Sorel countryside, her interlocked novels, *Le Survenant* (1945) and *Marie-Didace* (1947), translated together as *The Outlander* (1950), won the Governor General's Award along with both the Prix Duvernay and the Prix David in Quebec. With less tragedy but equal stress on cultural survival, Mabel Dunham (1881–1957) celebrated south-western Ontario Mennonite pioneers in *The Trail of the Conestoga* (1942) and the award-winning children's book *Kristli's Trees* (1948), while Winnipeg-based Olive Elsie Knox (fl. 1940–70) concentrated on western Canadian historical themes (*By Paddle and Saddle*, 1943; *Red River Shadows*, 1948). The lives of contemporary urban women in periods of radical social and emotional upheaval were the focus for Canadian-born but California-based Margaret Millar (1915–94), especially her depiction of a woman's descent into madness in *The Iron Gates* (1945). The emotional challenges of urban life are subjects of the two early novels of McGill instructor Constance Beresford-Howe (1922–), *The Unreasoning Heart* (1946) and *The Invisible Gate* (1949), and of media and stage producer Françoise Loranger (1913–95), the first Quebec woman to earn her living as a writer, in *Mathieu* (1949).

    Often described as forgotten, the seven women I want to consider to start with were a combination of early and late bloomers. Madge Macbeth, Irene Baird, Gwethalyn Graham, Elizabeth Smart, Winifred Bambrick, Gabrielle Roy, and Ethel Wilson wrote novels that appeared in the generation or generations before mid-century, and several continued to write for many decades. Most have been the subject of biographies, and almost all their work is available, in many cases through new editions. Such accessibility allows us to catch glimpses of their writing lives, to enter the milieu of national and international publishing agreements and conditions of circulation, to chart the differences between participation in and resistance to publisher's promotions, and, most of all, to perceive the immense scope and power of their realistic fiction. They span large, international as well as intimate, domestic casts of characters. Reproducing dialects, capturing incisive exchanges in Canadian and European settings, their narratives explore both timely and perennial topics. Along with apprehension as war looms in Europe, they humanize labour upheaval during the Depression and anti-Semitism in Westmount. They treat the bonds of middle-class marriage as well as the plangency of passionate longing.

Ottawa-based widow Madge Macbeth (1878–1965) wrote to support her two young sons. Author of more than twenty books, of which only *Shackles* (1926) remains in print, and "many more articles, short stories, book reviews, speeches, plays and skits" (Kelly 3), she maintained close associations with artists and other writers, and presided over the Canadian Authors Association from 1939 to 1941. Published both in Ottawa by the "short-lived cultural-nationalist press, the Graphic Publishers" (Kelly 35), which folded in 1932, and in 1927 in the United States by Waterson, the novel sold for two dollars; the author purchased the unsold copies when Graphic Publishers disappeared to avoid having them remaindered. Remarkable for its layers of insider knowledge, *Shackles* not only privileges the interior thoughts of wife and aspiring writer Naomi Lennox but also reveals Macbeth's own attitude towards her characters.

The three interrelated issues the novel addresses are sexuality, marital fidelity, and woman's independence, with startling observations in each case. Naomi views sex with her constantly chattering, oblivious husband as a form of prostitution. With ellipses emphasizing the predictable, repeated torment, she feels "soiled ... unclean ... unclean" (127), while Arnold "reduced the supreme act of love to a mere physical function which he performed as soullessly as he took his morning bath" (126). In wondering about "shattering these agreeable illusions," Naomi realizes that, "To demolish the particular niche in which he has placed himself would be to invite domestic chaos" (225).

The evidence of "woman's inherited sense of bondage" (228), as expressed by Naomi's suitor, the man whose offer of escape she refuses, is a stark reality: "Any excuse to put on the shackles, rather than shake them off" (228). The representation of the woman writer within this stagnant marriage is hardly a picture of exhilarating independence. The closing ironic exchange, Arnold's interrupting Naomi to tell her about the notice he is making "to hang on the door when you are writing and wish to be free from interruption" (318), underscores the momentary liberation Naomi can hope to experience in this stifling household.

The entrapment of poverty, unemployment, and anger is the focus of Irene Baird's (1919–81) *Waste Heritage* (1939). The novel is a modern-realist and fictionalized documentary treatment of the aftermath of the Vancouver sit-down strike of unemployed men outside the Art Gallery, the Georgia Hotel, and the Central Post Office, in May 1938, and their subsequent march to Victoria to demonstrate in front of the legislature. Published by both Macmillan in Canada and Random House in the United States, translated into French in 1951, reissued by Macmillan in 1974, and unjustly neglected, this second of her four novels is now available in a new edition from the University of Ottawa Press. *Waste Heritage* was nominated for the Governor General's Award, but lost to a historical novel, an indication, in Carole Gerson's view, that the Canadian Authors Association prized epic scale over social realism.[1]

The novel's raw naturalism is a curious hybrid of lived experience and mythic emplotment. Baird's visits to strike locations with Victoria's Medical Officer contribute to the text's gritty immediacy. So do the screeching fire trucks, clanging streetcar gongs, choked traffic, and raucous crowds of Vancouver. They become an "expressionistic projection of the internal states of Baird's conflicted characters" (Hill xxxii). The flophouses and junk dealerships of "Ye Olde English City" (162) of Victoria, which appear under the biblical names of Aschelon and Gath, an allusion to Israelite cities conquered by the Philistines (II Samuel 1:20), contribute to the sense of fatalism. In the "doomed secular covenant" between Matt and Eddy, Baird also alludes to the bond between David and Jonathan; importing into the text "a mythology of both brotherly love and fraternal mourning," she uses a "socialist modernist practice" through which the biblical illuminates the contemporary

(Rifkind 182). "Sympathetic to and critical of socialist organizing of the mass unemployed," the novel testifies, as Candida Rifkind argues, "to the sedimentation of leftist figures and forms in the aesthetic ground of modernism and the political ground of Canadian liberalism" (163).

In contrast to the polished subterfuge of the Lennox marriage, the exchanges between simple-minded Eddy and recently arrived Matt are blunt and heated. When Eddy confesses to lobbing a gas bomb into a candy store window, Matt explodes: "Maybe I should of left you to that cop after all!" (14). Eddy's "half childish, half cunning" (19) explanation, "Before I got beat over the head I wasn't crazy at all, I jus' made mistakes" (19), adds to the poignancy of this lopsided friendship. Baird's tragic narrative is saturated with gloomy omens. Matt's sense of responsibility for Eddy is intensified as another fellow proposes suicide in order to avoid institutionalization – "He'd a damnsite better walk right down an' lay his head on the tracks" (89). Omens are fulfilled: Matt beats a cop to death, and Eddy, calling in vain to his friend, "Jus save me this once, Matt! Jus this once more!" (275), steps into the path of an oncoming train sobbing "I gotta get away from here!" (275).

As Joan Sangster has analysed, Baird's last novel, *The Climate of Power* (1971), published after her retirement from three decades of work in the civil service and especially reflecting her experience as an information officer in the Department of Indian Affairs and Northern Development, is a satirical exposé of the male-dominated workplace and the paternalistic view of Indigenous peoples.

A writer's own experience is filtered in the work of Gwethalyn Graham (1913–65) as well. Despite the continental setting of her first novel, *Swiss Sonata* (1938), a Governor General's Award-winning publication, issued in England by Jonathan Cape and in the United States by Charles Scribner, succeeds in making the Pensionnat Les Ormes a recognizable and politically charged world. Certainly a more privileged milieu than the pavements and alleyways of *Waste Heritage*, the girls' finishing school contains its own drama: battles for control and curriculum among the teachers; girls dropped off and forgotten by parents or considered "mentally negligible" (84) by their brothers; proto-lesbian infatuations;

and, most prominently, bullying of Jewish and Bavarian Catholic students by the daughter of a German nationalist. The timing of the narrative, immediately before the January 1935 "plebiscite in the Saar, which was to determine whether this small territory [rich in coal], then owned by France, would remain under the aegis of the League of Nations or revert to Germany," is significant; the resultant decision to return to Germany enabled "the Nazis to manufacture military weapons, since coal was essential in making steel" (Cameron, "Introduction" ix–x). *Swiss Sonata*, blacklisted in Germany, was an amazingly mature production for the twenty-five-year-old novelist, who managed to combine aspects of her own experience along with contemporary politics and internment labour camp conditions in its continuous narrative.

Graham's upbringing in an upper-middle-class Toronto family devoted to refugee causes, schooling at Havergal College, four months at the "international finishing school Pensionnat les Allières" (Meadowcroft 62), and brilliant year at Smith College, all contributed to the reinvention of Gwethalyn Erichsen-Brown. Her university formation was halted by an elopement at nineteen, the birth of her only child, and divorce at twenty-one. As a novelist she adopted "the family name of the paternal grandmother she had never known" (Meadowcroft 48). Clearly Graham's four months at the Swiss boarding school were not wasted. She captured the microcosm of the Pensionnat on the hill overlooking Lausanne; the school was "the suspended little world" (4), a "Cat's cradle" of emotions and loyalties, "when your fingers are all tangled with crossed and re-crossed lines of string" (67). One element of cohesion is the lone English-Canadian student, Vicky Morrison, who appears to be supremely knowledgeable and self-confident; she manages to elicit information from a German student exhausted with worry about her brother sent to a labour camp. As adroitly as Baird folded in reportage about street conditions in Victoria in 1938, Graham manages to include facts about forced labour in 1934–5 Germany.

A comparable insider knowledge informs Graham's second novel, *Earth and High Heaven* (1944), another Governor General's Award winner, published in the United States by J.B. Lippincott and in London and Toronto by Jonathan Cape. "An overnight sensation," "the first English edition sold out on the day of publication"; although the novel sold more than a million copies, Graham's biographer, Barbara Meadowcroft, notes the observation of historian Jonathan Vance: "Canadian tax law of the time considered royalties to be unearned income, so the federal government took almost everything Graham earned; she never wrote another book, and when she died prematurely at age fifty, she was making ends meet by marking assignments for a Montreal high school" (Meadowcroft 119). Serialized in *Collier's Magazine* for $40,000, translated into fifteen languages, with an MGM option for film production, the novel of the romance between Westmount socialite-journalist Erica Drake and a Jewish lawyer from northern Ontario, Marc Reiser, was both well-promoted and topical – even though it strikes one later reader as "so inept that it ends up corrupting its own sincerity" (Lane 66).[2] Graham reveals the poisonous, polite reality of anti-Semitism in 1940s Montreal. As Marc clarifies for Erica's sister: "Erica was born on top ... If she marries me, she'll lose all that overnight" (183). *Earth and High Heaven* demonstrates how, through the force of Erica's independent personality, old sureties, like the bond with her father, who "felt that Erica was the only human being who really understood him" (31), melt away. Despite Erica's liberation from her father's influence, the novel does not address the "question that can't yet be asked: that of women's participation in the public world" (P. Coleman 168).

The contrastive structure of the novel traces the declining relationship with Charles Drake at the same time as Marc's ascent from reluctance to assurance about marrying Erica. Significantly, too, the struggle within Marc occurs during the Yom Kippur, Day of Atonement, services he attends with his parents. Only as a result of his brother's intervention does Marc recognize the patriarchal narrowness of his thinking: "like Charles Drake, he had considered himself to be in some mysterious way better qualified to decide what would be best for her in the long run than Erica was herself" (315).

Unlike Graham's almost-utopian romance, along with the narrative's pragmatic movement towards realization and its purposive dialogue, *By Grand Central Station I Sat Down and Wept*

(1945) by Elizabeth Smart (1913–86) offers a poetic, often discontinuous and fractured, expression of passionate longing. The novel's self-reflexive intrusions effectively dismantle the humanist conceptions of identity – prominent in the examples already mentioned – as complex but also stable, knowable, and somehow fixed. An impressionistic monologue directed both to an unnamed lover and to the reader, the text is a collage of allusions and voices, times and circumstances, exhilaration and vulnerability. The title is taken from the opening sentence of the last of the book's ten sections; the passage captures the sense of simultaneous desolation and resistance that has characterized the whole text.

> *By Grand Central Station I sat down and wept:*
>   *I will not be placated by the mechanical motions of existence, nor find consolation in the solicitude of waiters who notice my devastated face. Sleep tried to seduce me by promising a more reasonable tomorrow. But I will not be betrayed by such a Judas of fallacy: it betrays everyone: it leads them into death. Everyone acquiesces: everyone compromises.* (117)

The first-person voice admits being "mortally pierced with the seeds of love" (27), "in the trap" (36), "possessed by love [with] ... no options" (44), "as at sea, and as ignorant and mystified, as the first day I ever saw algebra" (47). She casts aside the appurtenances familiar to the Ottawa socialite Betty Smart – "the silver brushes with my name, the long gown, the car, the hundred suitors, poise in a restaurant" (48). In pursuit of poet George Barker, having "picked him out in cold deliberation" (112), she stoutly maintains the rewards of her action. Torment is part of the self-image, too, for in declaring that "love still uproots the heart better than an imagined landmine" (91), she is consumed "like a Saint Catherine's wheel of torture" (124). Smart's pain in following this married man by whom she bore four children has "operatic grandeur" (118). She wrote *By Grand Central Station* in 1941 while pregnant with her first child. Believing in "motherhood as an erotic and sexual triumph" (Sullivan, *By Heart* 198) and convinced that she "was made only for [Barker]" (78), she figures herself as the beloved in the *Song of Songs*, Isolde, Penelope, and Lot's wife, among others.

Published in London, when Barker was "more or less absent" and Smart "was trapped washing baby clothes and pushing prams" (Sullivan 153), *By Grand Central Station* was reviewed in the literary magazine *Horizon* as a work of "poetic imagination," without "self-pity" but "full of promise and belong[ing] to our time."[3] The novel was dramatized on BBC Radio. Some readers might quibble about including Smart in this pre-1950 period, especially since the work of this expatriate writer was not readily available in Canada until decades after its U.K. publication, although Smart had managed to post a few copies to friends. Smart's mother, an influential Ottawa hostess, complained about the "erotomania," bought and burnt copies sold in a local store, and prevailed on friends in External Affairs "to ensure that the book would not be imported into Canada" (Sullivan 229). The first American mass paperback from the Popular Library appeared in 1966; Deneau Publishers, in Smart's native Ottawa, issued the first Canadian hardcover edition in 1982; and the Vintage International edition of the work and its sequel, *The Assumption of Rogues and Rascals* (1978), appeared in 1992.

Smart's work has not only eluded censors; she herself has acquired a place in Canadian literature. She is the subject of Wendy Lill's play *Memories of You* (1989) and of Maya Gallus's film *Elizabeth Smart: On the Side of the Angels* (1991). The narrator of this film, Michael Ondaatje, who met Smart in 1982 when she was writer in residence at the University of Alberta and suffering from deteriorating eyesight, writes her into his novel *In the Skin of a Lion* (1996) as the blind Elizabeth who mentions a "tragic love affair" and instructs the protagonist, "Don't resent your life." Because *By Grand Central Station* mirrors and relates its monologist's life with such poetic intensity, Smart's biographer, Rosemary Sullivan, contends that the book is not autobiographical but "archetypal" (153).

As with Gwethalyn Graham and Elizabeth Smart, lived experience informs *Continental Revue* (1946) by Winifred Bambrick (1892–1969). Like Graham's *Swiss Sonata*, Bambrick's Governor General's Award-winning first novel, a saga of a year in the life of a large multinational travelling theatrical troupe, playing Rotterdam, London, Leeds, Hamburg, Berlin, Munich, Antwerp, and Amsterdam, unfolds amid the mounting tensions of pre-World War II Europe. From the intimate and minimalist subjects of *By Grand Central Station* we move to the vast stage of *Continental Revue* with its cast of 300. The novel was published in London by Faber and Faber and in the United States, as *Keller's Continental Revue*, by Houghton Mifflin. The second contrast with Smart is Bambrick's continuous, realist narrative relying on stable characterizations and progressively complicated story lines within and outside this theatrical community. Salutes of "Heil Hitler!" resound in the theatres, and Hitler and Mussolini reportedly meet in the Munich railway station. Ingenues in the company become bargaining chips for continued performance. The fragile, sparkling Austrian ballerina Kathi, "a baby with eyes not open" (414), is claimed as the tragic prize of a Nazi general.

Ottawa-born Bambrick, a concert harpist, had debuted in New York at the Aeolian Hall in 1913, "recorded for Thomas Edison in 1914," and in the 1920s "toured with John Philip Sousa's band," performing on "a small straight-board Wurlitzer" (Govea 20). She had played London's Alhambra Theatre from 1934 to 1936 before joining a circus troupe that was much like Keller's Continental Revue. She managed to book passage on the last train out of Leipzig in 1939. Bambrick's only novel combines a vivid, increasingly anxious sense of the locales, buildings, and streets frequented by the company with the persistent, not entirely discredited, creed of the secret power of the theatre as more compelling and unifying than dictatorship.

Gabrielle Roy's (1909–83) spectacular career testifies to her deeply rooted belief in the power of art, more precisely prose fiction, although she had been drawn to the theatre and had studied acting briefly in London in the late 1930s before returning to Canada. While most of her writing occurred after mid-century, her first novel, *Bonheur d'occasion*, appeared in 1945. The novel won the Prix Femina and a Governor General's Award; translated into English as *The Tin Flute* (1947),[4] and eventually into eight other languages, it was the choice of the Literary Guild of America, "the oldest and most prestigious book club in the US with its million members" (Ricard 264), as "book of the Month." This "model of the realistic mode in French Canada" (Shek 65) launched her public life as a writer.

Realist fiction, as we have noticed in the work of Graham, Baird, Smart, and Bambrick, is invariably informed by and refined through the experience of the writer herself. This situation does not justify exclusively biographical criticism, but it does prompt us to be aware of the convergences through which life nurtures art. In the case of Roy, one of the first superstars of Canadian writing, the subject of many volumes of criticism, and the author of a candid autobiography (*La détresse et l'enchantement*, 1984 [*Enchantment and Sorrow*, 1987]), it is important to allow for the osmotic influences of experience to enlarge our understanding of her fictional oeuvre.

After study and travel in Europe, Roy, a teacher on leave from her position in Saint Boniface, decided not to return to Manitoba but to settle in Montreal. As the petted youngest child of a family of nine, she knew her decision would disappoint her impoverished, widowed mother. Although her fiction will shuttle back and forth between urban Quebec (*Bonheur d'occasion*; *Alexandre Chenevert*, 1954) and rural Manitoba (*La petite poule d'eau*, 1950; *Rue Deschambault*, 1955) settings, the Montreal locale to which she was initially and, as she explains in the autobiography, forcefully drawn was the working-class quartier Saint-Henri:

> Its poverty moved me. Its poetry touched my heart, strains of guitars and other wistful scraps of music escaping beneath closed doors, the sound of the wind straying through warehouse passageways. I felt less alone here than in the crowds and bright lights of the city. (408)

The ambivalence of this attraction is noteworthy. The reading of the passage can colour our response to Gabrielle Roy. She overcame her internalized sense of "linguistic and cultural inferiority as a Franco-Manitoban" (Chapman 4), was determined to work and write her way out of the genteel poverty of her upbringing in Saint Boniface, but nevertheless felt, on her return in 1939, that she "had failed in everything, love, drama, writing" (*Enchantment and Sorrow* 403). She was accused of looking down from Westmount on the hovels of Saint-Henri to create "pernicious propaganda"

(Ricard 5).[5] In fact, one Saint-Henri native, Lise Payette, media star and Parti Québécois Minister of Cultural Affairs in the first Lévesque government (1976–81), has recorded the shock and shame she felt on reading *Bonheur d'occasion* as a teenager in 1954, causing her to see Roy as a spy mocking her and warping her view of the district:

> *J'ai regardé autour de moi avec ses yeux. Je nous ai vu pauvres, insignifiants, sans ambition et sans culture, 'nés pour un petit pain' et incapables d'en sortir, répétant de génération en génération les mêmes gestes et les mêmes erreurs. Je fus blessée au coeur. Je nous ai vus paresseux, nous contenant de peu et ne désirant rien d'autre.*[6]

Whatever lens we use in reading *Bonheur d'occasion*, dedicated to Roy's recently deceased mother, Mélina, and in whatever translation,[7] there is no denying the crushing reality of poverty, particularly as a response to the life-altering events of pregnancy and war. *Bonheur d'occasion* uses a linear, realist mode to trace the lives of the Lacasse family from March to June 1940. Mother Rose-Anna in the last trimester of her twelfth pregnancy, working as a cleaning woman and seamstress; father Azarius, an unemployed former taxi-driver, salesman, and carpenter; and Florentine, the nineteen-year-old eldest, a waitress in a five-and-dime, whose wages are the family's main income, are the principal characters. As their name indicates, poverty boxes in the Lacasse (*casse*: box) family, for whom any form of happiness (*bonheur*) is fleeting or second-hand (*d'occasion*). The English title refers to the request of the six-year-old Daniel, dying of leukemia, for a little toy: "'Tu m'apporteras une flûte, maman!'" (I: 123). That the child dies alone in hospital just before Rose-Anna goes into labour underlines the inescapable, pathetic sense of entrapment. A "prisoner of the urban wilderness" (Grace, "Quest" 197), Florentine belongs to the rouged girls who content themselves with romance novels, "des romans-feuilletons de quinze cents" (I: 13), "burning their fingers at the wretched little fires of what they took for love" (10); hence, her "reckless" and "imprudent ... running to meet happiness, all alone in this furious night" (36) with the social-climbing

Jean Lévesque is predictable and doomed. She scorns the sobering advice of Emmanuel Létourneau and his unwelcome kiss, wiping her mouth "as soon as he was gone" (142). Yet Emmanuel becomes the convenient husband to camouflage Florentine's pregnancy and to outfit her in new clothes before he leaves for the front.

From the vantage of the family's misery, Florentine is not the only one who sees the prospect of war as "a last resort" (19), "sa suprême resource" (I: 26). For his part, Azarius signs up to provide for Rose-Anna. "We never had that much money in our lives!" he claims, adding ruefully, "The best of all is, you're going to be rid of me" (371). The exhausted *mater dolorosa*, the infinitely loving mother whose 'poverty of spirit' will inherit the earth" (McPherson, "The Garden and the Cage" 52), Rose-Anna might appear to be the emblem of "maternal resignation" (Whitfield 23). However, she is a figure of action, insight, and resolve. It is she who finds a new lodging for the family every May, who trudges to the hospital to visit her dying son – now infatuated with an English nurse, who sews the party dress Florentine later scorns, and who prays to stay alive until the children are grown. It is her shocked cry at the sight of Azarius in uniform that is "lost as a screaming locomotive passe[s]" (372). Despite being muffled, Rose-Anna's anguish at Daniel's death, Azarius's departure, and Florentine's loveless marriage is a forceful, emotive indicator of the stunted prospects and foreboding gloom for the Lacasse family. Like the dry leaves "tortured among electric wires and clotheslines ... and shrivelled before they were fully out" (383), this poignant saga captures the reality of blasted promises, evanescent happiness.

In contrast to Roy's characters, who have suffered from the criticism that they are too grim and frustrated, the figures brought to life in the simultaneously appearing smaller ambit of the fiction of Ethel Wilson (1888–1980) are sometimes skewered for being too ebullient and purposive. Yet both stereotypes are misleading. Appearing in the same year as *The Tin Flute*, Wilson's first published novel, *Hetty Dorval* (1947), published when she was sixty years old, and her series of family vignettes, *The Innocent Traveller* (1949), introduce the narrative deftness and subtle irony that have come to be her hallmarks.

A teacher like Roy before turning to writing, rooted in the west coast rather than Manitoba and Quebec, and more diffident than Roy about promoting her work, Ethel Wilson remains, in the words of her biographer, David Stouck, "at once too obvious and too elusive, too full of doubt and too wise" (284). With great agility her fiction explores the contingency and elusiveness of language. Even though, true to the characteristics of her own avoidant temperamental style, she dismissed *Hetty Dorval* as "amateur" and "slight" and supplied her publisher Macmillan with the furthest thing from a "studio portrait," a blurred snap in which she is "windblown" and "squinting" (Stouck 124),[8] the novel does usher the reader into Wilson's world. She finds inspiration in John Donne, using three[9] quotations as epigraphs; the excerpt from "Communitie" is particularly telling, since the poet goes on to claim that "women deserve nor blame, nor praise" (line 18). The Donne excerpt proves to be curiously ambivalent when the reader meets the title character, a "woman of no reputation" (42), described as "a human cat" (33) and "the Menace" (52), but who is ultimately "hard to hate" (104). The fascination this exotic stranger exerts on the British Columbia schoolgirl Frankie Burnaby, the insightful, maturing first-person narrator, is both understandable and mysterious.

Hetty's self-absorption, so dramatically deflated in the recognition scene where her real mother reveals herself, is paralleled in the novel's structure with Frankie's dawning awareness of this woman's true nature. The British Columbia setting, particularly the village of Lytton where the Thompson and Fraser Rivers meet, is itself a symbolic presence of contrasting colours and temperaments, not merely a scenic backdrop: "the line where the expanse of emerald and sapphire dancing water joins and is quite lost in the sullen Fraser" (15). Unlike the natural scene of absorption, conquest, and amplitude, Wilson's narrative crafts intimate scenes of growing awareness for Frankie, as the young woman strives to discern "how much of Hetty was artful and how much was artless" (77).

The Edgeworth family stories, mirroring the history and personalities of her own genteel Bryant family that Wilson had been sketching for two decades before their appearance in *The Innocent Traveller*, trace a huge span of time in the life of the centenarian heroine, Great Aunt Topaz Edgeworth. Unmarried yet matriarchal, exuberant yet ironically untouched by her surroundings, this "small ancient being" with an "unquenched vitality" (255) suffuses the whole narrative. At the age of 100, having journeyed from a Victorian childhood where Matthew Arnold is a dinner guest to death in modern Vancouver, she "is still little Topaz Edgeworth with a strong infusion of *grande dame*, she is invincible" (271). Wilson's agile narratorial voice combines "Topaz's childish view of the world of adults" (R.D. MacDonald 65) with the final release of the frail, lace-bonneted figure as "a memory, a gossamer" (275). This stylish portrait is comparable to the satiric humour of Kenneth Grahame's evocation of the Olympians in *The Golden Age* and *Dream Days* or P.L. Travers's description of the Banks family in her *Mary Poppins* books. An aura of Arcadian innocence hovers over these vignettes of an "inviolably respectable" family without a single black sheep. As Blanche Gelfant remarks, "Families can be idyllic in Vancouver, but only if they belong ... to the past, like the Edgeworths" (20).

Wrestling with the Strictures of Marriage and Family

Along with the continuing careers of Gabrielle Roy and Ethel Wilson, women's fiction of the mid-century and beyond includes startling confrontations of the restrictive, ossified, and often perilous conventions of family and married life. When these fictional landscapes belong to the past, it is to no idyllic Arcadia but rather to a historic re-creation always filtered through questions, judgments, and criticism informed by the present. A bold scepticism impatient with pieties and norms propels this writing that branches into an array of geographies, time periods, and psychological interiors. While there is no single or standard metric with which to gauge the expanding, variable complexity of women's fiction, one sure feature is its sophisticated narrative audacity.

No better example of such a shift towards a staccato yet poetic narrative style exists than the fiction of Anne Hébert (1916–2000).

Although her career as novelist, short story writer, poet, essayist, and screenwriter stretched over five decades, her earliest fiction – the collection *Le torrent* (1950; *The Torrent*, 1973) and *Les chambres de bois* (1958; *The Silent Rooms*, 1974) – establishes the lineaments of all her subsequent work. Hébert explores psychological torment and analysis embedded within social themes of the rejection of religiously inculcated guilt and challenge of the restraints of marriage. Despite the fact that three of the five *contes* in *Le torrent* had appeared earlier in periodicals, the overall effect of this "inaugural" collection is of critical intensity and narrative power. "La maison de l'esplanade" [The House on the Esplanade] reveals the deadening influence of the *haute bourgeoisie*, as room after room in the ancestral home of Stéphanie Bichette is sealed off, and the only other living person in this mausoleum, the maid, Géraldine, dreams of closing the final door "à aligner des tombes et à bien ratisser les tertres" (109), to line up the graves and rake over the burial mounds. The title story, derived from a newspaper account of a gruesome rape and murder committed by a seminarian, is the most shocking, conveying the pent-up anger of an illegitimate son, forced into the seminary by his prostitute mother in an attempt to reclaim her reputation; the ex-seminarian's matricide and suicide testify to the explosive violence.

As well as recalling the dark alienation of her poetry collection, *Le tombeau des rois* (1953), Hébert's first novel, *Les chambres de bois* (*The Silent Rooms*), completed in Paris where she lived for most of her career, presents another form of abortive escape. The orphaned Catherine, responsibly raising three younger siblings, moves from an unnamed "town where blast furnaces flamed in the sky, day and night, like the dark palaces of the Apocalypse" (4) to the stifling enclosure of a wood-panelled apartment in Paris as the bride of the bourgeois, but effete and impotent, Michel. With his promiscuous sister forming a bizarre ménage à trois, and Michel insisting that Catherine perform no manual work, the virtually imprisoned bride becomes a pale shadow of herself, until her decision to rebel against this lifelessness. The country life with her peasant lover contrasts startlingly with the narrative's earlier urban gloom and enervating aesthetic.

Like many expatriate writers, Hébert narrates the life of her native province from a distance, most famously in her novel *Kamouraska* (1970; English edition 1973). Winner of the Paris Prix des Libraires and subject of the 1973 Claude Jutra film, her second novel experiments with narrative voice and point of view, taking readers into the labyrinthine psychic realities of Elisabeth d'Aulnières-Tassy-Rolland. The novel is based on some details of the 1841 trial of Joséphine Taché in Quebec City, accused and acquitted of the murder of her husband, whose manor home was Kamouraska, and her subsequent prolific marriage to a notary who was later a Member of Parliament. *Kamouraska* employs diverse narrative voices – Elisabeth herself, her maiden aunts, her mother – and first- and third-person points of view. From the abusive madness of Antoine Tassy, Sieur de Kamouraska, to the passionate embrace of Dr George Nelson, her lover, and the unctuous piety of Jérôme Rolland, her dying husband for whom she appears the model wife, Elisabeth is haunted by a "guilt-ridden religion" and "the injustices of an oppressive society" that "subverts the traditional connotations of 'primitive' and 'civilized'" (Anderson 47). Kamouraska has become her prison but also a defiant shield against accusing voices. Both polyphony and multiple personalities characterize Elisabeth's psychic divide. "Torn between opposing values, the fairy princess becomes a witch; the loving wife, a shrew; the mother, a murderess" (Sturzer 37). Aware of her own theatricalism, Elisabeth plays at madness and innocence. At the deathbed of her husband, Madame Rolland experiences no liberation but rather a sense of being "alone and hungry" (249). As Mary Jean Green and others have recognized, the closing allusion to La Corriveau, the wife hanged in 1763 for killing her husband, with her exposed corpse legendarily transformed into a tormenting witch, captures Elisabeth's isolation. Misperceptions abound and "doors shut tight" (249), barring her entry. The mulatta midwife, accomplice, and accuser, Aurélie, on the margins of the narrative as a minority and an ethnic presence, shares many of the restrictions hemming in her mistress, Elisabeth. As Roxanne Rimstead observes, "they are also bound to the maintenance of the manor and the great house as ordered spaces (according to bourgeois taste

[Bourdieu], the Father's house [Smart], and the cult of domesticity [McClintock]), even though they compete for men's attention within that space" ("Working-Class Intruders" 49).

Hébert's subsequent novels accentuate this sense of bleakness, ineluctability, and fatality. *Les enfants du sabbat / Children of the Black Sabbath* (1975, 1977), winner of the Governor General's Award for fiction and the Académie française prize, uncovers the effects of the Depression in 1930s Quebec. Perverse scenes of incest, rape, witchcraft, and demonic possession, many within the Convent of the Precious Blood, invert and thus challenge Christian principles of virtue and morality. Her fourth novel, *Héloïse* (1980), revisits the motif of enclosure and entrapment of *The Silent Rooms*, only this time underscoring an obsessive fascination with death that precludes escape. *Les fous de bassan / In the Shadow of the Wind* (1982, 1983), set in the fictional community of Griffin Creek, Gaspé, labelled accurately "l'enfer" (242), takes the diabolic to a new extreme in the figure of the rapist-murderer Stevens Brown. His chthonic presence in the novel's world of hostility, hate, jealousy, and lust for power, also captured in the 1987 film adaptation by Yves Simoneau, reinforces the linkage between "Griffin" and "griffer" (to claw), as characters claw one another for violent pleasure or erotic supremacy.

Hébert's expatriate contemporary and friend Mavis Gallant (1922–2014) has itemized their shared experiences, as she declared in her introduction to an edition of Hébert's *Collected Later Novels*:

> We were both from Québec, though from dissimilar backgrounds, hers in Québec City, mine in Montreal. We had been to convent schools run by the same order of nuns. We had both worked at the National Film Board, when it was still in Ottawa. We had both moved to Paris to live and to write. We had both decided to live for and on our writing, and we did. (xi)

But differences separate them, too. Writing in English and mainly, though not exclusively, in the genre of the short story, Gallant chose to stay in Paris rather than reside periodically, as Hébert did, in Quebec. For six decades, more than 100 of Gallant's short stories have appeared in *The New Yorker*. With international settings and characteristic irony, these strongly imagined, accomplished, and acclaimed narratives succeed in distilling a whole cast of characters or an emotional sequence into a brief passage. One of her early *New Yorker* stories, "By the Sea" (1954), is a subtle study of American, British, and German guests at the Villa Margate on the south coast of Spain. Though "bored with one another," they are observant enough to realize that the supercilious Mrs Parsters appears interested only in her dog, Bobby, "part of whose ancestry was revealed in a noble spitz tail he wore furled on his back like a Prince of Wales plume" (3, 4). But the widowed Mrs Parsters is herself quick to judge a May-December romance, sniffing at it with scorn.

> *Dr. Tuttlingen and Heidemarie stood ankle-deep. He held her by the waist and seemed to be saying, "Come, you see, it's not dangerous at all!" When Dr. Tuttlingen was not about, Heidemarie managed to swim adequately by herself, even venturing out quite far. On that occasion, however, she squealed and flung her arms around his neck as a warm, salty ripple broke against them on its way to shore. Dr. Tuttlingen led her tenderly back to the beach. "Of course they're not married," said Mrs. Parsters. "It fairly shouts! Damned old goat!"* (6)

The narrator's skilful use of dialogue conveys the mini-drama of Mrs Parsters's disappointed hopes of convincing Heidemarie to leave the "old goat" and return to England with her as her servant.

Gallant's first novel, *Green Water, Green Sky* (1959), set in Paris and Cannes, expands the capacity for character study; allusion to paintings becomes the medium through which to understand characters' views of themselves and others. As Lesley Clement observes, "the techniques of the visual artist" allow Gallant "to compose, metaphorically, the structures, patterns, and gyres within her novel" (71). Bob prizes his beautiful wife, Flor, "an object as cherished as anything he might buy," as an Impressionist woman, thus increasing "his sense of possession and love" (37). Sliding into a nervous breakdown, Flor, the infertile young wife who is commodified by both her husband and her oblivious, self-absorbed mother, is not a Biedermeier or an Impressionist or a Pre-Raphaelite heroine; rather, she is finally admitted to an asylum, not a museum.

Much of the fiction of the fifties by women writers – in the continuing careers of Ethel Wilson and Gabrielle Roy and the debut novel of Adele Wiseman (1928–92) – reveals differing constructions and illusions of happiness and the fragility of survival. The two novellas of Wilson's *The Equations of Love* (1952) concentrate on the role of deliberate misrepresentation along with either a lack of introspection or an alert cunning. Mort, a gardener, and Myrtle, a cleaning lady, are the central couple of "Tuesday and Wednesday"; they exist in a realm of fabrications and barely concealed hatred. "A complete mistress (or victim) of the volte-face ... one of the reasons for her control and enslavement of Mort," Myrtle "reserve(s) the licence to dislike him, to hate him even" (13, 16). The narrator ushers us inside the world of self-satisfying private accommodation, in which Mort can believe his own lies and intense, class-based suspicion. Mort sees his employer as "a rich man who no doubt made his money by graft" (23), and Myrtle judges a neatly dressed street-car passenger as "A society woman! ... I'll bet her husband's no good. They make me smile, they certny do, society women" (17). Mort's bringing home "a *bo*kay of real nice flowers" (actually scavenged from a funeral home) to appease Myrtle's anger at the dinner ruined by his lateness (caused by drinking beer with an army buddy) defines the basis of deceit and illusion in their marriage. The more resourceful central figure of "Lily's Story," a single parent, is another hard, determined character. Her mask as a loyal widow and devoted mother not only inhibits spontaneous speech and desire but also permits her moves to the position of treasured housekeeper in an aristocratic home and then a small hospital. Even Lily's abrupt departure to escape detection and her demotion to hotel chambermaid do not diminish her prospects for success. Wilson upends moral expectations, encouraging us to cheer for the comic triumph of this canny, though damaged and repressed, survivor.

Wilson's most celebrated novel, *Swamp Angel* (1954), is another survival narrative, highlighting the restorative power of the B.C. interior to bring about the liberation of Maggie Lloyd "as free of care or remembrance as if she had just been born (as perhaps she had after much anguish)" (34). Having manoeuvred her escape from marriage to Edward Vardoe with split-second timing, Maggie luxuriates in a reality far away from Vancouver. Sleeping on the porch at Three Loon Lake (Wilson's evocation of a favourite fishing lodge at Lac Le Jeune), amid the chuckle of owls and under the "draperies" of the Northern Lights, she feels the absence of "her tormented nights of humiliation between four small walls and in the compass of a double bed" (122). Compassionate and morally aware, Maggie does remember and replay the death of her first husband and child, "the dreadful thing she had done to Edward Vardoe" (41) and his "brown spaniel eyes" (140). She also fulfils the promise to throw the pearl-handled revolver, the Swamp Angel, into the lake. Her strong-armed, iconic gesture not only honours a pledge made to her deceased friend, Nell Severance, but traces the consecutive moments of break, stillness, and resumption which themselves outline the trajectory of her journey.

Wilson's last published novel, *Love and Salt Water* (1956), and the collection *Mrs Golightly and Other Stories* (1961) continue what George Bowering has aptly identified as "the problem of home" and "a girl or woman looking for the meaning of the term" (in the Afterword to *Swamp Angel* 215). For Ellen Cuppy in *Love and Salt Water* this search for meaning involves war service, familial estrangement, a romantic jilt, and a horrendous accident; the whole cavalcade of experiences underscores the narrator's observation that "Nothing is safe" (68). This notion of being on the brink also characterizes the diverse, subtly ironic stories and often exotic locales of *Mrs Golightly*.

With the novels of Gabrielle Roy's continuing career, narration is less concerned with life on the brink than with distinctions between rural and urban existence, primarily between the Manitoba of her youth and contemporary Quebec. Inspired by experiences in her first teaching positions in isolated Manitoba villages, Roy creates in *La petite poule d'eau / Where Nests the Water Hen* (1950, 1951) the frontier idyll of the Toussignant family – Luzina, Hippolyte, and their large family (twelve children, eventually) – living on an island in the Little Water Hen River. Luzina's campaign for a school and supplies, the building of the log school, the succession of three teachers, and Luzina's almost-yearly "holidays" to Rorketon after which she returns with a new baby sketch the elements of this tenderly nested account. The novel's charm consists in its innocent simplicity, seen in Luzina's delight in writing letters and her awe at the response of the teacher "in a beautiful handwriting absolutely straight and without erasures" (42). Ecumenical goodwill triumphs as Father Joseph-Marie's undaunted faith secures donations for his church from the Jew Isaac Boussorvski, the Methodist Mrs MacFarlane, the Presbyterian Kathy McGregor, and the Protestant president of the Canadian Pacific Railway, Mr MacDonald. The novel celebrates the warm, close family, where problem-free births and the absence of serious illnesses are taken for granted, where there is no boredom and no moping about. Such a picture of untrammelled existence is necessarily a moment in time. Even as her youngest child is learning the alphabet and helping to address letters to older siblings who have pursued careers in teaching, nursing, farming, and medicine, Luzina learns that "already life, to which she had given so abundantly, little by little was leaving her behind" (97).

While in their formative years the Toussignants lead sheltered, happy lives in northern Manitoba, Alexandre Chenevert, the paying teller ("caissier-payeur") at the Savings Bank of the City and Island of Montreal, is the overlooked urban time-server, "the little man in cage number two" (23) for eighteen years. Dyspeptic, insomniac, suspicious, and penny-pinching, locked within a joyless marriage as well, Chenevert, the central figure of Roy's third novel, *Alexandre Chenevert, caissier / The Cashier* (1954, 1955), bears "within him a terrible yearning for happiness" (52). His brief vacation at Lac Vert only reveals "the spot where he would like to die" (154). Relief or recognition is fleeting and ironic, deferred until the novel's close, when Chenevert is hospitalized and dying of prostate cancer. His agony strips the attending chaplain's faith "of all proud pretensions" (248), and the name of this forgotten man, "a thing tender and mysterious," is uttered "after these several years" (251).

In Roy's fourth novel, *Rue Deschambault / Street of Riches* (1955, 1957), which won her second Governor General's Award for Fiction, the Manitoba setting and family stories, this time a semi-autobiographical evocation of her Saint-Boniface childhood, combine both the idyllic features of a vanished past, reminiscent of *La petite poule d'eau*, and the disappointment and frustration associated with *Alexandre Chenevert*. The first-person narrator, the youngest child, Christine, nicknamed Petite Misère, is the maturing medium through whom the reader learns about the family dynamic. Those forces include the differences in age and disposition between the sunshine-loving, younger Maman and the melancholic insomniac Papa, forcibly retired from a position in the Ministry of Colonization. The family also includes a sister with "the soul of a revolutionist" (16) who becomes a nun, and another sister who is institutionalized and dies young. Christine's realization of her need to write and of her process of composition reflects her parentage, as she sees herself "partagée entre ces deux côtés de ma nature qui me venait de mes parents divisés par le jour et la nuit" (*Rue Deschambault* 240). Christine's extended story as a young teacher is the subject of *La route d'Altamont / The Road Past Altamont* (1966). The autobiographical or semi-autobiographical mode proved appealing to more Canadian women writers, as Claire Martin's (Claire Montreuil, b. 1914) *Dans un gant de fer / In an Iron Glove* (1965/6, 1968), Margaret Laurence's (1928–87) *A Bird in the House* (1970), and Alice Munro's (b. 1931) *Lives of Girls and Women* (1971) witness.

Adele Wiseman's two novels, *The Sacrifice* (1952) and *Crackpot* (1974), challenge the emergent conventions of women's fiction in startling ways. Though both are situated in Winnipeg, their concern is not with the contrasts of rural and urban living. Invoking biblical echoes, imbued with an unshaken belief in the significance of the writer as a moral witness, and writing "always as a Canadian, a woman, and a Jew who sought to explore the human condition" (Panofsky, *Force of Vocation* 5), Wiseman traces the linkages between Old and New Worlds, between moral principle and mortal desire. Refugee from a pogrom in which two of his sons are hanged, Abraham, the butcher and patriarch of *The Sacrifice*, carries with him the mystery the novel probes: "Who has to take a life stands alone on the edge of creation. Only God can understand him then" (42). Clashes with his only surviving son, Isaac, who in a reversal of the *Genesis* narrative ultimately sacrifices himself to save the Torah scrolls from a burning synagogue, revolve around the acknowledgment that "it's hard to be a Jew ... but it's still harder to be a human being" (153). *The Sacrifice* is an intricately recursive, haunting narrative, in which Abraham's murder of Laiah recalls the blasphemous sacrifice of the cow in the Old World at the novel's opening. Wiseman confronts the reader with the dilemma of grappling with Abraham's rationalization of his horrific act, how the killing of this prostitute can evoke the chorus of "Life" (360) from his three dead sons, and how he can indict himself as "creator and destroyer" (388). With Wiseman claiming "an abiding love for Abraham," *The Sacrifice* suggests a "patriarchal ideology ... that venerates the male and his progeny" (Panofsky, "Success" 333, 348).

Although this Governor General's Award-winning novel launched Wiseman's career, it is important to note the differences between its "authoritative, monological, and patriarchal representation of the world propagated by the protagonist Abraham" and the "multiple and decentralized vision explored by the protagonist Hoda in *Crackpot*" (Mack 134). As Jonathan Kertzer argues, the sharp contrasts involve "an unavailing sacrifice," "the blasphemy of broken forms" in the earlier novel and "the efficacy of self-sacrifice" in the later one ("Beginnings and Endings" 31). An oversize, ebullient, strong-minded survivor, Hoda the prostitute, who knows "they've been laughing at [her] all [her] life," stands at the heart of Wiseman's novel; Hoda becomes "something of a vested memory ... somehow still unrepentantly out of pitch with the rest of humanity" (244, 286). Fiercely loyal to her widowed blind father, Danile, for whom she is the sole support, she caters for the abundant sexual needs of her community and experiences its retributive venom. Not only does she adopt an instructive take on pious righteousness, she also shows the breadth of her moral compass by conducting her own acute, retrospective examination of right and wrong before agreeing to the provocative scene of incest. Blending "the Lurianic story of creation and the messianic promise of redemption" (Kertzer 17), *Crackpot* is a novel preoccupied with brokenness and, arguably, with mending and wholeness. As Francis Zichy sees it, "the very act by which mending is attempted can only be another act of breaking" (270). From the opening tale of Hoda's grandfather, the tinker, mender of broken pots, to the closing observation of the aware "fallen fat woman" (285) who confronts "the horrible deformities of the human vessel" (292), the narrative enacts Wiseman's interest "in describing people on the edge of society, people who are deformed either physically or psychologically" (Morisco 129). She uses the fracture between past and present to build new meanings.

However, not all fiction in this mid-century decade, coinciding with the dawn of second-wave feminism, dealt with outsiders. In fact, it was still mainly "middle class in its affirmation and rejection of values" (McPherson, "Fiction" 233). Appearing in an era stereotyped by "the image of carefree, conspicuous consumption" and women's acceptance that "their roles as wives and mothers provided happiness, or, at the very least contentment" (Korinek 233), the novels of Grace Irwin (1907–2008) and Phyllis Brett Young (1914–96) offer rich perspectives on the conflicts of women's emotional subjectivities. The first three of Irwin's seven[10] novels appeared in the 1950s; set in the Toronto of her own childhood and adult life, *Least of All Saints* (1952) and *Andrew Connington* (1954) revolve around Emmanuel College at Victoria University and the intellectual struggles of a young minister in a well-heeled downtown parish. Theology and hermeneutics are the source of tensions, not Andrew's relatively placid, though initially childless, home life. His love for his wife surprises him "rather by its revelation of the purity possible in intense passion than by any disclosure of unsuspected depths of sensuality in his nature" (*Least of All Saints* 270–1). A classics major at the University of Toronto, Irwin was a high-school teacher of Latin for thirty-nine years, all but one of them at Humberside Collegiate, experiences reflected in the depiction of teacher Aran Waring in *In Little Place* (1959). The second of Young's four[11] novels, *The Torontonians* (1960), deals with the quiet desperation of housewife Karen Whitney in a fictional Toronto suburb, where closet alcoholism, barbiturate use, and a sprinkling of affairs contribute to the "gilt-edged suburban labyrinth" (13). With controlling, single-character viewpoints, both Irwin's Waring and Young's Whitney explain and interrogate their physical, material spaces to understand, situate, and at times rationalize their emotional realities, recalling cosy flashes of childhood and genteel upbringing so at odds with the radical changes and urban sprawl of their world. In a sense both protagonists *are* outsiders. Unmarried Aran, first female department head, holds her own, as did Irwin, against hordes of invading educational theorists and opts for living "fully and excitingly in a fairly circumscribed area" (214). By contrast, Karen's experience of "women's geographical isolation" and "sharp gender division of labour" (Harris 166) fuels her escape from the enervating suburban patterns of conformity and desired return to work and life in the urban core.

Revolutionary Talents and Experiments

Into the 1960s, more first novels by women – Sheila Watson's *The Double Hook* (1959), Marie-Claire Blais's *La belle bête / Mad Shadows* (1959, 1960), Margaret Laurence's *This Side Jordan* (1960), and Patricia Blondal's *A Candle to Light the Sun* (1960) – expand narrative experimentation, highlighting both minimalism and density and critiquing family and community in bold, often poetic, fearful language.

Although Watson's (1909–98) first-written novel, *Deep Hollow Creek* (1992), was published sixty years after its composition, her first-published novel, itself preceded by short fiction in *Queen's Quarterly* and *The Tamarack Review*, had germinated in drafts for some time. As her biographer Fred Flahiff recounts, this spare, dense book "began in the isolation and loneliness of Dog Creek [Watson's first teaching assignment] ... grew out of voices heard on a street in Toronto [where she was pursuing doctoral studies with Marshall McLuhan], and the pain and loneliness of two years in Calgary – [and] reached its final form in the revisions that Sheila undertook in Paris" (167). Her Paris journals provide another lens on the storytelling of her modernist novel. Linda Morra argues that "her very illegibility, even anonymity, and her sense of alienation as expressed in the journals *is* the experience of women, the *flâneur*, and the modernist artist" (105). Set in the Cariboo, the symbolic novel opens with a son killing his mother, an act accomplished by the fifth line of the narrative. Although its dry-belt B.C. interior is desiccated in contrast to the luxuriance of *Swamp Angel*, Ethel Wilson nevertheless hailed this "non-realist yet non-Romantic" novel as "personal incandescence in a lighted mind ... an emergence from within" ("A Cat among the Falcons" 16). The title refers to the inescapable doubleness of all experience: "That when you fish for glory you catch the darkness too. That if you hook twice the glory you hook twice the fear" (61). Although the dominating, repressive figure of Mrs Potter haunts and paralyses the living, effecting daughter Greta's hate-filled self-immolation and son James's retreat from acknowledging responsibility, the narrative does convey a passage through ruin, flames, and return to redemption. "The mythic structure of *The Double Hook* is the archetypal pattern of redemption through death and rebirth, the religious ritual celebrating the re-entry of love into the wasteland" (Morriss 84). Spiritual regeneration, emblematized in the birth of Lenchen and James's child, called Felix, recognizes the role of suffering and rupture in this process. The closing voice of Coyote, both trickster and tricked one, encapsulates a benediction of sorts:

> *I have set his feet on soft ground;*
> *I have set his feet on the sloping shoulders*
> *of the world.* (134)

"Soft ground" and "sloping shoulders" convey the imprint of human weight, frailty, and need.

The other revolutionary work of the same year, the explosive *La belle bête* of the nineteen-year-old Marie-Claire Blais (b. 1939), shares the features of a disintegrating family and the threats of fire and water. But in *Mad Shadows* there is no hint of redemption or regeneration: the symbolic destruction of the family corresponds to the collapse of a social order. Topography is deliberately unspecific. However, the psychological realism of the characters is piercingly acute: the beauty-obsessed mother, Louise; the unloved ugly daughter, Isabelle-Marie; the empty-headed, soulless, but beautiful son, Patrice, on whom the mother dotes; and Louise's second husband, "the irresistible seducer" Lanz attracted to "an old doll" (26). The marriage of Isabelle-Marie to the blind Michel creates another dysfunctional family, as the birth of their daughter and Michel's sudden sightedness result in his revulsion at their ugliness. Fatality and disaster haunt this narrative. The succession of tragedies is unremitting. The accumulation involves Louise's pus-filled face cancer, Lanz's being trampled by a horse ridden by Patrice, and the beautiful idiot's disfigurement in scalding water at the hands of his sister; the tragedies expand to include Patrice's abandonment and commitment to an insane asylum, Isabelle Marie's torching of the ancestral home and walking into the path of an oncoming train, and Patrice's Narcissus-like drowning where "the Beautiful Beast found his soul at last" (128). Readers soon dismiss the flicker of insight in this last line of a black fairy tale; what stays with us is the throbbing picture of contempt and bitterness.

> Had Isabelle-Marie been a more simple creature, she might have grown up without malice ... Wickedness was her second self; she was like those beings who lead two separate lives, one by day, and a more sinister one by night. (53)

This is territory far removed from the acknowledgment of Gabrielle Roy's Christine about her temperamental inheritance from Maman and Papa.

With the encouragement of University of Laval sociologist Father Georges Levesque, *La belle bête* launched Blais's prolific career (more than twenty novels, five plays, three collections of poetry, and an autobiography, to date). Her fifth novel, *Une saison dans la vie d'Emmanuel / A Season in the Life of Emmanuel* (1965, 1966), with its Quebec location and repressed family struggles, identified her loyalties to the Quiet Revolution. The novel throbs with strong indictments of patriarchal, clerical control: the dead-eyed mother of sixteen children; her newest baby, Emmanuel, who sees his father raping his mother nightly; the consumptive son Jean-Le

Maigre; another son who loses his fingers in a boot factory accident; and a pedophilic priest. Two scenes succinctly convey the struggle for survival. Daughter Héloïse, dismissed as a novice from the convent and now a prostitute who services the town's worthies, views herself as "cast up on a sterile shore" and her solicitor-client "as a child, a big baby with primal appetites, suspended from her nipple" (118). The closing scene of Grand-mère Antoinette's forced cheer, "Everything is going well; we musn't lose heart. It's been a hard winter, but the spring will be better. We must thank heaven that Héloïse sends us a little money every week." (129), does not dispel the gloom.

The two longer narratives, Laurence's *This Side Jordan* and Blondal's *A Candle to Light the Sun*, both coloured by the authors' lived experience, explore moments of personal transformation prompted either by a political change or a movement away from a childhood setting. An ambiguity about the future in the Gold Coast colony about to become the independent republic of Ghana informs Laurence's debut novel; as well, travel writing, a short story collection, and translation emerged from her seven-year stay in Africa (eighteen months in Somaliland and five years in the Gold Coast). With language blending biblical allusion and coarse talk, the novel's third-person narration alternates interior monologues from the Anglo-Irish accountant in an export-import firm, Johnnie Kestoe, "the racist and sexist protagonist" (Stovel 136), and the Ghanaian teacher of African history at Futura Academy, Nathaniel Amegbe. Each viewpoint is full of complex apprehensions. For Nathaniel, "the English either ... despised Africans or they wanted to turn themselves into Africans" (153). Laurence maintained that "the keynote of this novel is change and growth"; she strove not merely to caricature the English, like "most of the British couples from [her] husband's firm," as "well-meaning human dinosaurs, old colonialists who couldn't recognize that their time was over in Africa, and who ... were terrified to go back to their own countries" (Stovel 137).[12] While ambitious Johnnie grudgingly tolerates the Africanization program in his company, whereby Africans replace British employees, Nathaniel, struggling to reconcile his tribal past with mission school upbringing and the new Africa, leaves his teaching post to return to a village.

The agony of the quest for identity leads Patricia Blondal's (1926–59) protagonist, David Newman, away from his native Manitoba small town of Mouse Bluffs, modelled on Blondal's own home town of Souris, to college in Winnipeg. A biographical connection links Blondal to Laurence and Wiseman; all three were students together at United College in Winnipeg, and Laurence was one of the first reviewers of Blondal's novel, hailing her "treatment of a Canadian prairie town" as "the best [she had] ever read" ("Small Town's Silences" 5). Blondal had died of breast cancer at the age of thirty-two. Among the remarkable features of this first of her two posthumously published novels (portions of *From Heaven with a Shout* [1963] had been serialized in *Chatelaine* in 1959) is the adroit interleaving of details, characters, and motifs, the "ripples of allusion and symbol" (Ricou, "Twin Misunderstandings" 68) from the first half set in the town and the second half in the city. *A Candle to Light the Sun* shuttles back and forth between realism and symbolism in weaving its meaning. Complicating the novel's overall tissue of reality are its portraits of a perceptive drunkard and privileged reprobate who are also positive and negative guides to emotional maturity. To locate identifying markers of belonging, genealogy, and direction, she depicts a river that can bridge or imprison memories, a house that can symbolize ambition and decay, and a labile tension between town and city. In her title this "poet's novelist" (Ricou, "Long Poem" 294) echoes both the Bible's apocalyptic promise of eternal light to obviate candle and sun (Revelation 22:5) and William Blake's reduction of presumed knowledge to "only hold[ing] a candle in sunshine" (*The Marriage of Heaven and Hell* plate 22). *A Candle to Light the Sun* exposes the lack of substance in the light of the candle and the sun. In broad strokes the preface reiterates mentions of thinness in the Depression-bound Mouse Bluffs of 1936; the scorching sun affects bleary eyes, parched lips, and unslaked thirsts. The novel's large cast of characters, with cautionary examples and scarring episodes exerting their effects in both settings, constitutes the tissue of reality and the wells of loneliness, loss, and frustration. The "untouching" (10) quality of the couples in Mouse Bluffs is perceptible, especially in view of the explicit treatment of sexuality, "the strangely contemporary ... examination of the psychological and the sexual" (van Herk, "Second Thoughts" C17).

Flowering Careers in the Sixties

Many careers either begin or flower in the sixties, from Jane Rule's (1931–2007) lesbian fiction, Margaret Laurence's (1926–87) quintet of Manawaka novels, Claire Martin's collections and novels, and Margaret Atwood's (b. 1939) savvy, ironic city novels to early collections by Alice Munro (b. 1931). Their questing female protagonists express the temper of the times in their bluntness, daring, attentiveness to nuance and detail, and chafing against received norms or expected types.

Rule's breakthrough novel, *The Desert of the Heart* (1964), adapted as a movie by Donna Deitch in 1985, sets a standard for the sixties and later in many ways. She convinced the young Margaret Atwood that a literary agent is "a necessity of life, rather than a mere luxury"; on the topic of acquiring an agent, Atwood included a postscript in submitting her debut novel, *The Edible Woman*, informing the publisher that "Jane DESERT OF THE HEART Rule said I ought to have one and kindly supplied me with hers" (Schuster 140).[13] Linda Morra examines Rule's "archive of activism" in dealing with agents and publishers to demonstrate that she "extended her expectation of agents to her publishers: she would not compromise her artistic integrity to accommodate their expectations" (136).

The alternating points of view of Rule's two female protagonists, Evelyn, the older married woman who comes to Reno for a divorce, and Ann, the younger Reno resident, a cartoonist and change girl at one of the clubs, propel the approach-avoidance dynamic. With allusions to Bunyan's *Pilgrim's Progress* complicating her text, Rule herself has commented that it is no "moral allegory" and that "there is no judgement of the characters except those judgements they make of themselves or each other" (233). When Evelyn looks "into her own vision of the desert," we have this access to her iconoclastic decision making, with new assurance emerging from disbelief:

> *Evelyn began to walk slowly back the way she had come, neither Faithful nor Christian. There is no allegory any longer, not even the allegory of love ... It's a blind faith, human faith, hybrid faith of Jack-ass and mare. That's the only faith I have. I cannot die of that. I can only live with it, damned or not.* (233)

Rule's posthumously published and ambiguously titled autobiography, *Taking My Life* (2011), uses a similar candid and critical scrutiny to review her first twenty-one years.

Often isolated within marriage and interrogating competing notions of intimacy and desire, Laurence's female protagonists embody immense vulnerability and determination. Admitting that "pride was [her] wilderness" (318), Hagar Shipley, nonagenarian first-person narrator of *The Stone Angel* (1964), recasts her life in this *Vollendungsroman* as a failed daughter, wife, and mother. In retrospect she wonders why she was "shamed" (81) by Bram's sexual desire and her own eager response: *"His banner over me was love"* (80). Even when she is released into mourning for her son, John, and on the point of death is calling herself a "stupid old baggage" (250), she crustily acknowledges "there's no one like me in this world" (250) and refuses to implore God: "Bless me or not, Lord, just as You please, for I'll not beg" (307).

The thirty-four-year-old elementary school teacher Rachel Cameron, living with her widowed hypochondriacal mother above a funeral home in Manawaka, is the narrator of *A Jest of God* (1966), the novel for which Laurence won her first Governor General's Award. Repressed, "bounded by trivialities," and "fluctuating in age between extremes," Rachel admits that she "hardly know[s] myself whether I am too young or too old" (88, 64). Through a summer romance Rachel comes to know herself, to fear and then embrace what she thinks is a pregnancy, and finally to decide to take up a new position in Vancouver. Her mind reeling with insightful observations and comments, she confronts herself and her appeasing ways: "Go on apologizing for ever, go on until nothing of you is left" (134). Rachel's learning to narrow the gap between thought and speech is comparable to Hagar's winding up and confessional. As James King notes, both novels return "in part to the literature of childhood": "Hagar appears to be a harsh crone but locked up within her is the beautiful woman who emerges at the conclusion of *The Stone Angel*; Rachel is a Sleeping Beauty who kisses herself back to life" (229).

The suburban Vancouver life of Rachel's thirty-nine-year-old sister, Stacey MacAindra, anxious, harried mother of four, is central in *The Fire-Dwellers* (1969). Manawaka people and stories are part of the narrative thread, as conversations mention or invoke Piquette Tonnerre's horrific death in a fire and Vernon Winkler's emergence as Thor Thorkalson, and flashbacks recall the Cameron Funeral Home and her father Niall's drinking. The real experimentation of the novel is Laurence's deft splicing of first- and third-person narrative voices with Stacey's inner monologues introduced by a dash, her fantasies in italics, and news broadcasts of 1967 in capitals. In this portrait of a troubled marriage with temptations and threats of infidelity lobbed back and forth, Stacey's inner voice combines understanding and anger. However, this voice also admits rising stakes: "We go on this way and the needle jabs become razor strokes and the razors become hunting knives and the knives become swords and how do we stop?" (147).

Recreating the childhood world of Vanessa MacLeod, the fourth book, *A Bird in the House* (1970), a collection of eight stories Laurence had been publishing since 1963, is "strongly autobiographical, a fictionalized depiction of the two immediate strands of Margaret's family: the Connors are based on the Simpsons and the MacLeods on the Wemysses" (Powers 327). Vanessa is as much Laurence's alter ego as was Christine for Gabrielle Roy. Moreover, until she leaves for university, Vanessa becomes aware of many of the same pains – deaths, family tensions, and secrets. One unforgettable image is the Connor house of the title, introduced as "the Brick House ... plain as the winter turnips in its root cellar, sparsely windowed as some crusader's embattled fortress in a heathen wilderness," and finally occupied by strangers, yet still viewed by

Vanessa as a reflection of Grandfather Connor, who, she concedes, "proclaimed himself in my veins" (11, 191).

The Diviners (1974), the culmination of Laurence's Manawaka quintet for which she won her second Governor General's Award, is a *tour-de-force* production, assembling elements and characters from all the previous texts and experimenting with such narrative forms as memorybank movies. Like the hold of the Connor house on Vanessa, Manawaka is inescapable for the central figure, writer Morag Gunn living in Ontario: "the town inhabits her, as once she inhabited it" (227). The memorybank movies are Morag's way of fictionalizing the past; *"everyone is constantly changing their own past, recalling it, revising it"* (60). Her continuous conversations with pioneer, botanist, and author of *Roughing It in the Bush*, Catherine Parr Traill, are another way of facing the river of then and now. Through her writing Morag, too, is up and doing –*"Look[ing] ahead into the past, and back into the future, until the silence"* (453). Facing her daughter Pique's charge, "You're so goddam proud and so scared of being rejected" (236), she must revisit and assess her relationship with Pique's father, Skinner Tonnerre, her shame and fear of the people who raised her, Christy and Prin, and the infantilism and denial of her marriage to Brooke. Morag Gunn, now "an established and older writer" (420), acknowledges "the necessary doing of the thing ... the gift, or portion of grace ... or Morag's magic tricks" (452).

Trajectories of Celebrity: Munro and Atwood

The careers of two of Laurence's slightly younger contemporaries, Alice Munro (b. 1931) and Margaret Atwood (b. 1939), both now internationally acclaimed, also began in the sixties. The first Canadian woman Nobel laureate,[14] Alice Munro has won virtually every major national and international award, including three Governor General's Awards, two Giller Prizes, the Canada Council Molson Prize for her contribution to Canadian culture, the PEN/Malamud Award, the National Book Critics Circle Award, the Man Booker International Prize for Lifetime Achievement, and, in 2013, the Nobel

Prize in Literature as the master of the short story. From 1976 on, readers of *The New Yorker* regularly encountered her stories, which appeared thereafter, sometimes with adjustments, in collections. Her perpetually reconstructed and revisited terrain of Morris Township, Huron County, in western Ontario, now called Alice Munro Country, extending to the Blyth-Clinton-Goderich nexus, leads readers to believe that we know the author. We can trace the trajectory of a career – from hardscrabble family life on a fox and turkey farm on the outskirts of Wingham, a former-schoolteacher mother chafing against poverty and community judgments and ultimately battling Parkinson's disease, a father who became an author himself, a bright daughter reading her way to a university scholarship, followed by early marriage, moves to Vancouver and Victoria and the births of four daughters, and then return to Huron County.

Yet throughout her thirteen collections of stories and single novel, along with three selections and compilations, Munro adroitly distinguishes autobiography and fiction. She alerts us in the colophon of *Lives of Girls and Women* (1971) that it is a "novel ... autobiographical in form, but not in fact; my family, neighbours and friends did not serve as models." Thirty-five years later her foreword to *The View from Castle Rock* (2006) explores the intermixture of genres and the permeable membrane between history and fiction in stories that "pay more attention to the truth of a life than fiction usually does":

> *But not enough to swear on. And the part of this book that might be called family history has expanded into fiction, but always within the outline of a true narrative.* (x)

Incorporating more than three decades of scholarship in his *Alice Munro: Writing Her Lives* (2011), Robert Thacker traces the facts of "Munro's cultural inheritance and life," and by interleaving these facts with "the texts that Munro has produced," looks "forward and backward, and both outside of the texts as well as inside them" (17).

The most discussed passageway into and through her personal fiction is the depth of the complex and richly layered events her stories offer. We are drawn to their dark human truths, their elements of mischief, their dialectic of past and present, and their deliberately unresolved, open format. Her stories "have the fantastic inevitability of fables, the profundity of myths, the sudden turns of fairy tales; the rhythm and authority of a story told out loud, repeated, passed on, altered" (Schine 26). The continuing subject of many full-length studies, by Louis MacKendrick (1983), E.D. Blodgett (1988), Ildikó de Papp Carrington (1989), Neil Besner (1990), Beverly Rasporich (1990), Magdalene Redekop (1992), James Carscallen (1993), Coral Ann Howells (1998), Ailsa Cox (2004), Deborah Heller (2009), and Ilsa Duncan (2011), Munro has also been the topic of international university-based symposia at Orléans in 2003, Siena in 2007, and Ottawa in 2014 and subsequent collections of essays. Gerald Lynch and Janice Fiamengo, editors of the collection emerging from the Ottawa symposium, *Alice Munro's Miraculous Art,* see their subject as a master of paradox: "Is her fiction compassionate or dispassionate, realistic or metafictional, domestic or grotesque?" (5). Amelia DeFalco and Lorraine York, editors of the collection *Ethics and Affects in the Fiction of Alice Munro*, concentrate on edgier, messier affective and ethical perplexities in her work.

Louis MacKendrick prefaces an early essay collection with an observation about the "exactitude of human feeling and observation"; "Munro's stories retain probability and authenticity, while they also delight the attentive reader with their fictionality" (1). Ted Blodgett's claim that Munro's is an art of "accommodating contradictions" (126) is echoed in Helen Hoy's assertion that Munro's stories "require a simultaneous acceptance of conflicting perspectives on reality" ("Unforgettable, Indigestible Messages" 20). While Magdalene Redekop attends to Munro's "overlapping stories constantly under revision" (233), James Carscallen dwells on Munro's "true reality: the ordinary made marvelous in its distinctness and the abundance of its life" (535). Her exceptional narrative scaffolding and attention to the architecture of her fiction are the focus of more and more calibrated comments, from novelist Richard Ford's understanding, in his introduction to a re-issue of *The Progress of Love* in 2006, that "hers is freedom to stray beyond the story's apparent unities and amenities and hard sides and never to come back unless she wants to" (xiii) to narratologist Isla Duncan's application of narrative theory to Munro's "hybrid, thickly imbricated stories" (6).

Munro declared early in her career that she is "not an intellectual writer" but "very, very excited by what you might call the surface of life" (Gibson 241). Expanding on this remark, Mark Levene sums up the benefits: "Intellectual or beyond intellectuality, Munro is free too, perhaps, of the constraints the word and the activity may conjure up for her" (151). Yet throughout Munro's stories the frequency of embedded allusions to the art and demands of writing is remarkable.

In "The Peace of Utrecht" in *Dance of the Happy Shades* (1968), the narrator's return with her two young children to her childhood home in Jubilee, a fictionalized version of Wingham, where her unmarried sister, Maddy, still lives, releases a cascade of revelations about a "secret, guilty estrangement" (201) at the same time as it reinforces the distance, the "desert" (190), between the sisters. Munro faces the challenge of representing this past through many registers of voice and experience. While the narrator recognizes "a queer kind of oppression" and "the dim world of continuing disaster, of home" (191), she and her sister regale Maddy's friend Fred Powell with a version of their childhood "which is safely preserved in anecdote, as in a kind of mental cellophane" (193). The narrator's observations about Maddy's containment within Jubilee and her visit with Aunt Annie and Auntie Lou both allude to the choices and burdens of writing – allusions that thread their way through all Munro's stories. The narrator contemplates "the restrictions of life in Jubilee" and Maddy's friendship with Powell: the thought of "unconsummated relationships" depresses her "so much that I find myself wishing for them to be honest lovers" (194).

This narrator's thoughts on the sex life, here of her sister, continue to surface through different voices in Munro's work. The "high erotic charge" extends, as Margaret Atwood observes, "like a neon penumbra around each character, illuminating landscapes, rooms, and objects" ("Introduction" xv). Del Jordan, curious about her parents' marriage, in "Princess Ida" in *Lives of Girls and Women* (1971), tries to extract an explanation from her mother, who appeared to be overcome with gloom "in the vicinity of sex" (65). "Wanting to get it settled for good," Del persists:

> *"Why did you fall in love?"*
> *"Your father was always a gentleman."*
> *Was that all? I was troubled here by a lack of proportion, though it was hard to say what was missing, what was wrong.* (67)

With "luxuriant optimism," the family narrator in *The View from Castle Rock* (2006) imagines what was missing in this fanciful depiction of her parents' early years:

> *I think that when they came and picked out the place where they would live for the rest of their lives, on the Maitland River just west of Wingham in Turnberry Township in the County of Huron, they were travelling in a car that ran well on dry roads on a bright spring day, and that they themselves were kind and handsome and healthy and trusting their luck.* (139–40)

But visions of the past are rarely idyllic. By the time of the title story of *Friend of My Youth* (1990), the narrator can pinpoint the difference between her mother's memory of a "maiden" lady who was bypassed for marriage twice as "a noble figure, one who accepts defection, treachery, who forgives and stands aside" and her own assessment of what makes this friend evil in her story "as just what made her admirable in my mother's – her turning away from sex" (22). This narrator explains the disparity, linking her mother's ideas "in line with some progressive notions of her times," while her own "echoed the notions that were favored in my time." The noteworthy coda here is the narrator's comment about germinating notions that the writer develops: "It's as if tendencies that seem most deeply rooted in our minds, most private and singular, have come in as spores on the prevailing wind, looking for any likely place to land, any welcome" (23).

The narrator's visit to the maternal aunts in "The Peace of Utrecht" recalls from two perspectives her mother's hospitalization with the "shaking palsy" and Maddy's refusal to take their mother home. From Aunt Annie and Aunt Lou, the tone is accusatory: "Lou and I thought it was hard." The narrating sister, cast in the role of reporter of events, queries the "last function of old women ... making sure the haunts we have contracted for are with us, not one gone without" (209). Enacting the sense of oppression, the second perspective is Maddy's; she also poses a question for herself. Despite her promise to go away, she asks, "*Why can't I?*" (210).

The difficulty, in fact the impossibility, of answering Maddy's question points to the emotional gamut of Munro's stories, where repressed guilt and anger can be as catalytic or imprisoning as the determination to escape. The ways in which Munro succinctly captures this range through metaphor are noteworthy. Del Jordan concludes *Lives of Girls and Women* with a paradox-filled image of "dull, simple, amazing and unfathomable" lives: "deep caves paved with kitchen linoleum" (210). Yet she also forecasts what she wants to capture in her projected future writing: "every last thing, every layer of speech and thought, stroke of light on bark or walls, every smell, pothole, pain, crack, delusion, held still and held together – radiant, everlasting" (210). In the *Bildungsroman* of *Who Do You Think You Are?* (1978), schoolgirl Rose, who grows up to be an actress, is punished for showing off her skill at memorization and forced to stay late to copy each line of the poem she can readily recite three times. Margaret Atwood comments on Rose's detention by extending it to all artistic aspirations.

> *Rose is not to believe she can escape from the common herd just because she can do some tricky, inessential thing most people can't. For actress, read writer; for memorizing a poem, read composing a story. The teacher's attitude is one that all artists in the Western society of the past two hundred years, but especially those in smaller and more provincial places, have found themselves up against.* (*Negotiating with the Dead* 27–8)

The cumulative pace of the project of writing and the ease with which it can be criticized or dismissed are both reflected in the voice of the narrator, the former wife of a writer, in "Material" in *Something I've Been Meaning to Tell You* (1974). Her caustic tone is evident at the outset in her view of university discussions led by "bloated, opinionated, untidy men ... cossetted by the academic life, the literary life, by women" (24). Although she deconstructs the publisher's blurb of her first husband's story, she has to admit – not without bitterness and jealousy – that an event from their shared past has been "lifted out of life and held in light, suspended in the marvelous clear jelly that Hugo has spent all his life learning how to make" (43). Despite the fact that Hugo does have "the lovely tricks, the magic, the art," Margaret Atwood underscores the ex-wife's perspective: "It doesn't compensate – or not in the wife's mind – for the filthy moral idiocy of Hugo" (*Negotiating* 105).

The vastness of this undertaking and the time required to recall and assemble it are the concerns of the young mother and would-be writer on a car trip from the west coast to visit, and show off the children to, both sets of Ontario grandparents, in "Miles City, Montana" in *The Progress of Love* (1986). At home, amidst "the jobs to be done and the phone ringing and the sociability of the neighborhood," she finds herself wanting to hide to "get busy at my real work, which was a sort of wooing of distant parts of myself" (88). With precise reconstruction of the beginning of an affair in the past interwoven with prophetic warnings and glimpses of present relationships for the former husband and wife, "White Dump" in the same collection reveals how suddenly "the way the skin of the moment can break open" (308).

Sudden moments of insight can be the products of seemingly everyday happenings. In "Family Furnishings" in *Hateship, Friendship, Courtship, Loveship, Marriage* (2001), the visit of the college-student narrator with Aunt Alfrida reveals that this figure of sophistication and glamour is not only a philistine but the partner with whom her father had an affair. When she returns to college the narrator expresses the happiness of being alone and thinking.

> *I did not think of the story I would make about Alfrida – not of that in particular – but of the work I wanted to do, which seemed more like grabbing something out of the air than constructing stories ... This was what I wanted, this was what I thought I had to pay attention to, this was how I wanted my life to be.* (105)

"In forging her identity as a writer," Deborah Heller observes, "the narrator leaves behind her family furnishings; and yet, transformed, they become the subject of her art" (34). The past also surfaces with ironic narrative twists, as in "Fiction" in *Too Much Happiness* (2009). The second half of this narrative revisits the first half's account of the break-up of a marriage, this time from the perspective of the daughter of the woman at the centre of the split. Now a published author, whose book launch the narrator attends, this daughter does not recognize the woman who was her music teacher and whose marriage her mother broke up. On reading the book, the narrator passes judgment about its re-creation of her own past. "Here was where the writer would graft her ugly invention onto the people and the situation she had got out of real life, being too lazy to invent but not to malign" (58). Despite the fact that she sees "not a scrap of recognition" in the young author's face and despite her assessment of the book's fictionality, the narrator regains sufficient composure to remark that "this might even turn into a funny story she would tell someday" (63).

Munro's stories carry many revealing echoes about the fluctuating sense of what is outside and what inside and about the equally variable state of being happy. In "Boys and Girls" in *Dance of the Happy Shades*, Del Jordan demarcates the inside of housework, "endless, dreary and peculiarly depressing" and the work done outdoors with her father as "ritualistically important" (117). Only her retrospective adult consideration of what she saw as her mother's "plotting to get me to stay in the house more" leads her to observe, "It did not occur to me that she could be lonely, or jealous" (118). She comes to realize that the outside is also a place of slaughter for the foxes and superannuated farm animals. The eleven-year-old Del's memory of opening the gate to release the high-stepping horse Flora who "reared at fences" (120) suggests a temperamental link between the girl and the horse. However, her brother's triumphant news about the capture of the horse – "We shot old Flora and cut her up in fifty pieces" – leaves Del in tears, hearing her father's dismissive absolution, "She's only a girl" (127). When, in "Deep-Holes" in *Too Much Happiness*, a middle-class mother finally meets with her son who has alienated himself from parents and siblings for decades, the understanding of what is outside shifts. Now grey and thin with a lined face and missing teeth, he squats in a condemned building with others who beg for money. Having changed his name to Jonah, he spends the limited time with his mother informing her of the need to overcome "the concept of 'mine'" (113) and disavowing all his earlier explanations of "my stinking self." "There isn't any inside stuff, Sally.... There is only outside, what you do every moment of your life. Since I realized this I've been happy" (115). His happiness deliberately excludes his mother, who leaves with the uncertainty about ever seeing him again. Even when meetings after many years occur, as in "The Moon in the Orange Street Skating Rink" in *The Progress of Love*, the present distances among three people who were friends and lovers fifty years ago are intensified. The cousin who had become a business success looks in a kind of disbelief on the woman who, as a girl, had been the maid-of-all work at the boarding house where the boys stayed, and his cousin, who had not ventured far but stayed local and married.

> *The moment of happiness he shared with them remained in his mind, but he never knew what to make of it. Do such moments really mean, as they seem to, that we have a life of happiness with which we only occasionally, knowingly, intersect? Do they shed such light before and after that all that has happened to us in our lives – or that we've made happen – can be dismissed?* (160)

Although the cousin, who has suffered a stroke, is now described by his wife as "happy," the illumination of their past closeness for the returning visitor is a moment of rare, exclusive clarity.

Mingled often with this retrospective understanding is the depiction of sadness and anger, gratitude and embarrassment. The figure of the "Gothic Mother" ("The Peace of Utrecht" 195) assumed to be the "enemy" ("Boys and Girls" 117) by Del is also the prophetic voice of warning: "Use your brains. Don't be distracted. Once you make that mistake, of being – distracted, over a man, your life will never be your own" ("Lives of Girls and Women" 147). The choices girlhood friends make about early marriage or university underscore growing divides. When Del meets Naomi on the street in Jubilee, a shamefaced puzzlement characterizes their encounter: "I felt that she had moved as far beyond me, in what I vaguely and worriedly supposed to be the real world, as I in all sorts of remote and useless and special knowledge, taught in schools, had moved beyond her" ("Baptizing" 162). The "shameful treachery" Del experiences in laughing at her previous boyfriend, an evangelical zealot, as not "Neanderthal" but "Cro-Magnon" (162) in "Baptizing" surfaces in the college-student narrator's account of her mother's bachelor cousin in "Wenlock Edge" in *Too Much Happiness*. Ernie Botts, a high-school graduate now a ticket supervisor for the railway, treats the student to Sunday evening dinner, yet she hopes "that nobody from the college would see us and think he was my boyfriend" (65). Nina, the well-dressed, worldly audit student who comes to share her room in the boarding house, who buys the best notebooks and pens but who takes no notes, is another person influencing the narrator's ambivalent reactions. Nina has "no pegs to hang anything on."

> *She did not know what Victorian meant, or Romantic, or Pre-Columbian. She had been to Japan, and Barbados, and many of the countries in Europe, but she could never have found those places on a map. She wouldn't have known whether or not the French Revolution came before the First World War.* (73)

Although Nina, "alert and ready to respond to the demands of this life ... once she understood what they were" (85), creates a short-lived romantic liaison with Ernie, the worlds of the essay-writing university student and the would-be hairdresser, Nina, do collide. It is one thing for the narrator to recite Housman's "On Wenlock Edge" for money from the old predator who controls Nina; it is another and later development to feel "the sticky, prickly shame" of her recitation and its moral weight after Nina has abandoned Ernie to return to her keeper. It seems that the "trouble" alluded to in Housman affects the once-confident reciter.

> *There, like through woods in riot,*
> *Through him the gale of life blew high;*
> *The tree of man was never quiet:*
> *Then 'twas the Roman, now 'tis I. (A Shropshire Lad,* XXXI)

With her variety of intellectual pegs, the scholarship-student feels obligated to counter the wrong done to Ernie by Nina and her insinuating, needy ways.

The deftness with which Munro fashions, animates, and scripts her characters and the aspects of ourselves we recognize in these people are among the hallmarks of her writing. In *Lives of Girls and Women* the differences are sharp and poignant between the discreet adventuress and boarder Fern Dougherty, who considers the unmarried music teacher "a poor thing ... only trying to catch a man," and operetta-loving Miss Farris *con brio* herself, who "hennaed her hair," "made all her own clothes," and whose death, "floating face down, unprotesting, in the Wawanash River, six days before she was found," is privately deemed a suicide ("Changes and Ceremonies" 102, 118). The now-ancient piano teacher, Miss Marsalles, in "Dance of the Happy Shades," appears to be easily ridiculed, looking "like a character in a masquerade, like the feverish, fancied-up courtesan of an unpleasant Puritan imagination" (217). Yet the condescension of the neighbour towards Miss Marsalles and her bedridden sister – "Oh well I feel kind of sorry for a couple of old ladies like them. They're a couple of babies, the pair" (218) – prompts some recalibration of the teacher. The neighbour's assessment of the Down syndrome pupils Miss Marsalles has invited to the recital – "nice little things and some of them quite musical but of course they're not all there" (221) – and the narrator's mother's wondering about the reason for inviting them "to listen to a procession of little – little idiots" (222) might also let us grasp our own misinterpretation. With her "grotesquely exaggerated" maternity, Miss Marsalles, as Magdalene Redekop observes, "look[s] on things that we do not see ... With this clownish mock mother, Munro puts herself deliberately at an ironic distance from the real-life mothers" (58, 59).

The intricate architecture of Munro's stories leads to curious intersections and often unresolved contrasts. In "Lichen," collected in *The Progress of Love,* a misogynous ex-husband with his current girlfriend arrives at his former wife's summer home spouting opinions about the "troll" she has become and convinced that women have a smell "when they know you don't want them anymore. Stale" (40). He presents his former wife with a Polaroid snapshot of the genitalia of his most recent very young girlfriend, who he knows is cheating on him. The ex-wife sees the photo as "the dark silky pelt of some unlucky rodent" (42). Yet discovering it days later, sun faded and deliberately left behind, she repeats her earlier judgment that it looks like lichen, "like moss on a rock" (41). Now, however, knowing all the "bog bad boy" behaviour of her former husband, "she felt the old cavity opening up in her" as she looks on "the black [that] has turned to gray, to the soft, dry color of a plant mysteriously nourished on the rocks" (55). Munro's narrative arc can illustrate the laws of retribution as movingly as sexual desire. In the first two of the trio of stories in *Runaway* (2004), "Chance," "Soon," and "Silence," a mother rejects her daughter only to be rejected herself by her daughter in the third. A single story, as in "Too Much Happiness," can illustrate a reversal, albeit belated in the case of Russian mathematician Sophia Kovalevsky. Though considered "a delightful freak ... with a mind most unconventionally furnished, under her curls" (250), this winner of the Bordin Prize was denied a professoriate in Paris since "they would no more think of that than of employing a learned chimpanzee" (267). Despite becoming the first female professor in Europe at the University of Stockholm, Sophia endures both frail health and the casualness of her lover, Maksim. However, her exuberant understanding of "events and ideas now taking on a new shape, seen through sheets of clear intelligence, a transforming glass" (299) prefigures a posthumous renown: "Sophia's name has been given to a crater on the moon" (304).

Subject of countless articles and more than a score of book-length studies[15] and international comparisons, Alice Munro is, according to A.S. Byatt, "the equal of Chekhov and de Maupassant and the Flaubert of *Trois Contes*, as innovatory and as illuminating as they are" (n.p.). Understandably, no single reading or overview can hope to capture the complete richness of her work. "Munro's house of fiction," Dermot McCarthy remarks, "is so complex a fabrication that there is no one view of it – critic's or author's – that sees, or seizes, it all" (19). "Meneseteung," Munro's re-creation of a Victorian lady-poet collected in *Friend of My Youth*, offers an illustrative example of this complexity, as her narrative construction of the past interleaved with observations about the life of the woman artist in the present. Almeda Roth, author of the poetry collection *Offerings* published in 1873, provoked comment in the local paper, the all-seeing and genteel *Vidette*, always quoted along with Munro's ventriloquizing of Almeda's poetry in italics, as a *"literary lady"* (58) and in her obituary as *"a lady of talent and refinement whose pen, in days gone by, enriched our local literature with a volume of sensitive, eloquent verse"* (71). The question of Almeda's eccentric sanity or insanity, integration or disintegration, and finding or losing her voice trickles throughout various readings of the story. For Ildiko de Papp Carrington, Almeda is a figure of "wasted artistic potentiality" (215). Concentrating on the images of throat, mouth, and tongue, Magdalene Redekop hears the sound of "menace" and "tongue" in Meneseteung and adds that "this conjunction directs us to Munro's reflections on the dangers surrounding the woman who finds her tongue" (227). Although she remarks that "the poet herself disintegrates in the harsh and multiple presence of the vivid life that surrounds her and that finally proves too huge and real for her," Margaret Atwood questions her own judgment: "Does she disintegrate or integrate? Does crossing the borders of convention lead toward insanity or sanity?" (*Moving Targets* 98).

Among the salient features of the vivid life surrounding Almeda is her back bedroom window facing the Pearl Street swamp, not the front-facing respectable Dufferin Street. In this "bushy, luxuriant" vista "she can see the sun rising, the swamp mist filling with light, the bulky nearest trees floating against that mist and the trees behind turning transparent. Swamp oaks, soft maples, tamarack, bitternut" (56). Her next-door neighbour, widower Jarvis Poulter, who has become rich through salt mining, initially supplies a romantic yet always cautious fantasy. "She doesn't want to get her hopes up too much, she doesn't want to make a fool of herself" (59). But the gaps between them widen. While Almeda comments on his occupation with a biblical reference – "the salt of the earth" – Jarvis's concerns are commerce and competitors. "She would be thinking about the ancient sea. That kind of speculation is what Jarvis Poulter has, quite properly, no time for" (61). His treatment of the drunk woman from Pearl Street – catching "the horrid hair close to the scalp ... shak[ing] her head slightly, warning her, before he lets go of her hair. 'Gwan home!'" (67) – seals the rupture between Almeda and Jarvis. As her blocked menstrual blood begins to flow and the strained grape pulp for jelly pools around her, "Almeda looks deep, deep into the river of her mind" (70).

Novelist, poet, short story writer, essayist, editor, activist, protector of rights, and promoter of the arts, Margaret Atwood is "the most written-about Canadian writer ever" (Howells, *Margaret Atwood* 5). A 2007 reference guide to her works, interviews, and reviews, covering less than twenty years, contains more than 3,900 entries,[16] "while the Margaret Atwood Society, an international association of scholars, teachers, and students, holds well-attended annual conferences and publishes a journal called *Margaret Atwood Studies*" (Gray, *The Promise of Canada* 193). "Omnipresent as a cultural commentator," Atwood has been, according to Robert Thacker, "what might be called a 'phe-nom,' that is, a phenomenal cultural presence, a public intellectual par excellence" ("Quartet" 359). Author of twenty-one works of short and long fiction, including twelve novels, and of fourteen collections of poetry, recipient of innumerable honorary degrees and major national and international prizes (two Governor General's Awards; the Booker and Giller prizes), Atwood is also an essayist, acclaimed lecturer, children's writer, literary critic, and editor; her work has been published in more than thirty-five languages.

Although she has remarked, "I think I would recognize an Alice Munro story in Braille, even though I don't read Braille" (*Moving Targets* 97), readers might actually say the same about Atwood herself. She shows and tells. When impersonating illustrator Charlatan Botchner and cartoonist Bart Garrard; cavorting with Dennis Lee as one half of the pseudonym Shakesbeat Latweed for the student magazine *Acta Victoriana*; editing Canadian verse, Canadian short stories, and a Canadian foodbook; or delivering the Clarendon Lectures at Oxford, the Empson Lectures at Cambridge, and the Massey Lectures for the CBC, Atwood is recognizable, audible, and visible. A capacious, kinetic intellect spices everything she writes; so does an alert sense of her Canadian identity, along with an often sardonic humour and, what can surprise, an intuitive compassion for her characters. Reversing the moral of the film *The Red Shoes* that one cannot be an artist and a woman, Atwood affirms that she writes "for the joy of it" and proclaims "It's exhausting but not a bad kind of exhausting" (Sullivan, *The Red Shoes* 315). She is particularly attuned to what she attributed to Susanna Moodie, "the inescapable doubleness of her own vision." Just as in *The Journals of Susanna Moodie* (1970) she presented her subject "as an old woman on a Toronto bus ... reveal[ing] the city as an unexplored, threatening wilderness" (64), so she scripts the message of Grace Marks, released after serving thirty years in the penitentiary, about her adjustments to the quilting pattern called the Tree of Paradise as a reflection of "the way life is." Marks declares in the concluding section of *Alias Grace* (1996),

> The Fruit of Life and the Fruit of Good and Evil were the same ... [I]f you did eat of it, you would be less bone-ignorant by the time you got around to your death. (459)

Adept at transporting the past to the present, Atwood's work fulfils the writer's passage from here to there and back again that she outlined in her Empson Lectures, *Negotiating with the Dead*:

> All writers must go from now to once upon a time; all must descend to where the stories are kept ... And all must commit acts of larceny, or else of reclamation, depending how you look at it. (178)

In her fiction Atwood is not only an expert adapter and borrower but a consummate architect of narrative. When her first novel, *The Edible Woman* (1969), was published, she had already won a Governor General's Award for poetry – in 1966, at the same time as Margaret Laurence for *A Jest of God* and Claire Martin for *Dans un gant de fer*. The narration of this debut novel, shuttling between first- and third-person voices, sketches in a preliminary way what will become salient markers of Atwood's style in a vast array of genres: the resistance of a woman to predetermined or conventional roles, here conveyed through a rejection of food; a pointed irony capturing both the chaos and consumerism of urban life; a wicked humour puncturing patriarchal assumptions about strength and control; and an assortment of characters of diverse backgrounds and often conflicting, satirized views. In the preface to the 1980 Virago reprint, Atwood herself has described the novel as protofeminist:

> *It's noteworthy that my heroine's choices remain much the same at the end of the book as they are at the beginning: a career going nowhere, or marriage as an exit from it. But these were the options for a young woman, even a young educated woman, in Canada in the early sixties.* (8)

Part One, told by market-research employee Marian McAlpin, displays her derisive awareness of the workplace, Seymour Surveys, as "an ice-cream sandwich" with her all-female department "the gooey layer in the middle" (19). Her room-mate, Ainsley, spouting feminist catchphrases about independence and wanting a baby but no husband, is quick to ridicule the "office virgins" (21) with whom Marian works; yet Ainsley is just as eager to use trickery to become pregnant. In the return to first person in the final scene with her ex-fiancé, Marian presents him with a cake in the form of a woman, charging "You've been trying to assimilate me ... This is what you wanted all along, isn't it?" (271). Throughout *The Edible Woman*, edgy humour enlivens and accentuates social critique.

The reliability of Atwood's narrators becomes an intriguing aspect of her fiction. The unnamed first-person female narrator of *Surfacing* (1972), an anti-heroine trying to explain or understand her father's disappearance in a northern Quebec lake, passes judgments on her companions, boyfriend Joe and married couple David and Anna. She also slowly discloses her own state of emotional decay exacerbated by a divorce, an abortion demanded by her married lover, and estrangement from her parents. A commercial artist engaged in illustrating *Quebec Folk Tales*, this woman sees the world in terms of victims and victimizers. Although Joe, "a mediator, an ambassador," comes back for her, calling her name, "offering [her] something: captivity in any of its forms, a new freedom" (192), her decision to accept or reject this offer is deliberately unformed. Without the entertaining, absurd wit of *The Edible Woman*, the conclusion of *Surfacing*, which contains its own quasi-mystical power, is ambiguous. Does she surface to a form of reintegration or continue in a breakdown? Atwood offers only the mounting annoyance in Joe's voice and the view of the lake and trees, "asking and giving nothing" (192).

Atwood's gifts for parody and satire have distinguished all her fiction, perhaps most prominently in *Lady Oracle* (1976), the first of her novels about the woman artist. Her protagonist stages her own death, sheds pounds, and re-creates herself as Louisa K. Delacourt, writer of "Costume Gothics." Past and present, life and fiction constantly jostle in this hop-scotching narrative, with interleaved drafts of Louisa's novels in italics. Living incognita in Rome, "Louisa" concludes with what seems to be a nod to the trajectory of Atwood's own career: "I won't write any more Costume Gothics, though; I think they were bad for me. But maybe I'll try some science fiction" (280). In her second *Künstlerroman* (development of the artist) novel, *Cat's Eye* (1988), Atwood's first-person narrator is painter Elaine Risley. Continuing the intricate association of past and present, art and life, the text is less jocular and parodic, more penetrating and dimensional. The narration opens by viewing time as "not a line but a dimension"; Elaine observes, "you don't look back along time but down through it, like water" (3). Time is actually a hinge in this novel; the adult Elaine, a successful artist, recasts her girlhood, under the thumb of the worldly so-called friend Cordelia, who is now suicidal and institutionalized. The cat's eye is both a cherished marble from childhood and the title of a painting, which itself captures the refractions and curvatures of time and space.

A related feature of Atwood's art is her ability to manage stories of interconnected relationships that ironically reveal the atomization and alienation of contemporary life. Toronto's Royal Ontario Museum, landmark buildings, and identifiable restaurants are the backdrops for many of the liaisons in *Life before Man* (1979). Despite this urban specificity, Atwood's characters, especially the palaeontologist Lesje, whose affair with a married man is one of the plot engines, are not predictable types. Contrasts between expectation and eventuality are just as strong as those separating stereotype and reality. Rennie, the Toronto-based freelance lifestyle journalist in *Bodily Harm* (1981), promises that her proposed piece on the Caribbean will be "nothing political ... [only] a good Fun in the Sun, with the wine lists and the tennis courts" (16). However, her actual experience on the fictional island of Saint-Antoine involves political intrigue and corruption, imprisonment, and misogynist violence.

The novel preceding *Alias Grace*, *The Robber Bride* (1993), illustrates her art in combining the Gothic fairy tale with an awareness of the power of female sexuality presented in the context of the feminism of the nineties. Her adaptation of the Grimms' tale of a serial-murderer bridegroom and his band of robbers is a tour-de-force of illusionist techniques. Military historian Tony, yoga instructor Charis, and business developer Roz, all former college students and residents of McClung Hall, are duped by their one-time fellow student Zenia, who appropriates, purloins, or otherwise claims their male partners. Although the women's residence is fictitious (named for the Canadian writer, reformer, and suffragist, one of the Famous Five who campaigned successfully to have women recognized as persons and therefore eligible to be judges and senators), the contemporary features of early nineties Toronto are precise and real. Atwood takes us inside the Goth-punk Queen Street bistro, Le Toxique, where her characters meet, Tony's home and refuge in the Annex, Charis's tumbledown cottage on "the Island," and Roz's constantly redecorated mansion in Rosedale. What is also on display in the expertly synchronized revelations of each of the novel's parts is Atwood's understanding of Tony, Charis, and Roz, not as easily hoodwinked women but as characters whose temperaments and family stories make them prey to Zenia's sympathy-evoking tales.

Although Roz's fifteen-year-old twin daughters propose a revamped tale of "The Robber Bridegroom," with women as both the murderer and victims, the insights the narrator discloses in this novel come from the three friends themselves. Zenia embodies a "*raw sexes war*," which is, Tony realizes, "a perfect palindrome" (456). The mirror play of words extends to the women whose partners Zenia snatches. Each faces her vulnerability and doubleness brought to light in Zenia's anger. Tony, whom Zenia labels a "little snot" and "the most awful two-faced hypocrite" (465), needs to protect the man who abandoned her; Charis, scorned as "a dipstick romantic" (480), senses the return of her former vengeful self, Karen, "a dark core" (483); and mothering, capable, problem-solving Roz, who according to Zenia "didn't own" Mitch as her "God-given *property*" (494–5), has to accept the care of Tony and Charis after her overdose. While the scene of the three women celebrating the scattering of Zenia's ashes in Lake Ontario pictures a form of rare sisterhood, the reader is invited to ponder the back-and-forth palindromic implications of Tony's questions: "Was she in any way like us? ... Are we in any way like her?" (528).

Even more trenchant satire informs Atwood's four dystopias, *The Handmaid's Tale* (1985), *Oryx and Crake* (2003), *The Year of the Flood* (2009), and *MaddAddam* (2013), horrific parables of the curtailment of women's voice and social agency, which Atwood prefers to label speculative fiction. As well as netting her second Governor General's Award, *The Handmaid's Tale* was adapted for film by Volker Schlöndorff in 1990, staged as an opera by composer Poul Ruders and librettist Paul Bentley in 2003, and re-created as a ten-episode television series by Bruce Miller in 2017, which was renewed for a thirteen-episode extension in 2018. Set in the patriarchal, theocratic, fundamentalist Republic of Gilead in the near future, the tale of the Handmaid Offred, who belongs to Commander Fred, outlines the different duties of women in this dictatorship. Fertile women are Handmaids, sex slaves, made to bear children, while infertile Wives join in simulation of the sex act, and older women are either Aunts, monitors who police the Handmaids, or Marthas, household servants. In the bordello known as Jezebel's, catering to officers and trade delegations, women prance about in "Government issue" Playboy costumes, but "nobody gets out ... except in a black van" (227–8). The coda, a symposium on Gileadean Studies convened in Nunavut in 2195, is an academic analysis of Offred's retrieved tape, a male-orchestrated discourse, which through innuendo and condescension actually continues the patriarchal domination.

The trilogy, *Oryx and Crake*, *The Year of the Flood*, and *MaddAddam*, presents a post-apocalyptic world of bio-engineered mutants and hybrids. The earliest novel is both bleak and unnerving, but not beyond belief. Concerned largely with men, it features the deranged scientist Crake (previously Glenn), who releases a pandemic and programs species to die at age thirty, and the narrator, his one-time best friend, Jimmy, who adopts the name Snowman. Women are ancillary at best; before he is killed by Snowman, Crake slits the throat of the prostitute Oryx. The second novel, depicting a period of time related to *Oryx and Crake*, focuses on women in a time following the lethal plague of the waterless flood. Members of an eco-religious, cooperatively egalitarian and vegetarian cult called God's Gardeners, Toby, a spa worker, and Ren, a pole dancer and prostitute, survive Crake's pandemic, reuniting with Jimmy. Both texts end ambiguously, with fire leading to doom or hallucination or something else. A distinctive feature of the ecological, communitarian *The Year of the Flood* is the Blakean-inspired hymns, ostensibly from *The God's Gardeners Oral Hymnbook*. Fredric Jameson draws attention to the fact that the "regressive primitivism" of God's Gardeners coexists with "computerized information and informers strategically planted among the elites" (8). Characters from both previous novels reappear in the conclusion, *MaddAddam*, itself another Atwood palindrome. Corrupt, venal corporations with slick, punning names are exposed; brutal Painballers are quelled; lovers and half-brothers find one another; and the building of the eco-cult of God's Gardeners moves forward.

The two novels that preceded *Oryx and Crake*, the Giller Prize-winning *Alias Grace* (1996), which also won the Italian Premio Mondiale, and the Booker Prize-winning *The Blind Assassin* (2000), both deal with the mystery of knowing the female protagonist. Not projected into the future but glimpsed merely through newspaper accounts of an 1843 trial in Lower Canada, piecemeal testimony, psychiatric assessments, and the protagonist's own disarming composure, "the true character of the historical Grace Marks remains an enigma" (465). A servant who is convicted at the age of sixteen of killing her gentleman employer and his mistress and who spends more than twenty-nine years in the penitentiary at Kingston before being pardoned, Grace herself offers no easy solutions: "People want a guilty person. If there has been a crime, they want to know who did it. They don't like not knowing" (90–1). Atwood's novel, released as a television series adapted by filmmaker Sarah Polley in fall 2017, complicates the figure of Grace and frustrates any assured sense of this woman's guilt or innocence.

Though set within a different class and time, in the fictional Port Ticonderoga, a blend of Paris, Elora, and St Marys, Ontario (Bemrose 55), *The Blind Assassin* also peels back the layers of public identity defining the narrator, Laura Chase Griffen. Her privileged childhood, the tragic death of her younger sister, presumed to be the author of a cult-classic novel called "The Blind Assassin," and clues about the real authorship and the love affair that surrounded it cast the novel as nested boxes of stories, all darkly interrelated. Laura's narrative probes the motives of memory, the desire to leave a mark.

Revelations or, more appropriately, glimpses of Atwood herself emerge from her long and short fiction, of course, but also from the multi-generic, experiment-filled miscellanies spanning several decades of her career. Prominent topics, also mirrored in her fiction and poetry, include the commodification of women, the links between art and commerce, and the importance of reaching readers in various formats, interspersed with continuous, invariably illuminating, reflections on the English literary tradition.

Illustrated with her own pen-and-ink drawings and collages, *Murder in the Dark* (1982), *Good Bones* (1992), and *The Tent* (2006) depart from fictional traditions; they are a mix of parables, fairy tales, autobiographies, horror stories, and prose poems ranging in tone from whimsical to mordant. Christl Verduyn reads *Murder in the Dark* as "a project in which the writer is a murderer and a liar destroying comfortable patriarchal reality and language ... to transform 'reality' into 'something else'" (130). Reversal of expectations, either abrupt or slowly cumulative, is the frequent agent of transformation. Nothing prurient seeps into the build-up in

"The Victory Burlesk." Atwood relies on and deflates the hint of naughtiness surrounding the ritual of the striptease at this Spadina Avenue landmark. Intrigued by the lighting, the fake names ("Miss Take," "Miss Behave"), she considers the still-clothed performers "moving as if they were swimming, mermaids behind glass." However, with the appearance of one stripper, who "was old," humour changes to shame: "I didn't want to look. I felt that I, not the woman on the stage, was being exposed and humiliated" (15). Silence fills the room as physiology replaces voyeurism. "The body up there was actual, it was aging, it was not floating in the spotlight somewhere apart from us, like us it was caught in time" (15).

The representation of the female anatomy is a topic of continuing interest in the seven parts of "The Female Body" in *Good Bones*. With adroit sequencing from autobiographical morning routines to the need to leash, lock, and chain this body, it illustrates how semiotics become more and more perilous. The hydrated, lubricated, powdered female body is both a topic – nearsighted, badly behaved, vulgar, aging – and an alliterative searcher, "hunting for what's out there, an avocado, an alderman, an adjective, hungry as ever" (40). Each section closes with a comparable twist, a return to the cerebral after the commercial.

Many connections link the pieces in these miscellanies, indications of Atwood's sustained attention. Consider the prose "Simmering" in *Murder in the Dark* and the poem "Bring Back Mom: An Invocation" in *The Tent*. Both feature kitchens as workshops, controlled by men in "Simmering" and by "a trapped drudge" (106) in "Bring Back Mom." The necessity of writing, a linkage that connects "Page" in *Murder in the Dark* and "The Tent," is among the most probing topics of these collections. While "Page" concentrates on the tactility of "a skin there to hold in" and the unseen, "what is beneath" (45), "The Tent" figures writing, "this graphomania in a flimsy cave" (146), as a primary condition of existence. The concluding section of "Page" reverses the sense of blankness: "it is you who are blank and innocent, not the page" (45). The pen is a scalpel incising the skin as "darkness wells through." Instead of surgery, the prominent image in "The Tent" is refuge; though surrounded by ruins and even when the "paper shelter" is ablaze, it is vital to "keep on writing anyway because what else can you do?" (146). *Good Bones*, which was republished together with *Murder in the Dark* (called *Simple Murders*) in 1994, provides a serio-comic observation on what is written. The poem "Let Us Now Praise Stupid Women" celebrates "the Eternal Stupid Woman" because "she's our inspiration! The Muse as fluffball!" (34–6). Adjusting Baudelaire, Atwood perorates:

> *Hypocrite lecteuse! Ma semblable! Ma soeur!*
> *Let us now praise stupid women,*
> *who have given us Literature.* (37)

The Penelopiad (2005) revisits the "myth" of Penelope and Odysseus; Atwood revises and refocuses the well-known account using the devices of an accomplished fiction writer. Acknowledging that she has "always been haunted by the hanged maids" (xv), her text adroitly alternates the voices of Penelope and the twelve maids through direct monologues, skipping rhyme, sea shanty, idyll, ballad, drama, and love song.

Atwood's reviews and especially her lectures supply additional, always witty, perspectives on literature, on her sense of the state of Canadian literature, and on her writing practice. She is not above having some fun at her own literary expense, although in the case of her first book-signing, at the Hudson's Bay Company in Edmonton, the humour reflects on the event's organizers as much as on the young author herself.

> *The signing was at a table set up in the Men's Sock and Underwear Department. I don't know what the thinking was behind this. There I sat at lunch hour, smiling away, surrounded by piles of a novel called The Edible Woman. Men in overcoats and galoshes and toe rubbers and scarves and earmuffs passed by my table, intent on the purchase of boxer shorts. They looked at me, then at the title of my novel. Subdued panic broke out ... I sold two copies.* ("Mortification," *Moving Targets* 407)

Taking the title of her fourth Clarendon Lecture, "Linoleum Caves," from Alice Munro's image of "deep caves paved with kitchen linoleum" in *Lives of Girls and Women*, Atwood fastens on "the idea of domesticity as simply a thin overlay covering a natural, and wild, abyss" (*Strange Things* 88). While she alludes to Marian Engel's *Bear* and Lou's "initiatory tattoo" (107), and mentions her own *Surfacing, The Journals of Susanna Moodie,* and stories in *Wilderness Tips,* Atwood's view of the north is ultimately that of an informed environmentalist.

The slippery, shadowy doubleness of the writer is one of the concerns in Atwood's *Negotiating with the Dead*. She admits, "I must have a slippery double"; yet she insists such a person "could never be imagined – for instance – turning out a nicely browned loaf of oatmeal-and-molasses bread" (36). (Interestingly, Atwood includes her mother's recipes for oatmeal-molasses bread and ginger cookies in *The CanLit Foodbook,* 140, 171.) Writing and, for Atwood, its attendant celebrity are also serious economic issues. As Lorraine York remarks about Atwood's fascination with art and money, "from the perspective of her fictional meditations on art and business, it is entirely predictable that Atwood should write a non-fiction commentary on money, finance, and the queasy state of debt, and it is entirely logical that she should rely primarily on literary texts to construct her discussion" (186). In her Massey Lectures on debt, *Payback,* Atwood promotes distinctive views of classic figures involved in financial crises: Shylock, Mr Micawber, and Mr Tulliver.

Atwood's engagement in arts, humanitarian, and environmental causes and her essays and projects contributing to fundraising for them underline her prominence as a citizen-artist. She is acutely aware that the range of topics and audiences she has addressed has been assisted by a variety of what she referred to as early as *Procedures for Underground* (1970) as "cool machines" ("Three Desk Objects"). Although she presented her electric typewriter with the ambivalence of avoidance and approach, "I am afraid to touch you / I think you will cry out in pain / I think you will be warm, like skin," she has embraced, Lorraine York notes, extensive experimentation with electronic and social media. "The various media she deploys – websites, Twitter, Facebook, blogs, the LongPen – echo, in their interconnecting, interactive workings, her public visibility, which, after all, comprises various relationships with agents, office workers, publishers, editors, website designers, accountants, lawyers, and many more" (*Margaret Atwood* 159).

Trying to fix Atwood, a writer on so many platforms, with a single image or perspective is impossible. Theodore Sheckels concludes his study of the political aspects of her fiction and its resistance of the constraints of institutionalized oppression by focusing on "the 'power down' in society because, here, one finds the victims and Atwood has always been more interested in the victims than the victimizers" (163–4). On the occasion of a symposium celebrating Atwood's sixtieth birthday, Nathalie Cooke rehearsed images of her as a literary lion, tiger, and pussycat, personifying Margaret as "the moral adventurer" and Peggy as the "stay-at-home-and-read type"; ultimately the labels themselves are restrictive. Atwood's creative energies and subjects, Cooke noted, continue to reveal and illumine "the endless possibility of transformation" ("Lions, Tigers, and Pussycats" 25–6).

The Tangle of Domesticity and Independence

Many of Munro's and Atwood's contemporaries concentrate on the tangled complications of either marriage and motherhood or independent adventures. The section to follow will consider the work of novelists Audrey Thomas (b. 1935), Marian Engel (1933–85), Aritha van Herk (b. 1954), and Carol Shields (1935–2003). Through a range of strategies and voices they not only explore the difficulties of embracing or rejecting domestic life, but they also grapple with the complexities of trying to capture the amplitude of women's lives in the actual or historical present. Their protagonists, many of whom are writers and mothers, can resort to disguise and deception; though not afraid to shock or challenge bourgeois smugness, they can be believably inconsistent blends of independence and vulnerability, awareness and naiveté.

In her fourth novel, *Blown Figures* (1974), Audrey Thomas uses the deliberate fragmentation of collage – stream-of-consciousness narrative often inter-cut with newspaper reports of weather, crimes and cure-alls, word games, folk tales, and cartoons – to sketch what Margaret Laurence called the "mind-map" and the "profoundly internal journey" (*"Blown Figures:* A Review" 100, 101) of wife and mother Isobel Carpenter. "Concerned with and aware of the inevitable shifting of identity in the slippage of the signified" and wrestling with "the interrelations between madness and articulation, insanity and aesthetics," Thomas's narrative dramatizes the self as "a palimpsest of shifting, layered languages" (Dorscht 223, 226).

> She was Isobel, wife of Jason, and mother of Mary and Nicholas (MA MA, MA MA, the breast), and yet sometimes from behind the invisible glass wall of her disguised madness she stared at the three of them as though they too were illusions. (22–3)

En route to West Africa, where she lost a child through a miscarriage, and invoking the abortion she had undergone at a lover's insistence earlier, events recalled but not repeated from Thomas's first novel, *Mrs Blood* (1970), Isobel is in every sense the writer's creation: malleable, quixotic, untethered. Aching for contact with her husband, who withdraws from sex, she is embarrassed by her post-parturition body. In its radical format *Blown Figures* evokes precariousness and longing, the fragility of blown glass, the unpredictability of being swept up by the winds of chance.

With deft strokes in the controlled space of her short stories Thomas articulates domestic realities, as in "Ted's Wife" from the collection *Real Mothers* (1981). The central character, a pining, frequently drunk academic wife, whom Thomas has labelled "a really nasty piece of work" (Wachtel 30), pities Ted the widower. She fantasizes about the special understanding she thinks she shares with him, and feels "shock" and "rage" when he returns from an extended sabbatical with a young woman. Her "drunken" voice cuts "across the congratulations ... with her best line yet. 'What are you going to do, adopt her?'" (59). A comparable and much more sympathetic understanding radiates through her novel *Intertidal Life* (1984), a hybrid *Künstlerroman* and domestic drama reproducing the commonplace-book record of the desertion of the protagonist's husband seven years ago. The text announces and investigates new ways of being for men and women in the late twentieth century, showing "the impact of feminist (conscious-raising) critique ... to be one of major cultural proportions" (Hutcheon, *Canadian Postmodern* 113). Alice, writer, mother of three daughters, and ex-wife of fine art professor and painter Peter, reflects on the transformation of Peter the Rock into Peter Pan; she herself "gradually apprehends a more feminized space" (Coldwell 148). To counter reader response favouring Peter, Thomas has remarked: "he's screwing around and being Mr. Bigshot and the whole idea that he's some ideal is nonsense" (Wachtel 59). What is clear, as Alice's daughters make their own decisions and as her women friends move on or desert her, is the peace she herself finds in the shore and tide pools. "She goes down because it soothes her and pleases her, all this wealth of life in the intertidal zone" (269).

Thomas's only work of historical fiction, *Isobel Gunn* (1999), might appear to be a departure. A clergyman narrator, Magnus Inkster, relates the real-life story of an Orkney Islands woman who signed on as a male labourer for the Hudson's Bay Company in 1806. Yet *Isobel Gunn* is really no aberration. Isobel's pregnancy and dismissal from the Pembina outpost, forced return to Scotland, and separation from her son are vivid details conveyed through the male contemporary's voice. Italicized ruminations ventriloquize Isobel's own thoughts. Now an old woman, destitute and forgotten, close to death, she remembers her son, "even the smell of him and the pull of his mouth on her breast" (217). Maternal memories and the inescapable lure of island life – "Is there a child on any of these islands who has not paddled in the tide pools or collected shells to use as animals or armies in his infant games?" (220) – connect nineteenth- and late-twentieth-century subjectivities.

The intersection of life in the real world and on the printed page is at the centre of Marian Engel's work: seven novels, two short-story collections, and two children's books. In fact, as Christl Verduyn argues convincingly, this tension informs all Engel's writing, including her private papers. "To read Engel's notebooks is to shift with the author from a commitment to a life of the imagination and writing to a commitment to the here and now" (Verduyn, *Lifelines* 43). The emergence and identity of the woman writer are key concerns. When thirty-year-old Sarah Porlock, PhD, resigns her teaching position at a Toronto university, in *Sarah Bastard's Notebook* (1968), to pursue writing full time, renaming herself Sarah Bastard in the process, she deliberately casts off the patriarchal norms of the academy and announces that "I ooze, booze, stink, feel human rather than feminine" (88). In *The Honeyman Festival* (1970), a forty-year-old mother of three, who is pregnant with her fourth child, replays her younger life and mentoring by the dead filmmaker-lover, Honeyman. "*The Honeyman Festival* is an effort," Christl Verduyn observes, "to demonstrate the discrepancy between the idealized puritan ethos and female reality" (81). Engel's Governor General's Award-winning *Bear* (1976), a radical attempt at integration, follows Toronto archivist Lou to a remote island in northern Ontario where she catalogues a nineteenth-century library, but also undergoes a fundamental change in perspective and personality. Lou's erotic relationship with the bear, on whose belly she lies, feeling him "to be wise and accepting ... rough and tender, assiduous, patient, infinitely, it seems to her, kind" (118–19), only concludes when, in arousal, he rips the skin on her back with one great paw. The sexual experience allows her to see her affair with the possessive, controlling director of the Institute as life-denying. A possible model is Sir Charles G.D. Roberts's *The Heart of the Ancient Wood* (1900), in which a young woman has a quasi-filial relationship with a black she-bear until the threatened life of her huntsman lover forces her to shoot the loved animal; Engel clearly repudiates the violence and patriarchal underpinnings of Roberts's novel. By blurring "the boundaries between man and beast," as Elspeth Cameron notes, "*Bear* shows the integration of an alienated personality through contact with a vital natural world beneath the social order" ("Midsummer Madness" 92–3). In *The Glassy Sea* (1978), Rita Heber seeks and finds integration through a different route. Ten years as an Anglican nun, marriage and motherhood, the death of her child, divorce, alcoholism, and eventually return to the Eglantine order of sisters are the stations of her journey. Introspective candour of the first-person voice makes this narrative an arguably more intimate exploration of the desire to heal discontinuities, through spirituality rather than sexuality. Her return as Sister Mary Pelagia to Eglantine House, now "a crawling mass of non-contemplative, cross, contentious humanity" (164), a hospice for women and their children, signals her need "not to serve, but to belong ... [to] do real, not toy, social work" (164–5). The sometime narrator of *Lunatic Villas* (1981), a harried single mother of seven and freelancer who writes a magazine column with the byline "Depressed Housewife," also performs constant, though chaotic, social work, even welcoming newcomers to her already-full Toronto townhouse. When Harriet Ross seeks a misremembered line by seventeenth-century poet George Herbert she realizes that

> *"Hope in the bottom lay" isn't there. Because it's rest, not hope, Harriet, you noodle. Rest is the pulley that hauls us up to God. You were always bad at memory work.* (251)

In "The Pulley" Herbert identified the lack of rest, "repining rest*less*ness," as the element that will haul us to the divine; it is also a determining, though secular, feature in the lives of the female characters created by Engel's contemporaries.

Hard-won independence characterizes Aritha van Herk's iconoclastic, plainspoken female protagonists, who size up men bluntly. Through narratives less overtly experimental than Thomas's, and less gynaecological than Engel's, her novels foreground resolute, determined women: Judith raises pigs (*Judith*, 1978); Jael cooks for a crew of uranium prospectors in Yukon (*The Tent Peg*, 1981); Arachne sells women's underwear in small Alberta towns and indulges in bar pickups and road jockeys (*No Fixed Address*, 1986); Dorcas, an international courier, hires her own assassin (*Restlessness*, 1998). As Robert Kroetsch reads his friend's work, "Van Herk's central characters like to live in a crisis situation, and that crisis is the risk of either love or death" (66).

Winner of the Seal Canadian First Novel Award, *Judith* traces a farm girl's return to rural roots. As the narrative shuttles back and forth between her life as an administrative secretary savouring "the capitivity" (143) of her boss, a possessive lover, and as a pig farmer on a property purchased with the inheritance from her deceased parents, Judith recasts and assesses her past, thanks, curiously, to the pigs. *The Tent Peg*'s assigning individual voices and chapters to the ten-person prospecting crew, including the lone female cook, is the narrative mechanism behind the turbulent but surprisingly successful summer exploration in Yukon. Feminist J.L. ends up fulfilling the quite conventional role of mesmerizing woman, playing siren in her gypsy skirt on the table top. "In their faces I see my transfiguration, themselves transformed, each one with the tent peg through the temple cherishing the knowledge garnered in sleep, in unwitting trust" (218–19).

Arachne Manteia, who sells (but does not wear) panties, is an altogether more engaging and fully realized protagonist. Although she feels an imposter in "the respectable world" (103) of cartographer and "Apocryphal" (173) lover Thomas, Arachne actually exults in this difference:

> *She does not mind dirt under her fingernails, she does not feel that deodorant is necessary every day. It shows on her face. Rebellion. Dissension. Trouble.* (98)

In her 1959 black Mercedes packed with Ladies' Comfort samples, criss-crossing the province, evading fraud charges at Lake Louise by slipping through the Crowsnest Pass, and continuing west and north to the Mackenzie Mountains, this picaresque heroine is a figure of movement and, ultimately, mystery. Even as a "missing person" (311) Arachne avoids detection, with dust-covered panties, "no end to the panties" (319) discovered. The unnamed inquirer (Thomas or the writer?) admits "there will be no end to this road" (319); Arachne herself reaches a self-styled apotheosis.

Finality for the woman traveller in *Restlessness* is more sombre, "the contemporary acting out of the melancholic's condition" (Kroetsch 65). This protagonist invites her subtle contract assassin, Atman, into her room in the Palliser Hotel in Calgary; their dinner conversation constitutes most of the deliberately non-teleological narrative. Despite his attempts "to deter [her] by making [her] tell him stories about [her] travels," she remains convinced: "I am a traveler on my way to bed, to sleep, perchance to dream" (192–3). But it is an escape that cannot be achieved; for

Kroetsch, the protagonist's longing "becomes at the same time a comedy, a traditional comedy of rebirth into a moment of blind innocence and the hidden pleasures (and terrors) of yet another chance" (72).

The multifarious ways of observing, layering, and arranging domestic lives and the possible erasure of domesticity in contemporary fiction concern Carol Shields. When addressing an audience at her alma mater, Hanover College in Indiana, she remarked on the narrative challenges of *not* concentrating on people in crisis. "Even the suggestion of a sound marital relationship," she realized, "posits the suspicion of what is being hidden and about to be revealed in the forthcoming chapter" ("Narrative Hunger" 33). She refused to equate "coupledom" with "boredom." Rejecting the flattening out of moral subtlety, Shields's ten novels, three collections of short stories, biography of Jane Austen, and three volumes of poetry investigate the human packaging of women's lives.

The woman writer, specifically the biographer, is a recurring figure in Shields's fiction. Her debut novel, *Small Ceremonies* (1976), can be read as an extended meditation on the links between biography and fiction. From the point of view of biographer Judith Gill, biography involves "enlarg[ing] on available data," while fiction presents the ways in which, through compressing and underlining, "our lives are steamed and shaped into stories" (52). Judith's borrowing the plot of an abandoned novel discovered in her family's rented sabbatical home in Birmingham and her later discovery, back in Canada, that her borrowed idea has been purloined by her creative writing instructor propel the narrative's ironic reflections on "crime within crime within crime" (108). The admission of the Birmingham householder that he has borrowed the letters between Judith's son and his daughter as the basis for his soon-to-be published novel completes the novel's Venn diagram template about adaptation.

A different overlap informs the companion novels *Happenstance* (1980) and *A Fairly Conventional Woman* (1982), republished in 1994 as *Happenstance: The Wife's Story, The Husband's Story*. A week in the lives of academic historian Jack and Brenda, a quilter who flies to the National Handicrafts Exhibition in Philadelphia, supplies the pretext for these interconnected narratives. Jack sees himself as "a wooly academic type," lacking Brenda's "specialized sensitivity to qualify as a decoder of modern life" (32). Academic temperaments and habits are a much more prominent feature of *Swann* (1987), subtitled "A Literary Mystery." Four interlaced narratives with vying academic biographers, a small town librarian, and a poetry publisher converge in their interest in the posthumous publication of the verse of Mary Swann, who was murdered and dismembered by her husband. As well as sending up academic obsessions about the truthfulness of biography, the text combines a series of narrative experiments: lengthy letters, a filmscript of the concluding Swann Symposium as "a ceremonial act of reconstruction, perhaps even an act of creation" (311), and a coda of the reconstructed work of Mary Swann. Fittingly entitled "Lost Things," it reflects on the manoeuvres, vanity, and lies of the preceding narrative. The symposium device itself recalls Laurence's memorybank movies from *The Diviners* and Atwood's Nunavut Symposium of Gileadean Studies in 2195 at the end of *The Handmaid's Tale*.

Large sagas and intimate portraits are the focus of Shields's four major novels. In tracing the inevitable union of Tom, three-times divorced, and Fay, survivor of three unsuccessful live-ins, *The Republic of Love* (1992) does not downplay the twists and detours of what is "after all, a republic, not a kingdom" (224). Riffing on the ideals of I Corinthians 13, the text provides and illustrates its own list of attributes:

> *Love is selfish. Love is dangerous, impractical, wasteful. Loving, we put a pistol to our heads. It burns, it makes us into fools, always it keeps us waiting. It sickens, it makes us sick, it's the start of a serious illness, it's illness itself.* (15)

The "fissured" and "discontinuous" (W. Roy, "Autobiography" 118) account of Daisy Goodwill Flett, *The Stone Diaries* (1993), is an engrossing narrative flitting between first- and third-person voices; "the recounting of a life is a cheat," the text asserts: "even our own stories are obscenely distorted" (28). Winner of the Governor General's Award, the Pulitzer Prize, and the National Book Critics' Circle Award, the text experiments with a range of devices:

among them Daisy's first-person account of her birth, interspersed family and archival photographs, family letters, and correspondence with Mrs Green Thumb (Daisy's journalist *nom-de-plume*). Daisy's parents haunt the narrative: Mercy, the "extraordinarily obese" (17) superb cook who dies giving birth, and Cuyler, the stone mason who memorializes his wife in a monumental tower. Shields's vast saga retains its unity throughout the vicissitudes of the central figure; the moment of the aged Daisy's death evokes Mercy as she "feels herself merge with, and become, finally, the still body of her dead mother" (358–9).

In a meteoric rise comparable to that of Cuyler Goodwill, the protagonist of *Larry's Party* (1997) emerges from the ordinariness of a Winnipeg flower-shop assistant to an Illinois-based landscape architect specializing in mazes. With each chapter prefaced by a maze pattern (recalling the quilting patterns of *Alias Grace*), Larry Weller has the special gift of landing on his feet; he embodies the novel's attitude, as Dee Goertz notes, "embracing chance and simultaneously seeking and promoting design" (242). The strongest element in this linear, third-person narrative is the deft control of dialogue. The finale, a party that brings together the people in Larry's life over twenty years, includes a seating plan, which functions as a stage set to recognize the speakers, and closes with thank-you notes.

Shields's last novel, *Unless* (2002), disrupts any grid of happiness, resolution, or contentment. "*Unless*," the narrator observes, "is the worry word of the English language. It flies like a moth around the ear, you hardly hear it, and yet everything depends on its breathy presence" (224). Married to "an ordinary man embedded in a family he loved" (8), Reta, mother of three daughters, accomplished translator, and blossoming novelist, must try to reclaim her eldest daughter, Norah, now mute and begging in downtown Toronto. In striving to grasp the full implications of the traumatic event that has unhinged and illuminated her daughter, Reta ends up living in searing detail the experience she had sketched as the premise for a possible novel: "This will be a book about lost children, about goodness, and going home and being happy and trying to keep the poison of the printed page in perspective" (16).

Rhizomes of Sexuality, Nation, Race, and Ethnicity

Varied, robust, and formally innovative, women's fiction writing since the seventies, and with increased urgency into the nineties and our century, continues to explore the intersectional challenges of growing up female – whether straight, lesbian, bisexual, two-spirited, or trans. Blended with the power politics of individual agency largely conveyed and queried through patriarchal family tensions, relationships, marriage, and motherhood, women's writing also interrogates the diversity of Canada's multicultural crosscurrents. Emerging, as Coral Ann Howells describes it, from "the intersection of postcolonial and feminist perspectives," contemporary Canadian women's fiction is involved in "a remapping of the nation space" ("Writing by Women" 195, 198). An understanding of history is a prime way of evaluating and creatively exploring this space. Women writers' "imaginative projection" to recover and speculate about the details of a female subject's life has become "a necessary corrective to the marginalization and patriarchal inscription of women in a linear ... male history" (Wyile 148).

This overview of women's writing must also acknowledge a wide variety in temperament and affiliation, in audience and scope. An example of a writer regularly omitted from academic studies, Alberta-based Janette Oke (b. 1935), can illuminate a neglected but loyal readership. Most of her more than eighty novels have been published by Bethany House, a Christian publishing company in Minneapolis, Minnesota. In light of Oke's faith-based readership, her novels' treatment of sexuality, Bible-inspired beliefs, and Indigenous-White relations is much less trenchant and critical, more oblique and conciliatory, than that of most of her contemporaries – Maria Campbell, Miriam Toews, Eden Robinson, Marilyn Dumont, Louise Halfe, and Tracey Lindberg, in particular – to be discussed in this project. In the pioneer setting of Oke's first novel, *Love Comes Softly* (1979), the slow relationship between the young widow and the lonely widower, who marry for initially practical housekeeping reasons, blossoms because of their shared, rock-solid beliefs. So successful was this first publication that it led to seven sequels, Hollywood movie adaptation, and immense sales for the eight-part boxed set. Her best-selling *When Calls the Heart* (1983), about a privileged eastern schoolteacher encountering conditions in Coal Valley (the mining towns of the Crowsnest Pass), is now the basis for a serialization lasting five seasons on CBC television. Oke's *Drums of Change: The Story of Running Fawn* (1986), set in different Blackfoot camps in southern Alberta from the arrival of the Northwest Mounted Police in 1874 to the time of the Riel Rebellion in 1885, illustrates her meliorist approach to First Nations encounters with missionaries. Not only does the protagonist, Running Fawn, willingly attend the mission school in Calgary and embrace baptism as "her first public step of obedience in her new faith" (225), her acceptance of the marriage proposal of fellow student Silver Fox signals a widespread and peaceful embrace of Christianity.

Most of Oke's women writer contemporaries in Canada, however, have embraced a thoroughgoing interrogation of their cultural identity within the nation, often questioning the solidity and efficacy of the concept of nation itself. From a range of perspectives reflecting personal suffering and redemption, women writers have reconsidered the nation not as "an essential social unit, or a mystical bond, or a spiritual soil" but as "a contested public space within which they must find whatever freedom and justice they can attain" (Kertzer, *Worrying the Nation* 158). For Indigenous women writers such a search must entertain the "politics of accountability" that "disrupts the all-too-persistent Western narrative of cultural triumphalism" (Hoy, *How Should I Read These* 200). In fact, these disruptions are effecting a rethinking of Canadian literature as a field of scholarly research. Diana Brydon sees Can Lit as moving "beyond older forms of nationalism and internationalism, and toward multiscaled visions of place – local, regional, national, and global – each imbricated within the other" (14). Although this overview cannot hope to be entirely inclusive, the following remarks aim to illustrate how these concepts and issues intermingle in women's fiction, shuttling back and forth between self-development and integration, challenging a broader neo-conservative political and economic climate, and giving voice to largely silenced groups.

Relying on semi-autobiographical elements and a mixture of first-person narration, journal entries, and letters, Beatrice Culleton Mosionier's (b. 1949) *In Search of April Raintree* (1983) invokes a restricted and fractured community. Set in Winnipeg, this account of two sisters, Cheryl and April, separated in two distinct foster homes, one stimulating and the other dehumanizing, "both invites and disrupts notions of the real and of the self, of authenticity and of identity, of truth." (Hoy, "Nothing but the Truth" 289). While the "novel attests to the importance of decolonizing mechanisms," Cheryl Suzack argues convincingly that it also demonstrates how "courts of law continue to function as intermediaries carrying out the government's illiberal, assimilative, and discriminatory ends" (62). Culleton Mosionier herself was raised in a foster home from the ages of three to sixteen; two of her sisters did die of suicide. Cheryl's jumping off the same bridge where her mother had ended her life underscores a tragedy-laden cycle. April's reading of Cheryl's journal account of her brutalization by a john who assaults and leaves her on the sidewalk and Cheryl's observation that "in the morning the garbagemen will take us all away, me and my friends" prompts anger and bewilderment within April.

> *Mostly, I guess the anger was for me. For being the way I was. Because it had caused Cheryl to feel so alienated from me that she couldn't share the most important event in her life with me. Cheryl's baby. Henry Liberty Raintree.* (205)

April's acknowledging that "it was tragic that it had taken Cheryl's death to bring me to accept my identity" (207) and vowing that tomorrow "would be better ... [f]or my people" (208) are precariously optimistic, obliterating, for the moment, all that has preceded – parental alcoholism, foster care for the sisters, and Cheryl's prostitution, alcoholism, and death. As Heather Zwicker notes, "the death of Cheryl marks the sisters' failure to turn biological connection into meaningful sisterhood" (334). Cheryl Suzack points to the root of failure in underlying conditions, since the novel leaves unanswered the question of "what justice obligations are owed [to Indigenous women] when legal mechanisms fail and social institutions exacerbate their vulnerability" (78).

Indigenous women's writing continues to reveal struggles for autonomy amid conditions of exploitation, brutality, and racism. Eden Robinson (b. 1968) uses the curious, street-smart, semi-rebellious voice of a teenaged narrator, Lisamarie Hill, to enquire about family secrets and cultural mysteries in *Monkey Beach* (2000). Haisla stories and language are key to reading the signs and grappling with the ambiguities of Robinson's narrative involving marital and residential-school abuse, adultery, rape, avenging murder, and unexplained disappearances. Despite the efforts of grandmother Ma-ma-oo to relate "old stories," to "really understand" them, she informs Lisamarie, "you had to speak Haisla"– a daunting prospect. As Lisamarie realizes, "even at one word a day, that was only 365 words a year, so I'd be an old woman by the time I could put sentences together" (211). Yet the fact that Ma-ma-oo sent her children to residential schools makes them "vulnerable to physical and cultural harm" (Suzack 50). Language and situation contribute to perplexity, and deliberately so, illustrating what Rob Appleford labels "the novel's strategic ambiguity and cultural *bricolage*" (87). The conclusion leaves the reader wondering if Lisamarie – lying "on the sand ... no longer cold ... so light I could just drift away" and in the distance hearing "the sound of a speedboat"– is alive and about to be rescued or in thrall to a b'gwus, "not quite human, not quite wolf, but something in between" (374).

The sixteen-year-old protagonist, Jared, who lives in his mom's basement and has a reputation as the weed "Cookie Dude" in Robinson's *Son of a Trickster* (2017), is both more secure and at the same time more vulnerable. Family secrets are now compounded by multiple partners and duelling Nanas. Enveloped by Coyote Trickster stories and appearances – real, dreamed, or hallucinated – of raven, bear, and otter along with the guide figure driving a burgundy Cadillac, "the little old Native lady with the monster hiding beneath her skin [whose] old name is Jwa'sins" (193–4), and Wee'git himself, the third-person account is full of narrative experiments. Raw dialogue and texting mix with savvy mythological explanations of cosmology. Jared's party-loving mother is fiercely protective yet often absent. While she can nail-gun the feet of one uptight, abusive boyfriend to the floor for breaking her son's ribs, when she sees Jared, now enrolled in AA and working flipping burgers at Dairy Queen, she considers him "a brainwashed robot" and admits, "I never thought I'd miss your smart mouth or your smug fucking attitude" (313). The women in this novel, whether guerilla mother Maggie, assumed Nana Sophia, real Nana Anita, monster Gran Jaw'sins, bisexual girlfriend Sarah, or neighbourly Mrs Jaks, who shelters Jared periodically, are the real emotional triggers of his slowly emerging consciousness. This first instalment of a projected trilogy is in development as a full-length feature by Indigenous actor and filmmaker Michelle Latimer.

Legal scholar Tracey Lindberg's debut novel, *Birdie* (2015), is another stirring narrative of the power of a "womenfamily" (245) to protect and heal the central character, Bernice ("Birdie") Mootoos, a Métis/Cree from fictional Loon Lake, Alberta. This beautiful, large, book-loving child, abused by a series of uncles, smothered by foster home gentility, living on the streets and under railway bridges in Edmonton, and finding a haven in a bakery in British Columbia, comes to realize that her real hunger is not about food. "She is hungry for family. For the women she loves. For the sounds of her language ... She misses the Cree sense of humour" (102). Only after a period of self-maintained starvation does Birdie come to the realization that by making a feast offering to the tree of life, *Pimatisewin*, with the help of her "madefamily," skinny sistercousin Freda, Aunt Val, and bakery owner and landlady Lola, can "the four of them set about making the feast that Bernice had been dreaming about her whole life" (245). The regeneration of the tree is life-affirming and illuminating in *Birdie*, the projected start of another trilogy.

Along with Indigenous writing, the transcultural work of autobiography and the attempt to reconstruct a woman's life can serve to critically reflect the nation state, as evidenced in the novels of Joy Kogawa (b. 1935), Hiromi Goto (b. 1966), Kerri Sakomoto (b. 1960), Larissa Lai (b. 1967), and Daphne Marlatt (b. 1942). Winner of the Books in Canada First Novel Award, Kogawa's *Obasan* (1981) recalls the period of internment of Japanese Canadians from 1942 to 1945 from the point of view of a young girl, Naomi Nakane, whose comfortable family life in Vancouver is shattered with the confiscation of their goods and removal of her father to a labour camp. As a school teacher in Cecil, Alberta, in the 1970s, Naomi revisits the sites of her past – childhood molestation by a neighbour, retreat with her brother and aunt to Slocan, and life on the beet farm in Granton – and finally learns of her mother's gruesome death after having been disfigured in the Nagasaki bombing. The Appendix, an excerpt from the Memorandum sent by the Cooperative Committee on Japanese Canadians to the House and Senate of Canada, in April 1946, identifies the orders-in-council for the deportation of Japanese Canadians as "a violation of International Law," a contemning of "the value of Canadian citizenship," "racial discrimination," and "a threat to the security of every minority in Canada" (272–4). Yet the Canada that emerges in Kogawa's narrative is an assimilating force: "Oh Canada ... We come from the country that plucks its people out like weeds and flings them into the roadside" (247).

Assimilation is more fluid and problematic in Hiromi Goto's *Chorus of Mushrooms* (1994) and Kerri Sakamoto's *The Electrical Field* (1998), both winners of the Commonwealth Writers' Prize for the Best First Book. Setting her story on a mushroom farm in Nanton, Alberta, Goto explores the impure myths of identity as her central narrator, Muriel/Murasaki, admits that she is "not erasing [but] re-telling and re-creating" stories (185). The female generational lineage of grandmother Naoe, mother Keiko (who prefers "Kay"), and daughter Muriel/Murasaki is a more complicated trio than in Kogawa. Rodeo star, bull riding Naoe sees her daughter as a woman who "has forsaken identity" (13), while this kindred spirit feeds forbidden Japanese snacks to her granddaughter and dreams of sex. The translation and intelligibility of language lie at the core of the tensions within the Tonkatsu family as depicted by Goto. For Sakamoto the legacy of internment camp survivors living in a Toronto suburb accounts for the violence and frustrated desires that subtly permeate the whole narrative. Poet and critic Larissa Lai generates languid, sensuous language to weave together the stories of different times and women in her two novels, *When Fox*

Is a Thousand (1995) and *Salt Fish Girl* (2002). Playing with gender fluidity, her debut novel connects the thousand-year-old Fox, Taoist poet and nun Yu Hsuan-Chi, and Asian American Artemis living in Vancouver. Maintaining the emphasis on relationships with women, *Salt Fish Girl* blends the narratives of nineteenth-century shapeshifter NuWa and the futuristic life of Miranda in the corporatized world of Serendipity in the year 2044.

Forecasting much of this intermingling of past and present, Daphne Marlatt explores the mysterious gaps and crannies in women's histories in *Ana Historic* (1988) by creating female voices that speak to one another across centuries and outside family connections. Working as a research assistant for her historian husband, Annie Richards imagines and vivifies the unrecorded details of the life of an early British Columbia schoolteacher, Mrs Richards ("Ana" Richards), whose existence appears to stop with her marriage. With jagged observations and fragments drawing connections between then and now about restricted gender roles, the invisibility of domestic life, the fraught relationships between mothers and daughters, and the possibilities of intimacy between women, Marlatt's text poses a deliberate challenge to our understanding of the novel: "a book of interruptions is not a novel" (37). It also contests the structuring of history on "a groundwork of fact" (134) that Annie's husband, "known for the diligent research behind his books" (134), upholds.

Through the admissions of different narrative voices, sweeping family sagas from Jane Urquhart (b. 1949), Ann-Marie MacDonald (b. 1958), and Camilla Gibb (b. 1968) can also uncover the hidden or marginalized lives of fictionalized women. Urquhart's Governor General's Award-winning *The Underpainter* (1997) relies on the first-person narration of octogenarian painter Austin Fraser as he reviews his life and acknowledges that he "panicked in the face of the possibility of happiness" (334). With a narrative that switches from Silver Islet Landing on the north shore of Lake Superior, where Austin has painted in the summer, to the New York gallery scene and the cold, drafty house in Rochester where he now lives, the novel reveals what the painter has lost or sacrificed in not accepting the love of Sara, his summer model and mistress. *The*

Underpainter builds on a series of closed parentheses: Sara's receipt of Austin's telegram at the outset and her skiing to join him, as he leaves when seeing her approach, at the close; his coldness in telling her "I have painted you enough" (323) and Sara's leaving her house to Austin in her will; Austin's mocking of the fine china painting of a self-taught artist and his painstaking reassembling of shards of this china in his old age. Fittingly, Austin's "most recent paintings ... referred to as *The Erasures* ... [are] ragged-edged episodes from [his] own life and the lives of the others" (107). Such erasures as Sara's autobiography, which he "tossed like shredded paper into the wind" (107), and his burying of images "under layers of paint [which] seems like a preparation for [his] own death" (183) chart the losses he only belatedly recognizes. From the plans of a parish priest to create a church on the hill in south-western Ontario to the execution of architectural designs for the Vimy Memorial in France, Urquhart's *The Stone Carvers* (2001) creates the interlaced story of a brilliant woman carver; she takes these plans to full expression, bringing "a personal retrospection to [the] monument ... allow[ing] life to enter it" (340) and installing her finally carved sculpture of the female saint on the altar of the church on the hill.

In MacDonald's *Fall on Your Knees* (1996), the effects of the physical, psychological, and sexual abuse of the four daughters and wife of James Piper stretch over generations from Cape Breton to New York. The murder mystery underpinning MacDonald's *The Way the Crow Flies* (2003), a fictionalization of the Stephen Truscott case, covers another large span of time, from the sixties to the eighties, as members of the McCarthy family, and particularly the youngest, Madeleine, face the issue of what constitutes honesty. The saga evokes life around the RCAF station in Centralia, Ontario, tangled in a web of guilty secrets: the unreported abuse of the teacher's After Three exercises for the girls, the schoolgirls' eagerness to please and be chosen, and the accusation of rape and murder against a handsome Métis foster child based on flimsy circumstantial evidence and lies. The slow unveiling of the truth relies on the changing perceptions of mangled lives and memory. As the narrator observes, "Mixed and multifarious ... story is memory rendered portable" (804). Although her most recent novel, *Adult Onset* (2014), concerns a single week in the life of author Mary Rose McKinnon, known as "Mister" (or "MR") it reaches back into childhood and early adulthood to include now-familiar MacDonald fictional and autobiographical story threads. Gaelic and Lebanese expressions reflect her parents' background in Cape Breton; family secrets enliven and exaggerate the protagonist's memories of childhood experiences in Germany, Hamilton, and Kingston; her comfortably renovated and child-proofed home, "somewhere between yuppy and dingy" (15), is in Toronto's Annex neighbourhood. As always, "you don't get the whole story," since "Mary Rose's life is stained with the dye of what can never be stated, a skein from which she spun stories while she still could" (370). Yet the novel does offer several comic and serious glimpses into MR. Assessed by her younger brother as living in "the middle-aged lesbian single-mother housewife sweetspot" (73), she spends a harried week tending to two-year-old Maggie and six-year-old Matthew on her own when her partner is directing a play in Calgary. While the scene of duct-taping winter boots onto uncooperative Maggie is funny, MR is anxious about work on her third book, reminding herself that "Alice Munro did some of her best work while her kids were sleeping" (293), and about the fidelity of her girlfriend, partner, wife. "Why isn't there a better word? Apart from the flagrant *lover*, sexless *partner*, and dowdy *spouse*" (108). The most searing recollections of MR's week alone concern her coming out to her parents, who had rather she were "a murderer," "burnt at the stake," or "had cancer" (205).

In the coda "A Bit of Background, a Lot of Thanks," Camilla Gibb calls her third novel, *Sweetness in the Belly* (2005), "a work of fiction inspired by research, relationships and, above all, imagination" (411). It was adapted and released as a film in March 2019, directed by Mehari Zeresenay. Drawing on Gibb's field work in Ethiopia for her Oxford PhD in social anthropology and narrated in the first person by the white Muslim protagonist, Lilly, the novel is set in Harar during the deposition of Emperor Hailie Salassie in 1974 and in Thatcher's London in the 1980s. As a White woman in Harar who teaches the Qu'ran and a veiled nurse and refugee worker in London, Lilly remains an observant outsider. Although her narrative includes accounts of female circumcision and HIV/AIDS, Lilly, the orphan of hippy parents, mainly searches for belonging and in the process comes to many realizations about herself. Looking back, she admits "how naïve I had been" (136), yet when she is without the passionate nearness of Aziz, the Indian doctor she loves who is also an outsider in Ethiopia, she longs for "an easier time, when being Muslim was rigid and rule-bound ... I wished there were something absolute in which to believe" (358). After their erotic consummation, Aziz, from whom she will be separated forever, convinces her that she has given him "sweetness in the belly" (374). The quest continues for Lilly, as it does for Gibb herself in her memoir *This Is Happy* (2015), to be considered in the non-fiction chapter.

Reflecting the multiplicity of landscape and identity, race compounds an understanding of home and homelessness, belonging and rootlessness, in the novels of Marlene Nourbese Philip (b. 1947), Dionne Brand (b. 1953), and Shani Mootoo (b. 1957). For Margaret, the fourteen-year-old Toronto-based narrator of Nourbese Philip's *Harriet's Daughter* (1988), home embraces both the known and the ancestral; she realizes the tension between her West Indian parents and the homesickness of Zulma, a girl recently arrived from Tobago. So successful is Margaret in liberating her mother from her overbearing father's control and in securing a plane ticket for Zulma's return home that she earns the new name connecting her with Harriet Tubman and the tradition of liberation activism. Brand's Trinidadian neo-slave narrative, *At the Full and Change of the Moon* (1999), extends from the early-nineteenth-century Le Chagrin plantation to late-twentieth-century Amsterdam, tracing the descendants of Marie Ursule and her daughter, Bola, through the detours of postcolonial exile and in search of the strange safety of Culebra Bay, Trinidad. A protracted romance complicated by a mysterious disappearance, Mootoo's *He Drown She in the Sea* (2005) alternates locales between Vancouver and the fictional Caribbean island of Guanagaspar. Class and race separate the childhood friends who become lovers, Rose Sangha (later Rose Bihar, wife of the Guanagasparian attorney general) and the Afro-Indian Harry St George, whose widowed mother cleans for the Sanghas. Although the narrative contests and ultimately bridges class divides, the attitude conveyed to the young Harry by another Sangha employee prevails in the Caribbean setting:

> *"You and she different, boy. That is Narine Sangha daughter. You and me is yard-boy material. She is the bossman daughter. Oil and water. Never the two shall mix."* (138)

However, with his transplanted acculturation on the west coast of Canada, Harry learns to challenge such divisions.

Extending the lesbian tradition of Jane Rule, the work of Mary Meigs (1917–2002), Nicole Brossard (b. 1943), and Gail Scott (b. 1945) creates a particular locus of authenticity about women's lives by experimenting with and probing what Erin Wunker terms "a multiplicitous subjectivity" (162). Meigs, who started publishing in her sixties, borrowed the name of the painter from Virginia Woolf's *To the Lighthouse* for her *Lily Briscoe: A Self-Portrait* (1981), an account of her life as a lesbian artist. The most directly autobiographical of this trio, Meigs fashioned *In the Company of Strangers* (1991) as a recollection of the experience of participating in the National Film Board feature *The Company of Strangers* (1990), a film by Cynthia Scott about eight elderly women stranded in the wilderness when their bus breaks down. Brossard's *Le désert mauve* (1987; translated as *Mauve Desert* [1990]) trains three related but distinct lenses on an exposition of desire by combining three novels in one: a fifteen-year-old girl's narrative of driving at great speed across the Arizona desert and her fascination with a woman who died during atomic bomb tests, the book's discovery by another woman, and her translation and re-visioning of the "original." Both Brossard and Gail Scott have actively promoted feminist publications. From 1965 to 1979, Brossard was affiliated with the journal she co-founded, *La Barre du Jour* (later *La Nouvelle Barre du Jour*, 1977–) to reveal the literary tradition and encourage innovation; a co-founder, too, of the feminist newspaper *Les Têtes de Pioche* (1977), she founded the publishing house L'Intégrale in 1982. A co-founder of the bilingual journal *Tessera*, along with Marlatt and academics Barbara Godard and Kathy Mezei, Scott has always been interested in the kaleidoscopic quality of language to reflect our relationship to the culture around us. The first-person narrator of Scott's *Heroine* (1987), suggestively identified as G.S., ruminates in a bathtub about the October Crisis, the bleakness of the 1980s, and with deliberate repetition in this work of "autobiografiction ... (fiction that self-consciously draws the reader's attention to the possibility that it is, perhaps, autobiographical) ... revisits the trauma experienced by a female subject" (Wunker 149). Nicole Markotic, reflecting on the need for repetition that probes experience but creates against finality, reads *Heroine* as "a palimpsest version of the self she must write again and again and again to get it right" (48).

The images of young women in the sex trade, as represented in the work of Evelyn Lau (b. 1971), Catherine Hanrahan (b. 1969), and Heather O'Neill (b. 1973), abandon theoretical terms for street talk from capable, perceptive participants. Fiction, Shawna Ferris maintains, has the potential to "resist the dehumanization of sex workers and other marginalized populations in Canada" (181). Lau's *Runaway: The Diary of a Street Kid* (1989), Hanrahan's *Lost Girls and Love Hotels* (2006), and O'Neill's *Lullabies for Little Criminals* (2006) humanize their first-person narrators in ways that allow trenchant critique and extreme vulnerability to coexist. The diary entries of *Runaway* by a smart drop-out who ends up as a junkie intensify a sense of victimization; the diarist acknowledges that her supposed protector, really her pimp, sees her as "no more than a fifteen-year-old foster kid he's having a fling with" (192). Yet with equal clear-sightedness she tells her analyst she could never satisfy her parents: "In prostitution, I mean, I can fulfill someone ... I mean, at home I could never please them. I could get 95 or do 6 hours of homework and never go out. Always hoping for something, you know. Some sign of love" (Gunew 255).[17] Alcoholic, drug-using, and promiscuous, Margaret, the platinum-blond Torontonian narrator of *Lost Girls* embodies the title in her desire to "sell [her] time and kill [her] body" (4) in Tokyo. Employed by the Air-Pro Stewardess Training Institute, which she nicknames "trolley-dolly boot camp" (7), Margaret also works in love hotels, participating in the fantasies of anonymous sex while she shuts down "the smart [self] ... the [self] she's pushed farther and farther back into [her] head" (52). Margaret's background involves parental infidelities, corrosive language, a gang rape, and a psychotic brother. Baby, the child savant in O'Neill's *Lullabies*, lives in the red-light district of Montreal with an addict father. Even as this story-spinning youngster drifts into prostitution, she retains an amazing candour: "Despite my lifestyle, I could still be pretty immature. I always asked little kid questions. I couldn't help it, as I was curious" (291). But she also admits dissatisfaction with this lowlife and where she's headed. "I didn't want to sit drinking beer with a bunch of teenagers who were going to be in grade seven for the next four years, who talked about stuff you would see on the cover of the tabloid newspapers. I wanted to be able to go home ... at the end of the day" (270–1).

As with the motivating backstories of young girls and women in the sex trade, the revisiting of an immediate or a distant past can also focus on a single character's exercise to make sense of her life. By concentrating on one family member within a limited time span, coming-of-age novels or *Bildungsromans* offer pseudo- or semi-autobiographies of girls and women exploring sexuality, contesting patriarchal dictates, and struggling to understand fidelity and its lapses. Franco Moretti traces the movement in the *Bildungsroman* between "self-development and integration," at whose point of encounter "lies that full and double epiphany that is 'maturity'" (18–19). The works of Gail Anderson-Dargatz (b. 1963), Lynn Coady (b. 1970), Miriam Toews (b. 1964), Marina Endicott (b. 1958), and Joan Crate (b. 1953) complicate the sense of maturity, making it less a moment of insight and more an intricate, cumulative series of observations and declarations.

Fifteen-year-old Beth Weeks, the narrator of Anderson-Dargatz's *The Cure for Death by Lightning* (1996), deals with a grizzly's murder and evisceration of a female classmate, an event that unravels the mystery of Coyote tales; she also faces the daily tensions between her recipe-recording mother and angry, abusive father. Set in the village of Turtle Valley in the British Columbia interior during World War II, the narrative is a mesh of secrets and frustrations: Beth's attraction to the sensual Métis girl Nora, her mother's communing with her grandmother, and her father's sexual abuse. Beth's decisions not to follow Nora to Vancouver but to "make paper for [her] own scrapbook ... to write everything down" signal her difference from her mother's "craziness, talking to a dead woman" and her belief that "if you could only get things out of yourself – speak them, or write them down, or paste bits of them into a scrapbook – then you could sort things out" (287). Her command to her father to "keep your goddamned hands off me" (290) conveys an independent position even as she stays within the family.

The experiences of pregnancy, post-partum depression in a psychiatric ward, and being forced to give up her baby for adoption shape and actually strengthen the teenaged central figure of Coady's *Strange Heaven* (1998), Bridget Murphy. She realizes her father's patriarchal control, her stalking boyfriend's belligerence, and the condescending superiority of an Ontario boy. Bridget's marginal reconciliation with her Cape Breton family does not disguise the fact that "as she grew, she had an increasing understanding that God cared nothing for people like Bridget" (187). Coady is equally agile in presenting male and female protagonists. The e-mail correspondence from hockey-enforcer-turned-teacher Gordon Rankin ("Rank") to his one-time friend who is writing a tell-all novel, which makes up *The Antagonist* (2011), captures the profane jock language of their shared past. Rank also comments on unflattering reflections: "It's like seeing pictures of yourself that you didn't even know anyone was taking – candid camera – a whole album of worst-moment closed-circuit stills" (195). The short stories of Coady's Giller Prize-winning *Hellgoing* (2013) are propelled with fierce wit and savvy characterization. In "Take This and Eat It," Sister Anita, a young pastoral care worker in a hospital, sizes up her colleagues and the patients with sardonic practicality. Of the social worker who professes that she's not religious at all, she observes that, "the quick way she straightens her back shows me a woman who was baptized, took communion and knows the Act of Contrition by heart" (74). To the teenaged religious fanatic who refuses to eat and insists that she is following the Bible, Sister Anita offers blunt advice: "Well, don't read the bible. That's what

Protestants do and look at them" (75). This nun is no intervening presence or bleeding heart. "Let them do as they please, the whole bunch of them. Eat and smoke and starve and stand on your head as far as I'm concerned ... I won't be the one to say a word" (87).

The Mennonite town of East Village, based on Miriam Toews's own Steinbach, Manitoba, is brought to life through the sixteen-year-old narrator, Nomi Nickel, the sensitive daughter and irreverent believer in the Governor General's Award-winning *A Complicated Kindness* (2004). Nomi understands the "complicated kindness" of East Village. "You can see it some times in the eyes of people when they look at you and don't know what to say" (46). But she also registers the effects of shunning, excommunication, and banishment that have led to the departure of her older sister, her mother, and finally her father, as well as the hypocrisy of her supposedly concerned English teacher. About her mother she longingly asks herself, "Did she live every day with the conundrum of wanting to raise her kids to be free and independent and of knowing that that's just the kind of kid a town like this chews up and spits out every day like happy hour?" (245). Alone, with the family bungalow to sell and the car to drive away, Nomi is for the moment immobile, "wondering who I'll become if I leave this town" (246).

The force of custom and grievance hemming in a woman's life is at the heart of Endicott's *Good to a Fault* (2008). Clara Purdy transforms her plain bungalow, unchanged since her mother's death two years ago, into a child-friendly arena when she decides to take in the homeless family whose car she hit in an accident. Clara's understanding of her motivation and needs underpins the novel. Although she quits her job to care for the three children, the cancer-stricken mother, the long-absent father, and the demanding mother-in-law, Clara still feels "stupidly ashamed of wanting to help" (24). Prompted by the children's curiosity about her past, she dredges up her marriage and his "multiple and humiliating adulteries" (213). "She had spent too long despising herself for being stupid, hating her mother for being accidentally right about him, despairing of regaining her father's respect" (214). Originally dismissing the charge of the recuperating mother ("You keep thinking you're better than me, even though you try not to") as "trailer-park ignorance" (301), Clara is also forced to admit her own impulses: "Tried to run their lives, and then sulked when they said no" (331). Despite the recriminations, trenchant observations, and quotations from Hopkins, Dylan Thomas, and the Bible by the budding love interest, an Anglican priest, *Good to a Fault* concludes as a promising romance. Another slowly emerging connection between gallery owner Hugh Argylle, "as open-hearted as an out-of-practice fiftyish man can be" (166), and Ivy Sage, visiting theatre actor who travels from gig to gig, enlivens Endicott's *Close to Hugh* (2015). Set in a fictionalized arts community in Peterborough, Ontario, during an eventful week in late October, the novel is a sprawling assortment of characters and narrative experiments. Amidst the insider theatre talk of productions of *Streetcar*, *Twelfth Night*, *Taming of the Shrew*, *The Importance of Being Earnest*, and even Judith Thompson's *Crackwalker*, on which "Ivy cut her teeth" (255), and the "finicky, fustian phrases" (290) of a self-styled impresario, Endicott inserts stream-of-consciousness segments and social media quips. Although the wordplays on Hugh are overdone ("Can't Buy Hugh Love," "A Hughlogy," "The Very Thought of Hugh"), a comic sadness envelops the novel along with charming, quirky scenes. A prime example is Hugh's climbing a ladder to feed Ivy ice cream through the peephole in the storm window in her rented room. Given the theatrical backdrop of the whole novel and the allusion to the Globe theatre, it is telling that Hugh "threads the spoon through the wooden O again, into her waiting mouth" (110).

Joan Crate's *Black Apple* (2016), relating the experiences of a young Blackfoot girl in a residential school, is a complex coming-of-age novel. Sinopaki, whose name gets changed to Rose Marie, endures brutality and racism within and outside the fictional St Mark's Residential School for Girls run by the Sisters of Brotherly Love. What is surprising about Crate's narrative, honouring those who confided in her and her own Indigenous heritage, is that the empathy extends both to Sinopaki and Mother Grace, the superior at the school who actually raises the girl from the age of seven. In showing "the many sides of human behaviour" (324), Crate illustrates not only physical and mental cruelty, such as a refusal to let the child see her dying father, but also a curious recognition of a shared understanding. As the nun meets Rose Marie's look of "world-weary resignation," the narrator comments, "It was as if the child could appreciate Mother Grace's frustration at the unseemly behaviour of the sisters" (78–9). After Sinopaki leaves the school and the village of Black Apple to begin anew on her reserve, the words of Rose Marie's letter, "*I hope I can forgive you*" (317), knock through Mother Grace's mind.

Canadian women writers' exploration of selfhood can be far removed from national settings, as in Aislinn Hunter's (b. 1969) *The World before Us* (2014), Alix Hawley's (b. 1975) *All True Not a Lie In It* (2015), and Madeleine Thien's (b. 1974) *Do Not Say We Have Nothing* (2016). All could be considered historical novels, unlike the Pembina locale of Thomas's *Isobel Gunn* or the servants' quarters influenced by Hamilton's Dundurn Castle in Atwood's *Alias Grace*. Hunter's second novel considers the mysterious disappearances of two British girls, one in 1877 and the other in 1991 from the viewpoint of the London-based archivist Jane Standen, from whose charge the five-year-old slipped from sight more than two decades ago. The curious connections between a Victorian lunatic asylum practising electroshock therapy and a wooded estate reflect "the problem of the historical record" (44). Along with the meticulously observed details of museum objects and curatorial practice, the salient feature of the narrative is Hunter's use of the first-person plural pronoun to include participant-observers in the past and the present. Since "we, all of us, are observers" (359), "we" signals the engagement not only of figments of Victorian dreams and fellow archivists in the now-closed small Chester Museum but the involvement of readers following Jane's progress. Together we share in the realization that "the narratives we have been trying to build our lives on are less fixed than we ever imagined, or peripheral to something else" (402).

Although Alix Hawley speaks in the voice of mythic woodsman Daniel Boone, her novel *All True, Not a Lie in It* also reflects the fluidity of a life narrative. The tale of Boone's being the first white man in Kentucky, widely circulated by the unscrupulous travelling documentarian William Hill, prompts Daniel's satirical acknowledgment: "I know I am whoring myself to Hill for land, but Hill is fond of whores, as I know well enough" (192). With allusions to *Gulliver's Travels* and the Trojan War throughout Hawley's imagined autobiography of a man who actually left almost no writing, this gripping exploration of restlessness, passion, and betrayal along with grisly details of scalping and torture follows the path of a protagonist "inviting Death to a fight ... an old knight crashing forward in a joust" (234–5).

Madeleine Thien's third novel, winner of the Governor General's Award and the Giller Prize, explores the intersections of geographies and histories. Her first novel, *Certainty* (2010), illustrates "the belief that histories touch," espoused by Thien's central character, a radio documentary producer, who "weaves together interviews, narration, music and sound in the hope that stories will not be lost in the chaos of never touching one another" (209, 210). *Do Not Say We Have Nothing*, a work of epic proportions, combining life stories during Mao's cultural revolution, the Tiananmen Square massacre, and contemporary Vancouver is, as narrator and daughter Jiang Li-ling admits, necessarily incomplete and continuing. "No one person can tell a story this large, and there are, of course, missing chapters in my own Book of Records" (462). In the international and intergenerational sweep of this novel, containing lessons in etymology, poems by Li Po, and homilies by Mao Zedong, a daughter who is a professor of mathematics moves towards an understanding of the suicide of her pianist father. It is a meditation on creativity and loss: friendships among a composer, a violinist, and a pianist at the Shanghai Conservatory lead to labour-camp deprivation and horror. Li-ling's hope buoys this sorrowful, beautiful narrative: "Mathematics has taught me that a small thing can become a large thing very quickly, and also that a small thing never entirely disappears" (463).

Extensions in 2017

The fiction published in 2017 by Gurjinder Basran (b. 1972), Heather O'Neill (b. 1973), Suzette Mayr (b. 1967), Alison MacLeod (b. 1964),

Kathleen Winter (b. 1960), and Barbara Gowdy (b. 1950) illustrates the maturity and continuing expansion of women's writing in Canada. O'Neill, Mayr, and Gowdy's current novels, featuring complicated, unsettling female protagonists relayed through third-person narration, are set primarily in Canadian cities – Depression Montreal for O'Neill, shadowed Calgary for Mayr, and downtown Toronto for Gowdy. Both MacLeod, a Canadian who now lives in the UnitedKingdom, and Winter, born in the United Kingdom but raised in Newfoundland and Labrador, create places on both sides of the Atlantic that, through first-person voices, oscillate between past and present, reminiscence and befuddlement. Basran's first-person narrator toggles between Punjabi communities on the west coast and in India. What unites all their work is probing the vulnerability of the self, shaped through childhood experience and trauma, often warped by institutions, and challenged for survival due to the influence of parents and lovers, absent as well as present.

Following the success of winning the Search for the Great B.C. Novel prize and the Ethel Wilson Fiction Award for her first novel, *Everything Was Good-bye* (2010), recounting an Indo-Canadian young woman's rebellion against Punjabi community expectations and her own sexual and cultural adventures, Gurjinder Basran continues to explore elements of a family saga in *Someone You Love Is Gone*. Simran, the narrator, mourns the death of her mother as she alternates between the tragic particulars of her mother's arranged marriage in India and the tension-filled family life of her parents and two siblings, Diwa and Jyoti, in Canada. Among the novel's remarkable features is the continuing presence of the mother, who flits in and out of the narration, reminding Simran "I'm always here. Always listening" (105). Diwa, the brother, whose handicap, delusions, and intervention to protect their mother from the father's rage led to his institutionalization, is the poetic centre of the family. As the siblings gather to scatter their mother's ashes in India, this now middle-aged man, a runaway who lived rough on the streets and rooming houses of Vancouver's Downtown Eastside, shares his creed of "what the poets tell us" with his sisters: "They speak of love and diversity and truth. That's real freedom" (232). Although he was clear that "religion wasn't his path home"

(241), Diwa opts to stay in his mother's native land since "something about the place feels familiar" (240).

Spanning a period from the outbreak of World War I to the onset of World War II, Heather O'Neill's *The Lonely Hearts Hotel* (2017) is a pain-filled yet ultimately hopeful account of abandonment, abuse, and exceptional love. Set decades earlier than *Lullabies for Little Criminals* (2006) in both Montreal and New York and stressing the bond between two often-separated children, the novel serves as a test of endurance and a sad triumph for these artistic lovers. In her Kreisel Lecture delivered at the University of Alberta in 2017, O'Neill has argued that "children are instructed at a young age how to play parts that will allow them to be accepted in the world as brilliant"; writing, she maintains, "is about reclaiming alienated personhood and valuing rule books from idiosyncratic groups as literature" ("My Education" n.p.). Orphans Pierrot and Rose, considered stillborn and left in the snow, are raised and brutalized by the nuns in a Montreal orphanage. Their world is without *Lullabies'* clumsy parental presence of the father, Jules, for his daughter Baby. The predatoriness of Sister Eloise, who introduces eleven-year-old Pierrot to oral sex and full penetration, is ugly and shocking. Her brutal beating of Rose for the infraction of dancing with a mop exposes Eloise's uncontrollable sadism. Feeling "like Samson ... Eloise felt she could just stand there whipping the girl again and again until she was dead" (49). Bonded to each other from the very beginning and solemnizing their union in a private marriage, Pierrot and Rose have rare musical talents – playing by ear for Pierrot who "was able to play much better than the Mother Superior herself" (13) and ballet dancing for Rose, which leads to her position as mistress in the home of heroin dealer and brothel owner Mr McMahon. Rose convinces herself of the perverse connection between self-loathing and "having sex with someone other than Pierrot"; as she sees it, "hating herself was part of what made it feel so good" (107). While the prettier Pierrot, who "would never get old" (376), overdoses on heroin, Rose becomes the confident owner of a hotel catering to single girls where no pimps will be allowed. The reflections she shares with Pierrot are part of the achievement of this narrative:

> *"I was an orphan, Pierrot. My body never belonged to me. You must have felt that too. If someone wanted to beat me, they could beat me. If someone wanted to lock me in the closet, they could. They didn't even have to have a reason. Childhood is such a perverse injustice, I don't know how anyone survives it without going crazy. But I have a chance to turn the tables. I have a chance to run the streets and be a very wealthy woman. No one is ever, ever, ever going to treat me with disrespect again."* (343)

Pierrot's funeral, "held in the tiny church where [he] and Rose used to go to get free soup during the Depression and where they were married" (378), is another kind of victory, a joyous bohemian celebration. Clowns are pallbearers and mourners; people strain on stoops and are "perched on the roofs of buildings ... to get a glimpse of the casket"; children weep "openly at the death of their hero" (379).

From O'Neill's fearless, confessional intimacy, Suzette Mayr's writing moves us to contemporary urban worlds of deftly interleaved, often irreverent, voices and perspectives. Through snippets and ruminations the narrative of *Venous Hum* (2004) packs momentous events into the aftermath of a twenty-year high school reunion, from a shaky same-sex marriage and extramarital affairs to vegetarian cannibalism. The two-week plot of *Monoceros* (2011) reveals the effects of the suicide of a bullied high school student at the fictionalized St Aloysius School in Calgary. Seeing *"u r a fag* scrawled in black Jiffy marker across his locker" (10) begins the novel as "The End" for seventeen-year-old Patrick Furey. The subsequent chapters relate the actions and responses of those left behind: his mean girlfriend, so-called boyfriend, mother who wanted her son to be normal, distracted English teacher, principal and guidance counsellor hiding their gay relationship, true friend and unicorn-obsessed Faraday, and her drag performer uncle, Crêpe Suzette. With the "gored, broken, and now empty" school destroyed by unicorns, "a wall of fury at full gallop" (261), *Monoceros* (Greek for unicorn) closes with a combination of retributive justice and magic realism. Mayr's recent satirical *Dr Edith Vane and the Hares of Crawley Hall* (2017) takes up another current (or perennial) topic, the cutthroat nature of the academy, here presented in the "Brutalist architecture" (84) of the University of Inivea, a stand-in for the University of Calgary. Edith Vane, "a woman in her forties with deadlines" (116), fights for recognition from a new dean anxious to advance the university's high-impact factor, the new hire in "Digital Humanities" who is treated like a god, her ex-girlfriend considered "a psychic hangnail" (81), and her former supervisor, who claims first authorship of Dr Vane's work from the University of Okotoks Press. The campus novel, associated with Randall Jarrell, John Williams, David Lodge, Brian Morton, André Dubus, Francine Prose, and Terry Castle, among others, has not been a popular genre among Canadian women writers, with the possible exception of Marian Engel's *Sarah Bastard's Notebook* (1968). Mixing biting humour and fatalism, Mayr's novel is studded with such alert portraits as the perogie heiress and philanthropist, "her fingers and earlobes chunked with diamond" (55), and the Shakespeare scholar who is now selling appliances. But as the mysterious deaths and disappearances mount, and grazing jackrabbits are everywhere, Edith is convinced that the building is possessed: "It's making all of us crazy" (165). The conclusion, a bizarre nod to magic realism, illustrates the depth of her disturbance as, burrowing underground, she assumes the traits of a leveret.

Whether animating exceptional personalities of the past, like Anne Bonny, the eighteenth-century pirate from Cork, in *The Changeling* (1996), or exploring an uneasy marriage during wartime in 1940s Brighton in *Unexploded* (2013), Alison MacLeod's precise attention to language and geography deftly probes the tensions and mysteries of her protagonists. These features also propel the short stories in her collection *All the Beloved Ghosts* (2017). She revisits the community surveillance and shock surrounding the drowning of a great-aunt in Cape Breton, "a young, unmarried woman" offered "a late-night lift home" ("The Thaw" 17) by her married employer who dared to motor across Sydney's frozen estuary. Crossing back and forth from Regent's Park Road to Nantucket, MacLeod communes and talks about recipes and cemetery placements with Sylvia Plath, "the American sweater girl who'd become a British poet," suggesting that she and Ted were "almost as winsome in literary London" as Jackie and JFK ("Sylvia

Wears Pink in the Underworld" 67). The collection's title story is a poignant depiction of ninety-one-year-old painter, musician, and writer Angelica Garnett (1918–2012) on the day of an awkward public interview. MacLeod's narrative shuttles between carefully realized pictures of Angelica Bell's Bloomsbury childhood and Mrs Garnett's sense that she is being positioned in the role of "a weathered castaway adrift in a new century" (224). The recollected childhood scenes are poetic and vivid, especially the tea preparations of the housekeeper, Grace, whose kitchen routine had "the restoring effect of a Vermeer" (220). Along with wedges of lemon and a pair of tongs, oatcakes for Duncan, and buttered toast for the children, she selects plums piled high for Vanessa's pleasure. "The plums are the colour of a Sussex sky before a downpour, and in this moment as Angelica gazes, she falls *into* their colour, into a dark pool of plumminess" (221). Angelica summons images of her mother, Vanessa, painting in the orchard, "still unaware, still so absorbed," and her aunt, Virginia, for whom "she posed as a Russian princess" (225). Yet despite these instances of being taken for granted as a child who only belatedly was informed of her paternity, Mrs Garnett realizes as "an old lady with red-rimmed eyes," that she is "not *un*interesting. How many people, after all, can say they married their father's lover?" (227).

The material specificity of Kathleen Winter's fiction enables her pursuit of troubling psychic interiors, first exemplified in *Annabel* (2010). The novel relates the birth of an intersex child in the remote Labrador village of Croyden Harbour; despite surgical alteration and the father's calling the child Wayne, the name Annabel supplied by the mother's friend provides emotional support as this protagonist strives for an independent yet ambiguous identity in St John's and Boston. Winter excels at accounts of loneliness and uncertainty, as revealed in her own journey following Franklin's route, in *Boundless: Tracing Land and Dream in a New Northwest Passage* (2014), and particularly in her recent novel, *Lost in September* (2017). Both transatlantic and transhistorical, the narrative, ostensibly in the voice of General James Wolfe, who returns to twenty-first-century Montreal to live the "eleven stolen days" (23) of his planned respite in Paris, which he lost in Britain's transfer to the Gregorian calendar, shifts between eighteenth-century England and contemporary Montreal and Quebec with a side trip to the Fisher Library in Toronto. Grounded but far from being bound by historical context, Wolfe's voice presents the cities as centres of exclusion and violence – from today's Montreal, where he views "the walking dead" at Costco and wonders "was it for them my blood poured out of three ragged holes?" (60), to his Quebec campaign where he "never confess[es] that my Redcoats scalped any Canadian they pleased: Indian, *habitant*, woman or babe" (97). Though laced with interconnections between then and now, what is remarkable about Winter's narrative is its exploration of the uncanny resemblance between James Wolfe and his ventriloquist, Jimmy Blanchard, a veteran damaged from tours in Ghundy Ghar, Afghanistan. Jimmy's climactic expedition to the Plains of Abraham intensifies the reverberation of voices. Not only does the creature of the Plains assert ownership of Wolfe, "*whom you wish to be but are not*," but this claim also prompts Jimmy's lingering question about himself: "If you hold Wolfe in your safekeeping, and he is not within me and I am not him, then who am I in the night, lost in September on his Plains of Abraham?" (250).

Continuing the exploration of the uncanny, Barbara Gowdy's fiction ushers us into unforgettable, strange places. In the eight stories of the collection *We So Seldom Look on Love* (1992), a sixteen-year-old confidently admits she is a necrophile, justifies her obsession with male corpses as "irredeemably abnormal," and surrenders "wholeheartedly now to [her] obsession" ("We So Seldom Look on Love" 154). A young wife who poses nude for a voyeur in the neighbouring apartment complex realizes that "in certain lights, desire sprang up out of nowhere" ("Ninety-three Million Miles Away" 100). When a woman discovers she is marrying a transsexual man, she confronts him: "Against all the visible evidence, she says, 'You're not a man'" ("Flesh of My Flesh" 193). Gowdy's narrative traces how this couple accommodates their expectations to "seem like two happily married, perfectly normal people" (209). Her novel about an anthropomorphized herd of elephants, *The White Bone* (1998), focuses on Mud, who, upon being impregnated, refuses to change her name to She-spurns. Becoming an adoptive member of the She-Ss, Mud, "a Visionary who is capable of seeing both the future and the distant present" (xvi), joins the quest for the relic of the White Bone in The Safe Place. Faithful to the complex genealogy and language of the Central Elephant Families, with their own religious hymns, Gowdy sustains the imaginative power of the matriarchal She-Ss, whose "precise, instantaneous measuring of the passage of time" (159) is one of their mysterious gifts. Along with drought, their most persistent adversary is the human bounty hunter known as the "hindlegger."

Although *The White Bone* invites readers to share a communal elephantine consciousness, *Little Sister* (2017) takes us into a single female psyche and the revelations that are hidden therein. Rose Bowan, thirty-four-year-old booking agent for a rundown Toronto repertory cinema started by her parents, deals with her mother, Fiona's, increasing dementia, while Rose herself periodically becomes another person, book editor Harriet Smith. "Not as a glint at the edge of Harriet's consciousness but as ... a fully integrated component," Rose feels "as if she had been waiting for this from the start" (94). Ironies abound. Rose realizes "memory by memory Fiona was losing herself, while she, in the most concrete way possible, was finding another self" (108). While Rose's boyfriend, Victor, is a routine-oriented meteorologist, she imagines she is having sex with Harriet's married lover; moreover, these connections are often triggered by a meteorological event like thunder. Gowdy re-creates scenes of Rose's childhood with the same exact detail as she constructs the present, regularly punctuated with movie allusions to themes of betrayal and guilt. The mystery gradually disclosed in tandem with Rose's integration into Harriet's life and dilemmas is Rose's sense of guilt for the death of her little sister, Ava, twenty-three years ago. But "piano wires snap in Rose's head" (299) when she encounters Harriet pushing a baby carriage; relief at the sight of the child whom Harriet has carried to term combines a sense of expiation and joy: "The infant soul she had privately mourned and paired with Ava in eternity was alive" (300).

These narratives all involve identities unravelled and exposed. A daughter learns to cherish her exceptional brother's insights; without her true soulmate an orphan becomes a determined survivor; an academic burrows in fear of hares; a nonagenarian artist resumes her place in a Bloomsbury past; a recuperating soldier strives for recognition in a historical identity; and a woman exhumes a sense of responsibility for her little sister's death. With insight and precision Basran, O'Neill, Mayr, MacLeod, Winter, and Gowdy conduct their meditations on the power of consciousness to reconstruct or annihilate or substitute existence. The spaces of their narratives are both detailed and amazingly shifting, vividly exterior and interior.

In a vast array of narrative formats stressing voice or pastiche or fluid space, women's fiction in Canada continues to explore the ways these elements connect with one another. From Elizabeth Smart's self-portraits to Daphne Marlatt's interruptions, from Anne Hébert's nightmare visions to Heather O'Neill's savvy street-kid language, their stories reach out and draw us into their imagined worlds. They leave us wondering about the next steps for their fully realized characters, about the fate of Maggie Lloyd and Luzina Toussignant, the prospects for Larry after his party and for Hoda after retiring from the street, and the possibilities for a relationship between Morag Gunn and her daughter. Would Engel's Lou continue her archival work, and what routes north would van Herk's Arachne take? Is there a future for adolescents Nomi Nickel, Lisamarie Hill, and the Weed Cookie dude? Will the Tree of Life continue to shelter Birdie? Will Jimmy Blanchard be comforted by the news that his handwriting and that of James Wolfe are found to be the same? Narrative art in all its registers creates these characters about whom we care and wonder. These fictional worlds attune us to the contradictions and passions, complexities, and re-visions of our lives.

chapter two

Film

"The art of film," Christian Metz reminds us, "is located on the same semiological 'plane' as literary art" (96). The close alliance between the art of writing and making films in Canada and the techniques of fiction is the topic of this chapter. Visual and auditory events of the "created spectacle" (Metz 43) of film engage us in the role of witnesses, absorbing details of design, setting, location, point of view, and dialogue or monologue; the work of women filmmakers in Canada offers "a resistant viewing position for the female spectator" (Dickinson 164) and arguably for any alert reader. Women filmmakers' films range capaciously across all genres and "in their relation to popular culture," as Kay Armatage affirms, are distinctively "avant-garde" ("Fluidity" 98). In original screenplays or adaptations of women's writing or documentaries, this accomplishment also involves "broadly cast networks of cinema-related practices that are directly connected with the history of feminism" (de Lauretis 9). Such practice, especially as it focuses on the voice and representation of the female as artist, lover, wife, narrator, mother, daughter, and/or citizen, further intensifies an understanding of Canadian cinema. As Armatage and her editorial colleagues observe in *Gendering the Nation*, "linking nation and gender together to think about cinema leads to a redefinition of place" (Armatage et al. 12), including social relations and identity formation. This re-examination "disrupts the imagined community of nation," calling "into question the often essentialized and romanticized community of women" (13). While attending to the politics of location and place-based identities, the cinema art of Canadian women filmmakers pictures place as both a fully realized, often bounded environment and a wished-for or attained porous space of liberation. In their rich and diverse body of work an extraordinary commonality is the search, frequently solitary and oppositional, for voice, recognition, release, and independence.

Original Screenplays

The Far Shore (1975) by painter, mixed-media artist, and filmmaker Joyce Wieland (1931–98) narrates the escape from a doomed marriage between the Québécoise Eulalie, who dreams of earning a living as a concert pianist, and Ross, a Toronto industrialist. As the film opens on a sunny pastoral riverbank scene in 1919 Quebec, Ross entrusts a little girl to deliver his note to Eulalie asking her to marry him. Their arrival, on a rainy evening the day after the marriage, in Ross's Rosedale mansion, heavy with mahogany and rosewood, presages the entrapment of stiffness and convention. The differences in language, directness, and values expand. He accuses her of being "a foreigner" and "thinking too much"; she dares to tell him his overlong speech announcing a holiday bores his employees. While Ross plans silver mining explorations, Eulalie plays Debussy. Her artistic talent is admired by painter Tom McLeod, a fictionalized version of Tom Thomson. Ross's rape of Eulalie signals the vivid contrast with Tom. The iris shots in this film are exceptional and revelatory. When Eulalie and Tom meet in his studio-cabin, each in turn uses a magnifying glass to talk to the other, a soundless but intimately magnified communication, with their animated faces filling the circle. As the camera closes in on Eulalie's face when Ross accuses her of thinking of her lover, the iris circle dissolves and widens to the scene of Tom canoeing. Her escape by plunging into the lake to join Tom leads both to their rhythmic, passionate lovemaking and to Ross's fierce chase to pursue them. Lake Mazinaw and its magnificent rockface in Bon Echo Provincial Park, where this chase was shot, is itself the far shore, an ironic recollection of the idyllic riverbank engagement scene. After two gunshots are heard, Tom's blood-soaked body appears, but the only evidence of Eulalie is her floating hat. Of this ambiguous ending Lauren Rabinovitz concludes that Eulalie, "not integrated into the dominant order," only accedes "to an as yet unactualized territory" (127). The contrasts between Ross's philistinism and Eulalie's "cultured modernism" lead Kay Armatage to view Wieland's melodrama as "a radical understanding of Canada's political and cultural history throughout the period of industrial modernization" ("Fluidity" 108).

Although the forceful symbolism and rupture of the ending of this full-length commercial film, with Canadian financing and cast and made by a writer-director better known for experimental films, did not result in box-office success, *The Far Shore* establishes an important platform for considering women's cinema in Canada. Filmmaking is a fluid process that extends our understanding of narrative and cultural and cross-cultural viewing. Through feature films, along with documentaries and artisanal and accented films, cinema has the capacity to represent liminal subjectivity and recognized as well as interstitial locations. With an emphasis on their original screenplays, the filmmaking careers, extensive and emerging, of Anne Wheeler (b. 1946), Patricia Rozema (b. 1958), Deepa Mehta (b. 1950), Mina Shum (b. 1966), Sarah Polley (b. 1979), and Sadaf Foroughi (b. 1976) contribute to a redefinition of Canadian cinema not only by their questioning of patriarchal and heterosexual norms but by their adroit control of the interplay between commerce and culture.

Anne Wheeler's work shows an acute awareness of the tenacity of women, their survival strategies, in the face of the odds stacked against them in both physical environment and social expectations. Her intense interest in the endurance of women is a salient feature, from the early National Film Board shorts *Great Grandmother* (1975) and *Augusta* (1976); the melodramas she wrote, *Loyalties* (1986) and *Bye Bye Blues* (1989); her direction of a television adaptation of Laurence's *The Diviners* (1992) and the witty romp set in the lesbian community of Vancouver, *Better Than Chocolate* (1999); to her television work in the historical romance *Mail Order Bride* (2008) and the breast cancer drama *Living Out Loud* (2009). Whether documenting the lives of indomitable Albertan pioneers (*Great Grandmother*), or an eighty-eight-year-old non-status Shuswap Indian living alone (*Augusta*), or the tension of Indigenous-White relations and allegiance in an upper-middle-class English family in Lac La Biche (*Loyalties*), or the romance of a young mother who sings for a dance band during World War II *(Bye Bye Blues)*, Wheeler's films declare their sympathies with the physical, passionate needs of the protagonists. Co-written with Sharon Riis, *Loyalties* explores the bond between the English doctor's wife, Lily, whose husband is a convicted pedophile, and the local Indigenous woman in an abusive marriage, Rosanne, whom she employs as a nanny. The fact that both women are given refuge in the small home of the nanny's mother, Beatrice, who fills the role of an Elder, underscores the motif of female generational comfort. Wheeler makes creative use of western locations, setting *Loyalties* in a visually stunning northern Alberta town and shooting the dance hall scenes of *Bye Bye Blues* in an Edmonton art-house cinema. She also revisits family stories, making her grandmother's pioneer experiences the basis for *Great Grandmother*, relying on her mother's grass widowhood during World War II for *Bye Bye Blues*, and dramatizing her father's letters while in a Japanese prisoner-of-war camp for the NFB feature-length docudrama *A War Story* (1981).

A different trio of women are the central characters in Rozema's *I've Heard the Mermaids Singing* (1987): art gallery owner Gabrielle and painter Mary are lovers, while the blithe, occasionally inept narrator, photographer Polly Vandersma, "the most closely aligned with Rozema's authorial voice" (Del Sorbo 130), looks on in fascination. Polly's quest to be recognized as an artist and literally to float above the world (in the film, to the strains of the flower duet from Léo Delibes's opera *Lakmé*) strikes critic Teresa de Lauretis as insufficiently political, preempting the "sociopolitical and subjective power" of feminism and lesbianism (20). Yet the closing reconciliation among the three and magical opening onto a green world affirm Rozema's belief that "fiction answers our need for utopias" (Pevere and Wise 23). Rozema's *When Night Is Falling* (1995) examines another female relationship between a young instructor, Camille, striving for tenure within a homophobic academy, and an artist/performer, Petra, with whom she joins the circus. The characterization of Fanny Price in Rozema's adaptation of Austen's *Mansfield Park* (1999) did not please all Janeites; instead of the shy, timid, avoidant Fanny concerned with appropriate behaviour, Rozema's character is an assertive, daring writer.

Deepa Mehta's directorial debut was *Sam & Me* (1991); "signaling the promise and the perils of cross-cultural dialogue" and "the uneasy relations between ethnic groups" (Banning 293, 294), the screenplay by Ranjit Chowdry traces the connections and misunderstandings between Sam, a Jewish widower in Toronto who wants to die in Israel, and Nik, a young immigrant from India with get-rich dreams, whose job is the caregiver for Sam, his employer's father. Although Mehta directed an adaptation of Carol Shields's *The Republic of Love* in 2003, the best-known and most controversial work by this filmmaker is her *Elements* trilogy, set in India and intimately concerned with the future of women. Educated in both India and Canada, Mehta could be included in the genre Hamid Naficy defines as accented cinema, where "by dint of their education, class affiliation, multilingualism, cosmopolitanism, and distance from the homeland, accented filmmakers are structurally outsiders, however much they desire to be considered insiders, either within their own native culture or in the host society" (70). *Fire* (1996) presents sisters-in-law in arranged marriages who find liberation in their relationship; *Earth* (1998), based on a novel by Bapsi Sidhwa, considers how the 1947 partition of India separated friends and lovers; *Water* (2005), based on Mehta's story with screenplay by Anurag Kashyap, follows the misfortunes of an eight-year-old girl, widowed in an arranged marriage, who is sent to an ashram for Hindu widows. The most polemical of the trio, *Water* depicts the arrangements and tensions among four ages of women: the girl-child Chuyla; the beautiful young woman Kalyani, who is prostituted to support the ashram; the literate widow Shakuntala, who shows maternal concern for the child; and the greedy older boss Madhumati, who, after the suicide drowning of Kalyani, sends Chuyla to replace her. In the realm of accented cinema, Mehta's trilogy contributes "to constructing both what is exilic and diasporic and what is national" (Naficy 70). These strands come together again in *Heaven on Earth*

(2008), her depiction of the abuse of Vibrant Chand, a Punjabi bride in an arranged marriage, who arrives in Canada to live in her husband's crowded extended-family home in Brampton, Ontario. Despite the help of a magical root with seductive powers, supplied by Vibrant's Jamaican co-worker, the resulting clashes do not resemble *A Midsummer Night's Dream*. Mehta's recent dramatic thriller *Beeba Boys* (2015) exposes the brutal Indo-Canadian drug-and-arms-war scene in Vancouver, as leader Jeet Johar and his "beeba boys" (good boys) compete to be "seen and heard."

Set in Vancouver's Downtown Eastside, Mina Shum's original screenplays and direction for *Double Happiness* (1994) and *Meditation Park* (2017), among others, deploy pathos and humour to illustrate the cultural conflicts and expectations of Asian-Canadian family life. Troubling conventional constructions of kinship and "offering an unsurpassed representation of South Asian-Canadian diasporic experience" (Banning 304), *Double Happiness* focuses on a twenty-two-year-old protagonist, Jade Li, as she tries to juggle her parents' expectations that she marry a Chinese boy and her own ambitions to be an actor and play Blanche DuBois. Arranged dates are disastrous, with one "approved" Chinese suitor admitting that he is pursuing the charade rather than tell his own parents that he is gay. Jade's meeting a Caucasian grad student intensifies the dilemma.

In *Meditation Park* a sixty-year-old homemaker, Maria, having made surprise preparations for a special meal to celebrate her husband, Bing's, sixty-fifth birthday, is shocked to find a lacey orange thong in his trouser pocket. She does not confront him; nor does she confide in her married daughter but rather announces her decision to get a job. Bing's responses, "my wife doesn't need a job" and "women over fifty are the most unemployed category," fuel her resolve. It is female Asian friends who help her to learn selling backyard parking spaces, an illegal activity, accountant Bing threatens, that carries a $5,000 fine. Maria's success in selling, along with riding a bicycle, are stages in her discovery of herself and her marriage. She befriends a neighbour, initially a parking-space competitor, when he confides in her that his wife is dying. Using her newfound resources, she hires a taxi to follow Bing's moves. The taxi driver's quietly hilarious question, "Are you some kind of detective, ma'am?," invokes the previous scene of Maria watching an old rerun of *Dragnet*. Pathetic and comic details intertwine; she graduates to a bicycle chase and is eventually confronted by the young mistress herself, who, recognizing Maria's ring and her face from Bing's wallet photo, ends the affair. The film poignantly avoids the clichés of irate wife squaring off against denying husband; instead, this wife actually asks the mistress to take Bing back. To emphasize the mounting female ascendancy, the daughter chastizes the father for bullying her mother, "the woman who has given you forty years of her life." Maria finds her voice, emerging from domestic shelter and refusing to be ruled by her husband. Two scenes capture the joy of this film. The first is a block party celebration as the Asian parking-space ladies gyrate and shimmy to silent disco music on headphones. The second reinforces Maria's determination to attend their son's wedding, which Bing had tried to forbid; alone she rolls her suitcase away from the house and, smiling serenely, boards the ferry.

Sarah Polley's filmography reflects her decades of involvement in television series and full-length features. As an actor she is recognizable in her large body of work, from roles in *Road to Avonlea* (1994–6) to movie roles in, among many others, Atom Egoyan's *The Sweet Hereafter* (1997), David Cronenberg's *eXistenZ* (1999), Thom Fitzgerald's *The Event* (2003), and Isabelle Coixet's *The Secret Life of Words* (2005). Most pertinent here is her art as filmmaker in the screenplay for *Take This Waltz* (2011), exploring the routes and impasses of communication in a marriage. (Her adaptations of Munro and Atwood are discussed below, and her film of family history is addressed in the non-fiction chapter.) Among the remarkable features of this film is its overt use of visual motifs to portray emotional states. The chance encounter between Margot and Daniel, her eventual lover (who happens to be a neighbour in Toronto), at a historical re-enactment at the Fortress of Louisbourg in Cape Breton, Nova Scotia, an enactment involving the flogging of an adulterer, starts the unravelling of Margot's playful but already static marriage to Lou. Margot's plan to stay faithful to her husband for thirty years and eventually reunite with Daniel at the lighthouse at Louisbourg emerges as a dream, shot in silhouette but in actuality unrealized. Polley subtly embeds Canadian allusions and landmarks throughout. As well as the historic site of Louisbourg, there are the aural cues of Leonard Cohen's singing the song which supplies the title and Feist's cover of his "Closing Time." Among the cinematic cues is Margot and Lou's fifth-anniversary celebration viewing of a film, Claude Jutra's classic *Mon Oncle Antoine*. The generously realized, passionately uncertain character of Margot, professing love for Lou yet unable to deny the magnetism of Daniel, illustrates how, in the praise of *New York Times* reviewer A.O. Scott, "Polley excels at managing the idiosyncrasies and contradictions of her characters so that our knowledge of them is both intimate and mixed with potential surprise." Margot's relocated life with Daniel shows traces of the same non-communication as her marriage, a situation conveyed in the final scene of Margot alone jostling from side to side in a late-night amusement park ride on Toronto's Centre Island.

Prospects are more sombre and even more ambiguous for sixteen-year-old Ava Vali in Iranian-Canadian Sadaf Foroughi's debut feature, *Ava* (2017). Cited as one of the ten best films of 2017 at the Toronto International Film Festival (TIFF) and winner of the TIFF Discovery Prize, the Persian-language film, shot in Tehran with English subtitles, presents the teenager's anguished attempts to break free of her professional parents' surveillance, especially that of her doctor mother. Ava's desire to study violin, amplified by her attraction to a handsome male pianist and the music of Purcell and Beethoven, does not match her mother's plans for her only child's future. The principal of the girls' school Ava attends, who lectures students about "animalistic desires" and wears white gloves to inspect their backpacks, and her mother herself, who takes her daughter to a gynaecologist to affirm her virginity, underscore the girl's isolation and need to flee.

Adaptations of Women's Writing in Canada

Since, as Peter Dickinson argues convincingly in his study of adapting Canadian literature to film, "different institutional and cultural codes" can be called upon, "questions of *infidelity, incoherence*, and *non-equivalency* often provide more productive starting points for adaptation studies than the traditional measuring sticks of *fidelity, coherence*, and *equivalency*" (211). Three examples, Lynne Stopkewich's *Kissed* (1996), an adaptation of Barbara Gowdy's short story "We So Seldom Look on Love"; Léa Pool's *Lost and Delirious* (2001), as adapted by Judith Thompson from Susan Swan's novel *The Wives of Bath*; and Sarah Polley's *Away from Her* (2006), an adaptation of Alice Munro's "The Bear Came over the Mountain," are the focus of this section.

Lynne Stopkewich (b. 1964) made *Kissed* as her MFA thesis at the University of British Columbia. The figure of the female necrophile in Gowdy's story, Sandra Larson, is still prominent in the film; no longer a first-person narrator, she fills the role of voice-over, telling the viewer mildly and softly that she has always been "fascinated with death," wanting "to get inside it" and "understand perfection." Instead of the middle-aged independent Sandra of Gowdy's story, the film presents a twenty-something Sandra along with recalled childhood scenes of Sandra wrapping a dead bird in toilet paper, burying a mouse, and massaging a dead chipmunk's blood on her throat. The fascination leads to her study of embalming and job at the funeral parlour as well as her encounter with the sometime med student, Matt, who becomes a sexual partner. "One of the most radical narrative treatments of non-normative heterosexual female desire in Canadian film," *Kissed* also succeeds in presenting "a more youthful and accessible figure of deviant desire" in line "with late feminism's preference for female icons who combine various degrees of surface empowerment with sexual availability" (Parpart 51). The visual medium is especially riveting when the funeral parlour owner demonstrates to a rapt Sandra how to vacuum the liquids by thrusting a cannula into a corpse and when a naked Sandra, experiencing orgasm over a body, tells us "I'm out of myself." The most startling image is the hanging naked body of Matt, who, having been convinced that "love is about crossing for transformation," finally offers his corpse for Sandra's delectation.

Homosexual female desire centres both Swan's *The Wives of Bath* (1993) and *Lost and Delirious*, the first English film by

Swiss-Québécoise filmmaker Léa Pool (b. 1950). The three teen-aged girls, Paulie, Victoria, and Mary, students at a private boarding school, are present in both texts. But differences in time, characterization, and plot, with which Swan declared herself in the introduction to a reissue of her novel "shamelessly satisfied" (ix), separate them. The film, shot on the campus of Bishop's University in Lennoxville, Quebec, sets the novel's 1960s narrative in the present. The combination of dramatist Thompson and filmmaker Pool, not concentrating on Paulie's desire to be seen as a man, turns the novel's murder and castration of the janitor into Paulie's suicide from the parapet of the school building in the film's breathtaking conclusion. Each girl experiences alienation: Paulie, adopted at birth, searches for her "blood mother"; Tori chafes against parental expectations that she will be "the perfect Junior League girl"; and Mary, initially "Mouse" and then "Mary Brave," mourns her dead mother. The newcomer to Paulie and Tori's room of "lost girls," Mary observes their lovemaking and narrates as the heterosexual other. Seeing Mary's role as working to "expel same-sex desires," Catherine Silverstone also interprets Paulie's borrowings from *Twelfth Night* and *Antony and Cleopatra* to try to regain Tori's love as "markers of unhappiness and melancholy" (n.p.) While Sara Ahmed views Paulie's descent as ascent, arguing that "she and the bird [the falcon whom Paulie nurses to health] rise above the heads of the teachers and schoolgirls who look upon the scene with passive horror and disbelief" (105), Silverstone sees the ending quite convincingly as sacrificing the threat to the community, occluding "Paulie as an embodied desiring queer subject" (n.p.). By tracing the philological root of "lost" to the Germanic root for "cut apart" and "delirious" to the Latin *delirare*, "to go off the furrow," Maria Anita Stefanelli concludes that *Lost and Delirious* "hints at a disjunction, a separation leading to somewhere off: off space, off time, off the mind" (364).

Sarah Polley has written and directed an adaptation of Alice Munro's "The Bear Came over the Mountain" from *Hateship, Friendship, Courtship, Loveship, Marriage* (2001) as *Away from Her*, along with a well-received television adaptation of Atwood's *Alias Grace*, which debuted on CBC in fall 2017 and on Netflix in

2018. Adaptations, as Linda Hutcheon reminds us, are "autonomous works ... deliberate, announced, and extended revisitations of prior works" (*Theory of Adaptation* xiv). Polley's *Away from Her* sets out to illustrate how the female protagonist, who is slipping into Alzheimer's, has what Munro identified as "the spark of life" ("The Bear Came over the Mountain" 275). Instead of referring to Fiona's privileged upbringing, the money and eventual home supplied by her cardiologist father, and her childlessness, the film concentrates on the aging beauty of the actor Julie Christie. The serial, somewhat programmatic philandering of the retired academic husband, Grant, as portrayed by Gordon Pinsent, becomes a deliberately muffled detail in the film. In the short story, Munro had commented on his affairs at length – "Many times he had catered to a woman's pride, to her fragility, by offering more affection – or a rougher passion – than anything he really felt" (Munro 285). Polley extends and visualizes memories and suggestions from Munro's text. Fiona's aesthetic recollection of skiing under the full moon where "they had heard the branches cracking in the cold" (Munro 279) emerges as a brilliant, moon-drenched, voiceless scene; Grant's preliminary exchanges with Marian, the wife of the resident at Meadowlake institution to whom Fiona has become attached, and his expectations of "the practical sensuality of [Marian's] cat's tongue" (Munro 321) play out in the film as a bed scene with Grant and Marian. Polley's adaptation, "repetition but without replication ... involves both memory and change, persistence and variation" (Hutcheon 173).

Documentaries

At an international women's film conference along with a film festival held in Vancouver in March 1999, four women documentary filmmakers participated in a panel about their work. Brenda Longfellow, known for her Genie Award-winning documentary on Gwendolyn MacEwen, *Shadow Maker* (1998), lamented that "where feminist documentary filmmaking was about building communities, especially in the first stages, like other kinds of political filmmaking, now with television it is also about commodification" (Levitin et al. 214). Fellow panelist Métis-Cree Loretta Todd, speaking from "within the community of Aboriginal expression, where song and dance and story and creating were available to everybody to do," separated from these ranks filmmakers "who embrace the role of visionary and dreamer ... to be able to interpret something back to the people" (Levitin et al. 215). In his detailed analysis of the filmmaking of Abenaki Alanis Obomsawin, Jerry White views her documentaries as "complex critical works, which balance the needs of a utilitarian, educational cinema with the larger political project of Native self-determination" (364). Documentaries can blend capacities to build community and envision futures by presenting a complicated version of the national self, disrupting "some basic assumptions about Canadian life" (White 373).

Joyce Wieland's landscape film, *Reason over Passion / La raison avant la passion* (1969), could arguably be considered a topographical documentary or an abstract journey. Provocative and politically complex, in its allusion to the motto then-Prime Minister Pierre Elliott Trudeau espoused in all his writing, the film is a series of glimpses and hypotheses about Canada, from Cape Breton to Vancouver. With the progressively jumbled letters of the title resembling a Scrabble board and electronic beeps supplying a heartbeat, *Reason over Passion*, shot largely from a hand-held camera through car or train windows, embodies movement, as it presents glimpses of highways, grain elevators, and, in the central portion, images of the 1968 Liberal convention. Drawing on Wieland's experience with collage and multi-media art, the film's ironic treatment of Trudeau shows his ambiguity through "its use of a post-Pop art approach" (Lellis 61). *Reason over Passion* demands multiple viewings, "far better on a moviola than on a screen ... when you can walk around the hall in which it is playing, glance up or away at will" (Lellis 62).

More deliberate and sustained viewing is necessary for the work of Loretta Todd, who helped to establish the Indigenous Arts program at the Banff Centre. The resilience of First Nations people is a central concern. She directed *The Learning Path* (1991) about residential school survivors, and wrote and directed both *Forgotten*

Warriors (1996), narrating the experiences of confiscated land and broken promises for Native soldiers returning from World War II, and *Kainayssini Imanistaisiwa: The People Go On* (2003). Todd's filmography deserves to be studied alongside the documentaries of Alanis Obomsawin, especially Obomsawin's quartet on the Oka crisis. The fourth instalment, *Rocks at Whiskey Trench* (2000), is discussed in the introduction to this book. With her voice-over commentary, *Kanehsatake: 270 Years of Resistance* (1993), Obomsawin's observational documentary, based on more than seventy hours of behind-the-scenes footage of the 1990 armed standoff at Oka, Quebec, between Mohawk protesters and Sûreté du Québec officers and Canadian Armed Forces soldiers, details the history of the appropriation of First Nations land and the centuries-old colonial devaluation of Indigenous culture. Her advocacy continues with such recent documentaries as *The People of the Kattiwapiskak River* (2012), focusing on the housing and infrastructure crises at the Attawapiskat First Nation; *Hi-Ho Mistahey!* (2013), addressing education on First Nations reserves; and *Our People Will Be Healed* (2017), highlighting the addition of Cree culture and history to the Manitoba curriculum at the Helen Betty Osborne Ininiw Education Resource Centre in Norway House. *Finding Dawn* (2006), a documentary by Métis Christine Welsh, professor of Indigenous cinema at the University of Victoria, narrates the stories of missing women, from Vancouver's Downtown Eastside to Saskatoon, symbolized by the title figure of Dawn Crey; insufficient DNA evidence was found at the Pickton farm to include her as one of Robert Pickton's victims.

As advocates, revisionists, and challengers of imposed representations, documentary filmmakers inform and, in fact, mediate cultural understanding. Bonnie Sherr Klein's (b. 1941) documentaries feature hard-hitting advocacy: the anti-pornography crusade of *Not a Love Story: A Film about Pornography* (1981), in which she is accompanied by stripper Linda Lee Tracy, and *Shameless: The Art of Disability* (2006), meditating on the changes in her own life after strokes limited her movement to a motorized scooter. For Maya Gallus, the documentary is an effective medium for conveying unconventional author biographies, as in *Elizabeth Smart: On the Side of the Angels* (1991) and *The Mystery of Mazo de la Roche* (2012). Her analysis of the women in roller derbies, *Derby Crazy Love* (2013), introduces what Iron Wench calls "the sisterhood" of this sport featuring Smack Daddy, Suzy Hotrod, Raw Heidi, and Kamikaze Kitten among its fully engaged participants. Brenda Longfellow's *Weather Report* (2007) displays the effects of global warming from the Arctic to India, Africa, and China. Her more recent *Offshore* (2013) is a full-length interactive documentary about the next chapter in oil exploration, when "the era of easy oil is over"; taking viewers along on helicopter investigations, the interactive possibilities allow viewers to open and read a classified incident report about an accident aboard a drilling rig. Based on her book of the same name, Naomi Klein's (b. 1970) *This Changes Everything* (2015) pursues the connection between capitalism and climate; illustrating examples from Montana's Powder Basin and Alberta's tar sands to sites in India and Beijing, she challenges the addiction to profit and fossil fuel consumption with the call to reclaim democracies.

The feature that links women filmmakers' original screenplays, adaptations, and documentaries is the engagement of their protagonists and narrators in the imagined power to illustrate situations vividly and suggest, effect, or envision change. From Joyce Wieland's avant-garde flickering reflections of Canada in 1968 to Brenda Longfellow's and Naomi Klein's indictments of resource extraction today, women's films convey personal exchanges and questions in alert, probing ways. Routes and roadblocks to political and individual self-determination remain at the heart of their work.

chapter three

Poetry

Knowing
One is the observer of,
made participant in,
momentarily
caught, stilled;
listens with every fibre.
— Margaret Avison, "Four Words," *Concrete and Wild Carrot*

The interior life and dialogue with the self, the rhythms of speech, the gravitational pull of emotions, and flashes of unexpected comparison – all glimpsed in the poetry of any era or nation – defy a single understanding or approach. Important for the intensity of life perceptible in it and for its insights beyond the world of appearances, poetry is open to sensual and imagined realities. Although critics have noted the "singular absence of defining characteristics" in the "richness and complexity" (Staines 153) of Canadian poetry, this chapter aims to trace some of the highlights of the imaginative continuum and resonant afterlife of women poets. In the poetic production of the 1950s in Canada, what Northrop Frye labels in his preface to *The Bush Garden* as "one of its crucial periods," he discerns "how the echoes and ripples of the great mythopoeic age kept moving through Canada, and taking a form there that they could not have taken elsewhere" (xxviii–xxix). Through a dazzling array of experiments and shimmering shapes, with verbal gestures ranging from the playful and plainspoken to the metaphysical and mythological, women poets were substantial contributors to this history. In fact, poet Di Brandt designates the modernist women of the fifties and sixties as "important makers" through their favouring of "more holistic, fluid, and sustainable relations with the natural world, and new forms of self-expression and community building" ("A New Genealogy" 13). Recognizing that women's poetry in Canada, like all poetry, originates in the senses, this necessarily selective sampling of their work, pausing to include two overviews of critical commentary about different generations, is arranged according to what strikes me as linked experiences of social circumstances, which can be dark or absurd, cryptic or mystery-filled.

Jaques, Livesay, Waddington, and Page: "fired in the kiln of endurance"

Like fiction writers, women poets were active before mid-century, often publishing in newspapers in the absence of literary periodicals. One of the most prolific and popular was Edna Jaques (1891–1978), whose career was launched with publications in the *Moose Jaw Times Herald* when she was a teenager living on the family homestead twenty-five miles from the city. Her autobiography, *Uphill All the Way* (1977), is a candid account of her family's move from Ontario to the west, the rigours of homesteading, the disappointment of her "just plain lazy" (142) husband, and her enjoyment of success; as she relates, "How I love to see my books sitting on a counter at Eaton's or Simpson's or Coles, smiling at me like a happy kid ... All told I have had twelve books published and have sold a quarter of a million copies" (242).

Jaques's popularity was based largely on her vernacular directness. The first-person voice conveys a neighbourly honesty, as in this admission in "Prairie Born":

> *I want the little sounds once more*
> *That common folk like me,*
> *Were raised to love and listen for,*
> *The droning of a bee.* (Prairie Born, Prairie Bred 10)

For all its beneficent cheer, the homespun style is not interested in "little foolish trivial things" like "curtains or the polish of a floor," but rather wants to probe beneath the surface.

> *I wanted to reach down and touch her heart*
> *Beneath the thin veneer that shut me out,*
> *And let our true selves speak ... to hear her tell*
> *The secret hidden things she dreamed about.* ("At a Tea," *Aunt Hattie's Place* 4)

"In Flanders Now," written in 1918, was among her most widely published poems; on display at the unveiling of the monument of the Unknown Soldier in Arlington Cemetery and sold in a booklet by the Federation of Women's Clubs in the United States for the restoration of the national library in Louvain, her answer to John McCrae's "In Flanders Fields" supplies the assurance that the torch has been taken up:

> *We have kept faith ye Flanders dead,*
> *Sleep well beneath the poppies red*
> *That mark your place,*
> *The torch your dying hands did throw*
> *We held it high before the foe*
> *And answered bitter blow for blow*
> *In Flanders fields.* (*Uphill All the Way* 129)

Most of Jaques's twelve books were published by Thomas Allen in Toronto, although undated chapbooks such as *Verses for You* and *Drifting Soil* were printed in Moose Jaw. *Verses for You* identifies Jaques as an honorary member of the Moose Jaw Writers' Club; in her foreword to this little book she praises the many beautiful things that have come from the prairies, "but none lovelier or of more grace than its poetry." In genuinely populist work Jaques spoke directly to women, yet, as Carole Gerson has remarked, her popularity was dismissed "among primarily male by gender and values" members of the academic literary establishment ("Sarah Binks and Edna Jaques" 66). E.K. Brown in his "Letters in Canada" review disliked her "cosiness," fearing the emergence of another "Eddy Guest," while his successor Northrop Frye judged her work as part of "the doggerel school."[1] Gerson points to these assessments as evidence of "some of the biases of class, gender and ethnicity that have been unquestioningly accepted by the profession that constructs literary value" (70).

In contrast to Jaques's model of the plainspoken, immensely productive but virtually lone poet developing her contacts with newspaper editors and publishers, other early women poets in Canada belonged to a supportive network. The remarkable and intertwined career trajectories of Dorothy Livesay (1909–96), P.K. (Patricia Kathleen) Page (1916–2010), and Miriam Waddington (1917–2004) share several features. "Fired in the kiln of endurance," as Livesay put it in "The Enchanted Isle: A Dialogue" (*A Room of One's Own*) their acclaimed poetry reflected the experience of different disciplines – social activism for Livesay and Waddington and visual art for Page. These women wrote to and about one another. As Waddington recalls her friendship of more than fifty years with Dorothy ("Dee") Livesay, "we sent each other our poems hot off our typewriters, and we each responded enthusiastically, analytically, and critically."[2] Seeing "Dee" as "a real pioneer ... a real innovator," Anne Marriott recalled that there was not "any other woman writing in the thirties as she did," while Waddington reflected on Livesay's whole career as flowing "from her daily life and her deep emotional interest in politics ... not politics so much as a hunger for justice and freedom in the world."[3] In distinctive ways they searched for a green world – playful, flourishing, light-filled, integral. They also contributed to publication venues that established long-standing traditions for Canadian poetry, as did the Contemporary Poets series initiated by Ryerson Press along with the Ryerson Poetry Chap-Books edited by Lorne Pierce.

Publishing essays and fiction as well as the poetry for which they are best known, they relied on and sustained small literary magazines. Some of their poetry first appeared in the New Writing series under the editorship of John Sutherland in the Montreal-based *Preview* (1942–5), which Page helped to edit, and *First Statement* (1942–5), which published Waddington's first collection in 1945.

These magazines joined forces to form *Northern Review: New Writing in Canada* in 1945, as its masthead declared, filling the express "need for a national magazine that could serve as a medium for new writers of poetry, fiction, and criticism." Dorothy Livesay and P.K. Page were among its regional editors. On the west coast Alan Crawley's *Contemporary Verse* (1941–52) was founded with the encouragement and assistance of Livesay and poets Floris McLaren (1904–78), Doris Ferne (1896–c.1975), and Anne Marriott (1913–97); its inaugural issue featured poems by Page. Livesay's commitment to poetry imbued her whole life; more than three decades later, during her tenure (1975–7) as the founding editor of *CVII* (*Contemporary Verse II*), she issued a call for poetry with "the authority of experience and action from all levels of society: the deprived, the enslaved, the sheltered, the brainwashed, as well as the fat, sleek, jaded" (Irvine 265). Disputing Frye's sometimes inconsistent claim about "Canadian poets [who] have written only one good book of poems, generally their first" (*Bush Garden* 235), the wide-ranging production of these foremothers and their successors continues to exert a generative influence on poetics in Canada.

Dorothy Livesay's experience as a social worker during the Depression and her affiliation with the Communist Party until 1939 coloured much of her poetry of this period. However, Livesay's first collections of lyrical verse, *Green Pitcher* (1928) and *Signpost* (1932), and her contemporary unpublished poems illustrate the puckish delight she took in disappointing readerly certainties.

> *Reader, if you are curious*
> *To find in this book my proper self,*
> *Warning! I, like the pepper-pot*
> *Live each day on a different shelf.* ("Where Is It?," *Archive for Our Times* [1998] 33)

Focusing, Brandt notes, "on the predominance of the natural world and the surrounding cosmos over our human activities" ("A New Genealogy" 12), she discerns genteel memories of her grandmother's house and parlour in "the rain as the feathery fringe of her shawl" ("Green Rain," *Signpost* 38). The more overt political concerns of her two major collections of the 1940s, *Day and Night* (1944) and *Poems for People* (1947), both of which won Governor General's Awards, resonate beyond imagism. They express her activist concern with all forms of oppression, using syncopated chant, adapted nursery rhymes, and prayer-book idioms to comment on union solidarity and ruminate on the possibilities for peace in a post-World War II world. The title piece of *Day and Night*, composed in 1935 during her period of membership in the Communist Party, throbs with the degradations of the mechanized, programmed movement of industrial life: "Men in a stream, a moving human belt / Move into sockets, every one a bolt" (16). In contrast to this caesural bluntness, the insistent Lenin-inspired pound of the dimeter refrains –

One step forward
Two steps back
Shove the lever
Push it back. (19)

– gives an audio intensity to the shop floor, its coal furnaces, rolling steel, and racist foremen. Her invocation of the prophet Daniel's Babylonian companions, Shadrack, Meshack, and Abednego, who refuse to eat unclean meat (Daniel 1:7) and therefore "burn in the furnace, whirling slow," reflects back to an account of archetypal oppression. This labour cantata closes with a far-off forecast of workers triumphing over capitalism:

One step forward
Two steps back
Will soon be over
Hear it crack! (21)

But in the struggle for a socialist society, the turning of life "the other way" remains an unfulfilled desire.

The assessment of Livesay's early poetry is a topic of critical debate. George Woodcock judges her agit-prop of the thirties as "turgid" (50) in its combination of "social awareness; a ranging honesty; [and] ... that almost-Manichean sense of the dual nature of existence" (58). Pamela McCallum views the aesthetic and social task of "Day and Night" very differently. Recognizing "Livesay's encounter with Black culture and forms of Black expressivity," McCallum sees in "the exhausting repetition of factory labour ... a dialectical movement in which advancement (one step forwards) will only be discovered as the layers of the past (one step back) are unravelled and reconfigured into new patterns" (209). Yet with what Woodcock terms "the sudden widening of Livesay's poetic capabilities" (59) in the late 1940s and beyond, the intimate language of womanhood and sexuality becomes salient. Her consideration of Emily Brontë, Emily Dickinson, and Emily Carr, "The Three Emilys" from the collection composed in 1953, *Faces of Emily*, and included in *Collected Poems*, positions the contemporary poet as possessing "much less" and remaining "uncomforted." The couplets of the opening two stanzas chart the differences between mid-century notions of female freedom and the artistic expansiveness and cosmic expressivity these Emilys exploited; although "these three / Cry to be set free,"

> *Yet they had liberty!*
> *Their kingdom was the sky: ...*
> *A lake their palette, any tree*
> *Their brush could be.*[4]

The erotic charge so evident in *The Unquiet Bed* (1967) accompanies a greater explicitness about love and the female self. The image of "softly ... melt[ing] down / into the earthy green / grass ... between my thighs" ("The Notations of Love") sharply contrasts the evocation of "Green Rain" almost four decades earlier; the rhyming dimeter of the title piece, "The woman I am / is not what you see / I'm not just bones / and crockery," declares a purposeful awareness (*Collected Poems* 302, 292). The advance of age, about which she wrote "with such a combination of tenderness and passion"

(Woodcock 60), may have tempered the heat of her socialist conscience, as she announced in a 1976 manuscript:

> *I don't politick:*
> *I hammer*
> *tap tapping lightly*
> *sometimes I bludgeon*
> *but I don't worm myself*
> *into the body politic*
> *to feed my ego*
> *and destroy others.*[5]

Another lifelong commitment to the arts of words radiates through the work of Miriam Waddington as she draws attention to the ironic contrast between a mind apparently at peace and its inner turmoil. Cadences of sadness and anger inform her evocation of a green world melding socialist yearning and an exploration of Jewish-Russian ancestry. As she presents her "homeless half-and-half soul" in *The Glass Trumpet* (1966),

> *I went out into the autumn night*
> *to cry my anger to the stone-blind fields*
> *just as I was, untraditional, North American,*
> *Jewish, Russian, and rootless in all four,*
> *religious, unaffiliated, and held*
> *in a larger-than-life seize of hate.* ("Fortunes" 24–5)

Tom Marshall locates Waddington "in an increasingly perilous and unobliging world," where "she is a survivor, not an explorer, and her weapons are wit and courage" (78). Such weaponry undergirds her steadfast pursuit of social justice and betterment in the face of ironic reversals and the neglect of love evident in all the lyrical grief of her poetry.

In the first collection, *Green World* (1945), she appears to be enfolded in "green rhythms," "a crystal chrysalis" that "under the intensely golden point / Warms, expands, / Until walls crack suddenly / Uncup [her] into large and windy space" (n.p.). This burgeoning, enveloping, cosmic spell suits "a poet becoming the enchanted land of herself" (Ricou, "Into My Green World" 147). But a bleak world encompasses this enchantment. Her affiliation with the snubbed and belittled shines through a portrait of the Jarvis Street Jewish whore – almost three decades before the print appearance of Winnipeg North End's Hoda in Adele Wiseman's *Crackpot*. Although Laurie Ricou sees "little metaphorical resonance in this poem" (151), it does use a deceptively simple but intense ballad metre to considerable effect. Waddington creates "a common rendezvous / Arranged by madness, crime, and race," as she suggests a post-Shoah kinship between two different Jewish working girls:

On Jarvis Street the Jewish whore
The Jewish me on Adelaide –
Both of the nameless million poor
Who wear no medals and no braid. ("The Bond")

Like Livesay, she comments on aging, but prefers aphorisms to bluntness, with the sing-song ballad metre of "Erosion" half-concealing a sly irony,

For life grows down and love wears thin
It comes from living merely
What if the heart still grieves within?
The mind's at peace, or nearly. (*The Second Silence* 43)

P.K. Page: Onlooker and Participant

The conclusion of P.K. Page's poetic tribute to Livesay, "But We Rhyme in Heaven," captures the sensual tonic in her friend's writing:

But her anguished, defiant phrase –
"We rhyme in heaven"
is like a balloon

that carries our anger up
to a rarefied air where rancour is blown away. (Kaleidoscope 202)

Poet, artist, diarist, essayist, P.K. Page is "English Canada's most important poet of the last fifty years" (McNeilly 423). The nineteen volumes of poetry she composed over her remarkable career, her Governor General's Award for *The Metal and the Flower* (1954), and her appointment as a Companion of the Order of Canada (1999) certainly affirm that she is distinguished. Yet even that epithet, according to editor and poet Eric Ormsby, "betrays her" because she remains "too vivacious, too cunning, too elusive to be monumentalized" (11). With the masks of her pseudonym Judith Cape novelist or visual artist P.K. Irwin, her married name, Page pursued a lifelong interest in what Douglas Freake terms "the problematics of the self"; he understands her work as moving "from an earlier emphasis on alienation as a condition of modern life ... to a new paradigm of the relation between self and world" (97). The editor of her *Collected Works* and her literary executor, Zailig Pollock, who organized a symposium at Trent University to celebrate "The Worlds of P.K. Page" in 2002, discovers "a great joy as well in her vivid sense of being in the world, a joy which, until the very end, continues to find its most powerful expression in her lifelong vision of magical renewal" (17).[6] Over decades of acquaintance and interviews, her award-winning biographer, Sandra Djwa, discerns in Page's "private quest for illumination ... the ferocious internal journey that she was undertaking" (237).

Written under the pseudonym "Judith Cape," Page's novella *The Sun and the Moon* (1944), which she began writing in 1939, depicts the psychological power struggle between married painters Kristin and Carl. This "modernist Künstlerroman" (Rackham-Hall 36) actually prophesies many of the conflicts about medium and style Page experienced in her career. Kristin and Carl are studies in contrast. Though loving Carl, Kristin takes over his painting; "her mind moved with his hands" (97) until there is a sense of complete possession: "the city that was Carl knew foreign leadership" (98). The novella climaxes with the transformative victory of Kristin, "exultant ... knowing her supremacy, knowing the re-creation of self in the united forgetfulness of self" (121). Kristin's withdrawal from Carl followed by his disillusioned departure and slashing of his painting reveals the impossibility of synthesizing the rhythm of his brush strokes with her organic impulse. As Sandra Djwa reads the symbols, "there is finally an eclipse of one force (the male sun) by the female moon" (66).

Stretching over decades, her poetry displays the questing self, wanting to understand, to penetrate mysteries, yet ultimately exulting in being free floating and unconfined. Viewing Jacob Epstein's sculpture in London in the 1930s led to her observation about the "unexpected entry / into the door of my mind" ("Ecce Homo" 21). As the wife of the Canadian ambassador to Brazil, Arthur Irwin, she contemplated the embassy garden after a storm and expressed her sympathy for the dejected Italian gardener, while also invoking the artist's wish to see past appearances and beneath glitter.

so that the whole may toll,
its meaning shine
clear of the myriad images that still –
do what I will – encumber its pure line. ("After Rain" 91)

Although P.K. Irwin the painter struggled to write poetry while in Brazil, and these canvases can be "an extension of her poetic output rather than a turn away from poetry" (Roy, "Visual Arts and the Political World" 63), Page herself experienced an almost guilty betrayal of her troth:

art is the highest loyalty
and to let
a talent lie about unused
is to break faith. ("Could I Write a Poem Now?" 99)

Graphic and poetic sketches, for Page, reveal the machinery of the mind.

I have only to fill my pen
And the shifting gears begin:

> *flywheel and cogwheel start*
> *their small-toothed interlock.* ("The Filled Pen" 159)

From her childhood in Calgary and ambassadorial postings in Australia, Brazil, Mexico, and Guatemala, to productive retirement in Victoria, Page offers a wry biographical assessment:

> *Such my preparation for a life of paradox –*
> *a borderland being, barely belonging,*
> *one on the outskirts, over the perimeter.* ("Hand Luggage" 220)

Whether her borderland placed her on the outskirts looking in to situations and dilemmas or casting her glance farther afield beyond the fixed frontier, her poetry, prose, sketches, and paintings always present vivid scenes from a range of perspectives. With the early poetry of her Montreal years and the influence of the *Preview* group, Page appears to be on the outside looking in. Reflecting her experience in 1942 as a clerk typist at Allied War Supplies in *As Ten as Twenty* (1946), she comments on the misery of fellow workers during wartime who have "no wind / for the kites of their hearts"; though efficient and sure, "they weep in the vault, they are taut as net curtains / stretched upon frames" ("The Stenographers" 29–30). Without pity she reflects on "terrible tourists with their empty eyes" who suspect that "the subtle mourning of the photograph / might later conjure in the memory / all they are now incapable of feeling" ("The Permanent Tourists" 61). As Rosemary Sullivan reads her work, "no Canadian poet has equaled [her] capacity for metaphorical language" (*Poetry by Canadian Women* xii). Mirroring Page's affair with poet F.R. Scott in "The Metal and the Flower," the intractability of "a garden of barbed wire and roses" contemplates obliquely the "profound division between two lovers" (Djwa 147).

The moves to various postings, especially Brazil from 1957 to 1959, accompanying her husband, provided a different, related outlet for Page's art. Mediated and carefully edited after the fact, her *Brazilian Journal* (1987) nevertheless presents lucid and evocative impressions of learning, as Michael Ondaatje observes, "how to live and how not to live in a foreign country."[7] Her crippling lack of fluency in Portuguese affects her: "Not only do I talk a kind of baby talk, with an appalling accent, but the things I actually say are often quite different from what I mean to say" (55). Yet, with what she calls "a literary pleasure," she admits, "I grow to love Brazil more each day – even the wide flat corner with some rather awful houses and no vegetation but grass cover" (107). Opportunities for adroit character sketches abound, such as a governor's silent wife who, in the protection of a chauffeured car and in the presence of women, begins talking nonstop: "It was as if she had been dammed up a very long time and now all the words rushed out, dragging me down with them, drowning me" (135). What sustains her most of all during the Brazilian adventure is painting; "so on fire am I," she notes, being "so absorbed in painting when I have a free minute" (198). Suzanne Bailey and Christopher Doody include sketches and examples in their (2011) edition of *Brazilian Journal*, while Wendy Roy discusses reproduced felt-pen and gouache illustrations in her contribution to the P.K. Page Issue of *Canadian Poetry* (2014).

Cry Ararat! (1967) announced Page's full-fledged return to poetry. The title poem, invoking the mountain where Noah's ark landed after the deluge (Genesis 8:4), is an uplifting call, a shout rather, for a true communion with nature.

> *when dreaming, you desire*
> *and ask for nothing more*
> *than stillness to receive*
> *the I-am animal,*
> *the We-are leaf and flower,*
> *the distant mountain near.* ("Cry Ararat!" 106)

The dove, emblem of the covenant by which the stability of the course of nature against catastrophe is assured (Genesis 9:9–16), is also the powerful harbinger of renewal.

> *The dove believed*
> *in her sweet wings and in the rising peak*
> *with such a washed and easy innocence.* (108)

Her collection of glosas, *Hologram* (1994), is an elegant display of technical mastery, with exquisite sound effects as the lines listen to themselves. In her foreword, Page described the form's "curious marriage – two sensibilities intermingling: the opening quatrain written by another poet; followed by four ten-line stanzas, their concluding lines taken consecutively from the quatrain; their sixth and ninth lines rhyming with the borrowed tenth" (9). "Poor Bird" takes its opening from Elizabeth Bishop's "Sandpiper" but adroitly enlarges the scope of the "obsessed" bird's search to include Page's own surprise.

> *But occasionally, when he least expects it,*
> *in the glass of a wave a painted fish*
> *like a work of art across his sight*
> *reminds him of something he doesn't know*
> *that he has been seeking his whole long life –*
> *something that may not even exist!* ("Poor Bird" 194)

As the decades lengthened Page's reflections of the journey from youth to age became more frequent. The title poem of *The Hidden Room: Collected Poems* (1997) depicts her girlhood friendship with Elizabeth Carlile, fellow student at St Hilda's school in Calgary, who was "better known as 'Fuzz'" (Djwa 31). This place "embodies all ... deeply hidden in my head ... in cellar or attic / matrix of evil and good." Much more than "a child's bolt-hole," it is a "prism / a magic square" ("The Hidden Room" 200–1).

Wilkinson, Brewster, Avison, and Macpherson: "clearing the hurdles of sleep"

Connections between generations and enduring contributions to literary culture mark the work of younger contemporaries: Anne Wilkinson (1924–61), Elizabeth Brewster (1922–2012), Margaret Avison (1918–2007), and Jay Macpherson (1931–2012). All creators of the "great mythopoeic age," they succeeded, as Wilkinson expressed it in "Three Poems about Poets" in *The Hangman Ties the*

Holly (1955), in "clearing the hurdles of sleep." Wilkinson served as literary editor for the short-lived Toronto arts magazine *Here and Now* in 1949 and "became a major patron of Canadian culture in helping to found, edit, and finance the *Tamarack Review* (1956–82) during its early years" (Irvine 233). Brewster, whose entry in a poetry competition in Saint John in 1940 was judged by P.K. Page, was a founding member of the literary journal *Fiddlehead*. Macpherson founded Emblem Books (1954–62), a small press that printed eight chapbooks, including in its number work by Livesay, Violet Anderson, Heather Spears, Dorothy Roberts, and Macpherson herself. In Wilkinson, whose life was sadly foreshortened, P.K. Page discerned "something almost unbearable – all that beauty and all that heartbreak."[8] Music inheres in and emerges from their work, too. Oscar Morawetz was inspired to create scores for five of Wilkinson's poems, while Livesay's poetry has prompted musical settings by Violet Archer, Barbara Pentland, and Carol Ann Weaver.

Wilkinson destabilizes and disassembles any prefab or childish notion of belief, fidelity, and joy. With allusions to folk ballads, nursery rhymes, and artists (Kafka, Klee, Woolf), her two volumes, *Counterpoint to Sleep* (1951) and *The Hangman Ties the Holly*, address the desires and growing impossibilities of returning to the green world, most poignantly narrated in "A Folk Tale, With a Warning to Lovers." Never "a simple tale," this "plight of two lovers ... scaled to commonplace dimensions" is based in "love's unreason" concerning "a space / Too rare to nourish root or green / the tree of grace." Scenes of wounded strife, with "their torn roots bleeding under eiderdowns," characterize the inescapable torment of "the home sweet hearth of hell" (*Counterpoint* 9). Judaeo-Christian religion, certainly the Anglicanism of her upbringing, offers little solace, as she clarifies in the meeting with a bearded, hairy man who swears his name is God, in "The Up and Down of It," a poem on which Page modelled her unpublished tribute to Wilkinson. The speaker of Wilkinson's poem calls herself "Mrs Bloom, the loitering Moon Goddess"; as God passes to his tower, "I, two steps at a time, / Jumped my way to grass" (13). This identification with growth and earth helps Wilkinson to see the world, especially the aspects of love and children, with "a woman's iris" and a "poet's eye" ("Lens," *The Hangman* 5). Echoing the rhythms of Dylan Thomas in her "In June and Gentle Oven," she evokes an image of lovers in a field walled in a "holy church of grass" and surrounded by insects, "Klee-drawn saints / And bright as angels are" (17). Moments of exaltation are few, however, as "sardonic parody" (Frye, *Bush Garden* 50) is more prominent. "Dirge," her version of the nursery rhyme of "Cock Robin," asks "Who killed the bridegroom?" and "Who killed the bride?," tolling the bell "For all whom love severs" (*Hangman* 28, 29). The childhood world of Christmas carols and folk rhymes is blasted and worm-filled: "Around my neck / The hangman ties the holly" ("Carol" 39). Citing only one commandment, "Mind the senses and the soul / Will take care of itself," an injunction that poet Douglas Barbour sees as akin to the sensibilities of Christina Rossetti, Emily Dickinson, and Edna St Vincent Millay ("Day Thoughts" 182), Wilkinson's "Letter to My children" is actually an apology for having "churched [them] in the rites / Of trivia" (48).

Elizabeth Brewster's career, comprising nineteen collections of poetry stretching over five decades, took her from New Brunswick to the west, Edmonton and then Saskatoon, where she was a professor of creative writing at the University of Saskatchewan. Experimenting with many tones, from witty to plangent, her work conveys an apologetic restlessness. In "To the Male Muse" she thanks this "faithful" lover:

> *Putting up with my restlessness,*
> *my moves here and moves there,*
> *always to boring places*
> *Sackville instead of Bangkok*
> *Saskatoon instead of Athens.* (*Collected Poems* II: 109)

In the work of Margaret Avison and Jay Macpherson, Christian liturgies along with biblical and mythological sources are pervasive, continuing influences. Showing a range of prosodic forms, Avison's Governor General's Award-winning *Winter Sun* (1960) also reflects her metaphysical grasp of totality, as "the huge bustling girth of the whole world / Turns in an everywhere of inwardness" ("Easter" 42). The Bible and Bunyan are repeated sources for Avison. As it accumulates detail, the tension-filled free verse of "Jael's Part" invokes the battles describing the defeat of the Canaanite king Sisera seeking refuge in Jael's tent and Deborah's song praising Jael's assassination of the enemy in Judges 5. The climax occurs in the scene framing the fatal hospitality of this Kenite wife as Sisera is "sprawled like a glutton ... / pegged to the dust under the smothering tentskins / by Jael" (67).

Avison has a tremendous capacity for zesty exuberance, as in her riff in *The Dumbfounding* (1966) on the exaltation of the biblical child (Luke 9:48), who "wakes to ice-cream-flavoured air; he possesses / the polka-dot, strut-singing, wave-suds, winking / wonder of off and out to / roads" ("A Child: Marginalia on an Epigraph" 32). Yet she acknowledges as well the mystery of speech "involving / heart-warmed lungs, the reflexes / of uvula, shaping tongue, teeth, lips, / ink, eyes, and de- / ciphering heart" ("Words" 23). A spiritual journey harmonizes all her work; for Avison "In the mathematics of God / there are percentages beyond one hundred" ("First" 51). As late as her Griffin Prize-winning *Concrete and Wild Carrot* (2002), the Easter liturgies remain a prominent feature. "On a Maundy Thursday Walk" has the effect of a seventeenth-century prayer by George Herbert, contrasting mortal disbelief in death with divine sacrifice.

> *How much more, that*
> *(suffering this*
> *creation to go under its Maker, and us all)*
> *He, the Father of love, should stake it all*
> *on a sufficient*
> *indeed on an essential*
> *pivot.* (72)

Macpherson's Christian mythology in *The Boatman* (1957), also a Governor General's Award winner, blends Elizabethan lyrics, Blake songs, hymns, riddles, and nursery rhymes. According to Northrop Frye, to whom it is dedicated, "this Noah's ark inside Noah" is "the most carefully planned and unified book that has yet appeared" in his review surveys (*Bush Garden* 74). The engagement of the reader, addressed several times, is key to the poem's "hermeneutic system," with Noah "as anagogic man/boatman/poet" (Weir 14) and the "gentle reader" pulled "through his navel inside out" (48). On experiencing the alternate rhymed quatrains of the Ark, "Articulate," "Anatomical," "Artefact," "Apprehensive," "Astonished," "Overwhelmed," and "Parting," the reader enters what Lorraine Weir perceives as "the sacramental community – not a static artifact – but a process of interaction, sharing, and exchange between poet and reader" (31). At the centre of Macpherson's second volume, *Welcoming Disaster* (1974), are Sumerian and Babylonian myth cycles along with a young girl and a Woolworths teddy bear. The interpretation of the text has been an embroiling issue for readers. Weir sees *Welcoming Disaster*'s voyage as "abortive" (27), where "redemption cannot occur" (30) and "fertility is not restored" (31). By contrast, W.J. Keith takes a cue from Michael Hornyansky's 1975 review to read the work as a balance of the sombre and the redemptive, "between the serious and the comic ... the psychologically crucial and the whimsically childlike" (38). The linkage between the teddy bear and the god Tammuz does suggest a traumatic need of reparation or transformation.

> *He is the Tammuz of my song,*
> *Of death and hell the key,*
> *And gone to mend the primal wrong,*
> *That rift in Being, Me.* ("Surrogate" 44)

Yet the epilogue to this enigmatic volume addresses the teddy bear, Tadwit or Tedward, and his signal though transitory importance as "Now ... a blank, as dumb as its stuffing. Magic like that runs out, it doesn't stay" ("The End" 59).

MacEwen and Atwood: "the slow striptease of our concepts"

Gwendolyn MacEwen (1941–87) and Margaret Atwood (b. 1939) are studies in like-minded art and friendship. They are also writers of long and short fiction, juvenile work, and drama, but their poetry is what concerns us here. There are differences in lengths of careers; autodidact MacEwen's deliberate refusal of both high school matriculation (a few weeks before the date) and university education (scholarships notwithstanding) contrasts with Atwood's formation at the University of Toronto and Harvard. However, what unites these two poets, who met at Toronto's Bohemian Embassy club in the Gerrard Street village in 1960, "two young mavericks starting out together" and sharing "a sense of being ... on the fringe" (Sullivan, *Shadow Maker* 68–9), is their anti-bourgeois determination to remove veils and perform what MacEwen called "the slow striptease of our concepts" ("Poem," *The Early Years* 82).

MacEwen's biographer, Rosemary Sullivan, captures her subject's zesty subversiveness at the time of the composition of MacEwen's most famous collection, *A Breakfast for Barbarians* (1966): "she was at play, like a hot wind ... she felt aggressive, hortatory, apocalyptic" (149). The metaphor of appetite is precisely appropriate for clinching the humour and iconoclasm of the mid-sixties. According to MacEwen, the book conveys an "essential optimism ... that joy that arises out of and conquers pain" (*The Early Years* 67). Masticating and destroying, barbarians "rock the universe" (70). The title poem depicts the meal as "the brain's golden breakfast / eaten with beasts / with books on plates"; included in this "cosmic cuisine" are "apocalyptic tea, / an arcane salad of spiced bibles, / tossed dictionaries" (69).

Underpinning the Rabelaisian satire of *Breakfast for Barbarians* is the probing search for a route to meaning through darkness and doubt. Though published after its original 1965 broadcast on the CBC, *Terror and Erebus: A Verse Play* (1974) is MacEwen's metaphysical dramatization of the fated Franklin Expedition for the Northwest Passage. Her Franklin is a hero more in quest of ontology than commerce:

> ... there is a meaning, a pattern
>   imposed on this chaos,
> A conjunction of waters
>   a kind of meaning
> Even here, even in this place. (*The Early Years* 106)

The voice of the later explorer Knud Rasmussen closes the play with an ambivalent query: "is it that you cannot know, / Can never know, /where the passage lies / Between conjecture and reality?" (119). The title poem of MacEwen's Governor General's Award-winning *The Shadow-Maker* (1969) expresses the insistence and melancholic pain of her address to the shadow-maker: "For I said I have come to possess your darkness, / Only this" (*The Early Years* 157).

Atwood's Governor General's Award-winning *The Circle Game* (1966), picturing encircling games themselves as restrictions from which the narrator longs to escape, also considers the underside of appetite, perceiving "the furtive insect, sly and primitive / the necessary cockroach / in the flesh / that nests in dust" and "gorges on a few / unintentional / spilled crumbs of love" ("A Meal" 33, 34). Love itself is an "awkward word":

Not what I mean and too much like magazine stories
in stilted dentists'
waiting rooms.
How can anyone use it? ("Letters, Toward and Away" 70)

The Journals of Susanna Moodie (1970) is Atwood's revelation of the vision of the Upper Canada immigrant, who "praises the Canadian landscape but accuses it of destroying her" (62). A subterranean menace pulses throughout this text, whether Mrs Moodie is picking strawberries –"surging, huge / and shining" – and realizes "anything planted here / would come up blood" (34), or whether she is projected in time as an old woman riding a bus along St Clair Avenue who threatens, "I have / my ways of getting through" (60). Nine collections later, in *The Door* (2007), Atwood's dedication to the "hot wire" of poetry is still charged: "You might as well stick a fork / in a wall socket" ("Sor Juana in the Garden" 27). While her reworking of Edward Lear, "Owl and Pussycat, Some Years Later," chronicles the signs of age, "No longer semi-immortal, but moulting owl / and arthritic pussycat," it also praises the indefatigable poetic impulse:

But sing on, sing
on, someone may still be listening

besides me. The fish for instance.
Any way, my dearest one
We still have the moon. (34)

Webb, Lowther, Marlatt, and Brossard: "the way any of us are tangled in the past"

One's past is a freight every artist, in fact every person, carries. Yet the work of Phyllis Webb (b. 1927), Pat Lowther (1935–75), Daphne Marlatt (b. 1942), and Nicole Brossard (b. 1943) grapples in especially forceful ways with what Marlatt in *The Given* (2008), her haunting long poem about the resonances of the death of her mother, identifies as "the way any of us are tangled in the past" (23). Contributing to the growing literary scene of the seventies (and, in most cases, beyond), their poetry also supplies valuable insights into the network of associations, friendships, and influences among these women.

Having published as early as the 1950s (*Trio* [1954], *Even Your Right Eye* [1956]), Webb focuses on, actually mirrors, the contradictoriness and paradoxes of existence. As she comments in "Lear on the Beach at Break of Day" on the lone figure "with dark small stones / in his crazed old hands,"

he hurls them now, as if to free
himself with them. But only stones drop
sullenly, with a hardened crop,
into the soft, irrational sea. (*The Vision Tree* 27)

Paradox is what Pauline Butling sees as the "operating principle ... at the heart of Webb's poems, first as the essence of experience, and then as the structural principle of the poems" ("Paradox and Play" 204). In the foreword to *Wilson's Bowl* (1980), about anthropologist Wilson Duff's study of west coast petroglyphs and his letters to Webb's friend Lilo Berliner, who left them on Webb's doorstep before her suicide, Webb lamented the prominence of male figures in her work. "They signify the domination of a male power culture in my educational and emotional formation so overpowering that I have up to now been denied access to inspiration from the female figures of my intellectual life, my heart, my imagination" (n.p.). However, the "fortuitous intersection" of her five-year association (1964–9) with CBC Radio, then under largely male direction, as program organizer and executive producer for *Ideas*, actually gave her wide scope as a public intellectual; the position provided a "starting point for much of her later work in poetry" (Butling, "Phyllis Webb as Public Intellectual" 248). As "Letters to Margaret Atwood," included in *Wilson's Bowl* and acknowledged as "an exception," admits, "Peggy: Sometimes I hear you screaming between the paragraphs and poems" (38). What the reader hears from Webb is the deep mystery entwining life and death, opening and closing, light and dark, as experienced in the petroglyph itself.

> *This is not a bowl you drink from*
> *not a loving cup.*
> *This is meditation's place*
> *cold rapture's.* (64)

While Webb considered Atwood's celebrity, Pat Lowther extolled the presence and support of Dorothy Livesay, who "makes spring in the ivory season / of her bones" ("Growing the Seasons," *Collected Works* 168). Lowther's three volumes of poetry, *This Difficult Flowring* (1968), *Milk Stone* (1974), and, posthumously, *A Stone Diary* (1977), imprint a present on the past. In recalling her life-of-the-party father, she remarks

> *Man it makes me old*
> *to see him fat and sixty*
> *doing his drinking sitting down*
> *while the lampshades*
> *stay on the lamps.* ("In Praise of Youth" 84).

The inheritance from her maternal grandmother of "tatting crocheting / yards and yards of / ecru and cream and white" prompts the contrast between Annie McCain's view of her granddaughter "pouring tea from a silver pot" and the reality that "I'd be something else / useless at owning things / up to my head in books" ("Inheritance" 189). Aware as she is, at the opening of *Milk Stone*, of "so many skins / of silence upon me" ("How Can I Begin" 113), Lowther later introduces violent imagery in such poems as "To a Woman Who Died of 34 Stab Wounds," "Kitchen Murder," and "Losing My Head." As her thoughtful editor, Christine Wiesenthal, remarks, these works almost prefigure the abrupt end of her "generously resourceful and creative life, by spousal homicide in September 1975" (15).

In collections from *How Hug a Stone* (1983) to *The Given*, which acknowledges how "contours of memory-landscape, significant features of its stories, shift with the years" ("Late in the Day," *The Given* 97), Marlatt's memories and invocations of her mother are prominent elements of her continuing search for ways to imagine and tell stories. The prose poems of *How Hug a Stone*, her account of a trip to England with her twelve-year-old son to reconnect with relatives, weigh the peril of small histories as "simply the shell we exude for a place to live in" against their potential to bury us: "stories," she observes, "can kill" ("Ellesmere" 51). From a variety of reports and recollections Marlatt reconstructs her mother's wrestling "with the angel authority of father, teacher, doctor, dentist, priest ... tearing at the placid assumptions of family ... and then lapsing, controlled, into silence" ("Pilgrim Cottage" 67). Marlatt's closing image of "wild mother dancing upon the waves" ("Feeding the Pigeons" 98) supplies another connection in the women writers' network; poet Di Brandt chooses this image as the conceptual framework for her study of maternal narrative, *Wild Mother Dancing*, seeing in Marlatt's "search for the absent mother ... a kind of 'spiralling,' going back and forth while moving into new space" (45). What Marlatt identifies as "mothertongue" is "language, a living body we enter at birth" (*Touch to My Tongue* 45). Significantly, birth is not an exit from the mother's body but rather an entry, with body and language, as in the erotic lesbian Demeter and Persephone poems of *Touch to My Tongue* (1984), continuously sliding together.

Another kind of coalescence occurs in *Steveston* (1974/1984) with Robert Minden's photographs and Marlatt's prose poems focused on a British Columbia fishing town with a largely Japanese-Canadian population. A decade after the first edition in 1974, Marlatt presented its story "as a single narrative told in two distinct modes that converse with each other"; her poems seek "to gather up the scattered threads of past and present ... run[ning] through layers of time, levels of meaning, into their conclusion" (93). This "onetime cannery boomtown" continues to generate ironic subjectivities.

While Brossard's location is firmly urban, her ideological position is that of a radical challenger of language. As she has reiterated, "a lesbian who does not reinvent the world is a lesbian on the path to disappearance" (Forsyth, "Introduction" 23). Brossard's more than thirty collections of poetry, beginning with *Aube à la saison* in 1965, ten novels, and numerous essays and articles have consolidated her path to international literary renown. She announces her theoretical dictate in "Vaseline" in *La Barre du Jour*, the periodical she co-founded: "Une grammaire ayant pour règle le masculin l'emporte sur le féminin doit être transgressée" (A grammar that has as a rule: the masculine prevails over the feminine, must be transgressed). In *Mécanique jongleuse, suivi de masculin grammaticale* (1974) she presents female desire, "l'ensemble des crues et des hauts cris" (the combination of floods and loud cries), as emerging – despite its grammatical gender – from a female source:

son désir	her desire
sur le masculin grammaticale	in the masculine singular
ramification des doigts malines	branching out of lacy fingers.[9]

The erotic charge of Brossard's poems creates "new realities absolutely removed from heterosexual and hetero-normative structures" (Forsyth, *Mobility of Light* xix) as illustrated in Robert Majzels and Erin Moure's translation of "Le dos indocile des mots" ("The Indocile Back of Words") from *Après les mots* (2007):

I long to lick sweet love and loukoum
long-time I leaned into this reading
of lyric lagoon and language long ago. (*Mobility of Light* 101)

Tostevin, Brand, Halfe, and Dumont: "their fragile, fragile symmetries of gain and loss"

The imbalance of loss and gain, exacerbated by cultural dislocation, the stifling of an Indigenous language, and the shifting rules of a diasporic identity, accounts for prominent tensions in the work of Lola Lemire Tostevin (b. 1937), Dionne Brand (b. 1953), Louise Halfe (b. 1953), and Marilyn Dumont (b. 1955). In the perpetual movement of the central figure in *Ossuaries* (2010), fleeing a past and living furtively, Toronto Poet Laureate Brand exposes the impossibilities of "to undo, to undo ... this infinitive / of arrears" as she contemplates "their fragile, fragile symmetries of gain and loss" ("Ossuary II" 21). While Brand examines the bones of fading cultures, many of her contemporaries are considering the disappearance or hybridization of language.

In collections from *Color of Her Speech* (1982) to *Site-Specific Poems* (2004), Franco-Ontarian Lola Lemire Tostevin addresses the echoes of hybrid discourse.

> *1 word French*
> *4 words english*
> *"tu déparles"*
> *my mother says*
> > *je déparle*
> > *yes*
> > *I unspeak.* (n.p.)

In *Color of Her Speech* the games and "badinage" of language can create distance rather than togetherness: "converse reverse / conserve reserve / the contradiction / à contre-temps / à contre-coeur."

Cartouches (1995) continues to blend English and French texts along with the wall art of ancient Egypt, in writing about the death of her father. *Site-Specific Poems*, another bilingual collection, positions travel writing – from north of North Bay to Spain – as a meditation on the sites of poetry, in memory, paper, ink, geography, and language. Thinking of "paper as site," she observes

> *The impulse to jot down. Index*
> *finger tracing paths through lampblack*

> *from burning oil and desiccated trunks*
> *of bouleaux blancs et épinettes [white birchwood and thornhooks from*
>   *hawthorns]*
> *split into printing blocks.* ("encre de chine" 23)

For Trinidad-born Dionne Brand the duality and hybridity concern Black suffering in the Americas. She declares in her eighth collection, the Governor General's Award-wining *Land to Light On* (1997):

> *I have to think what it means that I am here*
> *what it means that this, harsh as it is and without*
> *a name, can swallow me up. I have to think how I*
> *am here, so eaten up and frayed, a life that I was*
> *supposed to finish by making something of it*
> *not regularly made, where I am not this woman*
> *fastened to this ugly and disappointing world.* (9)

In "the terrifying poetry of newspapers" (13), or in the look of a girl, "a noticiary of pain" (29), waiting for a bus, or in the sidewalk preaching of a Baptist priestess whose "husband left her, took all her money / after she worked to bring him here" (30), Brand charts the events, faces, and voices of dislocation. The biggest gaps separate Island past and Canadian present. She recalls the surprised fascination as a child in being taken by aunts to a dance, "once they take we three to a dance," and realizing "I didn't know no dance could be so dark / and full of serious desire that frighten me / no arse" (58). She admits her address to relatives now, "as if I could not trust you / to understand my new language which after all I had made / against you ... bathe you in more blame, more sorrow," but telling them "nothing in return, my life was fine" (63). Yet she inches towards an understanding to encompass and foresee a kind of embracing sea change: "something holding us all, more than this / understanding we are caught in can say, how the circumference / of this world grips us to this place, how its science works, how / it will take a change of oceans shaking the other way" (64).

Lament for muffled Indigenous culture and language is at the heart of the poetry of Louise Halfe, whose Cree name is Sky Dancer, and Métis Marilyn Dumont. This sense of loss and playful, sardonic, hard-hitting gain (or regain) also connects their collections to a much larger network of acclaimed poets, including Emma LaRoque's *Writing the Circle* (1990), Rita Joe of Eskasoni's *Inu and Indians We're Called* (1991), Joanne Arnott's *My Grass Cradle* (1992), Katerii Akiwenzie Damm's *My Heart Is a Stray Bullet* (1993), Marie Annharte Baker's *Coyote Columbus Café* (1994), Jeannette Armstrong's *Whispering Shadows* (2000), and Lee Maracle's *Bent Box* (2000).[10] Straddling old and new worlds, Halfe's *Bear Bones and Feathers* (1994) recalls the black comedy of her childhood, with her mother always wearing "a black and blue shiner / every Friday and Saturday night, / those stupid fist marks / of his drama attacks" ("Loving Obscenities" 31). More searing because unrelieved by warmth of affection are the memories of school: eating bannock and fried rabbit "in the bathroom so white kids / wouldn't laugh at me" and being ridiculed "In the classroom / when I talk / when I write about the boosh / they laugh and scold me / make me stand in the corner" ("Thieves" 61). Sky Dancer's more extensive Cree Glossary appended to *The Crooked Good* (2007) is one indication of the greater prominence and centrality of Cree idiom to the story telling and pain conveyed in the recurring voice of "ê-kwêsît – Turn-Around Woman":

> *These gifted mysterious people of long ago,*
> *kayâs kî-mamâhtâwisiwak iyiniwak,*
> *my mother, Gone-For-Good, would say.*
> > *They never died. They are scattered here, there,*
> > *everywhere, somewhere. They know the language,*
> > *the sleep, the dream, the laws, these singers, these*
> > > *healers,*
> > *âtayôhkanak, these ancient story keepers.* ("ê-kwêsît –
> > Turn-Around Woman" 3)

Marilyn Dumont's defence of Cree culture and language, in *A Really Good Brown Girl* (1996), takes the form of challenging standards imposed by a Great Tradition and also by status insiders. In reconsidering "Eliot / and the Great White way of writing English," she exposes the racist underpinnings of a received standard with its "lily white words / its picket fence sentences / and manicured paragraphs" that has had "its hand over my mouth since my first day of school" ("The Devil's Language" 54). Just as dispiriting is the reaction of "this treaty guy from up north" who, on learning of her Métis ancestry, returns a look "that says he's leather and I'm naughahyde" ("Leather and Naughahyde" 58). The lyricism of Dumont's work, even when dealing with desperation, as in *Green Girl Dreams Mountains* (2001), is fuelled with a powerful sensuality.

> *My breasts were weasels' noses*
> *my hips narrow and firm*
> *In those days my body*
> *volunteered me, pulled me*
> *onward to dreams, verdant*
> *and monumental.* ("Green Girl Dreams Mountains" 59)

In *That Tongued Belonging* (2007), picturing the echoes of "once forbidden" and "now pronounced" Cree as continuing "to grow / like moss on our backs" (1) and always existing "on our cold side / and ache / like a phantom limb" (2) emboldens Dumont to reclaim territory, relatives, and reality.

you say, Canada,	I say, Turtle Island
you say, grandmother,	I say, *Nokum*,
you say, *General Dumont*,	I say, cousin,
you say, Rupert's *Land*,	I say, *home*,
you say, *treason*,	I say *self-defence*. ("Nomenclature" 6)

Taking her title from John A. Macdonald's name for the Métis, Dumont's *The Pemmican Eaters* (2015) blends free and metred verse along with prose poems to reimagine the period of the Riel Resistance. Language is deliberately hybridized: "He prays in Cree: Notahwenan; he prays in Michif: Li Boon Jeu; he prays English: Amen" ("The Black Mare" 48). Injustice is a permeating issue, both in "the number of Métis / less than one percent / who hold property from that scrip today" ("To a Fair Country" 53) and in the hanging of Riel:

> *They will regret taking our prince*
> *our prophet, the one among us gifted ...*

and when their children ask
what Louis did
they will have no answer. ("Our Prince" 61)

Crozier, Moure, Zwicky, Carson, Michaels, Bolster, and Shraya: "the truth likes to hide / out in the open"

Spanning a couple of generations, coming into prominence in the eighties, nineties, and beyond, and retaining a focus on everyday perceived or re-created materiality, the poetry of Lorna Crozier (b. 1948), Erin Moure (b. 1955), Jan Zwicky (b. 1955), Anne Carson (b. 1950), Anne Michaels (b. 1958), Stephanie Bolster (b. 1969), and Vivek Shraya (b. 1981) directs attention to the world and truths in front of us. As Anne Michaels remarks, in extending the diary of Nobel Prize-winning physicist Marie Curie after the death of her husband, Pierre, "the truth likes to hide / out in the open" ("The Second Search" 159). At times this openness is filtered through other texts or landmarks; at others, it emerges from intimate, powerful events or revelations.

Crozier's sixteen collections have garnered many prizes, including three Pat Lowther prizes and the Governor General's Award for her eighth collection, *Inventing the Hawk* (1992). An extended elegy for her father, the poems in this collection replay scenes of childhood and discontent with her father and his Sunday routine, "a little drunk," bringing home a pail of perch to be cleaned by her mother who "gutted them, scraped / the scales with a coke cap / nailed to a stick"; as the poet vows in "Cleaning Fish," "I swore I'd not do that / for anyone" (68).

What animates these recollections are the interjections from the perspective of the child and the adult poet – "swearing I would never be as unhappy / or alone as they / believing then / I'd keep every single vow I made" (69). All Crozier's work is suffused with the immediate engagement of precise language. In announcing "The New Poem," she devotes twenty-nine of its thirty-three lines to itemizing what the poem will *not* do: "not hate men," "not be a nursemaid," "not help you die," "not say *vagina*," "not forgive," "not save your children." The final four lines of testy welcome are worth the wait.

> *It will bark and growl*
> *and some days it might bite*
> *but always without fail,*
> *it will let you in.* (128, 129)

Her recent collection, *What the Soul Doesn't Want* (2017), is equally hospitable, as she meditates on age and dying. "God draws a life," she observes, "Then rubs it out with the eraser on his pencil" ("Time Studies" 14). Though punctuated with literary allusions – to Dickinson, whom she wishes she knew by heart; to Kafka, who found his body repulsive; and to the suicide of Tsvetayeva in Siberia – Crozier as the teacher of "mathematics at the school of the dying" notes "There are only so many numbers we need" ("The Least of Things" 46). Her virtual conversation, "Making Pies with Sylvia Plath," who confides "You make good pastry only if you're in love" (48), nicely complements Alison MacLeod's short story "Sylvia Wears Pink in the Underworld." Crozier's poem, however, concentrates on the kitchen scene as primary, not the journey along the Styx. Plath's evanescence underscores the motif of the passage of time at the same moment as it could hint at an intertextual allusion to Judith Thompson's play *Perfect Pie* (discussed in the chapter on drama).

Relying more on mixed media and verbal-image art than intertextuality, Erin Moure's poems on language, the body, citizenship, and community insist on a careful attention to word play and the ties of memory. As early as her first lyrical collection, *Empire, York Street* (1979), Moure has shown great ability in compacting history and geography, whether writing about working for the railway, friendships, or travel. The title poem traces the history of a specific urban site; the "history of empires, begun / when cities were named after reigning monarchs" to speculative land development for condos overseen by anxious, soon-to-be-displaced tenants watching "the man / who surveys his empire" (89). Moure compresses a series of perspectives about the disenfranchised or marginalized; she includes the immigrants' boats, "stubborn w/ flags & non-union labour," and the terrified tenants waiting "in an empire of rented rooms, / history of allegiance paid to landlords," along with the factory worker for whom "the empire of the body is rented / for small change." Her fourth collection, *Domestic Fuel* (1985), pursues more directly the boundaries of love and connection. Aware of the need to "call out, offering each other / our future absence, our private & immoderate discourse" ("Including Myself" 62), she recounts intimate longing: "My heart is a wild muscle, that's all, / open as the ocean / at the end of the railway, / a cross-country line pulled by four engines" ("Bends" 76). Marie Carrière discerns in Moure's "lesbian relational ethics ... an inscribed desire for spiritual redemption" (178). Moure's splicing of religious terminology and interspersed allusions to liturgical prayers fulfils an ironic role.

In her Governor General's Award-winning *Furious* (1988), erotic declarations and vulnerable avowals co-exist, as she details touching her lover "with my mouth,"

& our two cries flutter
impossible havoc, heat, haven, have-not of the body,
our tensions in its arms & folded openings in its centre. ("Aspen" 36)

It is remarkable how common the adverb "finally" is in this collection, as though the poet were breaking through to a hard-won clarity.

Finally there are no men between us.
Finally none of us are passing or failing according to
Miss Chatelaine. ("Miss Chatelaine" 34)

In the trilogy *Search Procedures* (1996), *A Frame of the Book* (1999), and *O Cidadán* (2002), Moure's continuing play with the labile nature of words leads to experiments with graphic design, a diversity of *mise en page* formats. *O Cidadán* also includes interjected snippets of translation from French, Spanish, and Portuguese texts, and extended, though deliberately disjointed, observations on her own place in Quebec society as a multilingual citizen.

> *I who have made myself strange in the arena of country and, here, come to Québec where I bear a strange tongue (yet hegemonic), allowed to be foreign, as foreign, to be, paradoxically but sensibly, a part of the body politic. To be a stranger (hospes or advena) here is to faire partie de tout ce qui comporte le civis.* ("Eleventh Impermeable of the Carthage of Harms" 82)

Another model of pastiche informs the work of Jan Zwicky. Readings in philosophy, specifically Ludwig Wittgenstein who, she notes in *Wittgenstein Elegies* (1986), "preferred to juxtapose dense often highly metaphorical fragments" (65), are catalysts for much of her poetry. As a participant in the "play of voices" (9), the narrator observes, "Words show us everything. How? Sense is / Vertical, position in the counterpoint" (16). The aim of all the accumulated reading and divagations on classical music, however, is to become simple.

> *If only thought as well as art could force*
> *The final gesture, that irrevocable moment of assent,*
> *When fragments, haloed, coalesce*
> *And the great space opens in the world*
> *To make us simple.* ("Rosro, County Galway" 60)

The strong directives of *Songs for Relinquishing the Earth* (1998), as in "You Must Believe in Spring," anchor their conviction not in Immanuel Kant, who "didn't like music" (17), but in each person's unique cognitive capacity: "Because it is the body thinking and Newt / Gingrich would like you not to" ("Kant & Bruckner: Twelve Variations" 76).

Philosophy is as suggestive of poetry for Zwicky as classical texts and the creativity of translating them are for poet, essayist, translator, and classicist Anne Carson (b. 1950), winner of the Griffin Poetry Prize for *Men in the Off Hours* (2001). She is best-known for hybrid work, such as *Autobiography of Red: A Novel in Verse* (1998) and *Decreation: Poetry, Essays, Opera* (2005). One of her most remarkable publications is the accordion-pleated, unpaginated, handmade book *Nox* (2010), which is both an artefact and an epitaph for her brother, Michael. Combining her translation of Poem 101 of Catullus, an elegy for his brother, with her own memories of Michael as a boy and an adult runaway, glimpsed through letters, scraps, and collages, Carson fills one side of the opening with lexicographical poetic prose and the other with meditations seeking to vocalize grief. Opposite her explanation of *"mos, moris"* as "an established practice, custom, usage," she notes, "Because our conversations were few (he phoned me maybe 5 times in 22 years) I study his sentences the ones I remember as if I'd been asked to translate them."

Writing novels and poetry are twin professions for Anne Michaels. The long narratives of her three collections, *The Weight of Oranges* (1986), *Miner's Pond* (1991), and *Skin Divers* (1999), show an unerring deftness in probing the emotional depths of stories. Among the most poignant re-creations of the past are her elegy for Adele Wiseman and her narratives of the widows of Antarctic explorer Robert Falcon Scott and physicist Pierre Curie. Proposing that history is "the love that enters us / through death," Michaels pictures Wiseman engaged in the plight of Jewish refugees: "You never forgot the floating ghettos: / landlocked in north Winnipeg, listening with your father / to the radio, while the boat was refused / at every port" ("The Hooded Hawk," *Poems* [2001] 169–70). Michaels gives voice to sculptor Kathleen Scott, who shaped clay, re-creating the faces of wounded soldiers to assist surgeons in grafting skin and copying features "to use scar tissue to advantage"; Scott also uses the tissue of grief to advantage, recalling the husband whom she "loved ... into stone" and declaring "I love you as if you'll return / after years of absence" ("Ice House" 166, 168). Nobel laureate Marie Curie recollects an intimate scientific partnership.

> *You laughed when I marked cookbooks*
> *with the same care as notes in the lab*
> *but for me it was the same: the same*
> *details of love – dissolving, filtering, collecting*

until truth is so small it fits
on the tongue. ("The Second Search" 161)

Animating photographs and paintings is at the centre of Stephanie Bolster's work. Her first collection, the Governor General's Award-winning *White Stone: The Alice Poems* (1998), extends and dialogues with photographs of Alice Pleasance Liddell Hargreaves, the "Alice" of *Alice in Wonderland,* while *Two Bowls of Milk* (1999) turns on the paintings of Jean-Paul Lemieux and, according to Bolster, on paintings in the National Gallery of Canada. Christine Wiesenthal identifies these talking pictures as ekphrastic poetry. "Rather than attempting faithfully to reproduce the aesthetic objects or external referents she takes as her subjects, Bolster's work thus throws its emphasis upon the essentially transformative nature of the encounter between viewer and viewed, poet and painting, self and other" (47). Taking her title *White Stone* from an entry in the diary of Charles Dodgson (Lewis Carroll) marking the day he met Alice "with a white stone" (15), which indicates a lucky day, Bolster re-creates Dodgson's darkroom; Bolster's Dodgson prompts Alice to convey "that desirous stillness / he required not posing but hinting" (16), and the "sullen adult eyes" (17) with which Alice at nineteen, when *Looking-Glass* was published, regarded him. Bolster even brings Alice together with Elvis, "Queen and King" (49), melting chronologies to insignificance with the claim "We are each a lens" (56). Her fourth and most recent collection, *A Page from the Wonders of Life on Earth* (2011), continues the encounter between viewer and viewed, concentrating on such troubled places as museums, zoos, and prisons.

The close-up photograph on the cover of transgender musician, novelist, and poet Vivek Shraya's *Even This Page Is White* (2016) announces that her collection is about skin and colour, as well as race and queerness. She takes up the topic in the opening poem, "white dreams": "even / this page / is white / so I protest this page" (14). With a directness forecasting her decision to sing a Whitney Houston song for her successful candidate talk in the English Department at the University of Calgary (Roberts n.p.), Shraya's poems are forceful declarations: *"how many times have I told you I am not a man*" ("birth certificate says m" 30); "brown life is an unbroken bearing of the weight and hollow of the active / absence of brown life" ("count the brown people" 50); "what if there is no right way to be brown / besides the brown you are / soil nut clove wheat bark pluto" ("brown dreams" 107).

Karen Solie: "poetic hipster"

The voice of Karen Solie (b. 1966), directing the everydayness she creates, is both energetic and caustic. Her five collections, *Short Haul Engine* (2001), which won the Dorothy Livesay Poetry Prize, *The Shooter's Bible* (2004), *Modern and Normal* (2005), the Griffin Poetry Prize-winning *Pigeon* (2009), and most recently *The Road In Is Not the Same Road Out* (2015), recast personal experience with postmodern juxtapositions. Solie's poetry is a sceptical, insightful collage of twenty-first-century culture expanding the categories and concepts of art. Allusions to Walter Benjamin and Ludwig Wittgenstein jostle with a bullet-riddled VLT, noxious weeds, and a cheap Niagara Falls hotel room. Wiped clean of sentimental or transcendental flourishes and removed from "the humanistic vocabulary that Canadian poets write in," her work is associated with "flinty reflection" and "self-mocking cheerlessness" (Starnino 217, 208, 213). While she was hailed early on as "a poetic hipster' (Pollock 85), Solie's more recent designation as "a contemporary prophet" (Bast n.p.) indicates the expanding enthusiasm for her development as a major poet in Canada. A selection of her poems, *The Living Option* (2013), has been published in the United Kingdom; according to British poet Michael Hofmann, Solie's poetry "runs the gamut from nervous, garrulous charm to the glory and shear of impersonal style" (27). Her work has been translated into French, German, Korean, and Dutch. International writer-in-residence at the University of St Andrews in 2011, Solie is an associate director of the Banff Centre's Writing Studio program.

One of the most insightful readers of Solie's poetry, James Pollock, has identified three salient features of her work: "satire of contemporary life, a balancing pastoral vision ... and sympathy for other human beings" (85). Her debut collection, *Short Haul Engine*, illustrates all these characteristics. A road stop during a prairie autumn is an occasion to reflect on its burnt-orange beauty as well as the disappointments of her love life. "It's a hinge of worlds, for you have loved poorly now / on both sides of the foothills" ("Java Shop, Fort MacLeod"). Her participation in a hotel-based conference on the humanities where "she will perform a theory / so dense it straightens her hair" ("Days Inn") is not only a sly comment on the impersonality of the exercise but a surprising moment to direct her interest to a non-participant in the next room. While "she is listening for the rustle / of a stranger, undressing," she contrasts her own compact script with the secret, mysterious sadness on the other side of the wall. "She wonders why the weight of a man / sobbing into morning frightens her." Solie's art is able to sketch a whole narrative in a few short lines about happy hour in "Alert Bay, Labour Day": "The waitress has a bruise / on her cheek. Walls here / are made of luck and girls / walk into them."

More, and more adept, self-characterizations appear in *Modern and Normal*, especially tracing the move from "purely agricultural" to becoming "a modern person." As she recounts in "Cardio Room, Young Women's Christian Association," a workout underscores the affirmation of change. "There was a time / I rolled like dough, plumped up / to be thumped down with artless yeasty / chemistry. Dumpling. Honeybun. / I sickened some. But evolved / in a flash, like the living flak / of a nuclear mistake." Her engagement with the pastoral also becomes more satiric. A trip south of the Alberta border, with stops in Missoula, Helena, Babb, and Havre, "backlit by gilt grasslands / of the Blackfoot nation," nevertheless distils into a recollection of "Corporate agriculture, franchise, and celebrity retreats / spread like cream across the counties" ("Montana"). In this collection Solie invokes earlier models to emphasize great difference. "Lines Composed a Few Miles above Duncairn Dam" alludes to Wordsworth's "Lines Composed a Few Miles above Tintern Abbey." Sharing the evocation of cottages, copses, and empty churches, Solie's speaker is, unlike Wordsworth, alone. The memory of the scene "above Tintern Abbey" is restorative; the scene "above Duncairn Dam" is "far more desolate" (Pollock 97).

Yet despite the rumour about "a pipeline leak below the lakebed" and the "little plank church" with "someone's junk ... in it," there is the lure of expansiveness: "To follow the sightline over the fields is a long, long / look." To highlight the poignancy of distance, geographical and altitudinal, and memory, Solie admits writing the poem on a plane "37,000 feet above / Lake Ontario. Above the cloud above Lake Ontario." Three repeated prepositions underscore both remove and recollection.

Solie is preoccupied with notions of mobility – from west to east coasts, beyond northern and southern borders, in her ancestral homeland of Norway – as a means of recording impressions, measuring distance, creating contact. Evan Jones describes her as "a sort of anti-flâneur, watching the world pass from motorized vehicles" (n.p.). "Medicine Hat Calgary One-Way" in *Pigeon* maps the route from the point of view of Solie, the Greyhound passenger; the trip also allows for conjecture about the unseen. "In the limitless / present of schedule 0063, you embrace / secret multitudes." The sense of sympathy with other passengers who rely on "the only way you can afford" stirs this question from the previously satirical observer: "As you leave with your bags / hire a taxi for the airport, is it not possible / to look with love upon your fellow travellers?" In *Pigeon* she re-creates the scene of the tragic mine explosion in the Crowsnest Pass more than a hundred years ago through the voice of a forgotten casualty. "They were carried out by the hundreds, / alive or dead ... all but me, Sidney Bainbridge, / the one man never found" ("Cave Bear"). Her impeccable ear for interlacing the soulful and the grim is on display in "Prayers for the Sick," combining the Catholic *Prayers for the Sick* with the experience of an emergency ward. "O Lord, you who cast low / and raise up also, and I empathize with the guy / in the bloody sleeve who stands every ten minutes / to yell down the hall and receive a straight answer / from nobody."

Her latest collection, *The Road In Is Not the Same Road Out*, is an important indication of Solie's interventions on "the corporatization of every aspect of individual life" (Bast n.p.). She continues to evoke depictions of the past to contemplate the world around us, fastening on elemental realities and uncertainty. "Bitumen," an "ekphrastic meditation on the environmental devastation of the Tar Sands" (Clarke n.p.), focuses on "An area roughly the size / of England stripped of boreal forest and muskeg, unburdened / by hydraulic rope shovels of its overburden." Adroitly Solie reflects on this site through allusions to romantic-era paintings of disaster: Géricault's *The Raft of the Medusa*, depicting a frigate that dashed on the rocks with 147 would-be survivors huddled on a raft (of whom only 15 survived), and Turner's *Disaster at Sea*, illustrating another wreck in which the captain abandoned the cargo of female convicts. This complex meditation directs attention to "the open pit where swims / the bitumen, extra brilliant, dense, massive, in the Greek *asphaltos* / 'to make stable,' 'to secure.'" In contrast to another romantic depiction, Caspar David Friedrich's *Wanderer above the Sea of Fog*, "a sensitive figure in the presence / of the sublime," Solie insists "you can smell it down here. Corrosive vapours unexpectedly distributed, caustic particulate infiltrates / your mood." Her allusion to the inventor of photography, "Light-sensitive bitumen of Judea upon which Joseph-Nicéphore Niépce / recorded the view from his bedroom," deliberately clashes with the contemporary work of industrial photographer Edward Burtynsky. "By elevated circumstance / of Burtynsky's drone helicopters, revolutionary lenses / pester Alberta's tar sands."

In this collection the look to the past is as revealingly sympathetic as the undecidability of what lies ahead. Solie determines to "leave the child [she was] alone" since "some of what you would warn her against / has not yet entered her vernacular" ("All That Is Certain Is That Night Lasts Longer Than the Day"). The connection with this past is deliberately, necessarily opaque. Remnants and shards continue to fuel her consciousness, as in the discovery of the ruins of the removal of a family of squirrels from an attic: "Shreds of paper, / insulation, twigs from the smoke bush, and the bitter / broken wood of the invasive tree of heaven" ("Roof Repair and Squirrel Removal"). In her recall of the drive in to "a prime-of-life / experience" coupled with her sense now of "an inaudible catastrophic orchestra," the poet finds herself at a highway intersection: "It yields / to traffic from both directions. / It appears it could go either way" ("The Road In Is Not the Same Road Out").

From the vernacular directness of Jaques to Solie's tart ironies, women poets in Canada cover a huge gamut of sensual, rational, and spiritual topics. Their tones and styles illustrate manifesto declarations, detached observation, ekphrastic allusions, and confessional utterances. The distances from the great mythopoeic age to contemporary laments of fading cultures and hybridized language chart the expansiveness of the field, through the inclusion of wider networks and diverse voices. With images of aesthetic speculation and instances of self-deprecatory humour, their work embodies captivating modes of breaking through the skin of silence.

chapter four

Music

The field of women's music composition is diverse, featuring many distinctive trailblazers and prize winners. The work of women composers in Canada is at home in a wide span of venues, from concert halls, chamber settings, and churches to open-air folk festivals and rock concerts. Compositions by Jean Coulthard (1908–2000) and Barbara Pentland (1912–2000) in neo-romantic and modernist styles, along with decades of neoclassical chamber pieces by Violet Archer (1913–2000), Ann Southam's (1937–2010) music for dance companies and acoustic instruments, and choral settings for adults and children by Ruth Watson Henderson (b. 1932) set pioneering benchmarks. They have influenced subsequent choral compositions by Nancy Telfer (b. 1950), Eleanor Daley (b. 1955), and Stephanie Martin (b. 1962). A prominent feature of contemporary musical composition is its multiplicity of styles. Consider the work of Janet Danielson (b. 1950), collaborating with poet Robert Bringhurst, setting an Ursuline carol, and creating a string quartet on the theme of war and peace; or the movie scores of Lesley Barber (b. 1962) for *Mansfield Park* and *Manchester by the Sea*, among others; or the sensuous chamber music of Kati Agócs (b. 1975). The fact that Jocelyn Morlock (b. 1969) won the 2018 Juno Award for Classical Composition for her orchestral work *My Name Is Amanda Todd*, celebrating the life of a young girl who was cyber-bullied and died by suicide, indicates the contemporaneous power of composition.

Because this project considers several forms of text, the discussion of music focuses more deliberately on the interaction between word and music in the interart convergence of singer-songwriting. Just as film evokes or adumbrates the language of fiction, so can song intensify or expand our understanding of lyricism. The musical, sonic, and verbal effects of the work of women singer-songwriters, combining linguistic and sound processes, prompt us to realize that "a song *is* a reading, in the critical as well as the performative sense of the term" (Kramer 127). Exploring the relationship between words and music not only recalls the affinity between the sister arts of music and poetry but vastly increases the cultural resonance and range of works deemed worthy of consideration. We recognize that while music and poetry call up powerful feelings, singing affects emotional centres, its temporal stress, repetition, and varieties of mood making pedestrian words meaningful. Although song lyrics are often considered a soft entry to arguably more literary poetry, these artists use the rhythms and tonalities of music, along with rhyme or blank verse and a large scope of images, metaphors, and allusions, to depict emotions and narratives. Their impressive vocal range is matched by the number of other artists who cover their songs. Moreover, like the work of poets, their lyrics and musical styles reflect the concerns of different generations and, increasingly, a blend of genres and disciplines.

Folk Singers Reclaiming Traditions

Folk artists Buffy Sainte-Marie (b. 1941), Edith Butler (b. 1942), Sylvia Tyson (b. 1940), Joni Mitchell (b. 1943), and Kate (1946–2010) and Anna (b. 1944) McGarrigle are among the first women singer-songwriters to gain popularity and international recognition. They write about cherished locations and those in need of protection; they all express ambitions and desires, trying to understand when relationships do and, more often, do not work.

Cree activist Sainte-Marie is known for the Indigenous topics in her songs, such as "Now That the Buffalo's Gone" (from the album *Native North-American Child: An Odyssey* [1974]), "He's an Indian Cowboy in the Rodeo" (from *Indian Girl* [1976]), and "Bury My Heart at Wounded Knee" (from *Coincidence and Likely Stories* [1992]).

"No, No Keshagesh" in *Running for the Drum* (2008) uses the Cree word *keshagesh* for "greedy guts" to comment on the commercialization and plunder of the planet by "business suits" who make "a dollar sign ... look so cute." "Got Mother Nature on a luncheon plate / They carve her up and call it real estate." By contrast she cites "the reservation out at poverty row" where "somebody's tryin' to save our Mother Earth," and resolves "I'm gonna help them to save it, and sing it, and pray it / Singing No, No Keshagesh / You can't do that / No more, no more, no more, no more." Her commitment and passion are undiminished; as the winner of the 2015 Polaris Prize (rewarding creativity and diversity in Canadian recorded music), she collaborated with the 2014 winner, throat singer Tanya Tagaq (b. 1975), to write and perform *You Got to Run (Spirit of the Wind)* (2017). Even though, as the lyrics declare, "I been so broken, so low that I kissed the ground," the uplifting, angry call reverberates: "You gotta take a stand."

Acadian songwriter and folklorist Butler also invokes her heritage, from *Chansons d'Acadie* (1969) and *De Paquetville à Paris* (1983) to *Un million de fois je t'aime* (2014). The album *Asteur qu'on est là* (1979), an affirmation of Acadian presence today with the term "*asteur*" as the contraction of "*à cette heure*," was an immediate success on both sides of the Atlantic. The tribute to her hometown of Paquetville, near Caraquet, New Brunswick, is a strongly inflected and deeply familiar praise of the village, which can sleep quietly in the knowledge that it taught her to play and dance and speak through whispers and actions. "Tu m'as tout joué tu m'as tout dansé / Tu peux ben dormir tranquille / Tu m'as tout joué tu m'as tout parlé / Tu peux ben dormir tranquille / Tu m'as chuchoté tu m'as tout montré / Tu peux ben dormir tranquille."

The artist's human journey to understand, explore, and, yes, grieve informs the folk songs of Tyson, Mitchell, and the McGarrigles. Tyson's "River Road" from *River Road and Other Stories* (2000) captures the need to escape and wander: "And here I go once again with my suitcase in my hand / I'm running away down River Road / And I swear once again that I'm never coming home / In my dreams I still run down River Road." Mitchell's "Both Sides, Now" from *Clouds* (1969) was inspired by her reading of

Saul Bellow's *Henderson the Rain King* while travelling in a plane and watching cloud formations. Since Mitchell considers herself a painter first and a musician second, it is possible to see and hear in this song "a meditation on reality and fantasy" (Wheeler n.p.), both youthful longing and mature assessment. "I've looked at love from both sides now / From give and take and still somehow / It's love's illusions I recall / I really don't know love at all." For the composing and singing duo of the McGarrigle sisters songs are subtle meditations on the appetite for love and its potential for destruction. "Heart Like a Wheel" from their debut album, *Kate and Anna McGarrigle* (1976), imagines a heart "just like a wheel, / when you bend it, you can't mend it." Noting that "it's only love / that can wreck a human being and turn him inside out," the lyrics declare "when harm is done no love can be won." Although it is tempting to read in the McGarrigle songs the fractiousness of Kate's marriage to Loudon Wainwright, III, who left their family of two young children, the lyrics also, as in "Dancer with Bruised Knees" from the 1977 album of the same name, convey a witty sense of coping with a partner who lets the dancer fall. "For years we had been one with the stars / A Pas de Deux of renown / I'd leap and he'd catch me on the fly / But once I came crashing down / Now I'm a weaver / Wall-hangings if you please / In every one I feature / A dancer with bruised knees."

The traditions of the north and of different Indigenous cultures inspire and fuel the work of many contemporary singer-songwriters. They are embedded in the folk songs of Inuk musician Susan Aglukark (b. 1967) and Inuk throat singer Tanya Tagaq. Aglukark's "Never Be the Same" from *Unsung Heroes* (1999) charts an ever-changing path – "Never be the same / I'm already changing / Never be the same again" – as it strives to find the language: "And if I could I'd tell them how I feel / Even if I had the words to heal." Accepting the Polaris Prize for her album *Animism*, Tagaq stunned the 2014 gala audience by projecting the names of 1,200 missing and murdered Indigenous women and girls. The title track of her most recent release, *Retribution* (2016), relies on a panting vocal pulse as she announces, "Our Mother grows angry; we squander her soul and suck out her sweet black oil to burn it." Now a standard feature for song releases, the video of "Retribution" opens with Tagaq smearing her face with oil, promising "retribution will be swift," and closes with choreographed, jump-cut sequences of angry screams.

The discography of Anishinaabe artist Leanne Betasamosake Simpson (b. 1971) and of Inuk Tiffany Ayalik (b. 1988) and transgender Ojibwe-Métis Grey Gritt, who are the duo Quantum Tangle, continues the use of multi-media and mixed musical styles. In "How to Steal a Canoe" from *f(l)ight* (2016), Michi Assgiig Nishnaabeg musician, poet, scholar-activist Simpson supplies the soft-voiced poetic soundscape as, along with violin accompaniment and animated figures, she sings to "a warehouse of stolen canoes," "bruised bodies" of "dehydrated rage." After smudging the spines of the canoes, emblems of appropriation and violence, with drops of water, she releases one canoe, sinking "her" with seven stones until she is "suspended in wet" as a form of dignified re-entry into the element. Combining blues and throat singing, technology and tradition, Quantum Tangle makes each of the tracks of *Shelter as We Go* (2017) a narrative of cultural reclamation, as the questions of "Tiny Hands" illustrate. "What have you seen in your short long life?" yields such answers as "Stretching, scraping, fixing and making, / Mending the skins that our souls fit within," "A witness to so many wrongs / Relocation, damnation, misinformation," and concluding with the repeated proclamation, "The traditional ways that are hidden away / Can be revived by the beat of a drum."

Punk, Pop, and Country

The crowded field of rock, indie-rock, and punk-rock, popular from the nineties on, is a bonanza for Canadian singer-songwriters. In "Calling All Angels," the indie rock lyrics and music of Jane Siberry (b. 1955), as sung by K.D. Lang on the Siberry album *When I Was a Boy* (1993), invoke the petitions of a litany of saints to light the way: "Calling all angels, calling all angels / Walk me through this one, don't leave me alone / ... / We're tryin', we're hopin' but we're not sure how this goes." "All I Want" from the break-through album *Jagged Little Pill* (1995) by Alanis Morissette (b. 1974) is a cry of greater alienation: "Slap me with a splintered ruler / And it would knock me to the floor if I wasn't there already." The singer longs for "intellectual intercourse, a soul to dig the hole much deeper," highlighting all she really wants as "a common ground, a wavelength," "some comfort," "some justice," "some patience," "deliverance." "Spill Yer Lungs," by the Acadian artist Julie Doiron (b. 1972), formerly known as Broken Girl, from her album *I Can Wonder What You Did with Your Day* (2009), indicates a considerable distance from the folk-inspired work of Edith Butler. The singer both approaches and avoids connection: "We could spend our hearts all over this town for nothing ... We could spill our wine all over this town for nothing ... We could scream our lungs out in this town for nothing ... We're gonna chase each other around this town for nothing." The lyrics of punk rocker Avril Lavigne (b. 1984) search for a similar distance in "Let Go" from her album *Complicated* (2002); although she claims "it's not worth it / to get in a mess over him," she continues to implore "would you leave me alone / before I lose my mind."

Pop and country music is another rich field for women singer-songwriters. K.D. Lang's (b. 1961) "Constant Craving" from her debut album *Ingénue* (1992) introduces both the sultry range of her voice and the concept of craving as "a great magnet [that] pulls / All souls to what's true." "Insensitive" by Jann Arden (b. 1962) from *Living under June* (1994) manages to address both the person left behind in a love story and the one who left her: "I'm out of vogue, I'm out of touch / I fell too fast, I feel too much / I thought you might have some advice to give / On how to be insensitive." The self-possessed lyrics of Arden's "Not Your Little Girl," from her album *These Are the Days* (2018), indicate how so-called popular music easily extends to serious affirmations, making the divide between popular and adult contemporary work tenuous. The assertions "I am big, I am strong / I am right where I belong" and "I am cool and I'm wise / And I'm larger than your life" empower the refusals, "You cannot rearrange me" and "You'll never pull me down." For Shania Twain (born Eileen Regina Edwards, 1965), "men are like shoes," as she sings in *The Will of a Woman* (2008). "Shoes" wittily surveys the types of shoes and men: "You've got your kickers and your ropers / Your everyday loafers, and some that you can never find / You've got your slippers and your zippers / Your grabbers and your grippers / Man, don't ya hate that kind? / Some you wear in, some you wear out / Some you wanna leave behind." Identical twins Tegan and Sara Quin (b. 1980) explore the difficulties of communicating with a self-absorbed person in "Frozen," from their first major album, *The Business of Art* (2000); the singers give voice to a reliably present but hemmed-in other figure: "When you're done whining / And taking things back / I'll be there as always feet submerged / And probably frozen." With a notion of promising encouragement they suggest that stopping in to say hi is "not far to go, it's not far at all." Although the rhythmic pulse of "1, 2, 3, 4" by Leslie Feist (b. 1976), co-written with the Australian singer Sally Seltmann on the Feist album *The Reminder* (2007), has contributed to its immense popularity among every age group, the song is much more than a number game; the plea, "Tell me that you love me more," previews a suspicion that love and "old teenage hopes" are fading: "Oh, ah oh, you're changing your heart / Oh, uh oh, you know who you are."

Realizations coupled with resolve characterize the lyrics of *Indian Ocean* (2014) by Frazey Ford (b. 1973), formerly a member of The Be Good Tanyas (2000–12). Rejoicing in women's support of one another at the same time as taking a firm stand, "Done" rejects being "taken for a goddamn fool, 'cause I'm not." Her insight injects strong emotion into the lyrics: "I used to think I hold the best parts of me / but sew the holes in your life and the cracks in your seams, / and I'm done, oh whoa, I'm done." In the latest album of the Indie-pop band Alvvays, *Antisocialites* (2017), vocalist and lyricist Molly Rankin (b. 1988) adopts a longing, nostalgic tone for "Dreams Tonite." With the video containing spliced footage of Expo 67, harmonic melodies and scenes of the past converge: "If I saw you on the street / would I have you in my dreams tonite?'

Adult Contemporary Styling

In adult contemporary lyrics by Sarah McLachlan (b. 1968), Chantal Kreviazuk (b. 1974), and Martha Wainwright (b. 1976), topics are more explicitly sexual. The title song of McLachlan's *Fumbling towards Ecstasy* (1993) celebrates release from fear, as "we will play / with chairs, candles and clothes / making darkness in the day." This sense of liberation entails a gamut of emotions: "And if I shed a tear I won't cage it / I won't fear love / And if I feel rage I won't deny it / I won't fear love." Kreviazuk's third album, *What if It All Means Something* (2002), looks candidly at the dynamics of a partnership. In "In This Life" the singer wants to "show you what I'm made of"; she declares to her partner, "I'll give you all the things that I never get, / Give you all I have and have no regret, / Take you to places that I've never been, / Forgive you all the things that you can't forget." Martha Wainwright, the daughter of Kate McGarrigle and Loudon Wainwright, III, makes the track "Bloody Motherfucking Asshole" in her self-titled 2005 album a way of talking back to her father's writing of songs about his family instead of caring for them. As interviewer Will Hodgkinson observes, Wainwright's "career might well be designed to irritate her family" (58). Building on her adolescent influences of Cyndi Lauper, Prince, and Leonard Cohen, she shifts her father's own words to accuse him of having "no idea how it feels to be on your own / in your own home." An ironic deflation of male bravado rather than female deference lies behind the wish that "I was born a man / So I could learn how to stand up for myself / Like those guys with guitars / ... / Who've been stamping their feet to a different beat." The singer's mood is anything but acquiescent: "I will not pretend / I will not put on a smile / I will not say I'm all right for you / For you, whoever you are."

A frankness in facing static circumstances or rejecting emotional blackmail unifies the different musical styles and tones of Jill Barber (b. 1980), Terra Lightfoot, and Mo Kenney (b. 1990). "Tell Me" from Barber's album *Mischievous Moon* (2011) shows her transition from the earlier pop sound to the clever jazz rhythms of the quasi-request at the heart of the lyric: "Did I do you wrong when I meant to do right? / Tell me what I can do to make it up to you." The powerful alto voice of guitarist and singer Lightfoot on her album *Every Time My Mind Runs Wild* (2015) underlines her determination, in "Emerald Eyes," to resist the movie-star looks of an unfaithful lover: "This gets older and older each time / Your lips shape the excuse." Kenney faces a dysfunctional long-distance relationship in "Telephones" from *In My Dreams* (2014), when she admits "I only talk to you by telephone / And rarely see you on my weekends home / I'd rather sit and watch my television shows / You know as well as me we're not in love."

The emotional space of women singer-songwriters in Canada is vast and complex, working through or out of relationships, reviving cultural memory and trauma, and rejecting notions of weakness or dependence. While their work ranges over a wide territory, its very existence and its candour, directness, and continuous expansion of media and topics testify to the determined art of these creators.

chapter five

Drama

Seeing your work come to life before your eyes is what's best about being a playwright.

– Carol Bolt[1]

Ringwood: Canadian Drama's Foremother

The career of Gwen Pharis Ringwood (1910–85), stretching over four decades and including both radio and stage plays, opens the door for Canadian women's dramatic writing. Born in Washington State and raised and largely educated in Alberta, she worked while completing her bachelor's degree at the University of Alberta as secretary for Elizabeth Sterling Haynes, director of drama for the Department of Extension, and subsequently as secretary for the Banff School of the Theatre. Her plays, firmly located in the west, establish the hallmarks of prairie regionalism. Regionalism need not be regarded "as narrow, limited, parochial, backward, out-dated or isolationist," but, argues Diane Bessai, as "rooted, indigenous, shaped by a specific social, cultural and physical milieu" (7). With "her characters and stories [taking] on the qualities of the climate and landscape in which they were placed," Ringwood "enriches her dramas with sound, music, and a new definition of space" (Ryga xviii). As Margaret Laurence noted, reviewing Ringwood's plays, "she saw, early on, the need to write out of our own people, our own land, and she has remained true to that vision" ("Foreword" xi).

A strong feature of Ringwood's work is her ability to create and interlace sharp, irreconcilable, and often tragic contrasts in character and affinity in an atmosphere of repression involving implacable or taciturn people. *Still Stands the House* (1938), which won first prize in the Dominion Drama Festival, resonates with the tension between sisters-in-law Ruth and Hester, their backgrounds in town and country, their desires for change or fixity, and ultimately their association with birth or death. From her first appearance, when she is described as "tall, dark, and unsmiling ... with bitter resentment in her dark eyes," forty-year-old Hester Warren, self-appointed keeper of her father's house, is the polar opposite of her brother's wife, Ruth, "small, fair-haired, and pretty" (28). Through telling exchanges Ringwood establishes Hester as the agent of the past and vengeance. Refusing to allow Ruth to place the blooming hyacinth in an old china bowl, Hester protests angrily, "I've asked you not to use that Wedgewood bowl. It was my grandmother's. I don't want it broken" (31). Not only does Hester resist Ruth's attempts to beautify and update the house, she actively destroys beauty, crushing one of the stalks of the hyacinth; yet she maintains her love of the land:

You have to love a place to make things grow. The land knows when you don't care about it, and Bruce doesn't care about it any more. Not like Father did. (32)

Her final act of spite, allowing Ruth to help her husband in a blizzard with a lantern Hester deliberately did not fill, feeds her delusion about the presence of her long-dead father; he had called her "the wise virgin," and she read him the proverb about the house that "fell not: for it was founded upon a rock" (43). These biblical passages (Matthew 25:1–13 and 7:25), likely recognized by Ringwood's audience, underscore Hester's crazed hypocrisy. This "wise virgin" is a killer, and the depiction of the house that stands is followed by the image of the house built upon sand that collapses (Matthew 7:27).

With their enveloping dread and sense of foreordained tragedy Ringwood's plays convey an almost-Euripidean agony. While in ancient Athens Euripides concentrated for about twenty plays on the cycle of Trojan war narratives, Ringwood focuses on the human costs of attachment to – or, more accurately, obsession with – the land. *Pasque Flower* (1939) and *Dark Harvest* (1945) have comparable story lines, in the triangle of a land-obsessed husband, long-suffering wife, and attractive brother-in-law beckoning the woman away from the farm; the contrasts between them reveal Ringwood's growing confidence in presenting complex human beings who speak not in biblical phrases but with directness and authenticity. As an undergraduate in Winnipeg in 1945, Margaret Laurence attended a performance of *Dark Harvest*, "the first Canadian play [she] had ever seen"; "it made a deep and lasting impression," she has affirmed, identifying the playwright in her foreword to Ringwood's *Collected Plays*, as "one of the writers who helped to shape ... a general Renaissance of Canadian literature" (xi). In *Pasque Flower* Lisa, when finally refusing her brother-in-law's offer of escape, interprets her husband's unacknowledged gift of flowers as an emblem of their marriage and need for one another: "I'm held here not by duty, David, as I thought, but something else; by some blind need Jake has for me and I for him" (56).

In *Dark Harvest* not only is Lisa more forthright throughout in expressing her views of her husband, Gerth, but the characterization of the remote Gerth is also more complicated and nuanced. She diagnoses her husband's "fever to buy land," realizes that "we're as far apart as strangers," and reminds him "that we had a child once ... and I lost it – but the ploughing got done that year" (70). Moreover, this wife admits her emotional quandary to her brother-in-law: "If only I could have loved him like he asked me to, instead of going through all the years needing you" (107). Yet it is Gerth who, in relating a dream, makes the most revealing confession about farming and marriage:

> *Lisa was in my dream, standing there, her eyes as blue as flax in the morning, and the wheat around her. But a hail storm came up. I saw it smashing the wheat back into the earth ... And I ran to where she was, because I didn't want the hail to hurt her. I wanted to keep it away from her, but when I got there, she wasn't there any more. She'd gone.* (110)

Gerth's saving of the wheat from the danger of a burning truck by driving it into the river puts a tragic-heroic cast on his suicide.

Situated in a variety of settings, Ringwood's later plays continue to explore ruptures within relationships and communities. In *The Stranger* (1971) the arrival of the Chilcotin woman Jana on a Palomino stallion signals trouble for the Shuswap, who insist that she leave. The realization that her common-law partner for five years and father of her child is engaged to marry the White ranch owner further isolates the Chilcotin woman. Jana's curse of her former lover is charged with the vehemence of a discarded woman:

> *For you I came to this place where they spit on me as a stranger ... Tell your white whore I'll send our child so she can look at him and know she'll never give you such a son ... Tell her I wish your children born blind and hideous and twisted with hate as I am now.* (397)

With an interspersed lullaby in Chilcotin and the chants of a chorus, the play fulfils its gruesome *Medea* prophecy.

Ringwood identifies the place of *A Remembrance of Miracles* (1980) as Willamont, a small western town; yet the topic, the censoring of a high-school English teacher's reading list by a committee of parents who refuse to read the books, resonates widely. In commenting on this play, first broadcast on CBC Radio in 1978, Margaret Laurence does not mention the fact that teacher Merrill Adams has included *The Diviners* on her list, but she does admit that, "I find this play unbearably poignant, as I happen to know only too well what the teacher is forced to go through" ("Foreword" xiv). Although Merrill's resignation might seem like capitulation to narrow-minded community standards and so-called "polite society," she makes her leaving the occasion for delivering a manifesto:

> *I believe that Art helps us to endure and to accept despair, maybe helps us to change the bad things, change the world. I don't think Art can deal with what is polite and pleasant and easy to swallow. To me and I hope to some of my students fiction can help us find our way, poems are shores of light.* (435)

Joudry, Henry, and Simons: Examining Emotions

Emotional involvement is a commonplace, built-in, aspect of drama. However, Patricia Joudry's *Teach Me How to Cry* (1955), Ann Henry's *Lulu Street* (1967), and Beverley Simons's *Crabdance* (1969) search into the development, insightfulness, and mystery of emotions in ways that are quite removed from Ringwood's prairie consciousness. In these plays there is no rift between city and countryside, no stifling of emotions but rather their blunt expression. The fibrillations of the self – however yearning, anguished, or disappointed – are central concerns. Both Joudry's and Simons's plays premiered in the United States, Joudry's in New York and Simons's in Seattle. The only identifiably Canadian locale is Winnipeg in Henry's play, although the 1919 General Strike stays in the background. What is in the forefront in all these dramas is talk about feelings, whether involving lonely adolescents, or a daughter forming judgments about her social activist father who stays on the sidelines during the strike, or a lusty yet compassionate older woman who welcomes male visitors in the afternoon.

Teach Me How to Cry opens with extensive notes on the characters that almost overshadow the action of the play itself. Emotionally suppressed high-school students Melinda Grant, illegitimate daughter of a distracted mother from whom she's alienated, and Will Henderson, whose mother is described as "invading his soul" (35), meet during rehearsals for a production of *Romeo and Juliet*. As their friendship progresses, they talk outside of school at a burnt-out bandstand, associated with the fatal tryst after which "Mrs" Grant was abandoned by her lover. The fact that Will suffers expulsion to defend Melinda's honour, causing Melinda finally to break down and sob in his presence, is the real breakthrough in the action. Will underscores the importance of the moment: "Some people say men don't like it when girls cry, but they're the kind of people that don't like girls to laugh either" (72). In addition to such mannered psychologizing, Joudry prefers hopeful endings, as this separated young couple vows to keep writing to one another.

After a decade in England (1962–73), where her plays were produced in London's West End, Joudry (1921–2000) returned to Canada, published three novels, and continued to write plays, one of the latest of which, *A Very Modest Orgy* (1981), premiered at the Canadian Theatre Today conference at the University of Saskatchewan. The rapid emotional turnarounds of this two-act comedy, in which a professor's wife, obsessed with the idea of "swinging," realizes that her husband is as faithful as she is, resolve potentially complex dilemmas with a superficial lightness and jocularity.

The view of the Winnipeg General Strike of 1919 presented in Henry's *Lulu Street* is one from the sidelines, yet the self-reflections expressed in the rundown rooming house reveal the emotional tolls of social activism. A novelist and reporter as well as playwright, Henry (1914–2000) was the first woman journalist to cover the Winnipeg Police Court and the Manitoba Legislature. Her keen sense of embedded stories and resentments propels the sparring of father and daughter, Matthew and Elly Alexander, in *Lulu Street*. Labour organizer Matthew tries to gain Elly's support for his rhetoric and dissuade her from thinking he "never cared" (80). As Elly reasons, even if her father were elected to Parliament, "I'd still be the daughter of a dirty Bolshevik. A friend of the Pollacks, Bohunks, Kikes. They spit on me on Lulu Street!" (81). Although another lodger tries to convince Elly that when Matthew was an earnest young preacher in England, "he was a firebrand," Elly clings to the anguish of her now-institutionalized mother.

> *My mother wanted to go to church and he wouldn't let her ... And then, when she needed him, when he had made her ... Sick ... And she couldn't stand it any longer ... He was out saving the world. Helping the poor, while she ... He knows it too. That's why he walks the streets at night and weeps in his room.* (115)

In contrast to the muffled or unacknowledged pain of Henry's realistic play, the absurd action of Simons's *Crabdance* conveys the ultimate vulnerability of Sadie Golden. As Simons (b. 1938) orchestrates the sequence of the afternoon, the three salesmen Sadie welcomes and the erotic innuendo of her desire to open their valises of merchandise reveal aspects of this lonely widow's past, her dead husband, and absent son. Amid the disjointed talk and occasionally slapstick, frantic movements, Sadie discloses shards of her life.

> *I wish my son could have heard you just now. He'd have learned a lot. Unfortunately he took after his father. A pig. Not a bad man. Dead. Don't misunderstand me. Decent, honourable, dependable. He adored me. Couldn't keep his hands off.* (36)

Sadie is by turns a figure of great pathos who admits "My fruit has fallen from me, rotted" (68), a woman who fantasizes about nurturance, "You don't know what a temptation helplessness is to a woman" (100), and an image of incompleteness, "trapped like a spirit in a white cave crying for a body to enter" (101). When the assembled tradespeople place Sadie in a coffin and proceed solemnly to carry it to the non-existent second storey of her house, they supply the strangely appropriate coda to Sadie's final "scream of loneliness and anguish" (103).

Pollock and Bolt: Re-viewing History and Power Politics

Both Sharon Pollock (b. 1936) and Carol Bolt (1941–2000) have been dynamic, transformative presences in the development of drama in Canada. Strong-minded and outspoken as playwrights, dramaturges, collaborators, mentors, and advocates of dramatic arts, they have looked critically at aspects of our history as well as the patriarchal structure of families and organizations. On- and off-stage they have contributed to theatre culture. In addition to being an award-winning actor and the founder of Garry Theatre in Calgary, Pollock has led the playwrights' colony at the Banff Centre and served as artistic director of Theatre Calgary and Theatre New Brunswick. Bolt was a founding member of Playwrights Co-op, which became Playwrights Canada Press; following her death from liver cancer, the Canadian Authors Association inaugurated the Carol Bolt Award for the best English-language play. In summarizing the double value they brought to the theatre scene, Bolt actually cited Pollock: "Sharon Pollock once said in an interview we were doing together that, in a way, we were both really lucky because when we started writing, theatres could produce our plays and get both a Canadian and a woman in their season in one shot!" (Rudakoff and Much, *Fair Play* 188).

The history these immensely productive playwrights revisit does not centre on documentary reportage but rather on acutely realized character studies of moral challenge. Working with both Theatre Passe Muraille and Toronto Free Theatre, Bolt connected issues of power with her fascination with larger-than-life, mythic characters.[2] They include the fictionalized "communist agitator" (38) Red Evans, who leads the Relief Camp Workers Union strike march to Regina in *Buffalo Jump* (1972), and the real-life Emma Goldman in *Red Emma, Queen of the Anarchists* (1974), who believes "in freedom, the right to self-expression. Everyone's right to beautiful, radiant things" (207). With a title invoking the Indigenous method of hunting buffalo by stampeding them over a cliff, *Buffalo Jump* contrasts the glib oratory of Prime Minister R.B. Bennett, "Iron Heel Bennett with an apple in his mouth" (66), who set up the relief camps, and the union organizer Evans, who knows that men "want a decent wage ... work that means something" (39). The "jump" occurs at Regina, when hunger and exhaustion caused the trekkers' riot on Dominion Day 1935 that was forcibly broken up by Mounties with guns, batons, and horses. As the Toronto audience filed out, they saw strikers handcuffed to policemen. Concentrating on the ideological positions, songs, and entwined love quarrels of the young anarchist, *Red Emma*, which was adapted and mounted as an opera by the Canadian Opera Company in 1995, presents a strong-minded, independent heroine. The truthfulness of words and authenticity of convictions are central issues. Early on Emma refuses to be a *porte-parole* for her one-time tutor and lover, Johann Most, telling him, "I speak for you, but I will not say your words" (182), and ultimately, as she is about to beat him with a belt, accusing him of hypocrisy: "Every principle you hold important, you deny" (206). Focusing on the complexity of interpersonal connections and the layered consequences of power politics, the contemporary urban realism of Bolt's thriller *One Night Stand* (1977), set in a Toronto high-rise, builds to its own eerily predictable fatality.

Sharon Pollock: "meaning through the making of theatre"

Sharon Pollock challenges Canadians to look at our history, to peel away the veneer of amiability and peacefulness. The editor of her *Collected Works*, Cynthia Zimmerman, includes Pollock's "Reflections" at the 2006 Playwrights Guild of Canada conference, where she acknowledges "a need to organize inconsistency and rupture in human affairs, to make meaning of it through the making of theatre." Playing with time and space is the lure for her, which involves "theatrically shuffling past, present, future, external locations and internal landscapes, inner thoughts and uttered words" (III: 15–16).[3]

Through more than five decades of work, garnering two Governor General's Awards and several honorary degrees, her plays "continue to explore the kinds of injustices which arise out of hypocrisy, bigotry, patriarchy and racism" (Coates 5). Offering "multiple answers, different perspectives on which questions matter, even different interpretations as to what actually happened," as Zimmerman remarks, they all "testify to her fascination with issues of power" (I: 7, 10). Using meta-theatrical devices, split subjects, offstage voices, and leaps of time and space, she investigates what Craig Walker identifies as the "recurrent theme of the role of memory in protecting individual integrity against deterministic forces" (199). Critical studies of her work have proposed various ways of seeing or staging such recurrence in her plays of ideas. Locating Pollock's two Governor General's Award-winning plays, *Blood Relations* and *Doc*, as "renegade play texts," Rosalind Kerr sees the centrality of their female characters as "an abrupt departure from the string of earlier plays which Pollock had written to force Canadian audiences to recognize the dominant ideologies underlying official government policies" (200, 204). By contrast, John Hofsess considers Pollock's popular success as "a sign that her plays are becoming bourgeois" (4) and longs for her return to the broader political scope of plays like *Walsh*. Yet in her reading of the diversity of Pollock's history plays, stretching from *Walsh* (1973) and *The Komagata Maru Incident* (1976) to *Fair Liberty's Call*

(1993), Anne Nothof emphasizes how the imposition of borders in these tragic plays confronts and destroys any bourgeois sense of contentment. Whether in the self-denial involved in enforcing government policies in nineteenth-century Cyprus Hills, or in an early twentieth-century Vancouver brothel, or in the justifications of slaughter in an eighteenth-century family of American loyalists in New Brunswick, the borders "between countries, between individuals – in the interests of securing or protecting property" express "the entrenched bigotry and greed of an established population" ("Crossing Borders" 475). Struggle with an establishment, moreover, has characterized Pollock's career itself. She was climbing the theatre ladder at a time when "the invisibility factor" excluded women from funding; as Pollock's biographer, Sherrill Grace, observes, "she was, for her time, one of the few women in Canada to succeed in the assault on this bastion of male power," adding "as her own opportunities to mentor others multiplied she often chose to encourage younger women, while also watching for creative ability in men" (*Making Theatre* 375).

The dramaturgical adroitness with which Pollock interleaves periods of time, stage techniques, and socio-political audience involvement remains the hallmark of her work. The first view of Walsh as a commissioner for Yukon in a Whitehorse saloon during the 1898 Klondike Rush presents him as a broken man, a technique "through which Pollock forestalls empathy and identification with the potentially charismatic Walsh by showing him in his later years" (Knowles, *Theatre of Form* 138). Such an opening highlights the disjunction that permeates the play – with allegiances formed then abrogated, policy questioned yet enforced, and sympathetic understanding leading to the dangers of friendship. The superintendent of the Northwest Mounted Police, Walsh, known as White Forehead Chief, promises Sitting Bull, Chief of the Hunkpapa Sioux, to honour his wish not to return to the United States. "I promise you, I'll stand by you," he declares (*Walsh* 57). Although, in an oral letter to his wife in Ontario, Walsh describes the Sioux as "an able and brilliant people ... crushed, held down, moved from place to place, cheated and lied to" (74), he is ultimately incapable of intervening in their starvation, brought about by the extinction of the buffalo. His final encounter with Sitting Bull, who is begging for flour, is explosive – "Cross the line if you're so hungry, but don't, for Christ's sake, come begging food from me!" (87) – as he throws the Chief to the floor, planting his foot in the middle of his back. When Walsh learns of the shooting death of Sitting Bull, dropped into a lime pit "so his people couldn't bury him proper" (94), the news intensifies his defeated realization that "Honour, truth, the lot [are] just words ... and they don't exist" (81). By dramatizing the denial of food aid to the starving band, Pollock shows that "Canadians were no better in their insidious complicity with American Indian policy and their desire to rid themselves of the troublesome Sioux" (Wasserman 21).

Pollock's art engages the conscience of her contemporary audiences as she uses the stage to "highlight the subjectivity of recorded history" (Belliveau 96). In its depiction of the exclusion of 346 Sikh and 30 East Indian immigrants from disembarking in the Vancouver harbour in 1914, *The Komagata Maru Incident* provides what Pollock terms in her introduction "a theatrical impression of an historical event seen through the *optique* of the stage and the mind of the playwright." Along with multiple locations and simultaneous narratives, Pollock introduces a Master of Ceremonies, T.S., who plays the role of carnival barker with gloves, hat, and cane. While T.S. opens in vaudevillian style with the pitch of "Three hundred and seventy-six Asians, to be precise, and all of them bound for Oh Canada, We stand on guard for thee!" (I: 101), he closes the play after the shooting death of Hopkinson, the Northwest Mounted Police officer hiding his own mixed-race heritage, with "a soft-shoe shuffle [and] a large but simple bow" (I: 137). His actions "implicate the paying audience in the incident; they become bystanders and participants in the racist side-show" (Belliveau 97). The questions and observations that frame *One Tiger to a Hill* (1980), about the 1975 hostage-taking at the Westminster, B.C., penitentiary, also implicate the audience. Everett Chalmers, a corporate lawyer who is brought in to mediate (and with the same name as Pollock's father, whose character and influence she will explore in *Doc*), is tonally very different from the sleazy T.S. Agreeable, family-oriented, middle-class but uninvolved in the proceedings at the "pen," located on the other side of the park from his own home, Ev opens with a confessional question and resolve, reflecting the experiences the play is about to reveal:

> *What if the things you hear, the things you don't want to hear, the things they won't let you hear, what if those things really happen inside? ... when we condemn men to that wastebasket we call the pen.* (I: 218)

The Métis prisoner Tommy Paul, involved in the hostage-taking and one of its two victims, presents his case about conditions inside to the intermediary Ev:

> *Lemma tell you somethin' ... in the last four years I spent over eight hundred days in the hole, solitary, top tier, concrete vault where they bury you. Eleven by six foot coffin. Four solid walls. Six inch window in a steel door. Light in the ceilin' they never turn off. I shower wearing steel shackles and cuffs. If I'm lucky I shave twice a week in cold water. My toilet bowl is my sink. That's right, I gotta wash in the crapper.* (I: 265)

Tommy's love of social worker Dede is not really reciprocated; he wonders "was everything bullshit therapy?" (I: 255), while she tries to explain, lamely, "I ... do love you, Tommy, but not in the way that you think ... I love you as ... a person who's been ... fucked up, and screwed around – but that's as far as it goes" (I: 273). As for what happens to us in witnessing these events, Ev's closing address to the audience leaves a sense of guiltily muted resolve: "What were the lies? (*He weeps*)" (I: 276).

Pollock's retrospective look at family tensions in *Doc* (1984) and the ambivalence of judgments about guilt and innocence in her meta-theatrical treatment of Lizzie Borden in *Blood Relations* (1980) do signal more intimate and interior dramatic explorations. Situating *Blood Relations* both in the 1892 circumstances of Lizzie Borden's actions and the re-enactment or re-visioning of them a decade later by an Actress playing Lizzie, Pollock takes on the role of Lizzie Borden's biographer, using play-within-a-play sequences and mirror talk to destabilize any certainty about what Lizzie Borden did or did not do and why. *Doc*, Pollock's quasi-autobiographical treatment of her own New Brunswick family and the play that won her second Governor General's Award, extends the techniques of *Blood Relations* in offering younger (Katie) and older (Catherine) representations of herself observing and judging an alcoholic mother and controlling physician father.

Her plays continue to illustrate that personal choices are invariably political. In *Whiskey Six Cadenza, Saucy Jack,* and *Fair Liberty's Call* they also involve extensions or adjustments of historical accounts. In speculating about the relationship between the actual rum-runner in the Crowsnest Pass, Emilio Piciarello, and the wife of his chauffeur, Filumena Lassandro, both of whom were hanged at the Fort Saskatchewan Penitentiary in 1923 for the murder of an Alberta Provincial Police constable, Pollock transforms them into Mr Big and Leah, his adopted "daughter," accomplice, and mistress. Mr Big both rationalizes his bootlegging activity and refuses to believe that Leah loves anyone else. It is Leah, however, who offers him the gun to "make it right" (II: 123). *Whiskey Six Cadenza* is full of what Mr Big calls "collidin' conjectures" (II: 123). For Anne Nothof the play emphasizes the struggles between prohibition and freedom through the figure of Mr Big, who engages in "an interrogation of the conflict between colonial power structures and individual resistance within an immigrant community" (*Sharon Pollock: Essays,* "Postcolonial Tragedy" 235).

Pollock's treatment of Jack the Ripper in *Saucy Jack* (1993) is not really an attempt to reveal his true identity but rather a subtle reversal of power separating the three male members of the cast from the female actor. While Eddy (Queen Victoria's grandson Prince Albert Victor), Jem (James Stephen, his Cambridge tutor), and Montague Druitt, teacher at a boys' school, rehearse and attempt to recall gruesome slayings, it is Kate who, through dramatizing a series of pictures, actually emerges as a potent survivor. In her notes to the play Pollock traces how Kate "acquires knowledge by listening" (II: 312). Kate "evolves from a silent, unknown, nameless figure to the only vital or potent figure or force in the play when the final blackout occurs" (II: 312). Kate lives; the men die.

The survivors in *Fair Liberty's Call*, commissioned by the Stratford Festival in 1993, challenge "the notion that the Canadian character is defined by peace, order, and good government," a model that Pollock sees as "valuing legality over justice, passivity over action in the face of injustice or corruption, and traditional form over authentic content" (II: 360). In 1785 the Roberts family deals with the aftermath of the American War of Independence and the transportation of civilian Loyalist families to what will become New Brunswick, whose legislative assembly is created that year. Of the Roberts children, one son has fought and died with the rebels and the other has committed suicide after fighting for the Loyalists; the daughter dresses as a man, assumes the identity of her dead brother, fights and kills for the Loyalists, yet loses her trust in the Loyalist leaders. The three figures through whom these losses are most palpably experienced are the mother, Joan; the daughter, Emily / Eddie; and the former scout, Wullie, who fought with Tarleton's Loyalist Legion. Although Wullie realizes that "fightin' for the Loyalists won't buy my freedom, 'less I be a runaway Rebel-owned slave" (II: 367), he is led to accept an indentured agreement for thirty-nine years. Emily / Eddie faces the establishment oligarchy intent on "restorin' order and rank and stability" with this question: "So our promised land, our great new province, this country will become the fiefdom of a few, is that it?" (II: 389). In a symbolic gesture of loss and mourning, Joan accepts and swallows the bowl full of dirt from "the red woman with the babe on her back" (II: 418). Instead of characterizing Joan as "a mother driven insane by grief," Kathy Chung suggests that "it is equally possible to see her behavior as the result not of grief but of an unhealthy community that refuses to recognize the losses and permit the mourning of all its members" (141).

The struggles of the artist protagonists of *Moving Pictures* (1999) and *Angel's Trumpet* (2001), Nell Shipman and Zelda Fitzgerald, against unhealthy or inhospitable communities crystallize the determination of the playwright herself. In *Angel's Trumpet*'s depiction of Zelda's psychiatric commitment, the verbal battles between Zelda and Scott question if one person's artistic expression must be sacrificed to allow for another's. The exchanges of the young actress, experienced middle-aged director, and older playwright Shipman in *Moving Pictures* present the hurdles of the woman artist. Although Pollock told the Playwrights Guild of Canada that she "generally hate[s] plays about art or artists," she admitted that her "female characters often are revealed and developed in action or interaction with themselves" (III: 17). This admission led her to a consideration, which she also hated, "whether the female playwright, me, is revealing and developing her own character by interaction with herself, her plays being that self." Like Shipman's younger incarnations who prompt her never to stop but to continue – "Alright. You've got me. Never! So – Play!" (III: 133) – Pollock revealed to her Playwrights Guild audience that "The work is something that must be done. No choice. No choice." Her dedication to theatrical work, her own and that of her contemporaries, and its enduring hold are exemplified vividly in her response to the fire in her Calgary home in the summer of 2008. Refusing to go to the hospital and insisting that her daughter drive her to the theatre, Pollock honoured her commitment to the role she was playing on stage that evening. "Sharon was performing the role of Margaret in Judith Thompson's *Habitat*" (Grace, "Biography and *the* Archive" 229), an elderly female resident in a house that burns down.

Ritter, Glass, Clark, and Lill: Enacting Vulnerabilities

Erika Ritter (b. 1948), Joanna Glass (1935–2006), Sally Clark (b. 1953), and Wendy Lill (b. 1950) bring multiple talents and experiences to play writing. Ritter has been a fiction writer, radio announcer, and stand-up comic, which experience is the basis of her *Automatic Pilot* (1980). Actor and novelist Glass re-creates family experiences of a resentful, delusional, alcoholic patriarch in *Play Memory* (1983/1986, premiering in Philadelphia and later Saskatoon). Clark adapts Franz Kafka to reflect on nightmarish bureaucracy in *The Trial of Judith K.* (1985). Journalist, broadcaster, and documentary writer Lill draws on her experience of Indigenous-White encounters in northwestern Ontario for her monodrama *The Occupation of Heather Rose* (1986).

From urban sex comedy and remembered family torment to scenes of death and disintegration, these plays – so different in tone – are united by their focus on the female protagonist and the realizations that she and the audience and readership reach about entrapment or liberation. The vulnerabilities they convey can involve emotional collapse and death, but on at least one occasion there is freedom from parental tyranny. Charlie, the stand-up comic in *Automatic Pilot*, expresses an insider's view of the Toronto show-business scene.

> Contracts ratified on waterbeds. People sucking up to power because it might rub off. Those macrobiotic people had it all wrong. Around here, you are who you eat. (18)

Strangely, though, the insights do not come from the queen of snappy one-liners. The final monologue of her cast-off younger lover, Gene, speaking to his microphone after watching Charlie's act, discloses the appeal, addiction perhaps, of her self-deprecatory humour: "telling stories that featured her as the perpetual underdog, perpetually disappointed ... the awfulness *was* the incentive" (56).

Glass's reworking of an earlier version of *Play Memory* focuses on the retrospection of daughter Jean, who comes to understand that her feckless, self-important father had done "the most admirable thing in his life" which was "to let us go" (61). Clark's unassuming bank clerk, Judith Kaye, finds herself "under arrest" (19) yet still permitted to lead her "ordinary and tediously boring life" (89); however, even though she is subjected to "indefinite postponement" for the rest of her days, her desire to live results in her death "like a dog!" (119). Lill's monologist, Heather Rose, idealistic nurse for Northern Medical Services, loses her illusions about the support of southern administrators, "those fucking high-paid whites coming through to help the Indians ... consulting on this, consulting on that, flashing their million dollar smiles" (86). Dejected on account of unanswered calls, undelivered supplies, and the death of a beautiful young sniffing addict, Rose admits "I've fallen apart" (91) and vows to occupy the nursing station.

Thompson and MacDonald: Performing Marginalization and Shape Shifting

Multiple award winners Judith Thompson (b. 1954) and Ann-Marie MacDonald (b. 1958) may seem to be a stylistically odd couple. In contrast to Thompson's disturbing yet compelling depictions of abuse, violence, and trauma are MacDonald's word plays and manipulating of literary conventions. But whether through extreme situations or serio-comic gender reversals, both playwrights are commenting on how we live and know ourselves, and on our endless pursuit of healing, wholeness, and forgiveness.

Though often spurred by supernatural presences, the reworking or challenging of reality in Ann-Marie MacDonald's plays occurs in situations of witty repartee and philosophical debate. The Governor General's Award-winning *Goodnight Desdemona (Good Morning Juliet)* (1990) introduces Shakespeare scholar Constance Ledbelly, who "slaved for years to get [her] doctorate, / but in a field ... that's so well trod, / you can run the risk of contradicting men / who've risen to the rank of sacred cow" (41). Seeing herself as "a failed existentialist" and "a fallen Catholic," and enslaved to a senior male professor whose papers she ghost writes, she is transported through warp effects to the worlds of *Othello* and *Romeo and Juliet*. Under Iago's influence, Desdemona doubts Constance's friendship, while Romeo and Juliet fight one another jealously for the love of the pretty boy they call Constantine. Constance manages to turn tragedies to comedies and in the process recognizes herself as "the Author" (86).

MacDonald sets *Belle Moral (A Natural History)* (2005) in late-Victorian Scotland, in a mansion (whose name supplies the title) outside of Edinburgh where secrets of a family's past abound. A philosophic morality play ironically invoking its title, *Belle Moral* is an endlessly inventive series of debate propositions about the complexities linking science and ethical responsibility. Through her central character, amateur scientist Pearl MacIsaac, MacDonald strives "to reconcile the extremes of rationalism and romanticism in an attempt to re-envision and to articulate afresh those core Enlightenment values that engendered the freedom and equality that we take for granted at our peril" (155). In uncovering the true story of her mother's suicide and the existence of a long-hidden sister, Pearl rejects the marriage proposal of the trusted physician and patronizing rationalist Dr Reid; he ultimately denounces Pearl and the whole MacIsaac family as "an unmarried woman with an illegitimate offspring surrounded by a pack of lunatics, sodomites, and vegetarians" (146). To rebut Reid's claim that he is "a child of the enlightenment" who resists "nothing that is rational" (155), Pearl argues for relational ethics influenced by quotidian events; as she insists, "Facts do not float in sterile solitude, they are embedded in reality, tainted with everyday life, stained with history; inextricable, like Darwin's web" (146). In contrast to Reid, who perceives only "an incoherent jumble" in Belle Moral, Pearl and MacDonald see "affinities. Patterns" (146).

Judith Thompson: "through the looking glass, darkly"

Thompson's fourteen multi-act stage plays, along with one-acts and screenplays, force us to look inside ourselves to acknowledge the pettiness, explosive anger, or aloneness we usually keep muffled and concealed. The repressed returns with visceral intensity in her work. As Craig Stewart Walker argues about Thompson's glimpses of death, judgment, heaven, and hell, "to transcend the barrier between our conscious selves and these four last things hidden deep within marks the first step towards transcending the barriers between us and our fellow human beings" (411).

From the striking debut of *The Crackwalker* (1980) with its fool saint Theresa to her one-woman *Watching Glory Die* (2017), fictionalizing the Ashley Smith tragedy in which a teenager took her life in an Ontario correctional centre, the dark corners of her plays, which have won two Governor General's Awards, continue to shock some readers. Thompson expresses her own surprise at this reaction:

> *I am always very, very shocked when people are shocked. The last thing I ever want to do is offend ... It just doesn't occur to me that these characters would*

> *offend anybody because they're people and I care about them. And you just don't care about people because they're nice or they're pretty.* (Rudakoff, "Judith Thompson: Interview" 29)

Among those Thompson cares about are the infanticide (Alan in *The Crackwalker*), the psychopath (Kevin in *Sled*), the murdered child and her murderer (Isobel and Ben in *Lion in the Streets*), the sacrificial suicide (Pony in *White Biting Dog*), and the rape victim and the epileptic amnesiac (Marie and Patsy in *Perfect Pie*). Urjo Kareda reminded us that "Thompson hears the poetry of the inarticulate and the semi-literate, embodying the colloquialisms, the brand names, the fractured but expressive syntax, with the urgency of their speakers" (9). She shows as much compassionate insight in scripting the monologue of a Canadian CSIS agent who cannot stop biting his nails as he tries to justify the torture of a fifteen-year-old Iraqi prisoner at Guantánamo Bay in *Nail Biter* (2008) as in the dialogue of two fifteen-year-old girls, one an Auschwitz survivor forty years later and the other a First Nations street gang member in *Such Creatures* (2010). With tremendous vividness Thompson explores the linkages of Eros and death, the extremes of physical abandonment, the festering of guilt, and the pervasiveness of misogyny.

Critical commentary on national and international performances of her work underscores the range of her innovative theatre and its unsparing language. Her characters "get into *our* blood," Robert Nunn observes; "they become the Other-within-us, and in the moment of recognition they remind us of something we are likely to resist: that we too are Other" ("Strangers" 29). Analysing British reviews of *The Crackwalker* and *Lion in the Streets*, Ann Wilson notes that reviewers' voyeuristic focus on what is perceived as "new-world despair" misses essential elements: "The failure to recognize the underlying religiosity of Thompson's work blinds the English reviewers to the notions of redemption, grace and forgiveness" (27). In "Judith Thompson's Ghosts" Claudia Barnett concentrates on the dead or ghostly characters to whom she gives voice, allowing them – despite their incorporeality – to gain the insight and agency after death they were denied in life.

Laura Levin argues for Thompson's rehabilitation of naturalism as avant-garde, proposing that she "radicalizes the naturalist aesthetic, exposing the experimental and politically enabling aspects of the genre" (172). A unifying feature within this new aesthetic, according to Diana Manole, is the exile resulting from alienation from the community to which one ostensibly belongs – the situations of Joe, Kevin, and Evangeline in *Sled*. Ideologies of gender can intensify the experience of alienation. Sharon Friedman's argument about "the brutal practices in communities engaged in violent conflict" (593), as in Thompson's triptych of monologues drawn from the written records of three public figures associated with the Iraq War, illustrates how monstrosity exists "not only in the oppressor but in the most ostensibly righteous victim" (603).

Thompson implicates her audience both through the harrowing, excoriating exchanges in her plays and through her own revelations about them. She describes her process as "the creation of other characters within a world that resembles our own, but, like Alice's Wonderland, is seen through the looking glass, darkly" ("Epilepsy & the Snake" 4). In acknowledging her history of epileptic seizures, which her elementary school vice-principal did not understand, she compares epilepsy to "a form of death" (6). Although *The Crackwalker* emerged from a combination of a summer job for the Ministry of Social Services in Kingston teaching life skills to unemployable adults, during which she heard about the death of a baby, and a workshop on channelling with masks at the National Theatre School where she was a student, this debut has prompted Thompson to wonder about the demonic characters in so much of her work.

> How can I represent people I abhor? Am I so morally and ethically runny inside? ... To face the dark hole, to reach inside the bucket, and pull out the rattlesnake and look it in the face; for me, this is the act of creation. (7)

Dedicated to the memory of her father, a psychology professor at Queen's University, *The Crackwalker* is a play that Thompson now finds difficult to watch. She has revised the climactic baby-murder scene, which was originally off-stage. In conversation with Cynthia

Zimmerman she admitted that making the scene of the build-up to the event more poetic "was wrong because it made Alan a madman rather than presenting his actions as resulting from the forces acting on him" (Zimmerman 19). A comparison of the original act two, scene six, as appended to the Playwrights Canada Press thirtieth anniversary reissue of the second edition in 2010, with the texts included in *The Other Side of the Dark* (1989) and *Late 20th Century Plays* (2003), reveals significant differences. In the original, the initial shocking reality of the act is followed by Theresa's screaming prayer, while directions in the revised version refer to Alan's "wooden state" and Theresa's "watching in wonder" (*Late 20th Century Plays* 75). Stage directions in the original describe Alan after the strangling as "still as a lizard" with tongue movement suggesting a petit mal seizure. Theresa, "not sure what to do," starts mouth-to-mouth, while her monologues invoking Mary, the mother of Jesus, bookend this scene, which closes with her word-perfect recitation of the Hail Mary and her repetition "He jus a baby" before "she reaches for the phone" (*Crackwalker* [2010] 113). In both versions the play's enactment of the discarded class who fall between the cracks also exposes the divides between tenderness and violence, perception and delirium, mercy and criminality. The last sight of Alan, crouching over a warm air vent with the unnamed First Nations Man whose bleeding he had attempted to staunch earlier by tying his shirt around the man's wrist and calling an ambulance, presents him now trying to escape the man's vomit. Commenting on a recent production thirty-six years after its debut, Nigel Irwin expresses ambivalence about the continued need for such a play, yet the actor playing First Nations Theresa finds hope in her character's strength in the face of loss and determination to carry on. In fact, Thompson's concluding scenes reverse judgmentalism at the same time as they exhort a probing consideration of circumstances. Sandra's defence of Alan and Theresa, who "will start blowin off old queers again for five bucks," draws attention to the baby's funeral, where the flowers around the infant's neck never hid the strangle – "They just made ya look harder" (101).

Thompson's plays force a harder look at conditions of devaluation, eruption, and loss as well as possibilities for innocence, grace, and forgiveness. In staging the north (at least as far as Algonquin Park), where murders occur, and the south of Toronto, where an incestuous reunion of half-siblings leads to pregnancy and suicide, *Sled* (1997) deconstructs the concept of Canada as "a peaceful nation defined by the 'north'" (Tompkins 9). The murders of Annie and Mike, the dying of their murderer, Kevin, and the suicide of the part-Cree Evangeline, pregnant with her half-brother Kevin's child, provoke mixed critical response. Sherrill Grace considers the play's conventional and unchallenged binaries of north and south "a disturbing representation of an individual and collective identity that finds little hope of redemption except in death" ("Going North" 162). By contrast, Penny Farfan, who understands Kevin as a "monstrous avatar of Canada's history as a settler-invader nation premised on violence," nevertheless sees the end of the play as revisionist and optimistic: "Thompson in effect replays the moment of contact not as brutal conquest but as a life-producing encounter between half-siblings of different races and, in doing so, she suggests the possibility of a new beginning through a revision of history" (48). The return of the repressed is the prominent motif in Robert Nunn's reading of Evangeline. Her "willingness to let herself be invaded by the uncanny brother/stranger," he argues, "comes out of her lifelong sense of being strange to herself, for she is and is not Indian" ("Strangers" 30–1). The sense of her life that Evangeline expresses to her neighbour, Joe, conveys a headlong, uncontrollable descent: "In a runaway sled down a mountain of ice, faster and faster and if I tip over I will break my neck and bones for sure but if I keep going, what's at the bottom, what's at the bottom Joe is the lake" (*Late 20th Century Plays* 380). With the Northern Lights on display and the sound of wolves in the forest air, the viewer or reader must decide if the heavily pregnant Evangeline's singing of a Cree lullaby as she lifts the dying, almost blind Kevin over her shoulder before she herself lies down on the mossy ground constitutes a cold death or a revisionist beginning. In the ambiguous, opaque lyrics of the resurrected Annie's closing song, "I move out of my dream and into this day as the fog it clears so slowly away to reveal ... to reveal ..." (401).

Just as Evangeline observes that "everyone wants to know their real family" (348), so too does Patsy in *Perfect Pie* (2000) labour to re-create a fast friendship of two girls, possibly to expiate her own sense of guilt. Patsy recalls that she and Marie "hung around together near Marmora, Ontario, like Siamese twins till you left town when you were fifteen or sixteen" (407). Patsy also knows from the first scene that Marie, ventriloquized as Francesca, an actor living in an urban high-rise for the rest of the play, is dead. "I know in my heart that you did not survive, Marie. So how is it? How is it that I see you there, out there, in the world?" (407). The play, which began as a monologue for Patsy, explores the lasting imprint of the event twenty years ago on the train tracks when both friends agreed to a suicide pact, but Patsy either reneged or was pushed aside by Marie as the train approached. Patsy's act of kneading the pastry for her pie is the accompaniment to or impetus for the series of revelations about their friendship, the rape and abuse of Marie by the boys at the party, and Patsy's sense of loss. She admits in the closing scene that her conversation with Francesca is "like you were a dream" (490) punctuated by the kneading of the dough. "I think I'm like making you. I like ... form you; right in front of my eyes, right here at my kitchen table into flesh" (490).

Thompson's themes of ambiguous subjectivity and the haunting power of the past propel *Perfect Pie*. Craig Walker pursues the implications of Francesca's presence being a dream. "Is Patsy's relationship to Marie more than a memory; is it a dark place of awful power hidden within herself that she revisits privately to reacquaint herself with the thrilling terrifying experience of being open to the 'unimaginable world'?" (406). Drawing connections between Patsy's description of her epileptic seizures (transferred from Marie) and Thompson's own experience of epilepsy, Jenn Stephenson sees Patsy as creating herself as an artist and a storyteller, as "a metafictional autobiographer, a playwright within the play, whose subject is her own life with a blank hole at its centre" (62). Although Marlene Moser presents epilepsy as a motif of the "dissolution of self" (93) in the play, she is one of the few readers who maintains the reality of Marie/Francesca, who, as a character, seeks subjectivity to the same degree and in the same way as Patsy does.

Thompson's characters, ambivalent yet recognizable, and environments, both natural and surreal, fashion ethical encounters for her viewing and reading audiences. In paying tribute to "the beautiful people who inspired" *The Crackwalker,* she also neatly pinpoints the continuing resonance of her whole gallery of subjects: "looking at and engaging with those whose very existence illuminates our insularity, our selfishness and greed, and worst of all, our abject fear of the Crackwalker in all of us" (*"The Crackwalker* Thirty Years Later" vii).

Gale, Sears, Mojica, Cheechoo, Nolan, and Clements: Recording "Documemories"

The work of African and Indigenous Canadian women playwrights reinvents traditional material to reflect contemporary life. In addressing their plays, Ric Knowles's terminology of "documemory" is both suggestive and compelling. His introduction to Djanet Sears's *Afrika, Solo* (2011 edition) glosses it as "the performing body as archive serv[ing] up embodied traces – scars – as documents of both individual and cultural memory"; his concept of "embodied cultural memory ... replac[ing] misrepresentation – or indeed lack of representation – in dominant Canadian (or Québec) historiography" (iv) supplies an apt introduction to the largely autobiographical plays of African Canadian and Indigenous women. Autobiography, in their plays, is both one woman's story and an emblem of the life of a community. The anthologizing efforts of Monique Mojica and Ric Knowles in *Staging Coyote's Dream* (2005)[4] and Daniel David Moses in *The Exile Book of Native Canadian Fiction and Drama* (2010) have made this drama more readily available.

The plays of Lorena Gale (1958–2009), Djanet Sears (b. 1959), Shirley Cheechoo (b. 1952), Monique Mojica (b. 1954), Yvette Nolan (b. 1961), and Marie Clements (b. 1962) represent either their own or other women's stories. The tone of their documemories is searing – in their depiction of violence, abuse, and neglect and in their indictment of the culture that condones or connives at this mistreatment. Anger about the consequences of what Djanet Sears identifies as "internalized racism" propels much of this work; as Sears observes about her childhood in England and Canada,

Although the ways in which each of us experiences internalized oppression are unique, no black person in this society has been spared. Internalized racism has been the primary means by which we have been forced to perpetuate and "agree" to our own oppression. (Afrika Solo, 1990 edition, Afterword 95)

Another shared element is a grievance for a lost, appropriated, or unknown homeland. The character Old Man in Margo Kane's *Confessions of an Indian Cowboy* (2001) puts it this way:

Our people been waitin for some kind of restitution from the government for a long time now. Their thievery of land and property that didn't really belong to them. They pushed us out. (II: 216)

Montreal-born actor and activist Gale, perhaps best known as the priestess Elosha in the TV series *Battlestar Galactica*, re-creates the history of the slave accused of setting fire to Montreal in 1734 in *Angélique* (2000) and reconstructs her own African-Canadian childhood in Montreal in *Je me souviens* (2001). Gale meshes timelines, intersecting past and present. *Angélique*, winner of the du Maurier National Playwriting Competition, depicts the domestic and sexual abuse of the Negro slave purchased and repeatedly raped by merchant François de Francheville, who has the "cocky confidence of a Donald Trump on a roll" (6). Although her mistress does not "know who set the fire" (64) and although the hubbub of the gossiping court is interrupted by the Reporter's voice announcing "dramatic new developments in the O.J. – I mean M.J. Angélique case" (69), the slave woman is hanged, strangled, and burnt at the stake. With dreams of her native Portuguese island of Madiere, Angélique closes the play with a powerful monologue invoking the "silent scream" of her brothers and sisters "arrested for their difference" and declaring "Someday, / some one will hear me / and believe / I didn't do it" (76). The performance essay *Je me souviens* recollects Outremont memories where "Anglo, franco and allophone children walk in / packs behind you, chanting: 'niggerblack, / niggerblack, niggerblack,' on the way to school" (38). When she returns as an adult and finds that Montreal "sags / like baggy stockings / around / an old woman's ankles" (86), she clings to the identity of her subtitle, "an expatriate Anglophone Montréalaise Québécoise exiled in Canada."

Related issues of absence and dislocation inform the work of Djanet Sears. *Afrika, Solo* (1990), a quest for a homeland, traces the search of Janet from recollections of her childhood in England and freezing winters in Saskatoon to an eye-opening journey through West Africa and a return to Canada. The play builds on contrasts. The directives of her blonde, English, one-time girlfriend demean her body: "So, one: Your bum is way too big to be a movie star ... Two: Your lips look like – well, your lips are – way too thick ... Your hair. Yes, your hair ... Well it's just so ... so woolly" (28); they clash significantly with her own discoveries in African market places:

> *I began to notice that a lot of the women, well – had behinds that were just like mine – very well developed. Yeh, they had these voluptuously developed hips. And their lips, their lips were sensuous and full. And their hair – oh, you should have seen some of the coifs and the many intricate styles of head wraps. God, this is beautiful!* (63–4)

Rap, calypso, and traditional West African rhythms move the action along, from sounding "like a Brit from Saskatoon" (40) to a soulful gospel anthem about being African Canadian. In the process of discovering herself as "an African of the Americas" and changing her name to Djanet after an oasis town she visits, she leaves behind an African lover, without regret or bitterness, for the sake of telling "lots of people back home who need to hear about this place, who need to hear how important they are" (88). Sears has started to fulfil this commitment in her anthology *Testifyin': Contemporary African Canadian Drama* (2000). A comparable quest for a transnational space is evident in the plays of Asian Canadian women writers, as explored in the studies of Eleanor Ty.[5] Among the strongest parallels with Sears are Mina Shum's autobiographical short film *Double Happiness* (1994), about a Chinese Canadian artist's struggle to explore her craft and face the demands of her family, and Elyne Quan's *Surface Tension* (1998), a one-act monologue in which she gradually re-dresses herself in her grandmother's outfit and finds that it is a perfect fit. "The piece works by exposing the gaps between her obviously Chinese physical appearance and her just as obvious enculturation as an English Canadian" (Demers and Kerr, "Introduction" 3).

The intersection of race and sex is much more complicated and fractured in Sears's Governor General's Award-winning *Harlem Duet* (1997). "A rhapsodic blues tragedy" (14) with three different time frames – 1860, 1928, and present day – *Harlem Duet* revisits *Othello* before Desdemona. It centres on the most prominent time of the break-up of the nine-year marriage of Billie, who is writing her Master's thesis, and Othello, who teaches at Columbia. Billie sees Othello, "so tired of this race shit," as "the mythical Negro" (55), while he accuses her of promoting "the Black feminist position" (70). The situation between them is at an impasse.

Othello: The message is, Black men are poor fathers, poor partners, or both. Black women wear the pants that Black men were prevented from wearing.

Billie: Which women? I mean, which women are you referring to? Your mother worked all her life. My mother worked, her mother worked ... I don't support you? My mother's death paid your tuition, not mine. (70–1)

Before Othello's marriage to Mona, Billie attempts revenge with her own version of the Shakespearean handkerchief business: "I've concocted something ... A potion ... A plague of sorts ... I've soaked the handkerchief ... Soaked it in certain tinctures ... Anyone who touches it – the handkerchief, will come to harm" (102). In the closing scene with Billie in a psychiatric ward being visited by her long-absent, alcoholic father named Canada, she struggles to express her emotions about Othello: "I hate him – I love him so – I forgive him now" (116).

For Kuna and Rappahannock playwright Monique Mojica, *Princess Pocahontas and the Blue Spots* (1991) is an opportunity to dramatize the historic realities and critique the stereotypes of First Nations and mixed-blood women. With two actors assuming many roles in the thirteen transformations of the play and the Blue Spots as "the 'doo-wop' girls who back up Princess Pocahontas and her band" (15), *Princess Pocahontas* combines anger with a call to arms to "Word Warriors" (59). The bitter humour of demeaning images fuels the Blue Spots' accompaniment of Princess Buttered-on-Both-Sides singing "à la Marilyn Monroe" about her happy enslavement to Captain Whiteman: "Oh Captain Whiteman, I'm your buckskin clad dessert" (26). As important as the time travel and the revisioning of conventional accounts is Mojica's emphasis on singularity. As Contemporary Woman #1 instructs, "I don't want to be mistaken for a crowd of Native women. I am one. And I do not represent all Native women. I am one" (59).

James Bay Cree playwright Shirley Cheechoo's autobiographical, one-woman play *Path with No Moccasins* (1993) re-creates the pain and loneliness of residential schooling. The torment includes the abuse of a teacher who "has bad breath that stinks worse than the dogs on the reserve" (11) and letters like this one, likely unposted, to her mother:

> *Dear Mrs. Lillian Cheechoo, in the bush, Ontario! I am writing this letter to prove that I can write now. You can come and get me now, mom. I can even speak English like the older kids ... So are you gonna come? Your friend, Shirley Cheechoo.* (13)

While the loss and pain she relates are wrenching, the way "to move towards ... healing without fear and into the new light" (48) is signalled by this declaration: "Every time I let go of something in my past, things seems clearer" (46).

For Algonquin/Irish Yvette Nolan and Métis Marie Clements, play writing is an opportunity to reclaim and rescue a past, not to let it go. Nolan's *Annie Mae's Movement* (1999, revised 2006) re-creates the final months of life of Mi'kmaq activist Anna Mae Pictou Aquash, who joined the American Indian Movement and was shot to death near Wanblee on the Pine Ridge Reservation in South Dakota in 1975. The "movement" of the title has a double meaning, recording Annie Mae's move away from her family in Shubenacadie, Nova Scotia, and the principles or causes she espouses with the Boston Indian Council and AIM. What separates this play from documentary treatment, as in the "positive energy" (Demers 309) of Mi'kmaq filmmaker Catherine Martin's *The Spirit of Annie Mae* (2002), is the haunting, ominous presence of the windigo figure Rugaru, "part man, part creature, big and hairy, obviously not of this world" (II: 139–40). Annie Mae faces suspicion, criticism, and ultimately betrayal within AIM. Lambasted for not accepting the scholarship to Brandeis – "You coulda been a lawyer, not some small potato survival school teacher" (II: 145) – and riddled with guilt about leaving her two daughters behind, she is under surveillance within and outside the Movement, itself infiltrated by FBI agents. Despite the pervasive sense of menace, there is also a tragic defiance. As she is being raped and before she is shot, Annie Mae declares her identity and genealogy: "My name is Anna Mae Pictou Aquash, Micmac Nation from Shubenacadie, Nova Scotia. My mother is Mary Ellen Pictou, my father is Francis Thomas Levi ... You cannot kill us all. You can kill me, but my sister lives, my daughters live ... You can kill me, but you cannot kill us all" (II: 169–70).

Relating the horrific murders of women in Vancouver's Downtown Eastside from 1965 to 1987, Clements's *The Unnatural and Accidental Women* (2000) illustrates how drama can be a forceful pastiche combining poetry, music, film clips, and newspaper reports as instruments of enlightenment and weapons of social justice. Clements repeats with sardonic intensity the coroner's verdict on these multiple murders as "unnatural and accidental" (I: 367). She also creates a community of caring and attentiveness linking these silenced women. One victim, the English immigrant Rose, "a switchboard operator with a soft heart but thorny" (I: 366), who on physical and emotional levels strives to make connections, explains her role: "As if every time I connected someone I had found an answer" (I: 423). The play itself finds an answer when, after the women have succeeded in slitting the culprit's throat, there is a "beautiful banquet," a celebratory "First Supper" involving "the long line of WOMEN as they take their trapping clothes off, their long hair spilling everywhere" (I: 459).

The letter of the young Shirley Cheechoo, the final words of Annie Mae Aquash, and Clements's depiction of a First Supper are all searches for collectivity capable of intervening in battles and producing galvanizing moments. They share some of the features

Jill Dolan labels as "utopian performatives," which "move and stir us because they're inevitably specific and local products of a here and now that passes into there and then even as we experience them" (169). In such gestures, as she observes, "hope adheres ... communitas happens ... the not-yet-conscious is glimpsed and felt and strained toward" (170).

MacLeod, Moscovitch, and Chatterton: Exploring Impasses

The strain of communication, which precedes and undergirds any sense of community, is a central concern in the recent plays of Joan MacLeod (b. 1954), Hannah Moscovitch (b. 1978), and Anna Chatterton (b. 1975). Although their careers position them in different generations of playwrights, what unites them is equally remarkable. MacLeod's *The Valley* (2014) and Moscovitch's *Infinity* (2017) rely on dramaturgic additives like an enacted Healing Circle bringing together the principals in *The Valley* and interludes of solo violin composed by Njo Kong Kie for *Infinity*. The primary device in Chatterton's *Within the Glass* (2017) is the increasingly heated conversational see-saw between genetic and gestational couples about the parenthood of an *in vitro* fertilization foetus. These devices significantly penetrate the impasses of communication between children and parents and wife and husband in all three plays, illustrating the specific troubles separating police service and mental illness in *The Valley*, the pursuits of physics and music in *Infinity*, and the uncertain future of an IVF child in *Within the Glass*. With different dialetics and interventions, these plays exhibit sober ways of dealing with complexity and vehement disagreement.

With a writing practice that always investigates conceptual and cultural dilemmas, MacLeod's plays have garnered many honours, including the Siminovitch Prize and the Chalmers Award. *Amigo's Blue Guitar* (1990), winner of the Governor General's Award, explores the family disruptions arising when a university student brings home a Salvadoran refugee with whom his sister falls in love. Family dynamics are also at the centre of

The Valley, set in Vancouver, with two intersecting – more accurately, colliding – units: a divorced mother helicoptering around her eighteen-year-old aspiring-novelist son who has dropped out of first-year university and a stressed policemen not listening to his wife's battle with postpartum depression. An unwillingness to listen characterizes all encounters. Initially disappointed with her son's enrolment in the University of Calgary, his mother lives with her own fantasies: "If you went to U of T, I could finally finish my master's. We could get a place, a two-bedroom in a house in the Annex" (4). When her son returns home, her question "are you finding school exhausting?" yields this blunt reply: "I find YOU exhausting" (13) and eventually "Stop being a fucking cheerleader" (79). The policeman who complains about his wife's "hanging out in ... pyjamas all day" (8) and about his work dealing "with crazy people fighting with other crazy people" (35) refuses to recognize the signs of his wife's depression, as she charges, "For five months I cried every day and you just wanted to pretend it wasn't happening" (47). A mistaken identity at the Skytrain station, resulting in the policeman's breaking the student's jaw, is the catalyst for the Healing Circle, which the policeman rejects as an idea the mother "dreamed up while doing yoga and talking to her shrink" (63). Ironically the policeman proves to be most in need.

An indicator of the international recognition of Hannah Moscovitch is the fact that, in 2016, she was the first Canadian playwright and first Canadian woman to be awarded the Donald Windham-Sandy M. Campbell Literary Prize adjudicated by Yale University. Unlikely encounters propel action in Moscovitch's plays – whether in the meeting of the son of a Nazi criminal who grew up in Paraguay and the daughter of an Auschwitz survivor in *East of Berlin* (2009) or in the chance connection of two graduate students, one in theoretical physics and the other in music composition, at a party, in *Infinity*. This basis of the drama is bookended by the funeral arrangements and final realizations of the couple's twenty-something daughter, preparing to do a PhD in mathematics, years later. Although the physicist is convinced that "musicians know about time ... that it doesn't exist" (11), the violinist allows that she "think[s] of music as a sculpture in time" (14). The glimpses of their marriage as an ongoing battle for recognition are interleaved with confessions from their now-adult daughter that she is "fucked up ... about love" (7). While the physicist maintains that he "like[s] to work," convinced that his PhD did not go "far enough" (43), the final hospital image of the dying man presents him "listening to [his wife's] violin suite on his headphones" (80). The juxtapositions and insights in this play about time emerge from the daughter, whose father has lectured her since childhood that "time itself doesn't have substance, because it's ... fake" (57); as "slow and pensive" music plays, she declares:

> *some thing you thought was ... fake, some thing you didn't listen to, that's it, you thought had no meaning is ... real. It's real. It is ... real.* (95)

She calls attention to the elision of time and truth and the need for introspective moments to make sense of one's past.

The two couples in Chatterton's *Within the Glass* are intensely focused on the present, a clinic mix-up that implanted the fertilized egg in the wrong woman, and the future parenting of this foetus. With her current role in the Playwright's Unit of Theatre Aquarius in Hamilton and past experience as playwright-in-residence at Nightwood Theatre and the National Theatre School, Chatterton tackles powerful topics – from her one-woman performance of the chasms between a single mother and her rebellious fourteen-year-old daughter in *Quiver* (her MFA project completed under Judith Thompson's supervision in 2011) to this exploration of infertility. The exchanges probe the nature of the family, the debilitating effects of fertility treatments, and the competing notions of ownership and adoption of the child. Chatterton captures the tension within the couples in an almost-operatic back and forth quartet, where the gestational "father" (writer Scott) complains to his pregnant wife, "you never tell me anything, you make family decisions all on your own," and simultaneously the genetic "father" (banker Michael) accuses his wife, "you refuse to think positively, you are the most dark – most black – little rain cloud I have ever met" (39). Predictably this evening of thrusts and barbs ends in frustration, with the impersonal Gestational Carrier contract torn up and the barren wife Darrah intoning "it's not real, it was never real, it was a mistake" (95).

The wide emotional register of women playwrights in Canada engages audiences and readers in irresistible ways – from the pathos of unrealized dreams and adolescent loneliness to exposure of the nation's racist, xenophobic history. Their plays make genuine demands and provoke lasting questions. In their re-enactments of trauma and rebellion, their reclaiming of embodied cultural memories, and their revelation of searing divisions, they compel us to attend soberly to who we have been and who we are.

chapter six

Writing for Children

In the field of Canadian writing for children, women are major contributors. Many of the writers discussed elsewhere in this study have produced work for children. Among them are Margaret Atwood, Maria Campbell, Marian Engel, Joy Kogawa, Margaret Laurence, Gwendolyn MacEwen, P.K. Page, Anne Wilkinson, and Adele Wiseman. This overview, however, will foreground authors, often librarians and teachers, who write primarily for young readers in the genres of fiction, fantasy, and verse.

The timelines for this study also coincide with a period of tremendous growth in the creation and marketing of children's literature in Canada. Presses devoted to a young readership have been established in this period, such as Kids Can, Annick, Tundra, Tree Frog, Women's, and Groundwood, along with presses focused on Indigenous publications: Fifth House, Pemmican, and Theytus. Another indication of the recognition of writing for children is the proliferation of national and professional awards for excellence. They include the Governor General's Literary Award for Juvenile Literature (1950–9) and the Canada Council Children's Literature Prize (1975–86), which was superseded by the Governor General's Award for Children's Literature from 1987. Several prizes recognize illustration, particularly the Amelia Frances Howard-Gibbon Illustrator's Award (1971–) commemorating a nineteenth-century pioneer in the field, and the Elizabeth Mrazik-Cleaver Canadian Picture Book Award (1986–) honouring the brilliant lino-cut work of this author-illustrator. Critical guides to and theoretical analyses of this literature by Sheila Egoff and Judith Saltman (1990), Roderick McGillis (1996), Perry Nodelman (1996), and Raymond Jones and Jon Stott (2000), along with commentaries by the founding editors of *Canadian Children's Literature*, Elizabeth Waterston and John Sorfleet, place this burgeoning production in international circulation. In 2009, with an expanded mandate, *Canadian Children's Literature / Littérature canadienne pour la jeunesse* became *Jeunesse: Young People, Texts, Cultures*.

Children's literature, Elizabeth Waterston comments, "is rooted in a universe of books, stories, fables, myths and songs" in which "there is no such thing as 'the child' in stasis" (228, 231). The continuous and aggregative nature of this universe and its insights account for many of the connections between adults and children. Young and older readers, according to John Sorfleet, "share some of the same needs: the need for more independence from outside control, the need for self-sufficiency, the need to assert and prove one's right to respect, the need to develop – *and live by* – a set of ideals" (223). Writers of children's fiction – realistic, historical, and fantastical – pursue these aims through a variety of narrative voices and techniques.

Fiction about Children and Young Adults

Lyn Cook's *The Bells on Finland Street* (1950) focuses on the ambition of young Elin Lauka to become a figure skater. Because of her father's accident at the Sudbury nickel mine, it is unlikely that her Finnish immigrant family will have funds to pay for skating lessons. As the first children's librarian in Sudbury, Cook (1917–2003) relies on her expert knowledge of the community, street names, stores, and surrounding lakes along with traditional recipes, holiday customs, and dances to provide a fully realized place. Her narrative also reflects a prescient understanding of Canadianness, as the skating teacher explains:

> "*In Sudbury there are no longer New Canadians. Every one of you, whether you're English, Irish, Czechoslovakian, Hungarian, Polish, or Finnish, every*

one of you, no matter from what far-away country your people have come, is a citizen of Canada, with a fair right to take part in all our Dominion has to offer." (85)

In addition to the pulpit aspect of Mr Crane's talk, several ameliorating features characterize Cook's text. The arrival of Elin's grandfather, a prize-winning figure skater from Finland, who encourages her at the start of a festival, and the fact that the mining company covers the doctors' bills for Elin's father contribute to the positive outcome. Sheila Egoff and Judith Saltman critique that even the slag heaps are beautiful, while "immigrants are shown as accepting, grateful, uncomplaining, and hard-working" (39). By contrast, Miriam Richter concludes that the stress on inclusivity makes *The Bells on Finland Street*, which was reprinted as "a classic" by Scholastic in 1991 and by Fitzhenry and Whiteside in 2003, an important forerunner and "co-producer of the Canadian national narrative of multiculturalism" (195). With a similar appreciation of cultural traditions, Cook's *The Little Magic Fiddler* (1951) recounts the story of the renowned Winnipeg-born Ukrainian violinist Donna Grescoe (1927–2012).

Jean Little (b. 1932) continues the strains of positive realism and the family story, but her first novel, *Mine for Keeps* (1962), is entirely non-specific about place. The protagonist, Sal, a child with cerebral palsy, returns reluctantly to her family after five years in a special school. What is remarkable about the narrative is its insight into the fears and perceptions of this young girl. In her more than forty-four published works Little, who is legally blind, has not concentrated on disability, yet the understanding of cerebral palsy emerging from Little's own teaching of special-needs children is pertinent and informed. As Sal tells her sister, "'it makes you so you can't walk and maybe your hands don't work just right. It makes you kind of stiff'" (14). Sal's wanting to return to the comfort of school, "back to where she was known and safe and never left alone for a minute" (16), is the major challenge her loving parents face. The book's lack of a Canadian locale and its depiction of Sal's relatively swift reintegration in family life meant that it did not receive a strong critical endorsement. In the first edition of her study *The Republic of Childhood*, Egoff pointed to its "contrived situations, quick and easy solutions, and the intimation that problems of magnitude could be solved completely" (186–7). Although Little went on to capture a Governor General's Award in 1977 for another novel, *Mine for Keeps* appeared before the explosion of the popularity of Canadian children's literature. Catherine Carstairs and Sydney Kruth observe that Little "fits uneasily into narratives that stress how the 'new nationalism' of the 1970s and the concurrent growth of small presses produced, for the first time, a worthwhile body of children's literature in Canada" (343). Parental care and determination are at the heart of the story. "I'm sorry if you are not happy here," Sal's father remarks, "but you are a part of our family and we feel you belong with us" (60). Not through parental dictates but rather encouragement and affection, assisted by the gift of a pet and finding new outsider friends, Sal learns to overcome her fears. Little's acute awareness of the child's growing sense of comfort along with the knowledge of "having cerebral palsy" means that Sal almost forgets relying on braces; with telling detail Little narrates this remembering:

> *Only once in a blue moon, when something startled you and you jumped harder than anyone else and your pencil flew out of your hand, or when the tip of your crutch slipped in some wet leaves and you fell flat on your face unexpectedly, or when everybody was waiting for you and you couldn't get the knee-lock of your brace done up, did you remember.* (128)

The novel presents family reunion, but no miraculous cure for cerebral palsy. A Japanese translation in 1965, *Goodbye, My Crutch*, changes the ending significantly to show Sal standing without crutches or braces (Carstairs and Kruth 353). The transformations in Little's novels are slower-moving and more subtle. One of her most poignant representations of childhood grief and loss is the protagonist, Jeremy, in *Mama's Going to Buy You a Mockingbird* (1984), who finally comes to terms with his father's death from cancer by slipping a favoured keepsake gift from his father into his mother's Christmas stocking. The result is a release, "a more difficult joy than he had known other years ... so real, so wonderful, that he felt almost afraid" (212).

Realistic fiction extending across different time periods, geographical locations, and language traditions is a prominent feature of women's writing for children in Canada. What unites this work, as Sorfleet suggested, are the shared experiences of loss and separation and the search for identity and independence. In *The Wooden People* (1976) by Myra Paperny (b. 1932) the repeated moves of the Stein family under the rule of a haunted but demanding patriarch, in the 1920s through western Canada, highlight the need for entertainment and escape. Winner of the Canada Council Prize for Children's Literature, the novel shows how the private world of the puppet theatre affords Teddy Stein an artistic release and permits a reconciliation with his father. Paperny has returned to Jewish themes more recently in *The Greenies* (2005), recounting the stories of six young concentration camp survivors fostered in Vancouver families in the 1940s. With more emphasis on sprightliness, Bernice Thurman Hunter (1922–2002) presents another picture of Depression-era childhood in her Booky trilogy: *That Scatterbrain Booky* (1981), *With Love from Booky* (1983), and *As Ever, Booky* (1985). Barbara Smucker (1915–2003) reveals her background as a Mennonite and a librarian in *Underground to Canada* (1977). Drawing on the real-life work of abolitionists Levi Coffin, hailed as the president of the Underground Railroad, and Canadian-born Alexander Ross, her story chronicles the journey of two girls, Julilly and her friend Liza, to a fervently hoped-for freedom in Canada; separated from their parents and hunted by a malicious slave owner, the girls find confidence in their Christian faith. Even though "this great new land of freedom" is not welcoming, the song-like words of Julilly's mother convey strong determination.

> "Freedom isn't easy. We black folks can't read and we can't write and the white people in St. Catharines don't want us in their schools. We are poor, but we are buildin' us a church and buildin' us a school. We are poor, but none of us is slaves." (137–8)

In *The Tin-Lined Trunk* (1980) Mary Hamilton (1927–2014) also deals with separation and journey, here involving Barnardo children sent to Canada as agricultural labourers. Polly the match girl and her brother, Jack, are true street children, rescued by

Dr Barnardo, "a little round man with sideburns and a beaming face," who warns them to "turn away from evil companions and wicked places like [the] theatre" (10). They are rescued and shipped to two different families in Stratford, Ontario, where Polly undergoes less harsh treatment than her brother, who is bruised and limping. Although both Polly and Jack are eventually accepted in the same household as domestic help, this brief novel sanitizes the experience of nineteenth-century rural life and does not interrogate the Barnardo movement. As historian Joy Parr relates, "more British boys and girls were taken away from their native country before the age of knowledgeable consent during the decade before the First World War ... than at any other time" (11). Exposing "a darker side of evangelicalism," the fate of Barnardo children often involved loneliness, frostbite, and "limbs lost to binders as well as to drill presses" (Parr 12).

The realistic fiction of Jan Truss (b. 1925) and Monica Hughes (1925–2003), based firmly in contemporary settings, concentrates on the discovery of talents and champions. Serious issues of identity complicate the outlook of the female protagonists of Truss's *Jasmin* (1982) and Hughes's *My Name Is Paula Popowich!* (1983). Living in a ramshackle rural homestead in an Alberta village, failing in school, and seeing her science fair project ruined by one of her six younger siblings, Jasmin Marie Antoinette Stalke has no sense of connection. "She watched the moon and thought *hate, hate, hate*. No private place. Nothing to call her own" (6). With a dream of following the bravery of John Keats's "Meg Merrilees," she slips away from home, encountering – with remarkable assurance – a bear, a coyote, a moose, a doe and fawn, and a cougar, and creating in a coyote's cave her "own wilderness" (66). Only after a full day does her mother, absorbed in TV soap operas, notice her absence and that of her affectionate, mentally challenged brother. The differences between the obliviousness of her family and the attention of the artistic couple who, even against her will, rescue her, and between the domestic chaos she has known and the order she instals in her cave refuge lead to a form of salvation for Jasmin. Although the rescuing photographer informs her that "the young man who wrote about that wild, proud Meg ended coughing up blood, dying slowly in a small room in a big city" (165), he also commends her remarkable talent as a clay sculptor of wild animals. Despite the photographer's caution, the romantic pathway of art through connection with nature opens for the girl.

In her more than thirty-five books, Monica Hughes is probably most identified with science fiction, especially the futuristic Isis trilogy (*The Keeper of the Isis Light* [1980], *The Guardian of Isis* [1981], and *The Isis Pedlar* [1982]). However, the psychological realism of *My Name Is Paula Popowich!* merits particular attention. The move of Paula Herman, the first-person narrator, from Toronto to Edmonton with her mother releases a series of cultural discoveries: her unknown father's Ukrainian background, her paternal grandmother's affection, and her delight in the mixture of German and Ukrainian cultures that she embodies. The Gregorian calendar Christmas celebrations introduce Paula to food that is "not a bit Christmas-y" but rather made without "meat or animal fat, out of respect for the animals in the stable who were the first to see the newborn Child"; she learns the meaning of the ejaculations "Khrystos Royvsia" / "Christ is born" and "Slavim Yoho" / "Let us glorify Him" (134). A liturgical cycle propels the novel, as Paula prepares for Easter by decorating her own pysanka for her mother, with whom relations have been strained. Although her grandmother calls the design "crazy" and "not Ukrainian," Paula defends her work: "It's a crazy mixed-up pysanka – sort of like me" (148). Considering what she has learned about her dead father, she concedes about imperfect grown-ups, "if they could be okay without being perfect then so was I" (148).

One of the most accomplished contemporary fiction writers for children, Kit Pearson (b. 1947), always succeeds in creating complex, individual, and flawed characters, as the jury of the British Columbia Lieutenant Governor's Award for Literary Excellence concluded in their judgment of her twelve books and in awarding her this prize in 2014. Although she is known for the time-shift fantasy *A Handful of Time* (1987) and the ghost story *Awake and Dreaming* (1996), for which she won the Governor General's Award, "even in her fantasies," as Jones and Stott observe, "Pearson's novels are marked by a strong realism" (386). Moreover, it is a realism fuelled by an attachment to books and the imaginative life. In *Awake and Dreaming* a conversation takes place between the lonely, unhappy child Theo (Theodora), searching for a family where she would really belong, and the ghost of a dead children's writer; the ghost offers this counsel: "I think an open book symbolizes imagination. Only imagination will save people from their narrow, cramped expectations of life" (199). For children's-librarian-turned-writer Pearson, such a formula energizes all her work.

The first novel, *The Sky Is Falling* (1989), of her war evacuation trilogy, compiled as *The Guests of War* (1998), illustrates the issues of separation and the discovery of allies – what Anne Shirley would call kindred spirits – for two English children evacuated to Toronto during the bombardment of World War II. The focus in the first instalment is on ten-and-half-year-old Norah and her acute observations about "Aunt" Florence Ogilvie and herself as she and five-year-old Gavin settle into life in Canada. Although the geographical locations for 1940s Toronto are recognizable (Hart House where the children are initially billeted, the Ogilvie home in Rosedale), with some fictionalized locales (the McNair branch of the Toronto Public Library where Norah finds refuge when she skips school and Brackley Hall, a snooty, strict private school), the revelations of the text concern Norah. During the children's period at Hart House, where a large room "had been set aside as a library," Norah finds herself "sheltering in a story" and so lost in adventures "that whenever the meal gong sounded she looked around, startled, as if she'd been a long way away" (67–8). When the librarian relates the tale of the wandering orphans Ivanoushka and Alenoushka, Norah is "pulled into the story as if by a magnet and she *became* Alenoushka, trying to stop her little brother from drinking water from the hoofprints of animals, and desperate when he did and turned into a little lamb" (75). In the Ogilvie mansion Norah pities Mrs Ogilvie's plain, plump, nervous daughter, Mary, from whom Mrs Ogilvie "seemed to have sucked all the colour" (86). It is Mary who actually keeps Norah's bedwetting a secret. But the connection with Aunt Florence is much more problematic; not only does Florence dote on Gavin as a child version of her dead son, her attempts to remake Norah leave the girl wondering if "she just want[ed] Norah to look respectable" (184). As Norah realizes "she had *never* taken care" of Gavin and "was planning to leave him behind in a strange country with a foolish woman to ruin him" (200–1), Aunt Florence also apologizes for her harsh words, promising "I will never send you away, Norah. You're one of the family" (207).

The family fiction of Sarah Ellis (b. 1952) also concentrates on young girls' insights about often-misjudged parents or guardians and personal mistakes. Although the teenaged heroine of *The Baby Project* (1986) is upset to learn of her forty-one-year-old mother's pregnancy, Jessica must deal with a greater change when the baby dies of sudden infant death syndrome. Finding friends in the city is the central challenge for the shy girl from a country town in *Next-Door Neighbours* (1989). In *Pick-Up Sticks* (1991), for which Ellis won the Governor General's Award, thirteen-year-old Polly comes to appreciate the work of her single mother, while in *Out of the Blue* (1994) another teenager learns to accept the half-sister her mother had given up for adoption.

Set in Cook's Cove, Newfoundland, *Seven for a Secret* (2001) relates the eventful summer of 1960 that changes the lives of three fifteen-year-old girls. Narrator Melinda has a pitch-perfect voice, whether commenting about her artistic cousin Rebecca, "spun tight as an anchor in deep water" (83), or about the legal marrying age of twelve, which means "I was past my prime" (165). Although this first of three Cook's Cove books by Mary C. Sheppard (b. 1952) is fuelled by sprightly talk, it does not shy away from tragic circumstances. While the marriage of now-pregnant Melinda, who has just turned sixteen, is a scene of frugal celebration, it also suggests loss; her widowed mother "never again mentioned anything about me becoming a nurse ... never again spoke of school or scholarship or university" (174). The situation of the girls' friend, fifteen-year-old Lottie, who "couldn't fit into a wedding dress by the time her Jamie was convinced to do the right thing and marry her" (115), is tragic; she dies in labour. At the funeral for mother and baby, hungover Jamie ogles young mourners.

Other Times and Space of Fantasy

As with much young adult (YA) fiction, in the realm of fantasy amenable conclusions are not standard fare. Characters and places can be strange, frightening, often disconnected, and uncanny. Endings are not uniformly optimistic, and locales are less stable or recognizable. Along with the greater presence of hazards and mystery is the exploration of the psychological makeup of the human actors, usually reflecting some form of disaffection or alienation. All of these features have contributed to impressive steps into other times and space in Canadian fantasy writing.

Foremost in the ranks of fantasy writers for young adults is Ruth Nichols (b. 1948), whose *A Walk Out of the World* (1969) and *The Marrow of the World* (1972) literally established the genre in Canada. Her novels are not concerned with the machinery or explanation of moves from one time or place to another but rather with the psyche and insight of her young journeyers. After a bad day in *A Walk Out of the World,* brother and sister Tobit and Judith, "silent children who never played with anyone but each other" (7), leave behind their apartment home in "a new city and an ugly one" (8) and find themselves in a deep forest following "a light in the wood" (20) as a dwarf conducts them to the bower of the Great-Great-Grandmother who "has been asking for [them]" (28). The maternal yet mysterious Lady Iorwen, who recalls a similar sage in George MacDonald's Curdie books, aids in instructing them about the legitimate king, driven out more than 500 years ago by the usurper Hagérrak. Although Judith considers that they have been "gone now for more than a week," when in actuality it's an hour, and "wonders what their parents must be thinking," the shuttling back to their known world only convinces her that "she belonged HERE: she had known it from the instant that she and Tobit stepped into the wood" (64–5). The lure of this other world is intense. "Whenever she thought of the brown brick school, of the antiseptic corridors of the apartment house, or the grey street lit for a tawdry, commercial Christmas, she felt a recoil that she could not explain" (65). The final climactic confrontation between Hagérrak and Judith involves revelations for both. While Judith understands "the gift of the silver eyes" (178), Hagérrak's suicide is the result of his facing the wilderness of his "bitterness and hatred" (180) for having killed his friend. Despite Judith's protests about returning to her "world which is still frozen in the instant of [her] leaving," the Lady Iorwen insists on the children's going back with the acknowledgment that "each soul is alone and wandering" (187). For novelist Audrey Thomas the world of folklore percolates in this "fine romance" which has "captured the Celtic sense of bittersweet and beauty" ("Bittersweet and Beauty" 93).

The stress on the female protagonist, an adopted sister, Linda, is even more prominent in *The Marrow of the World*. "All my life," she declares, "I've wanted something magical to happen" (6). In the journey she undertakes with her brother, Philip, into the world of the beautiful witch Morgan and good King Kyril Tessarion, where the speech is not English, she falls "naturally into the idiom of the land" (29) because she is "native to it" (43). As the abandoned child of Morgan and a woodsman, Linda has a double nature: a "witch half" and the "other self, the eyes of a young girl" (118–19). Her witch half-sister Ygerna entrusts her with the mission to reclaim their mother's portion of the Marrow of the World, "the earth from which all life sprang" (56). Nichols's descriptions of movement and encounters are riveting in this novel. Linda's quest involves passage through a cage of ribs, which resembles a dinosaur skeleton. Linda's discovery of the Marrow is a celebration of indigo. "All the blue Linda had ever seen seemed concentrated there: the brilliance of the peacock, the kingfisher, the sapphire, the fire-opal" (136). The final confrontation with Ygerna, as dramatic as the closing encounter in *A Walk Out of the World*, involves Philip, who intervenes to save his sister by consuming the witch half-sister in flames. Unlike Judith, Linda realizes "I don't *belong* here" (164). With more sustaining hope than the Lady Iorwen's depiction of aloneness, King Kyril leaves both brother and sister with a connecting brand on their wrists, which is "both a sorrow and a blessing" (165).

For Janet Lunn (b. 1928) time shifts and border crossings are the chief devices of her best-known work, the fantasy *The Root Cellar* (1981) and the historical novel *The Hollow Tree* (1997). Through wrenching a rusted lock on an almost-hidden door and entering an abandoned cellar, the unhappy orphan, twelve-year-old Rose, meets Civil War-era companions. The difference of more than 100 years vanishes as she realizes "I've shifted" (40). In addition to friendly comfort and adventure, the battlefield accounts of Will, who ran away to fight for the Union, are sobering reminders of the carnage of war. As the smoke and dust settle, he relates, "the vultures – them big ugly turkey vultures – starts to wheel and circle around in the sky, looking for their dinners, and the smell of the dead is something awful" (193). *The Hollow Tree*, winner of the Governor General's Award, is the prequel to the earlier novel. Once again, a girl, fifteen-year-old Phoebe Olcott, is the main character in events set during the American Revolution. The central concern is not time travel but rather the problematic distinctions between rebel and Loyalist; New Hampshire-born Phoebe honours a responsibility to her cousin, hanged as a British spy, to deliver his coded message hidden in a hollow tree to the British fort. Her crossing of the river involves not only defending herself against charges of spying but also coming to terms with what loyalty or divided loyalties mean. She strives to understand both sides. Of her rebel father she says, "I do not feel dishonoured by his embracing that cause" (222). Having delivered Gideon's coded message and faced many dangers, both physical and emotional, Phoebe is no longer a creature of timorousness: "She belonged to herself now" (252).

Continuous questions of belonging and affiliation percolate through *False Face* (1987) by Welwyn Wilton Katz (b. 1948). Family divisions simmer beneath the surface for the two central characters, thirteen-year-old Laney McIntyre and her fourteen-year-old friend Tom Walsh; Laney's parents are bitterly divorced and Tom's White mother does not understand his desire to pursue the Mohawk heritage of his dead father through a return visit to Ohsweken, the reserve of the Six Nations of the Grand River where they had previously lived. Laney's discovery of a mask in a bog, "a piece of genuine wilderness, surprising to find in the middle of a large Canadian city like London" (9), initiates the plot and reflects the underlying tensions. The false face mask is the mysterious presence, generating and exposing hatreds, "bog-thick and smothering" (139) sickness, and near-death experiences. The division between Laney's parents, antiques dealer mother and archaeology professor father, is fierce. The unearthing of the mask as "the only proof that a Neutral tribe had False Face Societies" (140) startles her father as an archaeological discovery, while for her mother it could represent a $10,000 sale. Their sparring is intense, as the dealer confronts the professor: "Your job is to moulder away in the classroom! Who promoted you to public defender?" (140). The young protagonists undergo internal conflicts as well. While Tom struggles with revealing or keeping private his ability as a painter of the mask, admitting that the promise of a gallery show stirred pride that "made the Indian part of him ashamed" (63), the dilemma about the eventual placement of the mask makes him wonder if "maybe he simply wasn't Indian enough to solve it" (96). Laney's intervention to wrest the mask from her mother and thereby save her father signals the loss of her mother. "And now that love was gone, buried in the wooden gaze of an Iroquois mask" (148). Unlike the comforting solutions of more traditional and less eerie family stories, *False Face* concludes with a Manichean perception of a sharply divided world: "The black and red, the hating and the loving, the two savages, eternal halves struggling beneath civilized appearances" (149).

Illustrated Narratives

Many children come to be readers not initially through longer fiction or fantasies but through engaging picture texts. An important segment of writing for children is the work of author-illustrators and careful versifiers through their rhythmic appeal to younger readers, including pre-literate listeners. The combination of the aural and the visual took particular advantage of the explosion of presses catering to children in the seventies, a movement signalled, Egoff and Saltman remark, by bringing to an end "abruptly and thankfully" the stream of textbook anthologies "with the appearance of *The Wind Has Wings: Poems from Canada,* selected by Mary Alice Downie and Barbara Robertson" (293). This 1968 collection, now followed by *The New Wind Has Wings* (1984), features the captivating lino-cut work of Elizabeth Cleaver (1939–85).

Among the most consistent contributors to authorship and illustration for the young is Ann Blades (b. 1947), whose *Mary of Mile 18* (1971), winner of the Governor General's Award, set a standard for illustration and text; it was declared Book of the Year by the Canadian Association of Children's Librarians. Drawing on her experience as a teacher at the small Mennonite farming community of Mile 18, north of Fort St John, British Columbia, Blades offers a prose account of the wish of the eldest Fehr child, Mary, that "the next day will bring something special" (n.p.). What illuminates the deliberately plain style are the full-page watercolour illustrations accompanying each page of text. Blades captures the cobalt beauty of the February sky with the northern lights crackling; in a mixture of terra cotta, vermilion, auburn, and gamboge, she takes readers and viewers inside the humble Fehr home. Heated by a wood-fed barrel, without running water or electricity, the interior reveals a scene of the children reading. Always helping with the necessary chores, the Fehr children are dutiful and excited by the arrival in the next month of a new baby. Mary's finding a wolf cub, which her father calls "useless," results in the child's obedient but lonely two-mile trek to the neighbours' farm to see if they will shelter the pup. The illustration of Mary's journey through uncleared forest, hemmed in on both sides by the winter trunks of trees with her back to the viewer and a small glimpse of the fur of the pup she is cradling, is both a riveting display of her determination and a cause for readers' concern for her safety. The wolf pup's saving of the henhouse from the raids of a coyote means that he will earn his keep. In the final illustration of Mary in her bedroom warming the wolf-pup in her arms, she looks out over the patchwork quilt covering both of them, a feature integrating all the interior and exterior colours of the story.

In more than twenty titles Blades's work as an author and illustrator, including a second Governor General's Award for her illustration of Betty Waterton's *A Salmon for Simon* (1978), continues to be extraordinary. The pictures she supplies for Michael Macklem's and then Kit Pearson's retelling of "Jacques the Woodcutter" in *The*

Singing Basket (1990) portray an Old Quebec cut-stone homestead and hearth, with husband and wife Jacques and Finette warmly united and without the daily visits of the gourmandizing seigneur. Significantly, the tall trunks of bare winter trees surround and, in this instance, protect the home. Her illustrations for Sue Ann Alderson's verse in *Pond Seasons* (1997) attend delightfully to the cycle of growth above water with mallards, butterflies, frogs, herons, and others, and below water, beaver and turtle. Blades's most stunning double-page illustration accompanies Alderson's summer time "Snake Birth," in which "belly to earth" the snake gives birth to twenty new snakes. Various shades of green flood the full opening, as do the pale brown twisting, encircling new snakes, some still emerging and not yet with the mature double striations of their mother. Blades's text and illustrations for *Too Small* (2000) show her familiarity with family dynamics, as two boys move to a smaller house with their mother and continue to complain: "There's nowhere to tumble / and wrestle and fall." The wonderfully detailed illustrations of the stuff of domestic life, both full-page and medallion vignettes on the opposite page, show how, by following a wise old neighbour's advice and adding pets, relatives, and birthday sleepover guests, the mother makes the house "a bedlam," with the effect that the boys' refrain becomes: "There's just enough room. / We think it will do."

Phoebe Gilman (1940–2002) is an author-illustrator attuned to the imaginative zest of family life, embodied in the heroine of her five books, begun in 1985, about the irrepressible Jillian Jiggs. Along with friends Rachel and Peter, Jillian and her younger sister love to dress up and play as dragons, trees, bad guys, witches, monsters, and canaries, which leads her mother to sigh at the mess and Jillian to promise to be neat: "'Later. I promise. As soon as I'm through, / I'll clean up my room. I promise. I do'" (*Jillian Jiggs* 4). The strong primary colours and full detail of Gilman's drawings make the mayhem much more enjoyable than the somewhat pedestrian verse. In her seventh book, *Something from Nothing* (1992), the retelling of a Jewish folktale set in a shtetl, Gilman creates a heartwarming story on several levels: text, characters depicted, village community, and, at the foot of almost every page, the running tale of the family life of mice below the floorboards emulating the life above the boards. With soft earth tones, her paintings in oil and egg tempera show nineteenth-century costumes and views of nursery, bedroom, kitchen, tailor shop, street markets, and the Sabbath meal; they carry the viewer into the home and village with tremendous affection. Little Joseph eventually must give up grandfather's initial gift of "a wonderful blanket" (1) because his mother tells him "it's frazzled ... worn ... unsightly ... torn" (3). With the "snip, snip, snip" of tailor grandfather transforming it each time into another piece of clothing (jacket, vest, tie, button) until the button is lost, the responsibility falls to Joseph. The "scritch scratch, scratch scratch" of the child's pen provides "just enough material here to make a wonderful story" (27–8).

With more than fifty titles to her credit as author-illustrator or illustrator, Marie-Louise Gay (b. 1952), winner of three Governor General's Awards, may be best known today for the seven books in the Stella and Sam series, begun in 1999, about a sister as high-spirited as Jillian Jiggs, who is eager to read to and instruct her younger brother, Sam. Gay "fully realizes the interplay of reality and fantasy in the lives of young children" (Sibley 271). In *Rainy Day Magic* (1987), translated from *Magie d'un jour de pluie* (1986), Victor, the narrator, and his friend Joey are confined to the basement because Dad has a headache. In the dark basement they travel through a jungle on a tiger's back, slide down a snake, encounter a starfish, and are swallowed by a great whale. The full-colour, full-spread openings contain elements of reality and fantasy. A sly humour enlivens every page, especially the final one picturing Joey with a mauve starfish in her red hair, as Victor comments: "I tried not to giggle, / I tried not to stare / when Daddy said, 'Joey! / What's that in your hair?!'"

The comic is also central to the work of Barbara Nichol (b. 1956) for children, especially in her poetry collection *Biscuits in the Cupboard* (1997). The dogs, principal characters, can be as clumsy as the pups Biggins, Baggins, and Boggins, as proud as Little Nonnie, as tame as Marauder, as fearful as Toughie, and as self-possessed as Canadian Jim. The subject of her longest poem, "The Tale of Canadian Jim," is a performing high fence walker. "He learned how to walk down the fence, did our Jim. / He was limber, and nimble, and spry. / He perfected a twirl and a leap for the end / And invited the crowds to drop by" (24). Nichol's light-hearted, conversational tone keeps the account of growing crowds and diminishing returns, from a dollar to a penny, moving at a predictable rate of decline before Jim's final announcement: "Jim heard their new offer from up on the fence / And answered with something quite clever. / 'I *will* take your penny, and here's what you'll see. / For a penny I'll leave here forever!'" (25).

The combination of text and illustration in graphic novels for older readers shifts the focus from cheerful protection to yearning and isolation. The acclaimed graphic novels of Mariko Tamaki (b. 1975), illustrated by her cousin Jillian Tamaki (b. 1980), centre on adolescent girls learning about sexuality and family discord. Winner of the New York Times Book Review Best Illustrated Children's Book and the Ignatz Award for Outstanding Graphic Novel, *Skim* (2010), as narrated by sixteen-year-old Kimberly Keiko Cameron (a.k.a. Skim), relates the experiences of a girl interested in Wicca, wanting a black not a white cast for her broken arm, feeling "like there's a broken washing machine inside [her] chest" (44), and seeing her school as "a goldfish tank of stupid" (45). Continuing the black-and-white manga style, *This One Summer* (2014) relies on the narration of thirteen-year-old Rose who, during the regular beach vacation, tries to understand why her parents, anorexic mother and concilating father, are fighting. Her father's dismissive attempt to explain, "Don't worry about any of this stuff, okay? It's all just adult junk that doesn't mean anything" (105), offers no comfort.

Whether depicted in recognizable or eerie settings, the acts of discovering oneself motivate all women's writing for children. Suitable for the reader who is never static but always developing, their writing also gestures towards a variety of futures, from the comfort of family security to the boldness of individual choices.

chapter seven

Non-fiction

Memoirists and Autobiographers

In *Le pacte autobiographique* theorist Philippe Lejeune distinguishes between autobiography, "a retrospective account in prose made by a person of his or her own existence, stressing ... the history of his or her personality," and memoir, in which the author as witness tells "the story of the social and historical groups to which the author belongs."[1] Women's life-writing in Canada blends and disturbs such neat categorization. Life-writing that is most sophisticated and thoughtful about the problems of inscribing the self in literature is not strictly autobiographical at all. As Shirley Neuman argues, "instead it crosses and recrosses the borders between auto/biography and fiction in order to question static and holistic conceptions of the writing subject" ("Life-Writing" 333). A related concern for locating the individual in the conjunction of categories and the gaps between them lies behind Helen Buss's use of the metaphor of the map to comment on Canadian women's autobiography. "Map making also involves a complex of individual and practical skills that offer a dynamic metaphor ... joining the activities of self-knowledge and knowledge of the world" (9). Inflected with creative re-enactments of the past, as recollections filtered from a writer in the present must be, the sampling of women's memoirs to be considered here conveys a range of social structures, cultural expectations, and familial strictures all attempting to define and invariably delimit the female self. Their memoirs – composites and hybrids of creative recollection, autobiography, and fiction – are, in many ways, acts of resistance and redefinition.

Accounts of triumph over oppression are especially moving reading experiences. The two volumes of autobiography by Claire Martin (b. 1914), *La joue gauche / The Left Cheek* (1965) and *La joue droite / The Right Cheek* (1966), which were translated together in English as *In an Iron Glove* (1968), relate the physical and mental trauma of living with her six siblings under the brutal tyranny of their widower father. Her *nom de plume* adopted the name of her mother's family rather than her birth name, Montreuil. She refers to the grotesque antagonist only as "my father," never with a first name. Her mother's death, for which her father orders "a second-class funeral" as "good enough," closes the first volume; treating it as "just an ordinary day" (186), this astonishingly cruel paterfamilias assigns jobs to his children: "If one of us seemed a little absent, he acted as though he didn't see any good reason for that" (190). In the second volume, the taunts of this insolent man and the insensitivity of the nuns who are supposedly educating her lead to more penetrating analyses of their shortcomings. "At the root of my father's injustice lay a profound ignorance of a child's mental development ... If we were too patently innocent, his bad humour knew no bounds" (282). Despite his ceaseless ravings, "like a bear in a cage," the second volume closes with the statement of a survivor: "He went on talking, but nobody listened" (357).

Martin's foreword remarked on the peril of her status: "To be a child or a woman will always be like being destitute or coloured – a hazardous situation." *Une belle éducation* (2006 [*Such a Good Education* 2010]), France Théoret's (b. 1942) autobiographically inspired novel set two decades later than Martin's autobiography, in 1950s Quebec, shows how durable the hazardous legacy remained. For the fourteen-year-old narrator, Évelyne, a gifted child whose poor household is ruled by an overbearing father full of delusions about get-rich schemes, prospects for her future are servitude and silence. "The moral education I receive at school is limited to very simple precepts. Give of yourself, serve others, vanquish pride and rebelliousness, and obey the authorities – these are the foundations of the Christian personality" (29). Her desire to learn is a form of liberation, "access to another way of thinking" (43). Interested in recording her mother's story three decades later, Évelyne encounters only the woman's silence, anger, and refusal – testimony to the strictures of pre-Quiet Revolution Quebec. "There is neither a first word nor a last word about the enigma that is my mother" (143).

Parents may appear plausible and known to the child, but they can become baffling to the adult memoirist. "That free wild perilous world" re-created by Fredelle Bruser Maynard (1922–89) in her memoir of childhood in small-town Saskatchewan and Manitoba, *Raisins and Almonds* (1972), has a gentler, more harmonious tone than the works of Martin and Théoret. A petted child of Jewish parents, with mother as an accomplished homemaker and father an unsuccessful merchant, she recalls the sights and smells of her mother's expert baking: "meringues the color of toasted almonds, crumbly rich shortbreads, pillows of puff paste dusted with sugar, tortes layered with nut creams and Turkish delight" (19–20). The steady decline of her father's stores contrasts with her prowess in school, even to the point of being strapped for correcting the teacher. Prefaced by a Yiddish cradle song about Freidele who "will read the Torah when she is grown," the memoir has curiously few mentions of religious ceremony. Maynard declares herself "woman and Jew," not bound by gender stereotypes yet positioned as "an actor in the cosmic drama that included Abraham and Isaac, David and Solomon, and Daniel and Job" (184). Her marriage to a Gentile seems to be an unproblematic closing to this volume. However, the continuation or second instalment of her memoir, *The Tree of Life* (1988), admits tensions and omissions: the conflicted relationship with her sister, the dominance of her mother, and separation and divorce from Max. She acknowledges that, "If *Raisins and Almonds* is a kind of sundial book, *The Tree of Life* is chiaroscuro, less lyrical and less blithe" (xxi). Her academic husband's bouts of drunkenness dot this confessional memoir, along with her own need for control. She waited until graduation from Harvard with a PhD before marrying and mailed the diploma to her parents, "another trophy of the hunt" (235). Though judging herself "a most imperfect mother – overprotective, overambitious, overinvolved" (237), the woman who made her living not as an academic but as a writer and lecturer about child care maintains an ironic optimism. The memoir by her daughter, Joyce, *At Home in the World* (1998), supplies a coda of sorts. She recounts the raging battles of her parents in their New Hampshire home, her own enduring obsession with J.D. Salinger (with whom as an eighteen-year-old she lived for a year after dropping out of Yale), and her mother's dying in Toronto. Assessing her mother as "a larger-than-life character" (306), she admits, "I still can't let my mother go" (307).

The focus broadens from a single character to a collage of accounts of struggle against stereotype and prejudice in the multiple voices Myrna Kostash incorporates in her memoir of Ukrainian-Canadians in the west, *All of Baba's Children* (1977). Though initially she granted only "a passing friendly nod" to her own Ukrainian origin, this well-travelled, Toronto-based freelance writer, "beneficiary of higher education" with a solid middle-class background, journeyed back to Alberta, to Two Hills, east of Edmonton, where "no Kostash had ever lived" (7–8). She not only interviewed local residents for four months but ended up buying a farm and naming it "Tulova" in honour of the Galician village of her family's heritage. These interviews, often quoted verbatim, and her parents' reminiscences are threaded throughout Kostash's account, which refuses both romanticization and trivialization of her culture. Citing her father's experience settling into his "ramshackle teacherage" in Hamburg yet within a month feeling "as much at home among the unsophisticated rural folk as ... among [his] schoolmates" (106), she also records the more burdensome jobs of his contemporaries, including,

> For thirty-five dollars a month cutting brush. Seven in the morning to nine at night without lunch ... Building granaries for $1.75 a day. Waitressing for ten-cent tips and working at the switchboard and taking in laundry. (209)

Kostash itemizes what she carries on from Baba; discounting language, habit, satisfaction, and faith, which she claims she has lost, she clings to otherness. "As the alien, the bohunk, the second-class citizen, and the ethnic, she passed on to me the gift of consciousness of one who stands outside the hegemonistic centre, and sees where the real world ends and the phantasma of propaganda begins" (399). However, more than three decades later, *Prodigal Daughter* (2010), recounting Kostash's journey to Byzantium in search of knowledge of the martyred St Demetrius, testifies to the renewal or rebirth of that faith; as she realizes, "my outer life – my life as a student, a citizen, and a writer well-settled in the world – was now struggling to find its way home to an interior form, rendering all that 'otherness' as a passage to the somnolent spirit within, and there opening 'the eyes of the heart'" (149–50). This travelogue cum memoir closes, fittingly, in Edmonton in her childhood Orthodox church, St John's, where the "intimate" liturgy (275) of remembering the dead centres her on an otherwise bustling Saturday "to land here, repeating ancient gestures from another civilization" (276).

Discovering and speculating about the muffled, overlooked details of women's lives serve as a reflection, often an indictment, of a national imaginary. Anger and determination pulse through Maria Campbell's (b. 1940) autobiography, *Halfbreed* (1973), the account of her first three decades – from the recalled degradation of Road Allowance people in Prince Albert, Saskatchewan, through a period of drug and alcohol addiction and prostitution in Vancouver, to community activism on the Saddle Lake Reserve in Alberta. Religion, specifically Catholicism, and schooling have been sources of punishment. The young Maria admits being "spellbound by the scarlets and purples" at liturgies, with the nuns' black robes reminding her "of 'the Lady of Shalott' floating down the river" (31); reality was less fanciful, as she also remembers the nuns pushing her "into a small closet with no windows or light" and locking her in "for what seemed like hours" for speaking Cree (44). The "constant stream of teachers" at Reserve schools she characterizes as "everybody else's rejects": "some got the girls pregnant and had to leave; others were alcoholic" (48). The guiding spirit throughout the narrative is her great-grandmother, Cheechum, a niece of Gabriel Dumont (who "fought with Riel during the Rebellion" [15]). This matriarch's lessons are proven by experience: "My Cheechum used to tell me that when the government gives you something, they take all that you have in return – your pride, your dignity, all the things that make you a living soul" (137). Cheechum's spirit of resistance imbues the concluding sense of solidarity: "Change will come because this time we won't give up ... I have brothers and sisters, all over the country" (157).

The 1970s saw the appearance of several memoirs by Indigenous writers, mainly dealing with the losses of language in residential schools and the constant struggle for respect for Cree, Métis, and Inu cultures. *Geneish: An Indian Girlhood* (1973) by James Bay Cree Jane Willis (b. 1940) is an autobiographical account of Anglican residential schools in northern Quebec. *Bobbi Lee: Indian Rebel* (1975) by Salish-Métis Lee Maracle (b. 1950) details political oppression from Vancouver to Toronto, while *My Name Is Masak* (1976) by Inuvialuit Alice Masak French (1930–2013) identifies the loss of both a native language and a name in the Anglican Mission residential school in Aklavik. *Life among the Qallunaat* (1978) by Inuit Mini Aodla Freeman (b. 1936) focuses on her childhood in the north, on Cape Hope Island, and less on her years in the urban south among White people or southerners ("Qallunaat"). Her published text was initially held in the basement of Northern Affairs, for fear of disclosures about residential schools; in 2015 an enlarged text including original omissions, edited by Keavy Martin, Julie Rak, and Norma Dunning, was published by the University of Manitoba Press.

As well as journeying back through cultural and racial communities, non-fiction reveals the temperament of the alert, observant memoirist herself within a family structure affected invariably by death, secrets, or distance. Margaret Laurence's posthumously published memoir, *Dance on the Earth* (1989), traces the kind and the exacting relatives of her Manitoba upbringing, her marriage, the birth of her daughter in Somaliland and her son in the Gold Coast, the divorce, her period in England, and the rigours of her writing career. It also discloses what links all these aspects of her life, the essential aloneness of this sociable woman and her sense of the particular threat she represents as a gifted writer.

> *The fact that a woman has children and is a devoted artist in no way lessens her sexual and adult emotional needs ... Still, male writers seem to have a*

kind of glamour attached to them while the reverse is usually true of female writers. (170)

Novelist Aritha van Herk revisits and explores landscapes to restore visibility and presence, blending genres of travel writing, literary analysis, and memoir in her hybrid "geografictione," *Places Far from Ellesmere* (1990). She traces memory-maps in her autobiographical journey from Edberg to Edmonton and Calgary, and meditates on the "escape" (77) to Ellesmere Island. With a copy of *Anna Karenina* as a prompt to her reflections, she resolves: "You must live up to your fictions, all there is to it; you must help yourself achieve geografictiones of the soul, moments of erasure only available in fiction and on desert islands" (87). "This geografictione, this Ellesmere" inscribes a new act of reading, "not introverted and possessive but exploratory, the text a new body of self, the self a new reading of place" (113).

The sense of place and belonging is itself a shifting reality. Whether born in Canada or choosing to reside here, Canadian women memoirists continue to explore the twists and turns of family relationships and their place as daughters or granddaughters. With a background as an economist and federal civil servant, Denise Chong (b. 1953) marshals the intricacies of her complex family history in *The Concubine's Children* (1994), winner of the Edna Staebler Award for Creative Non-fiction and the City of Vancouver Book Award. With compassionate insight she relates the lives of her grandfather Chan Sam and his two wives, May-ying, indentured as a waitress in a Vancouver tea house, and Huangbo in Kwangtung. Uncovered through old letters and emotional conversations, this family saga climaxes with Chong's convincing her mother to take a three-week trip to China where she meets her Chinese siblings. This "Portrait of a Family Divided" is a saga to which, as Chong admits, she brings "another shading of truth" (xi); but what stays with the reader in this history of uniting a family as one is the resonant importance of conversations and memories linking immigrants to one another.

Another intertwined family story underlies Rachel Manley's (b. 1947) Governor General's Award-winning *Drumblair: Memories of a Jamaican Childhood* (1996). Born in England, raised in Jamaica, and living now in Toronto, this daughter of the former Prime Minister of Jamaica, Michael Manley, concentrates on her childhood when she was raised by her paternal grandparents, Norman, chief minister and then premier of the West Indian Federation, and Edna, acclaimed sculptor, in the family home, Drumblair. These much-loved grandparents, whom she calls Pardi and Mardi, are central figures in the two decades of memory, and so are the housekeeper, Miss Boyd; the laundress, Edith; and the gardener, Batiste. Miss Boyd was the youngest of a large family whose mother died early and who accepted the role of caregiver for her aging father as well as the reality of "irreversible spinsterhood"; "four feet ten inches tall" (4), this "Aunta" is an additional motherly counsel for young Rachel as well as a foster parent for Miss Boyd's sisters' children and their children in turn. "Like homing pigeons the elder sisters would come back with their broken lives, and finally their old age and senility, and she would continue to nurse and care for them all, counting them like rosary beads through her fingers as they returned" (6). Edith, whose "fate had settled stealthily around her, giving her the appearance of a complete island setting sail whenever she embarked on a movement," was following her "inner light": "'When dat great bugle blow, me will be ready!' she'd say" (10). Tall and lean Batiste, who spoke mainly to the plants, "became a mediator, a slow-roving diplomat between the plants and the people of Drumblair" (13). As a student Rachel, emboldened by the campus radicals' critique of her elite and powerful family, "kept alternating between affection and pain, acutely irritated by [her grandparents] for not seeing things in a way that would make the students forgive them" (397).

Attending to the forms and tropes of culture through which we report ourselves to ourselves, experts in the theory of life-writing have also written their own memoirs. *Memoirs from Away: A New Found Land Girlhood* (1999) by Helen M. Buss / Margaret Clarke, a combination of her married, academic name and her middle and birth names, deftly weaves together the experiences of a young girl in St John's more than four decades ago with the penetrating analysis and questions of an English professor. A particularly vivid episode involves eleven-year-old Margaret's molestation by a male neighbour for whom she was babysitting. She rehearses her conflicted feelings. His promise not to tell his wife co-opts his young victim, as the memoirist admits. "It is only at this moment, as I write this through its third revision – trying for less reticence – that I realize the way in which he concocted our complicity, the way he assumed his desire was also mine!" (141). She never discloses the abuse to her mother, not even when she is an adult and a mother herself. However, she does move from blaming to understanding her parents. "Like all of us, they believed that with the new knowledge we were gaining in the twentieth century, the old human illnesses would be left behind" (145). Buss's memories of abuse and silence recall Sylvia Fraser's amnesia-stalled account of familial maltreatment in *My Father's House: A Memoir of Incest and of Healing* (1987).

Transplanted Australian Jill Ker Conway (b. 1934) was already an astute reader of life-writing with her study *When Memory Speaks: Reflections on Autobiography* (1998) and a best-selling autobiographer of her journey from sheep station to university, *The Road from Coorain* (1989); she had recounted her graduate work, marriage to a Canadian, and academic life in North America in *True North* (1994), before she embarked on the third instalment, *A Woman's Education: The Road from Coorain Leads to Smith College* (2001). Here she traces her route from a vice-presidency at the University of Toronto to her decade-long tenure (1975–85) as the first woman president of Smith College. The subtlety of her shifts in tone from public to private presence is exceptional – exulting in the fanfare of her first Smith convocation and then turning to the quietness of her husband's bipolar disorder and the sadness of her mother's unfulfilled potential. The ritual of convocation prompts observations on her own personality and the patriarchal traditions of the academy. "In my generation, one was always conscious on such occasions of the male portraits on the walls, the almost exclusively male faculty, and the weight of pushing back against that tradition to assert a place for oneself" (58). The anxieties and sadness of her widowed mother, who "would have shone in university-level study," filter through and colour the work of this accomplished academic: "I vowed to honour her frustrated intellectual dreams by seeing to it that older women students were given serious opportunities, and Smith gave me the chance to fulfill the vow" (75).

The circuitry between domestic and public life, especially high-profile public life in politics, broadcasting, and entertainment, is evident in the autobiographies and memoirs of these women: Barbara Frum's (1937–92) *As It Happened* (1976) and her daughter's memoir, *Barbara Frum* (1996); Deborah Grey's (b. 1952) *Never Retreat, Never Explain, Never Apologize: My Life, My Politics* (2004); Adrienne Clarkson's (b. 1939) *Heart Matters* (2006); and Shania Twain's (b. 1965) *From This Moment On* (2011). The family memoirs of filmmaker Sarah Polley, *Stories We Tell* (2012); novelist Camilla Gibb, *This Is Happy* (2015); and spoken word performer Ivan Coyote, *Tomboy Survival Guide* (2016) enrich our understanding of the symbiosis of artistry and autobiography. So full of conversations and exchanges, these memoirs of recognizably public figures illustrate the cogency of Oliver Sacks's observation that "memory is dialogic and arises not only from direct experience but from the intercourse of many minds" (21).

Narrating the daily challenges of the live CBC Radio current-affairs program she hosted, "As It Happens," Frum characterizes herself as Barbara Antagonistes who did not believe in charming her guests. "Being liked has never struck me as a pre-condition for an effective interview" (163). Her interview with Manson family member Sandra Good offers "a glimpse of the mad space that [Lynette] Fromme [who had attempted to shoot U.S. President Gerald Ford] and Good were in," as this portion of the exchange clarifies:

> Miss Good, do you think any –
> **Listen, woman –**
> Pardon?
> **Don't probe me like that. You listen to what I'm saying and you tone your manner of questioning down or I'll hang up. Do you understand me?**
> Well, I'm prepared for your hanging up. You know, that's one of the risks.
> **You're prepared for what you want to hear. You're not going to get what you want to hear. Listen, put me on to somebody else. I don't like you.** (167)

The memoir of Linda Frum (b. 1963) provides more insights into the criticism her mother faced as a woman in television news.

After Barbara Frum's June 1969 interview with Jacqueline Susann, her guest remarked, "What was the interviewer trying to do? Such a baby. I could have ground her to hamburger – but I'm here only once – poor thing she has to go on with the show every day" (105). When Linda Frum herself reviews the tapes of "The Way It Is" from 1969, she notes her mother's placement on the panel: "seated at the end of the semi-circle, she is just barely squeezed into the frame, the only one shot in profile" and comments about this future recipient of honorary degrees and multiple ACTRA awards that, "it is both funny and frustrating to see that my mother scarcely gets in a word, is interrupted whenever she does speak, and is never called upon for an opinion" (106).

The tradition of high-profile elected or appointed women politicians penning memoirs was well established by the time Deborah Grey published hers. Member of Parliament for Niagara Falls and minister in Lester Pearson's cabinet, Judy (Julia Verlyn) LaMarsh (1924–80), who established the Royal Commission on the Status of Women, published *Memoirs of a Bird in a Gilded Cage* (1968), while the Honourable Kim Campbell, following her prime ministerial role from June to November 1993, released *Time and Chance: The Political Memoirs of Canada's First Woman Prime Minister* (1996). Taking her title's directives from Nellie McClung, Grey, the first Member of Parliament elected for the Reform Party, who retired undefeated in 2004, recounts her fifteen years in federal politics. Like those of her forerunners, Grey's text is without any hint of a hovering ghost writer; it is spiced with the characteristic bluntness associated with this former English teacher and loaded with expertly recalled encounters. As a teacher about to start a new school year, she initially and strenuously resisted the invitation to be a candidate in the Beaver River riding with this refusal: "I don't want to be labeled a politician. Those pot-lickers disappear to Ottawa and then you won't see them again until it's election time" (75). For this motorcycle-riding politician of strong Christian commitment, passages from the Bible become prophetic preludes, as in the decision, influenced by the second chapter of Habakkuk, to rely on billboard advertisements in her campaign in Edmonton North and admitting, "I pray for many people, but I do not think it wise to appear above anyone else or sound superior" (181). Former Governor General Adrienne Clarkson's memoir concentrates on family, immigrant, and emotional histories, with allusions to literature, especially to W.B. Yeats, and accounts of university years, telecasting for CBC, and head-of-state travel providing recollections. Her title refers both to the irregular heartbeat that resulted in emergency surgery for a pacemaker in 2005 and to the linkage of this event with the overall meaning of her existence: "My physical heart, and the way it won't behave, makes me understand irregular events" (xi). One of the most poignant of these irregular events in Clarkson's highly successful life is the sudden death of her prematurely born twin daughter Chloe. Reflecting on "the misunderstandings and bad feelings that happened around the divorce" (119) and her estrangement from her children with whom she is now joyously reunited, Clarkson speculates about what Chloe would have been like: "Would Chloe have become a lawyer? My daughters have seemed to prefer structured professions as opposed to my totally unstructured life" (118). *Heart Matters* is a paean to the kind of existence Canada has afforded her: "As an immigrant myself, I cannot imagine what my life would have been like if I had not come to Canada; the genetic material would have been the same, but I wouldn't have been me" (249).

Shania Twain shines light on the challenges of the "glamorous" world of an entertainer. With agonizing disclosures about the domestic abuse she witnessed as a child, her peripatetic upbringing (seventeen schools before high-school graduation), and the ultimate betrayal of her ex-husband's affair with her former best friend, *From This Moment On* leaves no doubt about the circumstances that have shaped her life and career as a singer-songwriter. Candour and insight are the hallmarks of her style as she relates the ways the "Twain gang – five children from two mothers and four fathers – was off chugging through life, a crazy, happy, sad, dysfunctional, destructive, loving, violent roller-coaster ride, to a head-on collision" (14). The directness of this autobiographer's voice, so immediate and "so vulnerable," admits the necessity of "allow[ing] ourselves to feel our doom," as she explains: "From the time I was a little girl, I would write my feelings out of me ...

Expressing my emotions in a song or poem really helped me to see things more clearly and to come to terms with them" (364).

Sarah Polley spent five years documenting family history in her NFB production *Stories We Tell*. Disclosing the secret of her own paternity, the film adroitly splices interviews with actor-turned insurance man Michael Polley, Montreal producer Harry Gulkin, and her siblings with genuine and re-created home movies in which a look-alike actor (Rebecca Jenkins) stands in for Polley's mother, Diane. Acknowledging life-shaping circumstances is also at the core of Camilla Gibb's memoir *This Is Happy*. "Stories," she observes, "are how we make sense of our lives" (xi). As well as providing the lived, experiential background of Gibb's anthropology research in Ethiopia, so central to her novel *Sweetness in the Belly*, the memoir reveals her reliance on drugs and psychotherapy for a time as a treatment for depression. Her recollections of study at Oxford stress "the brain-in-a-box alienation" (61) she felt. Gibb's decision to mix creative and academic writing, her marriage to a supportive partner, and her pregnancy at forty-one, all face a severe impasse when her partner informs her that she is not coming home. With tremendous, moving honesty Gibb faces the challenges of brokenness, "what may never be fixable," and finding "some way to endure" (217). Balancing emotional polarities, she admits the love she feels for her child "does not mitigate or murder the anger" (155). She recognizes, too, that her new independence is fully dependent on her estranged brother's carpentry skills and the intuitive care of her Filipina nanny, with whose family she creates new happiness.

LGBTQ2S+ advocate Ivan E. Coyote (b. 1969), who uses "they/them" pronouns, reflects on the complexities of gender, sexuality, and identity in their autobiographical stories *One in Every Crowd* (2012) as they conclude about their Yukon childhood "that for all those years, in all those photographs of that little tomboy, there was only one member of my family wondering about me. And that was me" (69). Admitting in *Tomboy Survival Guide* that they first read the words "baby butch out loud in 1992 in the back stacks of Little Sister's bookstore" (112), they also acknowledge the slow journey towards top surgery at the age of forty-four: "I try every day to not let it break my heart that it took me so long" (113).

Commentators on Our World

Canada has been a generative base for many women commentators on our world. Along with academic studies and the work of journalists, broadcasters, and activists, the selective sample from approximately the last two decades to be considered here shows women using their professional expertise for a variety of aims. Moving beyond the elusive public image of women in our cultural past, historian Charlotte Gray (b. 1948) brings to life the private worlds of Isabel Mackenzie King in *Mrs King* (1997) and Susanna Moodie and Catharine Parr Traill in *Sisters in the Wilderness* (1999) as well as the interleaved stories of women in the Klondike in *Gold Diggers* (2010). In *Paris 1919* (2002) Margaret MacMillan (b. 1943) dramatizes the resonant tensions at work during and following the six-month project of devising the Treaty of Versailles at the end of World War I. Sally Armstrong's (b. 1943) *Veiled Threat* (2002) traces the changing prospects for women in Afghanistan from the imposition of Taliban rule to the events following 11 September 2001; her reporting on the generation of change is even broader in *Ascent of Women* (2013). As a self-styled "Muslim Refusenik," Irshad Manji (b. 1968) showcases the critique and calls for reform in *The Trouble with Islam* (2003). *Dark Age Ahead* (2004) by long-time urban activist Jane Jacobs (1916–2006) offers sobering forecasts about family economics, university education, and spiralling downturns. Christie Blatchford (b. 1951) details the bewilderingly complex situation of the occupation of Douglas Creek Estates in Caledonia, Ontario, by Mohawk Warriors in *Helpless* (2010). In her role as CBC foreign correspondent related in *All We Leave Behind* (2017), Carol Off charts the journey of her Afghan interviewee and then friend who, along with his family, was forced to flee the death threats of tyrannical warlords before finding sanctuary in Canada.

As a contributing editor to *Saturday Night* and *Elm Street* magazines, Charlotte Gray gained national attention with her first book, *Mrs King* (1997), which won the Edna Staebler Award for Creative Non-fiction. She personalizes and humanizes the childhood, marriage, and immensely influential motherhood of Isabel Grace Mackenzie King, daughter of the leader of the 1837 rebellion in

Upper Canada, William Lyon Mackenzie, and mother of Canada's longest-serving prime minister, William Lyon Mackenzie King. Gray presents Isabel not just as "a strong-willed matriarch" who held her aging bachelor son "in such thrall" (326) but as "the only person who ever came close to understanding him" (365). With a total of nine biographies, always probing the internal life, Gray has won the prestigious Pierre Berton Award for historical writing. *Sisters in the Wilderness: The Lives of Susanna Moodie and Catharine Parr Traill* (1999) traces the vastly different fortunes of the published, accomplished Strickland sisters as emigrants to Upper Canada "dream[ing] of taking their places within the landed gentry ... where their own children would be assured of a future" (48). Her sympathies for a person ahead of his time are on display in *Reluctant Genius: The Passionate Life and Inventive Mind of Alexander Graham Bell* (2006). Of Bell's "extraordinary invention" of the hydrofoil, she observes that its "technology would be rediscovered half a century later" (413). A gifted anthologist and communicator of Canadian history, Gray has published *Canada: A Portrait in Letters, 1800–2000* (2003), *The Museum Called Canada: 25 Rooms of Wonder* (2004), and *The Promise of Canada: 150 Years – People and Ideas That Have Shaped Our Country* (2016).

Since 2007 warden of St Antony's College at the University of Oxford, where she is professor of history, Margaret MacMillan, formerly professor at Ryerson University and provost of Trinity College at the University of Toronto, is acknowledged for her richly textured studies. What intrigues MacMillan about the exceptional quality of curiosity is that it seems to reside most particularly with women – "not that women are naturally more curious than men, but because so often it has been more difficult for them to follow their own paths" (*History's People* 219). As in *Nixon in China* (2006) and *The War That Ended Peace* (2013), *Paris 1919* nimbly combines character analyses and political motivations; the study won the Samuel Johnson Prize, the United Kingdom's most prestigious award for non-fiction. She concentrates on the personalities of Georges Clemenceau, Prime Minister of France; Vittorio Orlando, Prime Minister of Italy; David Lloyd George (who is her great-grandfather), Prime Minister of Britain; and Woodrow

Wilson, President of the United States. Her narrative is full of scenic gems, such as the meeting between the young British diplomat Harold Nicolson and the writer Marcel Proust, described as "white, unshaven, grubby, slip-faced" and "completely fascinated by the details of the work" (150). Wilson remains one of the most puzzling figures. "What is one to make of a leader who drew on the most noble language of the Bible yet was so ruthless with those who crossed him?" (6). The attempt in February on Clemenceau's life by anarchist Eugène Cottin leads to this refusal of the death penalty by the French prime minister: "I can't see an old republican like me and also an opponent of the death penalty having a man executed for the crime of lèse-majesté"; yet the reduction of Cottin's prison sentence from ten to five years was, MacMillan observes, "much to Clemenceau's annoyance, after the left took up his cause" (151). Noting the activities of Mussolini and Hitler in this postwar era, MacMillan is also alert to such continuing ironies as the fact that the Majestic Hotel, which was the headquarters for the British delegation, became two decades later "the headquarters of another foreign delegation, this time the German army in occupation in Paris" (485). The spectre of the next World War informs her whole narrative. She is adamant that things could have been different "if Germany had been more thoroughly defeated" or "if the United States had been as powerful after the First World War as it was after the Second" (494).

Former editor-in-chief of *Homemakers* magazine and contributing editor to *Maclean's* and *Chatelaine*, journalist and human-rights activist Sally Armstrong brings her passionate interest in the futures of girls and women to her account of the positive shift over a period of five years in Afghanistan. *Veiled Threat* traces the dramatic contrasts between a Taliban period when, as an example of practice, the religious police of the "Department of Enforcement of the Right Islamic Way and Prevention of Evil" stopped a "young bride who still had her manicure from her wedding ceremony ... and cut off her fingertips" (4), and the announcement of the appointment of Dr Sima Samar in December 2001 as one of the country's deputy prime ministers and minister of women's affairs. Although *Ascent of Women* includes accounts of rape in Kenya, Malawi, and Ghana;

polygamous abuse in Bountiful, British Columbia; and entrenched violence against Indigenous women, Armstrong also registers signs of hope. "From Molly Melching, the woman who invited the religious leaders to help her group lead the way to ending female genital mutilation in Senegal, to Hangama Anwari, the human rights commissioner who enlisted the mullahs in Afghanistan to reform family law, to Cindy Blackstock, the Canadian advocate for Aboriginal women ...all these people are seeking changes that are not only good for women but for men too" (224–5).

Born in Uganda and raised and educated in British Columbia, Irshad Manji directs the Moral Courage Project in the Graduate School of Public Service at New York University and presides over an organization promoting critical thinking, Project Ijtihad, which she founded. *The Trouble with Islam* challenges popular readings of the Qur'an and reconsiders Muslim history. "The Koran is not transparently egalitarian for women" (39), she remarks, noting passages where the fear of disobedience legitimates beating, and calling for a responsible reading that comes "clean about the nasty side of the Koran, and how it informs terrorism" (47).[2] Her contrast between the seventy libraries of Cordoba during Islam's golden age (750–1250 CE) and the martyr's prospect is trenchant: "That's one for every virgin today's Muslim martyrs believe they're pledged" (57). Manji's hope resides in transformation from within and in the potential of Muslim women themselves: "Supporting female entrepreneurs would be goal number one of Operation Ijtihad, a campaign to kick start change in Islam" (175).

The outlook of Jane Jacobs, who has been in the activist trenches a lot longer and began her residency in Canada in the year of Manji's birth, is less sanguine. The Rockefeller Foundation inaugurated the Jane Jacobs Medal in 2007 to honour her principles of activism and urban design, while the Canadian Urban Institute launched the Jane Jacobs Lifetime Achievement Award in 2010. Her last book, *Dark Age Ahead,* is a gloomy prognostic about lost values. No stranger to hard times, she recalls with admiration the struggles of her physician father in her native Scranton to make ends meet. "He told me one Saturday evening in 1936 that he had to earn $48 a day merely to pay for his office rent, his subscriptions to medical journals, office supplies, and the salary of his assisting nurse" (54). She is disheartened that the advent of "credentialism at the expense of education" has done little to address suburban sprawl and city traffic congestion (62–3). The gleam of hope tinged with warning that emerges in this book concerns cultural example and framework: "Any culture that jettisons the values that have given it competence, adaptability, and identity becomes weak and hollow" (176).

Journalist for the *Globe and Mail*, the *Toronto Star*, the *Toronto Sun*, and, since 2011, the *National Post*, Christie Blatchford has covered sports arenas, high-profile criminal cases, and military patrols in Afghanistan. Her time with the Canadian forces in Afghanistan's Kandahar Province led to *Fifteen Days: Stories of Bravery, Friendship, Life and Death from inside the New Canadian Army* (2007), for which she won the Governor General's Award for non-fiction. Her treatment of the Mohawk Warriors' occupation of Douglas Creek Estates in Caledonia is a controversial account of government inaction and buck-passing at many levels and Indigenous vandalism. As with all of Blatchford's books, the focus in *Helpless* is on the people. The riding's Conservative MPP, Toby Barrett, is dismayed that his letter warning of the seriousness of the situation in Haldimand-Norfolk, which includes the Six Nations Reserve of Ohsweken, sat undisturbed on the desks of Toronto media: "Nobody would listen to me. They thought it was just a little demonstration down here" (50). Longtime residents who had been neighbours, colleagues, and hockey parents are divided; the provincial government bulldozes a new home built on contested ground. Assessing the complex, distorted, and often bungled situation at Caledonia, Blatchford considers the consequences for journalistic responsibility as she weighs the outcome for terrorized, displaced former residents against the actions of the Six Nations band council.

A comparable assessment and interrogation of journalistic responsibility underlie Carol Off's *All We Leave Behind*. She acknowledges the consequences of having obtained an exclusive interview with former general Asad Aryubwal, for which she won awards and he faced death. Although for the CBC network the main aim was to feature "familiar and not foreign faces on the nightly news" so that "the public would be more engaged," she registers her own misgivings about this "dubious way to get people to care about the lives of others" (174). As the current host of *As It Happens*, Off supplies a bookend of sorts to Barbara Frum's memoir about inaugurating this weeknight radio show. Like Frum, Off struggles with the tensions between "personal impulses and professional codes" (185), ultimately deciding to return to Asad's side not "as a journalist" but "as a human being" (279). In crossing "the line that artificially separates a reporter from the story" (180), however, she also incriminates not only the warlords "prospering all over Afghanistan ... and killing those who opposed them" but the "Western countries, including Canada," who supported them (171).

Advisers and Observers

Another branch of journalism concerned with the broad human responsibility of health and well-being is writing about food. In advance of the steady stream of celebrity cooks today, Canadian women writers of cookbooks have enjoyed prodigiously loyal and large followings on radio and television, and in bookstores. Although this writing is customarily assigned to such categories as popular and non-elite, food is, as Margaret Visser reminds us in her *The Rituals of Dinner*, "the great necessity to which we all submit"; in fact, Visser argues, "it becomes an immensely versatile mythic prototype ... an art form, a medium for commercial exchange and social interaction, the source for an intricate panoply of distinguishing marks of class and nationhood" (2, 3). Without nostalgically invoking popular culture as a separate romanticized sphere or coralling cookbooks as "an elusive quarry" (Burke 65), my interest in this writing addresses both its sociological context and its necessary interimplication in all of our lives.

Borrowing, testing, and assembling recipes are exercises in creative collaboration. While the long-lived food writers sampled here, whose heyday occurred in the second half of the twentieth century, were all deeply indebted to relatives, neighbours, and church groups for securing their recipes, they were also independent, capable organizers of information and opportunity. Employed by newspapers that featured their regular columns or by such organizations as the Canadian National Exhibition (CNE), and often sponsored by flour and starch mills, drug and department stores, appliance companies, and pressure-cooker or microwave manufacturers, these shrewd businesswomen were usually prompted by personal circumstances to look after themselves and their families. Though not the first women to write about food, their careers overlap and extend beyond Elizabeth Driver's invaluable *Culinary Landmarks: A Bibliography of Canadian Cookbooks, 1825–1949*.

These self-starters were adept at turning challenges into advantages. Hamilton-based Mary Allen Moore (1903–78) wrote a daily cookery column for fifty years (1928–78) that appeared in twenty-two newspapers from St John's to Victoria. She started a canning company, Mary Miles Foods, and with the rationing of sugar during World War II experimented with recipes using syrup and honey. When the St Lawrence Starch Company offered her $1,200 if she "could come up with a booklet of recipes using Bee Hive Corn Syrup instead of sugar – inside of three weeks," she flew into "a cooking frenzy" and "met the deadline" (Driver 855), using the award as the down payment on the bungalow where, as a divorced mother, she lived for most of her life. According to her daughter, Moore "developed the first chocolate cake mix for Monarch Flour in the 1940s" (Driver 206); *The Mary Moore Cookbook* (1978), edited by her son, was published "days before she died" (Driver 220). Norma Bidwell (b. 1915) parlayed the experience of growing up in Moose Jaw in the company of excellent cooks and raising five children to help land her position as food editor for the *Hamilton Spectator*, a position she held for more than three decades (1951–85) until her retirement – and beyond. The *Spectator* published two of her cookbooks, *The Norma Bidwell Cookbook* (1993) and *The Best of Stoveline* (1994), and she produced her own retrospective glance in *Lifelines and Deadlines* (2002). Vancouver-based Mona Brun (1920–2013) moved from CBC Food Radio and Cuisine 30 to TV's Culinary Capers, sponsored by Woodward's Department Store. Selling more than 50,000 copies, *Cooking with Mona: The Original*

Woodward's Cookbook (1977) was reissued in 2003. With a degree in home economics from the University of Manitoba and further studies at the University of Minnesota, where she was employed by General Mills, Margo Oliver (1923–2010) returned to Canada as a food writer for the *Montreal Standard* and food editor for the widely circulated *Weekend Magazine* supplement; she wrote a total of eight books. As a divorced mother with two school-aged children to support, Jean Paré (b. 1927) opened a café in Vermilion, Alberta, where she quickly developed a reputation as a caterer. The first publication, *150 Delicious Squares*, of the Company's Coming Publishing Company, which she co-founded in 1981, led to the production of more than 200 cookbooks, with over 30 million copies sold by her retirement in 2011.

The three cookbook writers whose enduring popularity can be credited with creating media outlets for many who followed – Kate Aitken (1891–1971), Jehane Benoit (1904–87), and Edna Staebler (1906–2006) – were all strong proponents of home-made as opposed to pre-packaged ingredients and firm believers in personalizing their recipe narratives. "Mrs A.," as Aitken was known to her audiences at the CNE, where from 1938 to 1951 she was director of "Women's Activities," could properly be called a dynamo. Her multi-faceted experience of running a family farm in her native Beeton, Ontario, equipped her to serve as women's editor for the *Montreal Standard*, to do two live daily one-hour radio broadcasts on the CBC national network, and to supervise three restaurants. In addition to her *Kate Aitken's Canadian Cook Book* (1945), which appeared in annual reprints from 1965 to 1971 and is still available in the Classic Canadian Cookbook series, she wrote recipe pamphlets for the Ogilvie Flour Company, Canada Starch Limited, and Tamblyn drug stores, and, in retirement, two autobiographies, *Never a Day So Bright* (1956) and *Making Your Living Is Fun* (1959). The recipes in *Kate Aitken's Canadian Cook Book* are not only straightforward, relying on materials available in a well-stocked kitchen; she often appends a "Note to Brides." The conclusion of old-fashioned rice pudding advises, "Save the rice water; it's a grand starch for thin curtains, collars and cuffs" (115). For a lemon soufflé, "If the sides of the casserole are oiled, the soufflé slips as it rises; a soufflé can't be a clinging vine and be successful" (111). She expresses high hopes for the almond coffee ring: "this is a truly delicious roll, one on which you can build a reputation" (32). Aitken's practical directness is most in evidence with her comments about weight loss, "Eat and Keep Slim." Her regimen involves medical permission, the consumption of milk, and the total absence of dessert. The final directive is blunt and fully capitalized: "AND DON'T GO BACK TO NIBBLING, OR YOU'LL GAIN ALL YOU HAVE LOST" (264).

Graduate in food chemistry from the Sorbonne, author of thirty cookbooks, and a recognizable figure from appearances on CBC television, Madame Benoit is clearly the doyenne of Canadian cuisine. Always combining information and experiment with her great passion for food, her bold moves were avant-garde – in the 1930s opening a salad-bar restaurant and what became a very successful cooking academy, and in the 1970s embracing the new way of cooking of the microwave oven. The deluxe edition of the encyclopaedic *Madame Benoit's Library of Canadian Cooking* (1975), with combined French and English sales of more than 2 million, is a staple text for several reasons. Featuring recipes from every corner of the land and methods for the barbeque, pressure cooker, and canning bath, Benoit makes a strong case in her introduction, "The Food Tradition of a Country," for viewing recipes as a form of "culinary wit ... only a theme, which an intelligent cook can play each time with a variation" (15). As well as imparting the arithmetic of the kitchen and a glossary of culinary terms, she is concerned to contextualize cooking traditions: "The hunter, the trapper, the woman as well as the nun of Canada's Colonial period are responsible for many of the food traditions that still exist today" (13). Her examples include the Jesuits' introduction of apple and plum trees in the Georgian Bay district, their borrowing of the inclusion of wild fruits in bread from First Nations to produce "the first 'upside down cake,'" and their still at Sillery for "the first Canadian beer" (14). She argues convincingly that "by studying the cooking traditions of nations, we learn such things as the status of women in that particular society, the nutritional protection offered by the native diet as well as how such general characteristics as the degree of laziness, energy, aggressiveness, instability or industriousness have borne a direct relation to eating habits" (13).

In a total of eight books Edna Staebler conveyed her passion for food in swapped, invented, or Indigenous recipes by telling stories of their discovery and composition. A trusted contributor to *Maclean's*, *Chatelaine*, *Saturday Night*, the *Star Weekly*, and the *Reader's Digest*, she prefaced *Food That Really Schmecks: Mennonite Country Cooking* (1968) with a declaration of her familial but non-professional credentials: "I must warn you: I have absolutely no qualification for writing a cookbook except that (a) I love to eat, (b) my mother is a good cook and (c) I was born, brought up and well fed in Waterloo County, Ontario, where the combination of Pennsylvania Dutch-Mennonite, German, and modern cooking is distinctive and 'wonderful good'" (1). As Benoit borrowed from her grandmother, Staebler "borrowed [her] mother's and Bevvy's [Martin] little old black-covered notebooks with the handwriting faded and often obscured by splashes of butter or fat" (3). This University of Toronto-educated freelance writer, who had lived on an Old Order Mennonite farm and in a Hutterite colony in Alberta, a Nova Scotia Black orphanage, the Magdalen Islands, and a sword-fisherman's home in Cape Breton, is adept at supplying recipe narratives full of human interest. The engaging, almost light-hearted persona she conveys in the cookbooks is quite at odds with the more intimate narrative of her diaries, which she kept from the age of sixteen. Continually lacerating herself about not writing, she crystallizes this prime imperative in an entry on 6 January 1973:

> *I must never stop writing. I've done none, now for a very long time. And I hate myself for not doing it. It is a sort of denial of life, as if nothing is important enough, or exciting or interesting or beautiful enough to be recorded.* (Must Write 3)

Moreover, the self-possessed, independent cook she personifies is a figure who emerged after her divorce from an alcoholic husband in 1962 and her decision to make a winterized cottage her new home. As her journal relates, "I'd been married for twenty-eight years, had never lived alone, never paid household bills. At fifty-six I thought I was old and probably couldn't make it on my own. But I had to" (137).

Women writers as observers of their lives, real or imagined, who present their observations in the illustrated form of comics and graphic novels, grapple with a division similar to that experienced by Staebler between a public persona and a private reality. Their work also draws attention to the hybridity of the project of inscribing a life as it combines elements of autobiography and fiction. This divide is perhaps most strikingly realized in the career of comic writer Lynn Johnston (b. 1947), the creator of *For Better or For Worse*, which ran for twenty-nine years (1979–2008). Serialized in more than 2,000 dailies in twenty countries, the strip narrated the lives of the Patterson family, Elly and John and their children Michael, Elizabeth, and April. Housewife and homemaker Elly becomes a library volunteer and finally a bookstore owner, while her dentist husband runs his practice and plays with model trains. For Johnston, mother of a son and daughter and wife of a dentist, the strip was "a daily world of fantasy, which [she] slip[s] in and out of through invisible trap doors" (*The Lives behind the Lines* 1). Breakups happen in the Pattersons' snug middle-class neighbourhood, somewhere in southern Ontario, but the family remains sympathetic and secure. Though based on her own circumstances, the strip concealed as much as it revealed. Johnston's second divorce in 2007, her report about her abusive first marriage, and the surprise about her dentist husband's infidelity, all dissolved what she calls "a fantasy"; as she explained to journalist Anne Kingston, "I wanted to give [readers] a family behind the family in the strip that was together and communicated and could ... see each other through all the ups and downs."[3]

In contrast to Johnston's recognizable, if embellished and sentimentalized, aspects of family life stand the more confrontational and controversial strips and graphic novels by Montreal-based Julie Doucet (b. 1965). If Johnston's quotidian episodes closed with a learning nugget about acceptance or endurance or togetherness, Doucet's twelve segments of *Dirty Plotte* (*plotte* means "cunt"), for Drawn and Quarterly publishers from 1991 to 1998, deal with explicitly sexual escapades involving urban artists and friends. *My Most Secret Desire* (2006) illustrates with drawings and text "bad," "stupid" dreams about being mugged, giving birth to an animal, masturbating in space, and being a man.[4] Doucet works with collage, lino-cut, and exaggerated, often self-deprecatory drawings with no intent to glamorize or, apparently, fictionalize. Her diary of the year from November 2002 to November 2003, which appeared in English translation as *365 Days* (2007), features crowded and again unnumbered pages. Flitting between Montreal, Berlin, and Paris, she worries about the time it will take this book to be published: "what am I going to be living off in the meantime? from arts grants like half of the country? no thank you!! not full time!!!"[5] Unapologetically and entirely about the life and work of a contemporary woman graphic artist, the diary relates her difficulties in keeping the fridge stocked and being overheated in a room with letraset print, drinking beer and watching movies, and returning to Montreal to realize "nothing had changed at home ... god it's so quiet here!"

Diarist Doucet to the contrary, the breadth of women's non-fiction writing in Canada indicates a zesty, productive scene. Biographers and autobiographers excavate beneath the surface of appearance and received opinion. Through disrupting chronologies and relating personal stories, historians, ethnographers, activists, and journalists impart themselves into the complexity of their searches. Although cookbook writers occupy positions as culinary experts who have devised and succeeded with recipes, they can also, on occasion, admit to flops and foibles. For the creator of a syndicated comic strip about secure, if chaotic, family life to acknowledge its illusion demonstrates the true revelatory power of non-fiction.

Conclusion

Novelists, short-story writers, filmmakers, poets, songwriters, dramatists, and non-fiction writers realize the necessity, as Rinaldo Walcott has suggested, of thinking "contrapuntally within and against the nation."[1] The counterpoint of nation that emerges from the constant, productive, burgeoning energy of women writers in Canada in all genres over more than six decades reflects the hybridization of changing demographic, economic, linguistic, and community conditions. The enrichment of Canadian diversity through ever-growing immigrant and Indigenous populations plus the social media revolution influence women's writing that mirrors in distinctive ways the tensions of a palpable sense of national and intimate belonging. State-sponsored channels of recognition along with the growth of prizes, honours, and presses mean that "transnational and diasporic orientations ... co-exist with the struggle for full civic and cultural participation in local and national time-spaces and institutions" (Siemerling 360). Moreover, within and across genres, women writers' questioning, disruptive, feminist practice continues to be the hallmark of their vast array of work.

Locating a sense of belonging in time and space entails reflections on many homes and many pasts. As she announced at the 2013 Henry Kreisel Memorial Lecture, novelist Esi Edugyan (b. 1977) considers Canadian writing "post-post-colonial ... since a novel written from a 'minority' perspective ... has become the new dominant kind of narrative" (*Dreaming of Elsewhere* 7). This Canadian-born writer of Ghanaian parents incorporates different pasts in her work. The afterlife of the town of Amber Valley, Alberta, founded by free Black slaves, is the setting for *The Second Life of Samuel Tyne* (2004), while *Half-Blood Blues* (2011), winner of the Scotiabank Giller Prize, focuses on the struggles of an Afro-German jazz trumpeter, a Rhineland bastard, in Nazi Germany. Exploring "another kind of uprootedness, one in which we, as storytelling animals, are all complicit" (9), Edugyan concludes her lecture: "Dreaming of elsewhere is one of the ways we struggle with the challenge of what it means to be *here*, by which I mean at home, in ourselves" (32).

In fact, the roots and affinities of this project run deep, in tangled, interconnected ways. Its time-space has been necessarily flexible, looking back to work before mid-century and ahead to the sesquicentennial. Rather than charting a triumphalist or teleological march towards a present golden age, this slide-rule approach has aimed to show the continuing presence of the past filtered through variously adjusted lenses. While the backward glance has enabled the tracing of careers that expanded after 1950, as with the plays of Gwen Pharis Ringwood, the poetry of Dorothy Livesay, and the fiction of Gabrielle Roy, Ethel Wilson, and Anne Hébert, it has also led to observations about the pervasive trope of the position or displacement of the woman writer herself. From the struggles of Madge Macbeth's Naomi in a stagnant marriage (*Shackles*) to the fictionalized doppelgängers or spokespersons created by Alice Munro, Margaret Atwood, Audrey Thomas, Nicole Brossard, or Suzette Mayr in their daring to find space, medium, and language, women's depiction of emotional interiors has highlighted the challenge – at times, the perils – of writing. Moreover, through a range of temperaments, styles, and widely variable pacing, the work of relatively forgotten writers on both sides of the mid-century divide – from Irene Baird, Gwethalyn Graham, and Winifred Bambrick to Grace Irwin, Patricia Blondal, and Edna Jaques – also engages with the place of the woman writer.

Of equal importance is the second border, beyond 2017. Many continuities signal the move towards the end of the second decade of the twenty-first century, as asymmetric relationships and issues of belonging and estrangement remain prominent. Through philosophical supposition and ekphrastic narration poets Jan Zwicky and Stephanie Bolster sustain their probing of the ways we see and understand. Bolster's *A Page from the Wonders of Life on Earth* (2011) visits past and present gardens and zoos, including bombed examples in Kabul, Baghdad, and Dhaka, offering meditations on the landscape of contained things. Zwicky fashions the essays of *Alkibiades' Love* (2015) as a defence of lyric philosophy related to our grasp of music and metaphor. The historical ventriloquism of Kathleen Winter's protagonist in *Lost in September* (2017) illustrates and humanizes the aftermath of damage of the campaign in Afghanistan – an understanding shared through personal experience in the reporter's journey of CBC radio host Carol Off in *All We Leave Behind* (2017). Preserving the ferocity of her plays about sexual and environmental exploitation in *The Unnatural and Accidental Women* (2000) and *Burning Vision* (2003), Métis playwright Marie Clements's *Tombs of the Vanishing Indian* (2012) explores disappearance and displacement, focusing on three North American Indigenous sisters separated in different foster homes. Joan MacLeod's *The Valley* (2014) exposes our inept responses to mental illness. Shani Mootoo's fiction continues to examine the complexities of immigration and the fluidity of gender as her protagonist in *Moving Forward Sideways Like a Crab* (2014) shuttles between Toronto and Trinidad to connect with his estranged, transitioned parent. Family dysfunction is once again the revealing arena for Miriam Toews's characterization of two Mennonite sisters and the lure of suicide in *All My Puny Sorrows* (2014). Heather O'Neill returns to the Montreal underworld, in the radical entertainment scene of the 1930s, to follow the fortunes of two abandoned, immensely gifted orphans in *The Lonely Hearts Hotel* (2017), while both Winter's *Lost in September* and Barbara Gowdy's *Little Sister* (2017) enquire into the uncanniness of inhabiting another figure's body and life.

A longstanding feature of women's work is its appearance in many forms: multi-media art installations and films for Joyce Wieland; painting and poetry for P.K. Page; songwriting and painting for Joni Mitchell; and acting, filmmaking, and screenwriting for Sarah Polley. The worlds they represent can be real or imagined. Original screenplays and videos by Mina Shum and Vivek Shraya examine the lived experience of diasporic family life and transgendered existence. Documentaries by Alanis Obamsawin and Loretta Todd shine an informed light interrogating Indigenous conflicts. Filmmakers Lynne Stopkewich, Léa Pool, and Sarah Polley, adapting the work of women writers, enlarge the scope of fiction. Many topics intertwine and emerge in different genres, highlighting more and more the salient connections among artists and modes of expression. On the issue of land rights, consider the links joining the poetry of Louise Halfe and Karen Solie to the documentaries of Obamsawin and the songs of Tanya Tagaq and Leanne Simpson. On the topic of racism, the passages linking the plays of Sharon Pollock and Lorena Gale or the poetry of Dionne Brand and Marilyn Dumont suggest new ways of understanding. The subject of motherhood, responsibility, and reproductive ethics connects the fiction of Ann-Marie MacDonald, the YA novels of Mary Sheppard, and the graphic novels of Mariko Tamaki to the memoir of Camilla Gibb and the play by Anna Chatterton. The multi-project online platform Canadian Writing Research Collaboratory (CWRC), on which this study's bibliographic database resides (www.cwrc.ca/canwwrfrom1950), enables more lateral searches, which may be curiosity-driven, location- or date-specific, or key-word-centred, connecting *Women's Writing in Canada* with other projects.

Though not tracing an evolutionist path, this selective review of contemporary women's writing in Canada reveals the robustness of the field. Because the language on the page, the image on the screen, the sound on the album live in the reader/viewer/listener, a rich sampling of women's writing itself clarifies how their work leads to knowing and rethinking. In questioning the stereotypical image of Canada as a beacon of peace, order, and good government, in exposing the porous nature of social spaces, and in depicting multi-scaled, stratified, often exclusionary places, women's writing continues to challenge dominant mindsets. Before mid-century Dorothy Livesay was heralding "new prophets," and soon Anne Hébert was calling for day and light to discover and name, inhabit and possess life. The women writers of this more than six-decades span have gestured towards these futures, transforming Canadian cultural life in the process.

Timeline

1940s–1950s	Experiences and aftermath of World War II for Japanese Canadians in internment camps, and for Jews, European immigrants, and refugees
1945	End of World War II
1948	Louis Saint-Laurent (Liberal) replaces Mackenzie King as prime minister
1949–51	Work and report of the Royal Commission on National Development in the Arts, Letters and Sciences (the Massey Commission)
1950s	
1950–3	Korean War; UN forces assist South Korea in stopping the advance of North Korean communist troops; establishment of the Demilitarized Zone (DMZ)
1950–7	Margaret Laurence living in Africa: in Somalia (1950–2) and Ghana (1952–7)
1951	Amendment of Indian Act permits the Potlatch and the Sun Dance Founding of the National Ballet of Canada by Celia Franca Founding of Le Théâtre du Nouveau Monde in Montreal by Jean-Louis Roux and Jean Gascon

1952	Founding of CBC Television Vincent Massey appointed as first Canadian-born governor general Lester Pearson elected as first Canadian president of the UN General Assembly
1953	Founding of the National Library Founding of the Stratford Shakespeare Festival Opening of the Frederic Wood Theatre at the University of British Columbia Founding by Joy Coghill and Myra Benson of the Holiday Theatre in Vancouver, devoted to plays for children
1954	Establishment of the Crest Theatre and Canadian Players Distance Early Warning (DEW) line established across the Canadian north
1955	Founding of the Canadian branch of Actors' Equity Presidency of Irene Clarke at Clarke, Irwin Company, Ltd (1930–84), one of Canada's chief publishing houses
1956	Founding of the *Tamarack Review* Founding of the *Canadian Music Journal* Founding of the Canadian Theatre Centre with Mavor Moore as chairman Revolution in Hungary Suez Crisis
1957	Founding of the Canada Council Launch of McClelland and Stewart's New Canadian Library series Lester Pearson wins Nobel Peace Prize Elvis Presley bursts onto the rock 'n' roll scene John Diefenbaker (Conservative) becomes prime minister, ending a decade of Liberal rule Soviet Union launches Sputnik I
1958	Founding by Tom Hendry and John Hirsch of the Manitoba Theatre Centre Founding of the Canadian Opera Company in Toronto Founding of Miramichi Folksong Festival at Lord Beaverbrook Theatre, Newcastle, NB

1959	Establishment of the journal *Canadian Literature* Founding of Toronto Workshop Productions by George Luscombe St Lawrence Seaway opens Beaverbrook Art Gallery established in Fredericton, by Max Aitken, Lord Beaverbrook
1960s	
1960	Jean Lesage becomes premier of Quebec and inaugurates the Quiet Revolution
1960–3	Dorothy Livesay teaching in Zambia Opening of National Theatre School in Montreal
1961	Berlin Wall goes up
1962	Discovery by Francis Crick and James Watson of the molecular structure of nucleic acid and its significance for information transfer in living material (DNA) Opening of the Trans-Canada Highway Cuban Missile Crisis, escalation of the Cold War
1962–9	Opening of new theatres: Shaw Festival, Niagara-on-the-Lake (1962); Neptune, Halifax (1963); Vancouver Playhouse (1963); Arts Club, Vancouver (1964); Charlottetown Festival (1964); Citadel, Edmonton (1965); Globe, Regina (1966); Theatre Passe Muraille, Toronto (1969); Theatre Calgary (1969)
1963	Assassination of U.S. President John F. Kennedy
1964	The Beatles burst onto the North American scene
1964–6	Audrey Thomas in Ghana
1965	Adoption of the Maple Leaf flag in Canada Co-founding of literary avant-garde magazine *La Barre du jour* by Nicole Brossard in Montreal; became *La Nouvelle Barre du jour* (1977–90)
1966	Adoption of Medicare in Canada (universal access to most medical services)

1967	Canadian centennial celebrations: Expo 67, Montreal Start of Talonbooks, specializing in drama, in Vancouver Establishment of Tundra Books in Montreal by May Cutler, to create children's books as works of art
1968	Federal election. Liberals form the government, with Pierre Elliott Trudeau as prime minister Invasion of Czechoslovakia by Warsaw Pact forces; march of Soviet Army through Prague Assassinations of U.S. Senator Robert Kennedy and anti-racism and human-rights activist Reverend Martin Luther King, Jr
1969	U.S. manned space mission to the moon. Neil Armstrong walks on the moon Anti-Vietnam War protests and large-scale emigration of U.S. draft evaders to Canada Formation of Theatre New Brunswick by Walter Learning, Fredericton Opening of National Arts Centre, Ottawa
1970s	
1970	Invocation of the War Measures Act by Prime Minister Pierre Elliott Trudeau, following kidnapping of British trade commissioner James Cross and kidnapping and murder of Pierre Laporte, Quebec's minister of labour First Report of the Royal Commission on the Status of Women in Canada
1970–2	Establishment of new theatres in Toronto: Factory Theatre Lab (1970); Tarragon (1971); Toronto Free Theatre (1972)
1972	U.S. President Richard Nixon goes to China and meets with Chairman Mao Tse-tung Formation of Playwrights' Co-op in Toronto, under direction of writer/editor Daryl Sharp, to publish and distribute new Canadian plays in typescript at rate of two per week Founding of Alberta Theatre Projects by Douglas Riske and Lucille Wagner, in Canmore Opera House, Heritage Park, Canmore, specializing in plays on Canadian history

1973	Watergate hearings (wire-tapping scandal that brought about U.S. President Nixon's resignation)
	Founding of Kids Can Press in Toronto by small group of women, to produce Canadian books for Canadian children
1974	Establishment of Studio D for women's productions at the National Film Board
	Symons Report, *To Know Ourselves: Report of the Commission on Canadian Studies*
	Re-establishment of Press Gang Publishing (originally established 1970) by a feminist printing collective in Vancouver, as a women-only, anti-capitalist collective (bankruptcy declared 2002)
1975	Establishment of Annick Press in Toronto by Anne Millyard and Rick Wilks to produce books that address the world of the child; establishment of Les Éditions de la Pleine Lune by a feminist collective in Montreal, dedicated to the production of Québécois writers (directrice littéraire: Marie-Madeleine Raoult)
1976	Founding of NeWest Press in Edmonton and of Les Éditions du Remue-ménage by a collective in Montreal to mark International Women's Year (1975)
1977	Berger Commission Report, *Northern Frontier, Northern Homeland*
	Formation of Guild of Canadian Playwrights in Calgary, to improve working conditions for playwrights
1978	Establishment of Social Sciences and Humanities Research Council of Canada
	Establishment of Groundwood Books in Toronto by Patsy Aldana, dedicated to producing children's books in Canada, the United States, and Latin America
1979	Formation of Playwrights Canada, Inc., a non-profit arts service organization

1980s

1980	Announcement of chosen architects for National Gallery (Moshe Safdie) and Canadian Museum of Civilization (Douglas Cardinal)
	Incorporation of Ragweed Press, in Charlottetown, by Harry Baglole and Libby Oughton, to reflect Atlantic Canada's life and culture
	Founding of Longspoon Press, Department of English, University of Alberta
1982	Passing of the Constitution Act, patriating the constitution (signed by all provincial premiers except Quebec's René Lévesque), and of the Canadian Charter of Rights and Freedoms
	Amalgamation of Playwrights Canada and Guild of Canadian Playwrights to form Playwrights Union of Canada
1983	Establishment of the Centre for Women's Studies in Education (CWSE), at the University of Toronto, to advance interdisciplinary and multidisciplinary feminist research
1984	Assassination of Indira Gandhi, President of India
1985	Air India crash
1987	Negotiation of Meech Lake Accord by Prime Minister Brian Mulroney and the provincial premiers. The proposed amendments to the Constitution would recognize Quebec as a distinct society, increase provincial powers, and require provincial approval of the amending formula within three years
1988	Opening of the National Gallery, Sussex Drive, Ottawa
1989	Opening of the Museum of Civilization, Gatineau, Quebec

1990s

1990	Oka Crisis (armed stand-off between Mohawk Nation of Kanesatake protesting plans for a golf course on sacred burial ground and Quebec police and, eventually, the Canadian Army)

	Elijah Harper, Red Sucker Lake Chief and Manitoba MLA, refuses to support Meech Lake Accord because of non-involvement of Indigenous peoples in the process; Newfoundland Premier Clyde Wells refuses to present the accord to Newfoundland Legislative Assembly for approval, thus effectively killing the Meech Lake Accord
1990–1	Gulf War (to liberate Kuwait, which had been invaded by Iraq; decisive UN coalition victory)
1993	Signing of North American Free Trade Agreement (NAFTA); Canada, the United States, and Mexico create the world's largest free trade area
1996	British Columbia Supreme Court decision that Canada Customs agents had acted contrary to the Charter in seizing material bound for Little Sisters Book and Art Emporium, Vancouver
1997	Death of Diana, Princess of Wales
1999	Adrienne Clarkson becomes Governor General of Canada Launch of Aboriginal Television Network Establishment of Nunavut, "Our Land" (including most of the Arctic Archipelago, all the islands in Hudson Bay, James Bay, Ungava Bay, bordered by the North West Territories to the west, Manitoba to the south, with aquatic borders in Manitoba, Ontario, and Quebec; capital: Iqaluit)
2000s	
2001	9/11 terrorist attacks on World Trade Centre in New York City and the Pentagon in Washington, D.C. Signing of Nisga'a Treaty in British Columbia (guaranteeing open democratic, and accountable Nisga'a self-government and management of lands and resources) Incorporation of Playwrights Canada Press as Canada's oldest and largest exclusive publisher of drama titles
2002	Beginning of war in Afghanistan Renaming of Playwrights Union of Canada as Playwrights Guild of Canada

2003	U.S. invasion of Iraq and deposing of dictator Saddam Hussein
2003–6	Capture of Saddam Hussein by U.S. forces, subsequent trial for crimes against humanity (by the Iraq Special Tribunal), and execution
2004–6	Sponsorship scandal and appointment of Justice John Gomery to investigate misuse of federal funds to promote federalism in Quebec
2005	Same-sex marriage is legalized throughout Canada
2006	Swearing in of Prime Minister Stephen Harper's minority Conservative government Establishment of the Ad Hoc Coalition for Women's Equality and Human Rights as a response to actions taken by the Canadian government (including changes to the mandate of Status of Women in Canada and budget reductions affecting services for women)
2008	Federal government officially apologizes for the systematic abuses of Indigenous children in the residential school system General election results: Stephen Harper leads Canada's third – and the Conservatives' second – consecutive minority government Eva Aariak is selected as the new premier of Nunavut
2009	U.S. President Barack Obama makes his first foreign trip by visiting Canada
2010s	
2010	Government of Canada sends DART to Haiti to help in the aftermath of the earthquake The Truth and Reconciliation Commission begins hearings on residential school abuse Governor General Michaëlle Jean issues an apology to Rwanda for inaction during the 1994 Rwandan genocide

2011	Election results: Stephen Harper's Conservatives win a majority government, ending the longest period of minority government in Canadian history
	Osama bin Laden is killed in Pakistan by American military special operatives
	The Occupy Wall Street protest movement begins in New York
2012	Queen Elizabeth celebrates her Diamond Jubilee
	Barack Obama is elected to a second term as U.S. President
2013	Death of Nelson Mandela
	Alice Munro wins the Nobel Prize for Literature
2014	Malala Yousafzai becomes the youngest-ever person to be awarded the Nobel Peace Prize
2015	Same-sex marriage is legalized across the United States by the U.S. Supreme Court, ruling state bans as unconstitutional
	Election results: the Liberal party, led by Justin Trudeau, wins a majority in Parliament, following the longest election campaign since 1872
	The Truth and Reconciliation Commission issues its ninety-four "Calls to Action" (July) and the Final Report (December), *Honouring the Truth, Reconciling for the Future*
2016	The seventeen Sustainable Development Goals of the United Nations officially come into force
	The Government of Canada launches the National Inquiry into Missing and Murdered Indigenous Women and Girls
2017	Donald Trump is inaugurated as President of the United States
	Following the inauguration of Donald Trump, millions of people around the world participate in the Women's March, an international protest for human rights, women's rights, and more
	Canada celebrates its 150th anniversary of Confederation

Notes

Introduction: Imag(in)ing the National Terrain from the Mid-twentieth Century to the Sesquicentennial

1 Dorothy Livesay, Dorothy Livesay Fonds, Bruce Peel Special Collections Library, University of Alberta, 1. 40, Box 2, also reproduced in *Collected Poems*, 156; Wilson, *Hetty Dorval*, 11; Hébert, *Poèmes*, 71 (Our country is at the age of the earth's first days. Life here is to be discovered and named; this unknown face we have, this silent heart that is ours, all these lands before man waiting to be inhabited and possessed by us, and our confused talking begun in the night, all this calls for day and light).
2 As calculated in Hill Strategies, *A Statistical Profile of Artists and Cultural Workers in Canada*, 7 October 2014.
3 Michaels, "Reading to Hold"; Gordon, "The Joy and Comfort of a Well-stocked Library"; Gallant, "The Spirit of the Time," in D. Schaub, ed., *Reading Writers Reading*, 156, 144, 71.
4 Brossard, "L'ivresse du livre"; Blais, "Fécondité austère," in D. Schaub, ed., *Reading Writers Reading*, 87, 99. Hébert, "Mystère de la Parole," *Poèmes*, 68.
5 It is worth noting that in addition to novels by Atwood and Shields, male respondents considered Michael Ondaatje's *The English Patient*, Ian McEwan's *Enduring Love*, and John Fowles's *The French Lieutenant's Woman* to be "female reads" because of the dust-jacket copy or the cover design.
6 See www.cwrc.ca/canwwrfrom1950 and click on "reading surveys."
7 In *What's Sex Got to Do with It? Tax and the Family*, Claire Young comments on "the changing demographics of the family in Canada today, including a decrease in marriage rates, and increase in the number

of lone parent families and an increased state recognition of lesbian and gay relationships" (109). Amendments (1985) to the Indian Act restored status and membership rights. Amendments to the 1924 Copyright Act (1988), which were extended to music in 1993 and are continuing in Phase II involving digital media, assert the right of the artist to be compensated for the reproduction of her or his work.

8 Patron of the arts and philanthropist Vincent Massey supported the Hart House String Quartet, "helped found the Chamber Music Society in Toronto, took on the presidency of the Toronto Symphony Orchestra, and became chairman of the Dominion Drama Festival"; see Maria Tippett, *Making Culture*, 121.
9 The charismatic Franco-Ontarian archbishop of Montreal, Joseph Charbonneau, suffered more consequences than Georges-Henri Lévesque for his pro-labour role. Charbonneau resigned his position as archbishop, likely under some duress (although reasons of health were cited), and relocated to Victoria, British Columbia, where he served as chaplain in a Catholic nursing home until his death in 1959.
10 Probably in recognition of her exceptional service as the principal author of the *Report*, Massey provided Neatby with a small subvention (approximately $2,500) to assist in the publication of her best-selling but scathing indictment of Canadian education, *So Little for the Mind* (1953), in which she averred "Culture in its traditional sense of intellectual and moral cultivation is as unfashionable as is scholarship" (16).
11 See Marika Morris, "New Federal Policies Affecting Women's Equality: Reality Check." *Canadian Research Institute for the Advancement of Women* 8 (November 2006): 1–8.
12 https://laws-lois.justice.gc.ca/eng/const/page-15.html (accessed 15 Dec. 2016).
13 https://laws-lois.justice.gc.ca/eng/acts/c-18.7/page-1.html (accessed 15 Dec. 2016).
14 "Text of Harper's residential schools apology," *The Globe and Mail*, 11 June 2008.
15 Smart writes: "Par leur énergie, leur élan créateur, leur façon de jouir de la vie, leur sagesse et leurs amitiés entretenues et savourées depuis plus de cinquante ans, elles sont modèles pour les générations de femmes qui les suivent, et des phares dans le paysage culturel brumeux de cette fin de siècle."
16 *Manifeste refus global*. http://www.mbamsh.qc.ca (accessed 12 Dec. 2016).
17 In addition to the manifesto, *Le refus global* included two other Borduas texts, three dramatic pieces by Claude Gauvreau (selected from the

twenty-six pieces of *Entrailles* [1944–6]), essays by Bruno Cormier and Françoise Sullivan, and a one-page manifesto by Fernand Leduc.
18 It is worth noting that Gérard Pelletier, editor of *La Presse* and co-founder of the magazine *Cité Libre*, did not accept the tenets of *Le refus global*, citing his belief in sin as the reason: "Nous n'acceptons pas la règle de l'instinct parce que nous croyons au péché"; quoted by Ellenwood, 152.
19 Based on his paper, "S'il te plaît, dessine-moi une passé! La forme de l'expérience historique canadienne," at the symposium "Rethinking Identities in Contemporary Canada / Repenser les identités dans le Canada contemporain," sponsored by the Royal Society of Canada at the Congress of the Humanities and Social Sciences, at Carleton University, 27 May 2009.

1. Fiction

1 Gerson, "The Canon between the Wars," 46–56.
2 In reviewing the bestsellers of 1945 Lane finds no redeeming qualities in number nine, *Earth and High Heaven*. The book is in his view "crummy," with Graham "blithely doing her worst by writing prose." Although Lane declares it unreadable, his blistering comments indicate that he must have skimmed it at least. He also indulges in some unwarranted sarcasm about "the raw tongue of Canada, lashing the art of fiction into a fresh new lather" (63).
3 Review of Cyril Connolly, *Horizon*, 12, no. 68, 1945, quoted by Sullivan, 228–9.
4 Unless identified as the Hannah Josephson translation (Reynal and Hitchcock, 1947), quotations from *The Tin Flute* will be based on Alan Brown's translation (McClelland and Stewart, 1980) and identified parenthetically.
5 Ricard quotes "Un controverse sur *Bonheur d'occasion*: Saint-Henri présenté sous un mauvais jour," *La Voix populaire*, Montreal, 25 June 1947: 1.
6 Payette, *Des femmes d'honneur*, I: 68. "I looked around me with her eyes. I saw us as poor, insignificant, without ambition or culture, born to stay humble and incapable of escaping, repeating from generation to generation the same acts and mistakes. I was mortally wounded. I saw us as lazy, content with little and desiring nothing more."
7 Hannah Josephson, the first translator for the Reynal and Hitchcock edition (1947), was an American who occasionally missed the idiomatic sense of Quebec expressions. The most notorious error is her translation

of Roy's description of drifting snow, "la poudrerie se déchaîna" (I: 153), as "the powderworks exploded" (98). For an extensive, illuminating treatment of translation, see Chapman, *Between Languages and Cultures*, 181–96.
8 Stouck quotes Wilson's assessment from the preface to the Alcuin edition of *Hetty Dorval* and describes the author photo.
9 Wilson uses excerpts from *Devotions upon Emergent Occasions* (Meditation 17), "The good-morrow" (line 11), and "Communitie" (line 14).
10 The three novels in the Connington saga, *Least of All Saints* (1952), *Andrew Connington* (1954), and *Contend with Horses* (1968), all McClelland and Stewart imprints, were translated into German to considerable acclaim. In addition to *In Little Place* (1959), her other novels are a biography of the reformed slave ship captain John Newton, *Servant of Slaves* (1961), *The Seventh Earl* (1976), and her undergraduate novel, *Compensation* (2003), written when she was twenty and published more than seven decades later. She also published an autobiography, *Three Lives in Mine* (1986).
11 Young's four novels are *Psyche* (1959), *The Torontonians* (1960), *The Gift of Time* (1962), and *Undine* (1964).
12 Stovel cites Laurence, "Precis of *This Side Jordan*," York University Archives, 3.
13 Quoted by Schuster from the Jane Rule papers, Box 19, folder 7, University of British Columbia Rare Books and Special Collections Library.
14 Saul Bellow, born in Lachine, QC, won the Nobel Prize for Literature in 1976.
15 See Mazur and Moulder, *Alice Munro: An Annotated Bibliography of Works and Criticism*.
16 See Hengen and Thomson, *Margaret Atwood: A Reference Guide 1988–2005*.
17 Gunew is quoting from a 1993 CBC film, *The Diary of Evelyn Lau*, directed by Sturla Gunnarson. The scene re-created here is based on *Runaway*, 86, 154, 225.

3. Poetry

1 E.K. Brown, "Letters in Canada." *University of Toronto Quarterly* 5 (1935–6): 367; Frye, "Letters in Canada."
2 Waddington, "Foreword," in Livesay, *Archive for Our Times*, 9.
3 Ibid.
4 "The Three Emilys," Dorothy J. Livesay Fonds, Bruce Peel Special Collections Library, University of Alberta, 1.54, Box 3.

5 "The Unquiet Bed," Dorothy J. Livesay Fonds, Bruce Peel Special Collections Library, University of Alberta, 1.83, Box 4.
6 Zailig Pollock, ed., "Introduction," *Kaleidoscope: Selected Poems of P.K. Page*. All references to the poems will be based on this readily available edition, with page numbers included after the title.
7 Ondaatje's praise is included in the publisher's blurb on the back cover of The Porcupine Quill edition (2011) of *Brazilian Journal* (1987).
8 "Anne Wilkinson Remembered," With P.K. Page and Louis Dudek. *Anthology*, CBC Radio, 14 November 1984. Quoted in Wilkinson, *Heresies* (Irvine, ed.), n87, 47.
9 Brossard, "Vaseline," *La Barre du Jour* (automne 1973); reprinted, *Double impression*, 43. Brossard, poem from *Mécanique jongleuse*, suivi de *Masculin grammaticale*, 47, in *Mobility of Light*, ed. L. Forsyth, 20, 21. Translations by Nicole Brossard.
10 Excerpts from all these texts are included in Jeannette C. Armstrong and Lally Grauer, eds, *Native Poetry in Canada: A Contemporary Anthology*.

5. Drama

1 James, "Close Up: The Queen Bee of Canadian Playwrights," 16.
2 All references are from Zimmerman, ed., *Reading Carol Bolt*.
3 *Sharon Pollock: Collected Works*. 3 vols. Ed. Cynthia Zimmerman (Toronto: Playwrights Canada Press, 2005–8). All references will be based on this edition.
4 All references to Kane, Nowlan, and Clements will be based on this two-volume collection.
5 See *The Politics of the Visible in Asian North American Narratives* (2004), *Asian Canadian Writing beyond Autoethnography* (2008), and *Unfastened: Globality and Asian North American Narratives* (2010).

7. Non-fiction

1 As translated from Lejeune's *Le pacte autobiographique* (Paris: Seuil, 1975), 14, by Patricia Smart, Introduction to Martin, *In an Iron Glove*, xix.
2 For a historicized investigation of key Qur'anic texts about women as companions of the Prophet and as teachers, see Asma Afsaruddin's *Islam, the State, and Political Authority: Medieval Issues and Modern Concerns* (London: Palgrave Macmillan, 2011) and *Contemporary Issues in Islam* (Edinburgh: Edinburgh University Press, 2015).
3 Kingston, "Macleans Interview: Lynn Johnston," 27 August 2008.

4 Doucet, "If I Was a Man," in *My Most Secret Desire*, unnumbered pages. At the end of this dream, the female Julie walks through the mirror to have intercourse with the "male" Julie.
5 Doucet, "I will carry on anyway," in *365 Days*, unnumbered pages.

Conclusion

1 Winfried Siemerling quotes Walcott's fitting suggestion from *Black Like Who? Writing Black Canada* (2003, 22) in *The Black Atlantic Reconsidered: Black Canadian Writing, Cultural History, and the Presence of the Past*, 360.

Works Cited

Primary Texts

Aglukark, Susan. *Unsung Heroes*. EMI Music Canada, 1999.
Aitken, Kate. *Kate Aitken's Canadian Cook Book*. 1945. Introduction by Elizabeth Driver. Essays by the Aitken Family. North Vancouver: Whitecap Books, 2004.
– *Making Your Living Is Fun*. Toronto: Longmans, Green and Company, 1959.
– *Never a Day So Bright*. Toronto: Longmans, Green and Company, 1956.
Alderson, Sue Ann. *Pond Seasons*. Illus. Ann Blades. Toronto: Groundwood / Douglas and McIntyre. 1997.
Anderson-Dargatz, Gail. *The Cure for Death by Lightning*. Toronto: Alfred A. Knopf Canada, 1996.
Arden, Jann. *Living under June*. A&M Records, 1994.
– *These Are the Days*. Digital Distribution Serbia, 2018.
Armstrong, Jeannette C., and Lally Grauer, eds. *Native Poetry in Canada: A Contemporary Anthology*. Peterborough, ON: Broadview Press, 2001.
Armstrong, Sally. *Ascent of Women*. Toronto: Random House Canada, 2013.
– *Veiled Threat: The Hidden Power of the Women of Afghanistan*. Toronto: Viking Penguin, 2002.
Atwood, Margaret. *Alias Grace*. Toronto: McClelland and Stewart, 1996.
– *The Blind Assassin*. Toronto: McClelland and Stewart, 2000.
– *Bodily Harm*. Toronto: McClelland and Stewart, 1981.
– *The CanLit Foodbook: From Pen to Palate – A Collection of Tasty Literary Fare*. Toronto: Totem, 1987.
– *Cat's Eye*. Toronto: McClelland and Stewart, 1988.
– *The Circle Game*. Toronto: Anansi, 1966.
– *The Door*. Toronto: McClelland and Stewart, 2007.

- *The Edible Woman.* Toronto: McClelland and Stewart, 1969; London: Virago, 1980.
- *Good Bones.* Toronto: Coach House Press, 1992.
- *The Handmaid's Tale.* Toronto: McClelland and Stewart, 1985.
- "Introduction." *Alice Munro's Best: Selected Stories.* Toronto: McClelland and Stewart, 2006.
- *The Journals of Susanna Moodie.* Toronto: Oxford University Press, 1970.
- *Lady Oracle.* Toronto: McClelland and Stewart, 1976.
- *Life before Man.* Toronto: McClelland and Stewart, 1979.
- *MaddAdam.* Toronto: McClelland and Stewart, 2013.
- *Moral Disorder.* Toronto: McClelland and Stewart, 2006.
- *Moving Targets: Writing with Intent 1982–2004.* Toronto: Anansi, 2004.
- *Murder in the Dark.* Toronto: Coach House, 1983.
- *Negotiating with the Dead: A Writer on Writing.* Cambridge: Cambridge University Press, 2002.
- *Oryx and Crake.* Toronto: McClelland and Stewart, 2003.
- *Payback: Debt and the Shadow Side of Wealth.* Toronto: Anansi, 2008.
- *The Penelopiad.* Toronto: Alfred A. Knopf, 2005.
- *Procedures for Underground.* Boston: Little, Brown and Company, 1970.
- *The Robber Bride.* Toronto: McClelland and Stewart, 1993.
- *Selected Poems.* Toronto: Oxford University Press, 1976.
- *Strange Things: The Malevolent North in Canadian Literature.* Oxford: Clarendon, 1995.
- *Surfacing.* Don Mills, ON: General Publishing, Paperjacks, 1972.
- *Survival: A Thematic Guide to Canadian Literature.* Toronto: Anansi, 1972.
- *The Tent.* New York: Nan A. Talese, Doubleday, 2006.
- *The Year of the Flood.* Toronto: McClelland and Stewart, 2009.

Avison, Margaret. *Always Now: The Collected Poems*, Vol. 1. Erin, ON: The Porcupine's Quill, 2003.
- *Concrete and Wild Carrot.* London, ON: Brick Books, 2002.
- *The Dumbfounding.* New York: W.W. Norton, 1966.
- *Winter Sun.* London: Routledge and Kegan Paul, 1960.

Baird, Irene. *The Climate of Power.* Toronto: Macmillan, 1971.
- *Waste Heritage.* 1939. Edited with an introduction by Colin Hill. Ottawa: University of Ottawa Press, 2007.

Bambrick, Winifred. *Keller's Continental Revue.* Boston: Houghton Mifflin Company, 1946.

Barber, Jill. *Mischievous Moon.* Outside Music, 2011.

Basran, Gurjinder. *Everything Was Good-bye.* Salt Spring Island, BC: Mother Tongue Publishers, 2010.
- *Someone You Love Is Gone.* Toronto: Viking, 2017.

Benoit, Jehane. *L'encyclopédie de la cuisine canadienne*. Montreal: Les Messageries du Saint-Laurent, 1963.
– *Madame Benoit's Library of Canadian Cooking*, Vol. I of *The New and Complete Encyclopedia of Cooking*. Deluxe Edition. Montreal: Les Messageries du Saint-Laurent, 1975.
Bidwell, Norma. *The Best of Stoveline*. Hamilton, ON: The Spectator, 1994.
– *Lifelines and Deadlines*. Burlington, ON: North Shore Publishing, 2002.
– *The Norma Bidwell Cookbook*. Hamilton, ON: The Spectator, 1993.
Blades, Ann. *Mary of Mile 18*. Montreal: Tundra Books, 1971.
– *Too Small*. Toronto: Groundwood / Douglas and McIntyre, 2000.
Blais, Marie-Claire. *Mad Shadows*. 1960. Translated by Merloyd Lawrence. Afterword by Daphne Marlatt. Toronto: McClelland and Stewart, 1990, 2008.
– *A Season in the Life of Emmanuel*. Translated by Derek Coltman. Introduction by Edmund Wilson. New York: Farrar, Straus and Giroux, 1966.
Blatchford, Christie. *Fifteen Days: Stories of Bravery, Friendship, Life and Death from Inside the New Canadian Army*. Toronto: Doubleday, 2007.
– *Helpless: Caledonia's Nightmare of Fear and Anarchy, and How the Law Failed All of Us*. Toronto: Doubleday Random House Canada, 2010.
Blondal, Patricia. *A Candle to Light the Sun*. 1960. Introduction by Laurence Ricou. Toronto: McClelland and Stewart, 1976.
Bolster, Stephanie. *A Page from the Wonders of Life on Earth*. London, ON: Brick Books, 2011.
– *Two Bowls of Milk*. Toronto: McClelland and Stewart, 1999.
– *White Stone: The Alice Poems*. Montreal: Véhicule Press, Signal Editions, 1998.
Bolt, Carol. *Reading Carol Bolt*. Edited by Cynthia Zimmerman. Toronto: Playwrights Canada, 2010.
Brand, Dionne. *At the Full and Change of the Moon*. Toronto: Alfred A. Knopf Canada, 1999.
– *In Another Place, Not Here*. Toronto: Alfred A. Knopf Canada, 1996.
– *Land to Light On*. Toronto: McClelland and Stewart, 1997.
– *Ossuaries*. Toronto: McClelland and Stewart, 2010.
– *What We All Long For*. Toronto: Alfred A. Knopf Canada, 2005.
Brewster, Elizabeth. *Collected Poems*. 2 vols. Ottawa: Oberon, 2003–4.
– *Selected Poems, 1944–1977*. Introduction by Tom Marshall. Ottawa: Oberon, 1985.
Brossard, Nicole. *Le désert mauve: Un roman*. Montreal: L'Hexagone, 1987.
– *Double impression. Poèmes et textes 1967–1984*. Montreal: Éditions de l'Hexagone, 1984.

- *Mauve Desert, A Novel*. Translated by Susanne de Lotbinière-Harwood. Toronto: Coach House Press, 1990.
- *Mécanique jongleuse*, suivi de *Masculin grammaticale*. Montreal: Éditions de l'Hexagone, 1974.
- *Mobility of Light: The Poetry of Nicole Brossard*. Selected with an introduction by Louise Forsyth. Waterloo, ON: Wilfrid Laurier University Press, 2009.

Brun, Mona. *Cooking with Mona: The Original Woodward's Cookbook*. 1977. North Vancouver: Whitecap Books, 2003.

Burnford, Sheila. *The Incredible Journey*. London: Hodder and Stoughton, 1961.

Buss, Helen M. [aka Margaret Clarke]. *Memoirs from Away: A New Found Land Girlhood*. Waterloo, ON: Wilfrid Laurier University Press, 1999.

Butler, Edith. *Asteur qu'on est là*. Les Éditions TricTrac, 1979.

Campbell, Kim. *Time and Chance: The Political Memoirs of Canada's First Woman Prime Minister*. Toronto: Doubleday, 1996.

Campbell, Maria. *Halfbreed*. Toronto: McClelland and Stewart, 1973.

Carson, Anne. *Nox*. New York: New Directions, 2010.

Chatterton, Anna. *Within the Glass*. Winnipeg: Scirocco Drama, J. Gordon Shillingford Publishing, 2017.

Cheechoo, Shirley. *Path with No Moccasins*. Box 59, West Bay, Ontario POP IGO, 1993.

Chong, Denise. *The Concubine's Children; Portrait of a Family Divided*. Toronto: Viking, Penguin Group, 1994.

Clark, Sally. *Saint Frances of Hollywood*. Burnaby, BC: Talonbooks, 1996.
- *The Trial of Judith K*. Toronto: Playwrights Canada, 1985.

Clarkson, Adrienne. *Heart Matters: A Memoir*. Toronto: Viking Penguin, 2006.

Clements, Marie. *Tombs of the Vanishing Indian*. Vancouver: Talonbooks, 2012.
- *The Unnatural and Accidental Women*. 2000. In Mojica and Knowles, eds, *Staging Coyote's Dream*, vol. I, 363–459.

Coady, Lynn. *The Antagonist*. Toronto: Anansi, 2011.
- *Hellgoing. Stories*. Toronto: Anansi, 2013.
- *Strange Heaven*. Fredericton: Goose Lane, 1998.

Conway, Jill Ker. *The Road from Coorain*. New York: Alfred A. Knopf, 1989.
- *True North: A Memoir*. New York: Alfred A. Knopf, 1994.
- *When Memory Speaks: Reflections of Autobiography*. New York: Alfred A. Knopf, 1998.
- *A Woman's Education: The Road from Coorain Leads to Smith College*. New York: Vintage Books, 2001.

Cook, Lyn. *The Bells on Finland Street*. Toronto: Macmillan, 1950.
- *The Little Magic Fiddler*. Illustrated by Stanley Wyatt. Toronto: Macmillan, 1951.

Coyote, Ivan E. *One in Every Crowd*. Vancouver: Arsenal Pulp Press, 2012.

– *Tomboy Survival Guide*. Vancouver: Arsenal Pulp Press, 2016.
Crate, Joan. *Black Apple*. Toronto: Simon and Schuster Canada, 2016.
Crozier, Lorna. *Inventing the Hawk*. Toronto: McClelland and Stewart, 1992.
– *What the Soul Doesn't Want*. Calgary: Freehand Books, 2017.
Culleton Mosionier, Beatrice. *In Search of April Raintree*. Edited by Cheryl Suzack. Winnipeg: Portage and Main Press, 1999.
de la Roche, Mazo. *Jalna*. Toronto: Macmillan, 1927.
Doiron, Julie. *I Can Wonder What You Did with Your Day*. Endearing, 2009.
Doucet, Julie. *My Most Secret Desire*. Montreal: Drawn and Quarterly, 2006.
– *365 Days*. Montreal: Drawn and Quarterly, 2007.
Downie, Mary Alice, and Barbara Robertson, eds. *The Wind Has Wings: Poems from Canada*. Illustrated by Elizabeth Cleaver. Toronto: Oxford University Press, 1968.
Dumont, Marilyn. *Green Girl Dreams Mountains*. Lantzville, BC: Oolichan Books, 2001.
– *The Pemmican Eaters*. Toronto: ECW Press, 2015.
– *A Really Good Brown Girl*. London, ON: Brick Books, 1996.
– *That Tongued Belonging*. Cape Kroker Reserve, Wiarton, ON: Kegedonce Press, 2007.
Edugyan, Esi. *Dreaming of Elsewhere: Observations on Home*. Kreisel Memorial Lecture. Edmonton: Canadian Literature Centre and University of Alberta Press, 2014.
– *Half-Blood Blues*. London: Serpent's Tail, 2011.
– *The Second Life of Samuel Tyne*. Toronto: A.A. Knopf, 2004.
Ellis, Sarah. *The Baby Project*. Toronto: Groundwood, 1986.
– *Next-Door Neighbours*. Toronto: Groundwood, 1989.
– *Out of the Blue*. Toronto: Groundwood, 1994.
– *Pick-Up Sticks*. Toronto: Groundwood, 1991.
Endicott, Marina. *Close to Hugh*. Toronto: Doubleday Canada, 2015.
– *Good to a Fault*. Calgary: Freehand Books, 2008.
Engel, Marian. *Bear*. Toronto: McClelland and Stewart, 1976.
– *The Glassy Sea*. Toronto: McClelland and Stewart, 1978.
– *The Honeyman Festival*. Toronto: Anansi, 1970.
– *Lunatic Villas*. Toronto: McClelland and Stewart, 1981.
– *Sarah Bastard's Notebook (No Clouds of Glory)*. Don Mills, ON: Longmans, 1968. New York: Harcourt Brace and World, 1968.
Feist, Leslie. *The Reminder*. Polydor Records, 2007.
Ford, Frazey. *Indian Ocean*. Nettwerk, 2014.
Foroughi, Sadaf. *Ava*. Sweet Delight Pictures, 2017.
Fraser, Sylvia. *My Father's House: A Memoir of Incest and of Healing*. Toronto: Doubleday Canada, 1987.

Freeman, Mini Aodla. *Life among the Qallunaat*. Edmonton: Hurtig, 1978.
– *Life among the Qallunaat*. Edited by K. Martin, J. Rak, and N. Dunning. Winnipeg: University of Manitoba Press, 2015.
French, Alice Masak. *My Name Is Masak*. Winnipeg: Peguis, 1976.
Frum, Barbara. *As It Happened*. Toronto: McClelland and Stewart, 1976.
Frum, Linda. *Barbara Frum: A Daughter's Memoir*. Toronto: Random House, 1996.
Gale, Lorena. *Angélique*. Toronto: Playwrights Canada Press, 2000.
– *Je me souviens: Memories of an Expatriate Anglophone Montréalaise Québécoise Exiled in Canada*. Vancouver: Talonbooks, 2001.
Gallant, Mavis. "By the Sea." *The New Yorker*, 17 July 1954. In *In Transit*, 1–14. Toronto: Penguin, 1988.
– *Green Water, Green Sky*. Boston: Houghton Mifflin, 1959.
Gallus, Maya. *Derby Crazy Love*. Red Queen Productions, 2013.
– *Elizabeth Smart: On the Side of the Angels*. Red Queen Productions, 1991.
– *The Mystery of Mazo de la Roche*. National Film Board, 2012
Gay, Marie-Louise. *Rainy Day Magic*. Toronto: Stoddart, 1987.
Gibb, Camilla. *Sweetness in the Belly*. Toronto: Doubleday Canada, 2005.
– *This Is Happy: A Memoir*. Toronto: Doubleday Canada, 2015.
Gilman, Phoebe. *Jillian Jiggs*. Toronto: Scholastic, 1985.
– *Something from Nothing*. Richmond Hill, ON: North Winds Press, 1992.
Glass, Joanna M. *Play Memory*. *NeWest Plays by Women*. Edited by Diane Bessai and Don Kerr. Edmonton: NeWest Press, 1987.
Goto, Hiromi. *Chorus of Mushrooms*. Edmonton: NeWest Press, 1994.
Gowdy, Barbara. *Little Sister*. Toronto: Harper Collins, 2017.
– *We So Seldom Look on Love*. Toronto: Somerville House Publishing, 1992.
– *The White Bone*. Toronto: Harper Collins, 1998.
Graham, Gwethalyn. *Earth and High Heaven*. 1944. Introduction by Norman Ravvin. Toronto: Cormorant Books, 2003.
– *Swiss Sonata*. 1938. Introduction by Elspeth Cameron. Toronto: Cormorant Books, 2005.
Gray, Charlotte. *Canada: A Portrait in Letters, 1800–2000*. Toronto: Doubleday, 2003.
– *Gold Diggers: Striking It Rich in the Klondike*. Berkeley, CA: Counterpoint, 2010.
– *Mrs King: The Life and Times of Isabel Mackenzie King*. Toronto: Viking Penguin Canada, 1997.
– *The Museum Called Canada: 25 Rooms of Wonder*. Toronto: Random House, 2004.
– *The Promise of Canada: 150 Years – People and Ideas That Have Shaped Our Country*. Toronto: Simon and Schuster Canada, 2016.

– *Reluctant Genius: The Passionate Life and Inventive Mind of Alexander Graham Bell*. Toronto: Harper Collins, 2006.
– *Sisters in the Wilderness: The Lives of Susanna Moodie and Catherine Parr Traill*. Toronto: Viking Penguin Canada, 1999.
Grey, Deborah. *Never Retreat, Never Explain, Never Apologize: My Life, My Politics*. Toronto: Key Porter Books, 2004.
Halfe, Louise. *Bear Bones and Feathers*. Regina: Coteau Books, 1994.
– *The Crooked Good*. Regina: Coteau Books, 2007.
Hamilton, Mary. *The Tin-Lined Trunk*. Toronto: Kids Can Press, 1980.
Hanrahan, Catherine. *Lost Girls and Love Hotels*. Toronto: Penguin Canada, 2006.
Harris, Christie. *Once upon a Totem*. Toronto: McClelland and Stewart, 1963.
Hawley, Alix. *All True Not a Lie in It*. Toronto: Alfred A. Knopf Canada, 2015.
Hay, Elizabeth. *Late Nights on Air*. Toronto: McClelland and Stewart, 2007.
Hébert, Anne. *Les chambres de bois*. Paris: Seuil, 1958.
– *Children of the Black Sabbath*. Translated by Carol Dunlop-Hébert. Don Mills, ON: Musson, 1977.
– *Collected Later Novels*. Introduction by Mavis Gallant. Translated by Sheila Fischman. Toronto: Anansi, 2003.
– *Les enfants du sabbat*. Paris: Seuil, 1975.
– *Les fous de bassan*. Paris: Seuil, 1982.
– *Héloïse*. Paris: Seuil, 1980.
– *In the Shadow of the Wind*. Translated by Sheila Fischman. Toronto: Stoddart, 1983.
– *Kamouraska*. 1970. Translated by Norman Shapiro. Toronto: General Publishing, 1973.
– *Poèmes*. Paris: Editions du Seuil, 1960.
– *The Silent Rooms*. Translated by Kathy Mezei. Don Mills, ON: Musson, 1974.
– *Les songes en équilibre, poèmes*. Montreal: Les Éditions de l'arbre, 1942.
– *Le torrent*. Montreal: Editions Beauchemin, 1950.
– *The Torrent*. Translated by Gwendolyn Moore. Montreal: Harvest House, 1973.
Henry, Ann. *Lulu Street*. 1967. Vancouver: Talonbooks, 1975.
Hughes, Monica. *My Name Is Paula Popowich!* Toronto: James Lorimer, 1983.
Hunter, Aislinn. *The World before Us*. Toronto: Doubleday, Random House Canada, 2014.
Hunter, Bernice Thurman. *As Ever, Booky*. Richmond Hill, ON: Scholastic, 1985.
– *That Scatterbrain Booky*. Richmond Hill, ON: Scholastic, 1981.
– *With Love from Booky*. Richmond Hill, ON: 1983.

Irwin, Grace. *Andrew Connington*. Toronto: McClelland and Stewart, 1954.
– *In Little Place*. Grand Rapids, MI: Wm B. Eerdmans, 1959.
– *Least of All Saints*. Toronto: McClelland and Stewart, 1952.
Jacobs, Jane. *Dark Age Ahead*. Toronto: Random House Canada, 2004.
Jaques, Edna. *Aunt Hattie's Place*. Toronto: Thomas Allen, Limited, 1941.
– *Drifting Soil*. Moose Jaw, SK: The Times Company, Limited, n.d.
– *Prairie Born, Prairie Bred: Poetic Reflections of a Pioneer*. Saskatoon: Western Producer Prairie Books, n.d.
– *Uphill All the Way*. Saskatoon: Western Producer Prairie Books, 1977.
– *Verses for You*. Moose Jaw Writers' Club, n.d.
Johnston, Lynn. *The Lives behind the Lines: 20 Years of* For Better or For Worse. Kansas City: Andrews McMeel Publishing, 1999.
Joudry, Patricia. *Teach Me How to Cry*. New York: Dramatists Play Service, Inc., 1955.
– *A Very Modest Orgy*. Toronto: Playwrights Canada, 1981.
Kane, Margo. *Confessions of an Indian Cowboy*. In Mojica and Knowles, eds, *Staging Coyote's Dream*, vol. II, 205–22.
Katz, Welwyn Wilton. *False Face*. Vancouver: Groundwood / Douglas and McIntyre, 1987.
Kenney, Mo. *In My Dreams*. Pheromone Recordings, Fontana North, 2014.
Klein, Bonnie Sherr. *Not a Love Story*. National Film Board, 1981.
– *Shameless: The ART of Disability*. National Film Board, 2006.
Klein, Naomi. *This Changes Everything*. Klein Lewis Productions, 2015.
Kogawa, Joy. *Obasan*. Toronto: Lester and Orpen Dennys, 1981.
Kostash, Myrna. *All of Baba's Children*. Edmonton: Hurtig Publishers, 1977.
– *Prodigal Daughter: A Journey to Byzantium*. Edmonton: University of Alberta Press, 2010.
Kreviazuk, Chantal. *What if It All Means Something*. Columbia, 2002.
Lai, Larissa. *Salt Fish Girl*. Toronto: Thomas Allen, 2002.
– *When Fox Is a Thousand*. Vancouver: Press Gang Publishers, 1995.
LaMarsh, Judy. *Memoirs of a Bird in a Gilded Cage*. Toronto: McClelland and Stewart, 1968.
Lang, K.D. *Ingénue*. Warner Brothers, 1992.
Lau, Evelyn. *Runaway: Diary of a Street Kid*. Toronto: Harper Collins, 1989.
Laurence, Margaret. *A Bird in the House*. 1970. Afterword by Isabel Huggan. Toronto: McClelland and Stewart, 1989.
– "*Blown Figures*: A Review." *Room of One's Own* 10 (1985–6): 99–102.
– *Dance on the Earth: A Memoir*. Toronto: McClelland and Stewart, 1989.

– *The Diviners*. 1974. Afterword by Timothy Findley. Toronto: McClelland and Stewart, 1990.
– *The Fire-Dwellers*. New York: Alfred A. Knopf, 1969.
– "Foreword." *The Collected Plays of Gwen Pharis Ringwood*. Ottawa: Borealis, 1982.
– *A Jest of God*. 1966. Afterword by Margaret Atwood. Toronto: McClelland and Stewart, 1988.
– "Small Town's 'Silences' Not Mere Hypocrisy." *The Vancouver Sun*, 21 January 1961: 5.
– *The Stone Angel*. Toronto: McClelland and Stewart, 1964.
– *This Side Jordan*. 1960. Afterword by George Woodcock. Toronto: McClelland and Stewart, 1989.
Lavigne, Avril. *Complicated*. Arista Records, 2002.
Lightfoot, Terra. *Every Time My Mind Runs Wild*. Sonic Unyon, 2015.
Lill, Wendy. *The Occupation of Heather Rose*. NeWest Plays by Women. Edited by Diane Bessai and Don Kerr. Edmonton: NeWest Press, 1987.
Lindberg, Tracey. *Birdie*. Toronto: Harper Collins, 2015.
Little, Jean. *Mama's Going to Buy You a Mockingbird*. Toronto: Penguin Canada, 1984.
– *Mine for Keeps*. Boston: Little, Brown and Company, 1962.
Livesay, Dorothy. *Archive for Our Times: Previously Uncollected and Unpublished Poems of Dorothy Livesay*. Edited by Dean J. Irvine. Vancouver: Arsenal Pulp Press, 1998.
– *Collected Poems: The Two Seasons of Dorothy Livesay*. Toronto: McGraw-Hill Ryerson, 1972.
– *Day and Night*. Toronto: Ryerson, 1944.
– Fonds, Dorothy J. Livesay. Bruce Peel Special Collections Library, University of Alberta, 4 boxes.
– *Green Pitcher*. Toronto: Macmillan, 1928.
– *Poems for People*. Toronto: Ryerson, 1947.
– "The Secret Doctrine of Women" and "The Enchanted Isle: A Dialogue." *Room of One's Own. The Dorothy Livesay Issue* 5 (1979–80): 117–23.
– *Selected Poems of Dorothy Livesay 1926–1956*. Toronto: Ryerson, 1957.
– *Signpost*. Toronto: Macmillan, 1932.
– *The Unquiet Bed*. Toronto: Ryerson, 1967.
– "Voices of Women: A Suite." *A Room of One's Own: The Dorothy Livesay Issue* 5 (1979–80): 63–9.
Longfellow, Brenda. *Offshore*. Helios Design Labs, 2013.
– *Weather Report*. National Film Board, 2007.

Lowther, Pat. *Collected Works*. Edited by Christine Wiesenthal. Edmonton: NeWest, 2010.
Lunn, Janet. *The Hollow Tree*. Toronto: Knopf Canada, 1997.
– *The Root Cellar*. Toronto: Lester and Orpen Dennys, 1981.
Macbeth, Madge. *Shackles*. 1926. Edited with an introduction by Peggy Lynn Kelly. Ottawa: Tecumseh Press, 2005.
MacDonald, Ann-Marie. *Adult Onset*. Toronto: Alfred A. Knopf Canada, 2014.
– *Belle Moral [A Natural History]*. Toronto: Vintage Canada, 2005.
– *Fall on Your Knees*. Toronto: Alfred A. Knopf Canada, 1996.
– *Goodnight Desdemona (Good Morning Juliet)*. Toronto: Playwrights Canada, 1990.
– *The Way the Crow Flies*. Toronto: Alfred Knopf Canada, 2003.
MacEwen, Gwendolyn. *A Breakfast for Barbarians*. Toronto: Ryerson, 1966.
– *The Poetry of Gwendolyn MacEwen: The Early Years*. Edited by Margaret Atwood and Barry Callaghan. Toronto: Exile Editions, 1993.
– *The Poetry of Gwendolyn MacEwen: The Later Years*. Edited by Margaret Atwood and Barry Callaghan. Toronto: Exile Editions, 1994.
– *The Shadow-Maker*. Toronto: Macmillan, 1969.
MacLeod, Alison. *All the Beloved Ghosts*. Toronto: Penguin Canada, 2017.
– *The Changeling*. London: St Martin's Press, 1996.
– *Unexploded*. London: Hamish Hamilton, 2013.
MacLeod, Joan. *Amigo's Blue Guitar*. Toronto: Summerhill Press, 1990.
– *The Valley*. Vancouver: Talonbooks, 2014.
MacMillan, Margaret. *History's People: Personalities and the Past*. Toronto: Anansi, 2015.
– *Nixon in China: The Week That Changed the World*. Toronto: Penguin Books Canada, 2006.
– *Paris 1919: Six Months That Changed the World*. New York: Random House, 2002.
– *The War That Ended Peace: The Road to 1914*. Toronto: Allen Lane, 2013.
Macpherson, Jay. *The Boatman*. Toronto: Oxford University Press, 1957.
– *Welcoming Disaster*. Toronto: Saannes Publications, Ltd, 1974.
Manji, Irshad. *The Trouble with Islam: A Wake-up Call for Honesty and Change*. Toronto: Random House Canada, 2003.
Manley, Rachel. *Drumblair: Memories of a Jamaican Childhood*. Toronto: Alfred A. Knopf, 1996.
Maracle, Lee. *Bobbi Lee: Indian Rebel*. Richmond, BC: LSM Information Centre, 1975.
Marlatt, Daphne. *Ana Historic*. Toronto: Coach House Press, 1988.

– *The Given*. Toronto: McClelland and Stewart, 2008.
– *How Hug a Stone*. Winnipeg: Turnstone Press, 1983.
– *Touch to My Tongue*. Edmonton: Longspoon Press, 1984.
– *The Vision Tree: Selected Poems*. Edited by Sharon Thesen. Vancouver: Talonbooks, 1982.
Marlatt, Daphne, and Robert Minden. *Steveston*. 1974. Edmonton: Longspoon Press, 1984.
Martin, Catherine Anne. *The Spirit of Annie Mae*. National Film Board, 2002.
Martin, Claire. *In an Iron Glove: An Autobiography*. 1968. Translated by Philip Stratford. Introduction by Patricia Smart. Ottawa: University of Ottawa Press, 2006.
Maynard, Fredelle Bruser. *Raisins and Almonds*. Toronto: Doubleday Canada, 1972.
– *The Tree of Life*. Toronto: Viking Penguin, 1988.
Maynard, Joyce. *At Home in the World: A Memoir*. New York: Picador, 1998.
Mayr, Suzette. *Dr. Edith Vane and the Hares of Crawley Hall*. Toronto: Coach House Books, 2017.
– *Monoceros*. Toronto: Coach House Books, 2011.
– *Venous Hum*. Vancouver: Arsenal Pulp Press, 2004.
McGarrigle, Kate, and Anna McGarrigle. *Dancer with Bruised Knees*. Warner Brothers, 1977.
– *Kate and Anna McGarrigle*. Warner Brothers, 1976.
McLachlan, Sarah. *Fumbling towards Ecstasy*. Nettwerk, 1993.
Mehta, Deepa. *Beeba Boys*. Hamilton-Mehta Productions, 2015.
– *Earth*. Cracking Earth Films, Canada, 1998.
– *Fire*. Trial By Fire Films, 1996.
– *Heaven on Earth*. National Film Board, 2008.
– *Sam & Me*. Sunrise Films, 1991.
– *Water*. Mongrel Media, 2005.
Meigs, Mary. *In the Company of Strangers*. Vancouver: Talonbooks, 1991.
– *Lily Briscoe, A Self-Portrait: An Autobiography*. Vancouver: Talonbooks, 1981.
Michaels, Anne. *Poems*. New York: Alfred A. Knopf, 2001.
Mitchell, Joni. *Clouds*. Reprise Records, 1969.
Mojica, Monique. *Princess Pocahontas and the Blue Spots*. Toronto: Women's Press, 1991.
Mojica, Monique, and Ric Knowles, eds. *Staging Coyote's Dream: An Anthology of First Nations Drama in English*. 2 vols. Toronto: Playwrights Canada Press, 2005, 2008.
Moore, Mary. *The Mary Moore Cookbook*. Edited by Peter Moore. Toronto: Mary Moore, 1978.

Mootoo, Shani. *He Drown She in the Sea*. Toronto: McClelland and Stewart, 2005.
– *Moving Forward Sideways Like a Crab*. Toronto: Doubleday Canada, 2014.
Morissette, Alanis. *Jagged Little Pill*. Maverick Recording Company, 1995.
Moscovitch, Hannah. *East of Berlin*. Toronto: Playwrights Canada Press, 2009.
– *Infinity*. With original music by Njo Kong Kie. Toronto: Playwrights Canada Press, 2017.
Moses, Daniel David, ed. *The Exile Book of Native Canadian Fiction and Drama*. Holstein, ON: Exile Editions, 2010.
Moure, Erin. *Domestic Fuel*. Toronto: Anansi, 1985.
– *Empire, York Street*. Toronto: Anansi, 1979.
– *Furious*. Toronto: Anansi, 1988.
– *O Cidadán*. Toronto: Anansi, 2002.
Munro, Alice. *Dance of the Happy Shades*. Foreword by Hugh Garner. Toronto: Ryerson Press, 1968.
– *Friend of My Youth: Stories*. Toronto: McClelland and Stewart, 1990
– *Hateship, Friendship, Courtship, Loveship, Marriage*. Toronto: McClelland and Stewart, 2001.
– *Lives of Girls and Women. A Novel*. 1971. Introduction by Jane Smiley. Toronto: Penguin Canada, 2005.
– *The Progress of Love*. Toronto: McClelland and Stewart, 1986.
– *The Progress of Love*. Foreword by Richard Ford. Toronto: Penguin Random House Canada, 2006.
– *Something I've Been Meaning to Tell You*. Toronto: McGraw-Hill, Ryerson, 1974.
– *Too Much Happiness*. Toronto: McClelland and Stewart, 2009.
– *The View from Castle Rock. Stories*. Toronto: McClelland and Stewart, 2006.
– *Who Do You Think You Are?* Toronto: Macmillan, 1978.
Nichol, Barbara. *Biscuits in the Cupboard*. Illustrated by Philippe Beha. Toronto: Stoddart Kids, 1997.
Nichols, Ruth. *The Marrow of the World*. Toronto: Macmillan, 1972.
– *A Walk out of the World*. Toronto: Longmans, 1969.
Nolan, Yvette. *Annie Mae's Movement*. 1999; rev. 2006. In Mojica and Knowles, eds, *Staging Coyote's Dream*, vol. II: 137–70.
Nourbese Philip, Marlene. *Harriet's Daughter*. Toronto: Women's Press, 1988.
Obamsawin, Alanis. *Hi-Ho Mistahey!* National Film Board, 2013.
– *Kanehsatake: 270 Years of Resistance*. National Film Board, 1993.
– *Our People Will Be Healed*. National Film Board, 2017.
– *The People of Kattawapiskak River*. National Film Board, 2012.
– *Rocks at Whiskey Trench*. National Film Board, 2000.

Off, Carol. *All We Leave Behind: A Reporter's Journey into the Lives of Others*. Toronto: Random House Canada, 2017.
Oke, Janette. *Drums of Change: The Story of Running Fawn*. Minneapolis, MN: Bethany House, 1996.
– *Love Comes Softly*. Minneapolis, MN: Bethany House, 1979.
Oliver, Margo. *Margo Oliver's Weekend Magazine Cookbook*. Montreal: Montreal Standard Publishing, 1967.
O'Neill, Heather. *The Lonely Hearts Hotel*. New York: Riverhead Books, 2017.
– *Lullabies for Little Criminals*. Toronto: Harper Perennial, 2006.
– *Wisdom in Nonsense – Invaluable Lessons from My Father*. Kreisel Memorial Lecture. Edmonton: Canadian Literature Centre and University of Alberta Press, 2018.
Page, P.K. *As Ten as Twenty*. Toronto: Ryerson, 1946.
– *Brazilian Journal*. 1987. Edited by Suzanne Bailey and Christopher Doody. Erin, ON: The Porcupine's Quill, 2011.
– *Cry Ararat! Poems New and Selected*. Toronto: McClelland and Stewart, 1967.
– *The Hidden Room: Collected Poems*. 2 vols. Erin, ON: Porcépic, 1997.
– *Hologram*. London, ON: Brick Books, 1994.
– *Kaleidoscope: Selected Poems*. Edited by Zailig Pollock. Erin, ON: The Porcupine's Quill, 2010.
– *The Metal and the Flower*. Toronto: McClelland and Stewart, 1954.
– *Planet Earth: Poems Selected and New*. Edited by Eric Ormsby. Erin, ON: The Porcupine's Quill, 2002.
– *The Sun and the Moon and Other Fictions*. 1944. Toronto: Anansi, 1973.
Paperny, Myra. *The Greenies*. Toronto: Harper Collins Canada, 2005.
– *The Wooden People*. Boston: Little, Brown, 1976.
Paré, Jean. *150 Delicious Squares*. Vermilion, AB: Company's Coming Publishing, 1981.
Pearson, Kit. *Awake and Dreaming*. Toronto: Viking, Penguin Group, 1996.
– *The Guests of War Trilogy*. Toronto: Penguin Books Canada, 1998.
– *A Handful of Time*. Markham, ON: Viking, 1987.
– *The Singing Basket*. Pictures by Ann Blades. Toronto: Groundwood, 1990.
– *The Sky Is Falling*. Toronto: Viking Kestrel / Penguin Group, 1989.
Polley, Sarah. *Away from Her*. Echo Lake Productions, 2006.
– *Stories We Tell*. National Film Board, 2012.
– *Take This Waltz*. Magnolia Pictures, 2011.
Pollock, Sharon. *Collected Works*. Edited with an introduction by Cynthia Zimmerman. 3 vols. Toronto: Playwrights Canada Press, 2005-8.
– *Three Plays: Moving Pictures, End Dream, Angel's Trumpet*. Introductory essay by Sherrill Grace. Toronto: Playwrights Canada, 2003.

– *Walsh*. Vancouver: Talonbooks, 1973.
Pool, Léa. *Lost and Delirious*. Cité-Amérique, 2001.
Quan, Elyne. *Surface Tension*. 1998. In Demers and Kerr, eds, *Staging Alternative Albertas: Experimental Drama in Edmonton*, 3–15.
Quantum Tangle. *Shelter as We Go*. Coax Records, 2017.
Quin, Tegan, and Sara Quin. *The Business of Art*. Vapor Records, 2000.
Rankin, Molly, with Alvvays. *Antisocialites*. Royal Mountain Canada, Polyvinyl USA, 2017.
Ringwood, Gwen Pharis. *Collected Plays*. Edited by Enid Delgaty Rutland. Biographical Note by Marion Wilson. Foreword by Margaret Laurence and George Ryga. Ottawa: Borealis Press, 1982.
Ritter, Erika. *Automatic Pilot*. Toronto: Playwrights Canada, 1980.
Robinson, Eden. *Monkey Beach*. Toronto: Alfred A. Knopf Canada, 2000.
– *Son of a Trickster*. Toronto: Alfred A. Knopf Canada, 2017.
Roy, Gabrielle. *Alexandre Chenevert, caissier*. Montreal: Éditions Beauchemin, 1954.
– *Bonheur d'occasion*. 2 vols. Montreal: Éditions Beauchemin, 1945.
– *The Cashier*. Translated by Henry Binsse. Toronto: McClelland and Stewart, 1955.
– *Enchantment and Sorrow: The Autobiography of Gabrielle Roy*. Translated by P. Claxton. Toronto: Lester and Orpen Dennys, 1987.
– *Rue Deschambault*. Montreal: Éditions Beauchemin, 1955.
– *Street of Riches*. Translated by Henry Binsse. Toronto: McClelland and Stewart, 1957.
– *The Tin Flute*. Translated by Alan Brown. Toronto: McClelland and Stewart, 1980.
– *The Tin Flute*. Translated by Hannah Josephson. New York: Reynal and Hitchcock, 1947.
– *Where Nests the Water Hen*. Translated by Henry Binsse. Toronto: McClelland and Stewart, 1951, 1989.
Rozema, Patricia. *I've Heard the Mermaids Singing*. National Film Board, 1987.
– *Mansfield Park*. BBC Films, 1999.
– *When Night Is Falling*. Alliance Communications Corp., 1995.
Rule, Jane. *The Desert of the Heart*. Toronto: Macmillan, 1964.
– *Taking My Life*. Introduction by Linda Morra. Vancouver: Talonbooks, 2011.
Sainte-Marie, Buffy. *Running for the Drum*. Gypsy Boy Music, 2008.
Sainte-Marie, Buffy, with Tanya Tagaq. *You Got to Run (Spirit of the Wind)*. Blue Art Media, 2017.
Sakamoto, Kerri. *The Electrical Field*. Toronto: Alfred A. Knopf Canada, 1998.
Scott, Gail. *Heroine*. Toronto: Coach House Press, 1987.

Sears, Djanet. *Afrika Solo*. Toronto: Sister Vision, 1990.
– *Afrika, Solo*. Edited by Ric Knowles. Toronto: Playwrights Canada Press, 2011.
– *Harlem Duet*. Toronto: Scirocco Drama, 1997.
Sears, Djanet, ed. *Testifyin': Contemporary African Canadian Drama*. Toronto: Playwrights Canada Press, 2000.
Sheppard, Mary C. *Seven for a Secret*. Toronto: Groundwood / Douglas and McIntyre, 2001.
Shields, Carol. *A Fairly Conventional Woman*. Toronto: Macmillan, 1982.
– *Happenstance*. Toronto: Penguin, 1980.
– *Happenstance: The Wife's Story, The Husband's Story*. New York: Penguin, 1994.
– *Larry's Party*. Toronto: Random House of Canada, 1997.
– "Narrative Hunger and the Overflowing Cupboard." In Eden and Goertz, eds, *Carol Shields, Narrative Hunger, and the Possibilities of Fiction*, 19–36.
– *The Republic of Love*. Toronto: Random House of Canada, 1992.
– *Small Ceremonies*. Toronto: McGraw Hill Ryerson, 1976.
– *The Stone Diaries*. Toronto: Random House of Canada, 1993.
– *Swann: A Literary Mystery*. Toronto: Stoddart, 1987.
– *Unless*. Toronto: Random House of Canada, 2002.
Shraya, Vivek. *Even This Page Is White*. Vancouver: Arsenal Pulp Press, 2016.
Shum, Mina. *Double Happiness*. National Film Board. 1994.
– *Meditation Park*. Mongrel Media, 2017.
Siberry, Jane. *When I Was a Boy*. Reprise Records, 1993.
Simons, Beverley. *Crabdance*. Vancouver: Talonbooks, 1969.
Simpson, Leanne Betasamosake. *f(l)ight*. RPM, 2016.
Smart, Elizabeth. *By Grand Central Station I Sat Down and Wept*. London: Editions Poetry London, 1945.
Smucker, Barbara. *Underground to Canada*. Toronto: Clarke Irwin and Company, 1977.
Solie, Karen. *The Living Option: Selected Poems*. Hexham, Northumberland: Bloodaxe Books, 2013.
– *Modern and Normal*. London, ON: Brick Books, 2005.
– *Pigeon*. Toronto: Anansi, 2009.
– *The Road In Is Not the Same Road Out*. Toronto: Anansi, 2015.
– *The Shooter's Bible*. Toronto: Junction Books, 2004.
– *Short Haul Engine*. London, ON: Brick Books, 2001.
Staebler, Edna. *Food That Really Schmecks: Mennonite Country Cooking*. Toronto: Ryerson Press, 1968.
– *Must Write: Edna Staebler's Diaries*. Edited by Christl Verduyn. Waterloo, ON: Wilfrid Laurier University Press, 2005.

Stopkewich, Lynne. *Kissed*. Samuel Goldwyn Company, Orion Pictures, 1996.
Swan, Susan. *The Wives of Bath*. 1993.Toronto: Vintage Canada, 2001.
Tagaq, Tanya. *Retribution*. Six Shooter Records, 2016.
Tamaki, Mariko, and Jillian Tamaki. *Skim*. Toronto: Groundwood, House of Anansi Press, 2010.
– *This One Summer*. Toronto: Groundwood, House of Anansi Press, 2014.
Théoret, France. *Such a Good Education*. Translated by Luise von Flotow. Toronto: Cormorant Books, 2010.
Thien, Madeleine. *Certainty*. Toronto: McClelland and Stewart, 2006.
– *Do Not Say We Have Nothing*. Toronto: Alfred A. Knopf Canada, 2016.
Thomas, Audrey. "Bittersweet and Beauty: A Review of *A Walk Out of the World*." *Canadian Literature* 43 (1970): 92–4.
– *Blown Figures*. Vancouver: Talonbooks, 1974.
– *Intertidal Life*. Toronto: Stoddart, 1984.
– *Isobel Gunn*. Toronto: Viking, The Penguin Group, 1999.
– *Mrs Blood*. Vancouver: Talonbooks, 1970.
– *Real Mothers*. Vancouver: Talonbooks, 1981.
Thompson, Judith. *The Crackwalker*. 1980. Toronto: Playwrights Canada, 1981. Second edition, 2010.
– "Epilepsy & the Snake: Fear in the Creative Process." *Canadian Theatre Review* 89 (1996): 4–7.
– *Late 20th Century Plays 1980–2000*. Toronto: Playwrights Canada, 2003.
– *Lion in the Streets*. Toronto: Playwrights Canada, 1992.
– *Nail Biter: A One-Act Play*. In *Omar Khadr, Oh Canada*, edited by Janice Williamson, 165–73. Montreal: McGill-Queen's University Press, 2012.
– "Offending Your Audience." In Knowles, ed., *The Masks of Judith Thompson*, 50–1.
– *The Other Side of the Dark*. Toronto: Coach House Press, 1989.
– *Perfect Pie*. In *Late 20th Century Plays 1980–2000*, 407–90. Toronto: Playwrights Canada, 2002.
– *Sled*. Toronto: Playwrights Canada, 1997.
– *Such Creatures*. Toronto: Playwrights Canada, 2010.
– *Watching Glory Die*. Toronto: Playwrights Canada, 2017.
– *White Biting Dog*. Toronto: Playwrights Canada, 1984.
Todd, Loretta, *Forgotten Warriors*. National Film Board, 1996.
– *Kainayssini Imamistaisiwa, The People Go On*. National Film Board, 2003.
– *The Learning Path*. National Film Board, 1991.
Toews, Miriam. *A Complicated Kindness*. Toronto: Knopf Canada, 2004.
– *All My Puny Sorrows*, Toronto: Knopf Canada, 2014.
Tostevin, Lola Lemire. *Cartouches*. Vancouver: Talonbooks, 1995.

– *Color of Her Speech*. Toronto: Coach House Press, 1982.
– *Site-Specific Poems*. Toronto: The Mercury Press, 2004.
Truss, Jan. *Jasmin*. New York: Atheneum, 1982.
Twain, Shania. *From This Moment On*. New York: Atria Books, Simon and Schuster, 2011.
– *The Will of a Woman*. Mercury Records, 2008.
Tyson, Sylvia. *River Road and Other Stories*. Independent / Outside Music, 2000.
Urquhart, Jane. *The Stone Carvers*. Toronto: McClelland and Stewart, 2001.
– *The Underpainter*. Toronto: McClelland and Stewart, 1997.
van Herk, Aritha. *A Frozen Tongue*. Sydney: Dangaroo Press, 1992.
– *In Visible Ink: Cryptofrictions*. Edmonton: NeWest Press, 1991.
– *Judith*. Toronto: Seal Books, McClelland and Stewart, 1978.
– *Mavericks: An Incorrigible History of Alberta*. Toronto: Penguin, 2001.
– *No Fixed Address: An Amorous Journey*. Toronto: McClelland and Stewart, 1986.
– *Places Far from Ellesmere*. Red Deer, AB: Red Deer College Press, 1990.
– *Restlessness*. Red Deer, AB: Red Deer College Press, 1998.
– "Second Thoughts: A Nation Reflected in the Tensions of a Small Town." *The Globe and Mail*, 7 September 1991: C 17.
– *Stampede and the Westness of West*. Calgary: Frontenac House, 2016.
– *The Tent Peg*. Calgary: Red Deer Press, 1981.
Waddington, Miriam. *Collected Poems*. Toronto: Oxford University Press, 1986.
– *The Collected Poems of Miriam Waddington. Critical Edition*. Edited by Ruth Panofsky. Ottawa: University of Ottawa Press, 2014.
– *The Glass Trumpet*. Toronto: Oxford University Press, 1966.
– *Green World*. Montreal: First Statement Press, 1945.
– *The Second Silence*. Toronto: Ryerson, 1955.
Wainwright, Martha. *Martha Wainwright*. MapleMusic, Zöe Records, 2005.
Waterton, Betty. *A Salmon for Simon*. Illustrated by Ann Blades. Vancouver: Douglas and McIntrye, 1978.
Watson, Sheila. *Deep Hollow Creek*. 1992. Afterword by Jane Urquhart. Toronto: McClelland and Stewart, 1999.
– *The Double Hook*. 1959. Afterword by F.T. Flahiff. Toronto: McClelland and Stewart, 1989.
– *A Father's Kingdom: The Complete Short Fiction*. Afterword by Glenn Willmott. Toronto: McClelland and Stewart, 2004.
Webb, Phyllis. *The Vision Tree: Selected Poems*. Edited by Sharon Thesen. Vancouver: Talonbooks, 1982.
– *Wilson's Bowl*. Toronto: Coach House Press, 1980.

Welsh, Christine. *Finding Dawn*. National Film Board, 2006.
Wheeler, Anne. *Bye Bye Blues*. Allarcom, True Blue Films, 1989.
– *Great Grandmother*. National Film Board, 1975.
– *Loyalties*. Loyalties Film Productions, Inc., 1986.
– *A War Story*. National Film Board, 1981.
Wieland, Joyce. *The Far Shore*. Far Shore, Inc., 1975.
– *Reason over Passion*. Corrective Films, 1969.
Wilkinson, Anne. *The Collected Poems of Anne Wilkinson and a Prose Memoir*. Edited by A.J.M. Smith. Toronto: Macmillan, 1968.
– *Counterpoint to Sleep*. Montreal: First Statement Press, 1951.
– *The Hangman Ties the Holly*. Toronto: Macmillan, 1955.
– *Heresies: The Complete Poems of Anne Wilkinson 1924–1961*. Edited by Dean J. Irvine. Montreal: Véhicule Press, 2003.
Willis, Jane. *Geneish: An Indian Girlhood*. Toronto: New Press, 1973.
Wilson, Ethel. "A Cat among the Falcons: Reflections on the Writer's Craft." *Canadian Literature* 2 (1959): 10–19.
– *The Equations of Love*. 1952. Afterword by Alice Munro. Toronto: McClelland and Stewart, 1990.
– *Hetty Dorval*. 1947. Afterword by Northrop Frye. Toronto: McClelland and Stewart, 1990.
– *The Innocent Traveller*. 1949. Afterword by P.K. Page. Toronto: McClelland and Stewart, 1990.
– *Love and Salt Water*. 1956. Afterword by Anne Marriott. Toronto: McClelland and Stewart, 1990.
– *Mrs Golightly and Other Stories*. 1961. Afterword by David Stouck. Toronto: McClelland and Stewart, 1990.
– *Swamp Angel*. 1954. Afterword by George Bowering. Toronto: McClelland and Stewart, 1990.
Winter, Kathleen. *Annabel*. New York: Black Cat, 2010.
– *Boundless: Tracing Land and Dream in a New Northwest Passage*. Toronto: House of Anansi, 2014.
– *Lost in September*. Toronto: Alfred A. Knopf Canada, 2017.
Wiseman, Adele. *Crackpot*. 1974. Afterword by Margaret Laurence. Toronto: McClelland and Stewart, 1978, 2008.
– *The Sacrifice*. 1952. Afterword by Anne Michaels. Toronto: McClelland and Stewart, 2001.
Young, Phyllis Brett. *The Torontonians*. 1960. Introduction by Nathalie Cooke and Suzanne Morton. Montreal: McGill-Queen's University Press, 2007.
Zwicky, Jan. *Alkibiades' Love: Essays in Philosophy*. Montreal: McGill-Queen's University Press, 2015.

– *Songs for Relinquishing the Earth.* London, ON: Brick Books, 1998.
– *Wittgenstein Elegies.* Ilderton, ON: Brick Books, 1986.

Secondary Sources

Adam, Julie. "The Implicated Audience: Judith Thompson's Anti-Naturalism in *The Crackwalker, White Biting Dog, I Am Yours* and *Lion in the Streets.*" In Knowles, ed., *Judith Thompson: Critical Perspectives on Canadian Theatre in English*, vol. 3: 41–6.
Afsaruddin, Asma. *Contemporary Issues in Islam.* Edinburgh: Edinburgh University Press, 2015.
– *Islam, the State, and Political Authority: Medieval Issues and Modern Concerns.* London: Palgrave Macmillan, 2011.
Ahmed, Sara. *The Promise of Happiness.* Durham, NC: Duke University Press, 2010.
Anderson. Michèle. "Toward a New Definition of Eroticism: Anne Hébert's *Kamouraska.*" In Pallister, ed., *The Art and Genius of Anne Hébert*, 40–53.
Appleford, Rob. "'Close, very close, a *b'gwus* howls': The Contingency of Execution in Eden Robinson's *Monkey Beach.*" *Canadian Literature* 184 (2005): 85–101.
Armatage, Kay. "Fluidity: Joyce Wieland's Political Cinema." In Austin-Smith and Melnyk, eds, *The Gendered Screen*, 95–112.
Armatage, Kay, Kass Banning, Brenda Longfellow, and Janine Marchessault, eds. *Gendering the Nation: Canadian Women's Cinema.* Toronto: University of Toronto Press, 1999.
Atlantic Monthly. Supplement on Canada. November 1964.
Austin-Smith, Brenda, and George Melnyk, eds. *The Gendered Screen: Canadian Women Filmmakers.* Waterloo, ON: Wilfrid Laurier University Press, 2010.
Backhouse, Constance. *Colour-Coded: A Legal History of Racism in Canada.* Toronto: University of Toronto Press, 1999.
Banning, Kay. "Playing in the Light: Canadianizing Race and Nation." In Armatage et al., eds, *Gendering the Nation*, 293–310.
Barbour, Douglas. "Day Thoughts on Anne Wilkinson's Poetry." In Neuman and Kamboureli, eds, *A Mazing Space: Writing Canadian Women Writing*, 179–90.
Barnett, Claudia. "Judith Thompson's Ghosts." *Canadian Theatre Review* 114 (2003): 33–7.
Bast, Laura. "Modern and Doomed: On Karen Solie's *The Road In Is Not the Same Road Out.*" *Maisonneuve*. n.p. 1 May 2015. Web. 25 July 2016.

Beard, William, and Jerry White, eds. *North of Everything: English-Canadian Cinema since 1980*. Edmonton: University of Alberta Press, 2002.

Beecroft, Alexander. *An Ecology of World Literature from Antiquity to the Present Day*. London: Verso, 2015.

Belliveau, George. "Investigating British Columbia's Past: *The Komagata Maru Incident* and *The Hope Slide* as Historiographic Metadrama." *B.C. Studies* 137 (Spring 2003): 93–106.

Bemrose, John. "Margaret's Museum." Review of *The Blind Assassin*. *Maclean's*, 11 Sept 2000: 54–6.

Bentley, David M.R. *The Gay]Grey Moose: Essays on the Ecologies and Mythologies of Canadian Poetry, 1690–1990*. Ottawa: University of Ottawa Press, 1992.

Berger, Thomas R. *Northern Frontier, Northern Homeland: The Report of the Mackenzie Valley Pipeline Inquiry*. Ottawa: Minister of Supply and Services Canada, 1977.

Besner, Neil. *Introducing Alice Munro's* Lives of Girls and Women: *A Reader's Guide*. Toronto: ECW Press, 1990.

Bessai, Diane. "The Regionalism of Canadian Drama." *Canadian Literature* 85 (1980): 7–20.

Bissoondath, Neil. *Selling Illusions: The Cult of Multiculturalism in Canada*. Toronto: Penguin, 1994.

Blake, William. *The Marriage of Heaven and Hell*. Introduction and commentary by Sir Geoffrey Keynes. London: Oxford University Press, 1975.

Blodgett, E.D. *Five-Part Invention: A History of Literary History in Canada*. Toronto: University of Toronto Press, 2003.

Blumenberg, Hans. *Shipwreck with Spectator: Paradigm of a Metaphor for Existence*. Translated by Steven Rendall. Cambridge, MA: The MIT Press, 1997.

Borduas, Paul-Émile. *Le refus global*. Montreal: Éditions Mithra-Mythe, 1948.

Bothwell, Robert. *The Penguin History of Canada*. Toronto: Penguin Canada, 2006.

Bowering, George, ed. *Sheila Watson and* The Double Hook. Ottawa: The Golden Dog Press, 1985.

– *Stone Country: An Unauthorized History of Canada*. Toronto: Penguin Canada, 2003.

Brandt, Di. "A New Genealogy of Canadian Literary Modernism." In Brandt and Godard, *Wider Boundaries of Daring*, 1–25.

– *Wild Mother Dancing: Maternal Narrative in Canadian Literature*. Winnipeg: University of Manitoba Press, 1993.

Brandt, Di, and Barbara Godard, eds. *Wider Boundaries of Daring: The Modernist Impulse in Canadian Women's Poetry*. Waterloo, ON: Wilfrid Laurier University Press, 2009.

Brown, E.K. "Letters in Canada." *University of Toronto Quarterly* 5 (1935–6): 367.

Brown, Russell Morton. "An Opening." In Schaub, ed., *Reading Writers Reading*, xi–xiii.

Brydon, Diana. "Metamorphoses of a Discipline: Rethinking Canadian Literature within Institutional Contexts." In Kamboureli and Miki, eds, *Trans.Can.Lit*, 1–16.

Buchanan, Fiona. "OECD Education Report: Canada Ranks First for Higher Education but Falls behind for Public Funding." *The National Post*, 25 June 2013, n.p.

Burke, Peter. *Popular Culture in Early Modern Europe*. New York: Harper and Row, 1978.

Buss, Helen M. *Mapping Our Selves: Canadian Women's Autobiography in English*. Montreal: McGill-Queen's University Press, 1993.

Butling, Pauline. "Paradox and Play in the Poetry of Phyllis Webb." In Neuman and Kamboureli, eds, *A Mazing Space*, 191–204.

– "Phyllis Webb as Public Intellectual." In Brandt and Godard, eds, *Wider Boundaries of Daring*, 237–52.

Butling, Pauline, and Susan Rudy. *Writing in Our Time: Canada's Radical Poetries in English (1957–2003)*. Waterloo, ON: Wilfrid Laurier University Press, 2004.

Byatt, A.S. "A.S. Byatt Hails Alice Munro." *The Guardian*, 11 October 2013, n.p. Web. 26 July 2016.

Calder, Alison, and Robert Wardhaugh, eds. *History, Literature, and the Writing of the Canadian Prairies*. Winnipeg: University of Manitoba Press, 2005.

Cameron, Elspeth. "Introduction." *Swiss Sonata*, by Gwethalyn Graham. Toronto: Cormorant, 2005.

– "Midsummer Madness: Marian Engel's *Bear*." *Journal of Canadian Fiction* 21 (1977–8): 83–94.

– "The Wrong Time and the Wrong Place: Gwethalyn Graham, 1913–1965." In Cameron and Dickin, eds, *Great Dames*, 145–64.

Cameron, Elspeth, and Janice Dickin, eds. *Great Dames*. Toronto: University of Toronto Press, 1997.

Carrière, Marie. *Writing in the Feminine in French and English Canada: A Question of Ethics*. Toronto: University of Toronto Press, 2002.

Carrington, Ildiko de Papp. *Controlling the Uncontrollable: The Fiction of Alice Munro*. DeKalb, IL: Northern Illinois University Press, 1989.

Carscallen, James. *The Other Country: Patterns in the Writing of Alice Munro*. Toronto: ECW Press, 1993.
Carstairs, Catherine, and Nancy Janovicek, eds. *Feminist History in Canada: New Essays on Women, Gender, Work, and Nation*. Vancouver: University of British Columbia Press, 2013.
Carstairs, Catherine, and Sydney Kruth. "Disability and Citizenship in the Life and Fiction of Jean Little." *Histoire sociale / Social History* 45.90 (November 2012): 339–59.
Chapman, Rosemary. *Between Languages and Cultures: Colonial and Postcolonial Readings of Gabrielle Roy*. Montreal: McGill-Queen's University Press, 2009.
Chivers, Sally. *From Old Woman to Older Women: Contemporary Culture and Women's Narratives*. Columbus: Ohio State University Press, 2003.
Chung, Kathy K.Y. "Loss and Mourning in Sharon Pollock's *Fair Liberty's Call*." In Coates, ed., *Sharon Pollock: First Woman of Canadian Theatre*, 127–46.
Clarke, Laura. "Karen Solie on Absurdities and Privileges." *The National Post*, 30 October 2015. Web. 25 July 2016.
Clement, Lesley D. "Artistry in Mavis Gallant's 'Green Water, Green Sky.'" *Canadian Literature* 129 (Summer 1991): 57–73.
Clemente, Linda M., and William A. Clemente. *Gabrielle Roy: Creation and Memory*. Toronto: ECW Press, 1997.
Coates, Donna, ed. *Sharon Pollock: First Woman of Canadian Theatre*. Calgary: University of Calgary Press, 2015.
Cohen, Matt. "Notes on Realism in Modern English-Canadian Fiction." *Canadian Literature* 100 (1984): 65–71.
Coldwell, Joan. "Natural Herstory and *Intertidal Life*." *Room of One's Own* 10 (1985/6): 140–9.
Coleman, Daniel, and Smaro Kamboureli, eds. *Retooling the Humanities: The Culture of Research in Canadian Universities*. Edmonton: University of Alberta Press, 2011.
Coleman, Patrick. "Grounds for Comparison: The Geography of Identity in Françoise Loranger and Gwethalyn Graham." *Quebec Studies* 21–2 (1996): 159–76.
Conway, John. "What Is Canada?" In *Atlantic Monthly*, Supplement on Canada, November 1964, 100–5.
Cooke, Nathalie. "Lions, Tigers, and Pussycats: Margaret Atwood (Auto-) Biographically." In Nischik, ed., *Margaret Atwood: Works and Impact*, 15–27.
– *Margaret Atwood: A Biography*. Toronto: ECW Press, 1998.
– *Margaret Atwood: A Critical Companion*. Westport, CT: Greenwood Press, 2004.

Corbett, Mike. "I Dreamed I Saw Hilda Neatby Last Night: *So Little for the Mind* after 50 Years." *McGill Journal of Education* 39.2 (2004): 159–82.

Cox, Ailsa. *Alice Munro*. Horndon, Tavistock, Devon: Northcote House Publishers, 2004.

Dallaire, Roméo, with Brent Beardsley. *Shake Hands with the Devil: The Failure of Humanity in Rwanda*. Toronto: Random House Canada, 2003.

Damrosch, David. *What Is World Literature?* Princeton, NJ: Princeton University Press, 2003.

Davey, Frank. *Canadian Literary Power*. Edmonton: NeWest, 1994.

Davies, Robertson. "Educating for the Future." In *Atlantic Monthly*, Supplement on Canada, November 1964, 140–4.

DeFalco, Amelia, and Lorraine York, eds. *Ethics and Affects in the Fiction of Alice Munro*. Cham, Switzerland: Palgrave Macmillan, 2018.

de Lauretis, Teresa. "Guerilla in the Midst: Women's Cinema in the 80s." *Screen* 31.1 (1990): 6–25.

Del Sorbo, Agata Smoluch. "Feminist Filmmaking and the Cinema of Patricia Rozema." In Austin-Smith and Melnyk, eds, *The Gendered Screen: Canadian Women Filmmakers*, 127–40.

Demers, Patricia. "Location, Dislocation, Relocation: Shooting Back with Cameras." In Cheryl Suzack, Shari M. Huhndorf, Jeanne Perrault, and Jean Barman, eds, *Indigenous Women and Feminism: Politics, Activism, Culture*, 298–314. Vancouver: University of British Columbia Press, 2010.

Demers, Patricia, and Rosalind Kerr. "Introduction." In Patricia Demers and Rosalind Kerr, eds, *Staging Alternative Albertas: Experimental Drama in Edmonton*, iii–iv. Toronto: Playwrights Canada Press, 2002.

Dickinson, Peter. *Screening Gender, Framing Genre: Canadian Literature into Film*. Toronto: University of Toronto Press, 2007.

Djwa, Sandra. *Journey with No Maps: A Life of P.K. Page*. Montreal and Kingston: McGill-Queen's University Press, 2012.

Dolan, Jill. *Utopia in Performance: Finding Hope at the Theatre*. Ann Arbor: University of Michigan Press, 2005.

Dorscht, Susan Rudy. "Blown Figures and Blood: Toward a Feminist / Post-Structuralist Reading of Audrey Thomas' Writing." In Moss, ed., *Future Indicative*, 221–7.

Driver, Elizabeth. *Culinary Landmarks: A Bibliography of Canadian Cookbooks, 1825–1949*. Toronto: University of Toronto Press, 2008.

Duncan, Isla. *Alice Munro's Narrative Art*. New York: Palgrave Macmillan, 2011.

Edemariam, Aida. "The Books That Move Men." *The Guardian*, 6 April 2006: 14.

Eden, Edward, and Dee Goertz, eds. *Carol Shields, Narrative Hunger, and the Possibilities of Fiction*. Toronto: University of Toronto Press, 2003.

Edwards, Justin D. *Gothic Canada: Reading the Spectre of a National Literature*. Edmonton: University of Alberta Press, 2005.

Egoff, Sheila. *The Republic of Childhood: A Critical Guide to Canadian Children's Literature in English*. Toronto: Oxford University Press, 1967.

Egoff, Sheila, and Judith Saltman. *The New Republic of Childhood: A Critical Guide to Canadian Children's Literature in English*. Second edition. Toronto: Oxford University Press, 1990.

Eichhorn, Kate, and Heather Milne, eds. *Prismatic Publics: Innovative Canadian Women's Poetry and Poetics*. Toronto: Coach House Books, 2009.

Elder, Kathryn, ed. *The Films of Joyce Wieland*. Toronto: Toronto International Film Festival Group, 1999.

Ellenwood, Ray. *Egregore: A History of the Montreal Automatist Movement*. Toronto: Exile Editions, 1992.

Farfan, Penny. "Monstrous History: Judith Thompson's *Sled*." *Canadian Theatre Review* 120 (2004): 46–9.

Ferris, Shawna. *Street Sex Work and Canadian Cities: Resisting a Dangerous Order*. Edmonton: University of Alberta Press, 2015.

Findlay, Len M. "Extraordinary Renditions: Translating the Humanities Now." In Coleman and Kamboureli, eds, *Retooling the Humanities*, 41–57.

Flahiff, F.T. *Always Someone to Kill the Doves: A Life of Sheila Watson*. Edmonton: NeWest Press, 2005.

Forsyth, Louise. "Introduction." *The Mobility of Light: The Poetry of Nicole Brossard*. Waterloo, ON: Wilfrid Laurier University Press, 2009.

– *Nicole Brossard: Essays on Her Works*. Toronto: Guernica, 2005.

Freake, Douglas. "The Multiple Self in the Poetry of P.K. Page." *Studies in Canadian Literature* 19 (1994): 94–114.

Friedman, Sharon. "The Gendered Terrain in Contemporary Theatre of War by Women." *Theatre Journal* 62 (2010): 593–610.

Frye, Northrop. *The Bush Garden; Essays on the Canadian Imagination*. Toronto: Anansi, 1971.

– "Conclusion." In Klinck et al., *Literary History of Canada*, second edition, vol. 3: 318–32.

– "Letters in Canada." *University of Toronto Quarterly* (1953): 263.

Fuller, Danielle. *Writing the Everyday: Women's Textual Communities in Atlantic Canada*. Montreal: McGill-Queen's University Press, 2004.

Galway, Elizabeth. *From Nursery Rhymes to Nationhood: Children's Literature and the Construction of Canadian Identity*. New York: Routledge, 2008.

Garcia Zarranz, Libe. *TransCanadian Feminist Fictions: New Cross-Border Ethics*. Montreal: McGill-Queen's University Press, 2017.

Garneau, David. "Imaginary Spaces of Conciliation and Reconciliation: Arts, Curation, and Healing." In Robinson and Martin, eds, *Arts of Engagement*, 21–41.
Gaston, Lise. "How Difficult Could It Be to Stay Here? Karen Solie's *The Road In Is Not the Same Road Out.*" *Arc Poetry Magazine* 79 (Winter 2016): n.p. Web. 28 July 2016.
Gelfant, Blanche. "Ethel Wilson's Absent City: A Personal View of Vancouver." *Canadian Literature* 146 (1995): 9–27.
Gerson, Carole. "The Canon between the Wars: Field-Notes of a Feminist Literary Archaeologist." In Lecker, ed., *Canadian Canons*, 46–56.
– "Sarah Binks and Edna Jaques: Parody, Gender, and the Construction of Literary Value." *Canadian Literature* 134 (Autumn 1992): 62–73.
Gerson, Carole, and Jacques Michon, eds. *History of the Book in Canada*, Volume 3, *1918–1980*. Toronto: University of Toronto Press, 2007.
Gibson, Graeme. *Eleven Canadian Novelists*. Toronto: Anansi, 1973.
Gidney, Catherine. "Feminist Ideals and Everyday Life." In Carstairs and Janovicek, eds, *Feminist History in Canada*, 96–117.
Gilbert, Pamela K. "Sex and the Modern City: English Studies and the Spatial Turn." In Warf and Arias, eds, *The Spatial Turn: Interdisciplinary Perspectives*, 102–21.
Godard, Barbara. *Canadian Literature at the Crossroads of Language and Culture*. Edited by Smaro Kamboureli. Edmonton: NeWest, 2008.
Goertz, Dee. "Treading the Maze of *Larry's Party*." In Eden and Goertz, eds, *Carol Shields, Narrative Hunger, and the Possibilities of Fiction*, 230–54.
Govea, Wenonah Milton. *Nineteenth- and Twentieth-Century Harpists: A Bio-Critical Sourcebook*. Westport, CT: Greenwood Press, 1995.
Grace, Sherrill. "Biography and *the* Archive." In Coates, ed., *Sharon Pollock: First Woman of Canadian Theatre*, 213–35.
– *Canada and the Idea of North*. Montreal: McGill-Queen's University Press, 2002.
– "Going North on Judith Thompson's *Sled*." *Essays in Theatre / ÉtudesThéâtrales* 16 (1998): 153–64.
– *Making Theatre: A Life of Sharon Pollock*. Vancouver: Talonbooks, 2008.
– "Quest for the Peaceable Kingdom: Urban/Rural Codes in Roy, Laurence and Atwood." In Squier, ed., *Women Writers and the City*, 193–209.
Green, Elizabeth, ed. *We Who Can Fly: Essays and Memories in Honour of Adele Wiseman*. Dunvegan, ON: Cormorant, 1997.
Green, Mary Jean. "Léa Pool's *La femme de l'hôtel* and Women's Film in Québec." *Québec Studies* 9 (1989–90): 49–62.
Griffiths, N.E.S. *Penelope's Web: Some Perceptions of Women in European and Canadian Society*. Toronto: Oxford University Press, 1976.

Gunew, Sneja. "Operatic Karaoke and the Pitfalls of Identity Politics." In Verduyn, ed., *Literary Pluralities*, 254–62.
Hammill, Faye. *Literary Culture and Female Authorship in Canada, 1760–2000.* Amsterdam: Rodopi, 2003.
Harris, Richard. *Creeping Conformity: How Canada Became Suburban, 1900–1960.* Toronto: University of Toronto Press, 2004.
Heble, Ajay, Donna Palmateer Pennee, and J.R. (Tim) Struthers, eds. *New Contexts of Canadian Criticism.* Peterborough, ON: Broadview, 1997.
Heller, Deborah. *Daughters and Mothers in Alice Munro's Later Stories.* Seattle, WA: Workwomans Press, 2009.
Hengen, Shannon, and Ashley Thomson. *Margaret Atwood: A Reference Guide 1988–2005.* Lanham, MD: The Scarecrow Press, 2007.
Hesse, M.G. *Gabrielle Roy.* Boston: Twayne, 1984.
Higgins, Charlotte. "A Tale of Two Genders: Men Choose Novels of Alienation, While Women Go for Passion." *The Guardian,* 6 April 2006: 9.
Hill, Colin. "Introduction." *Waste Heritage* by Irene Baird. Ottawa: University of Ottawa Press, 2007.
Hodgkinson, Will. "'They Fuck You Up, Your Mum and Dad.'" *The Guardian,* 18 March 2005: 58.
Hofmann, Michael. "All Fresh Today." Review of *The Living Option: Selected Poems* by Karen Solie. *London Review of Books,* 3 April 2014: 27–8.
Hofsess, John. "Sharon Pollock Off-Broadway: Success as a Subtle Form of Failure." *Books in Canada,* April 1983: 3–4.
Housman, Alfred Edward. *A Shropshire Lad.* London: J. Lane, 1906.
Howells, Coral Ann. *Alice Munro.* Manchester: Manchester University Press, 1998.
– *Contemporary Canadian Women's Fiction: Refiguring Identities.* New York: Palgrave Macmillan, 2003.
– *Margaret Atwood.* Second edition. Houndmills, Basingstoke: Palgrave Macmillan, 2005.
– "Writing by Women." In Kröller and Howells, *The Cambridge Companion to Canadian Literature,* 194–215.
Howells, Coral Ann, ed. *The Cambridge Companion to Margaret Atwood.* Cambridge: Cambridge University Press, 2006.
Howells, Coral Ann, and Eva-Marie Kröller, eds. *The Cambridge History of Canadian Literature.* Cambridge: Cambridge University Press, 2009.
Hoy, Helen. "Alice Munro: Unforgettable, Indigestible Messages." *Journal of Canadian Studies* 26.1 (1991): 5–21.
– *How Should I Read These? Native Women Writers in Canada.* Toronto: University of Toronto Press, 2001.

– "'Nothing but the Truth': Discursive Transparency in Beatrice Culleton." In Suzack, ed., *In Search of April Raintree*, 273–93.
Hudson, Aïda, and Susan-Ann Cooper, eds. *Windows and Words: A Look at Canadian Children's Literature in English*. Ottawa: University of Ottawa Press, 2003.
Hulan, Renée. *Northern Experience and the Myths of Canadian Culture*. Montreal: McGill-Queen's University Press, 2002.
Hunter, Lynette. *Outsider Notes: Feminist Approaches to Nation State Ideology, Writers/Readers, and Publishing*. Vancouver: Talonbooks, 1996.
Hutcheon, Linda. *The Canadian Postmodern: A Study of Contemporary English-Canadian Fiction*. Toronto: Oxford University Press, 1988.
– "The Novel." In New et al., *Literary History of Canada*, vol. 4: 73–96.
– *A Theory of Adaptation*. New York: Routledge, 2006.
Ignatieff, Michael. *True Patriot Love: Four Generations in Search of Canada*. Toronto: Viking Canada, 2009.
Ingersoll, Earl G., ed. *Waltzing Again: New and Selected Conversations with Margaret Atwood*. Princeton, NJ: Ontario Review Press, 2006.
Irvine, Dean. *Editing Modernity: Women and Little-Magazine Cultures in Canada, 1916–1956*. Toronto: University of Toronto Press, 2008.
Irvine, Dean, and Smaro Kamboureli. *Editing as Cultural Practice in Canada*. Waterloo, ON: Wilfrid Laurier University Press, 2016.
Irvine, Dean, Vanessa Lent, and Bart Vautour, eds. *Making Canada New: Editing, Modernism, and New Media*. Toronto: University of Toronto Press, 2017.
Irwin, Nigel. "Cracks in the Stage of Aboriginal Life." *The Nation Magazine* 23.12 (2016): 21–3.
James, Noah. "Close Up: The Queen Bee of Canadian Playwrights." *Miss Chatelaine*, January 1978: 16–17.
Jameson, Fredric. "Then You Are Them." *London Review of Books*, 10 September 2009: 7–8.
Johnston, David, and Tom Jenkins. *Ingenious: How Canadian Innovators Made the World Smarter, Smaller, Kinder, Safer, Healthier, Wealthier, and Happier*. Toronto: Signal, McClelland and Stewart, 2017.
Jones, D.G. *Butterfly on Rock: A Study of Themes and Images in Canadian Literature*. Toronto: University of Toronto Press, 1970.
Jones, Evan. "The Living Option: Selected Poems by Karen Solie—A Review." *The Guardian*, 6 June 2014 (online).
Jones, Raymond E., and Jon C. Stott. *Canadian Children's Books: A Critical Guide to Authors and Illustrators*. Toronto: Oxford University Press, 2000.
Judt, Tony. *Reappraisals: Reflections on the Forgotten Twentieth Century*. London: Penguin Books, 2008.

Justice, Daniel Heath. *Why Indigenous Literatures Matter*. Waterloo, ON: Wilfrid Laurier University Press, 2018.

Kamboureli, Smaro. *Scandalous Bodies: Diasporic Literature in English Canada*. Don Mills, ON: Oxford University Press, 2000.

Kamboureli, Smaro, and Roy Miki, eds. *Trans.Can.Lit: Resituating the Study of Canadian Literature*. Waterloo, ON: Wilfrid Laurier University Press, 2007.

Kareda, Urjo. "Introduction." *The Other Side of the Dark: Four Plays by Judith Thompson*. Toronto: Coach House Press, 1989, 9–13.

Keahey, Deborah. *Making It Home: Place in Canadian Prairie Literature*. Winnipeg: University of Manitoba Press, 1998.

Keith, W.J. "Jay Macpherson's *Welcoming Disaster*: A Reconsideration." *Canadian Poetry* 36 (1995): 32–43.

Kelly, Peggy Lynn, ed. "Introduction." *Shackles* by Madge Macbeth. Ottawa: Tecumseh Press, 2005.

Kerr, Rosalind. "Borderline Crossings in Sharon Pollock's Out-Law Genres: *Blood Relations* and *Doc*." *Theatre Research in Canada* 17.2 (1996): 200–15.

Kertzer, J.M. "Beginnings and Endings: Adele Wiseman's *Crackpot*." *Essays on Canadian Writing* 58 (1996): 15–35.

– *Worrying the Nation: Imagining a National Literature in English Canada*. Toronto: University of Toronto Press, 1998.

King, James. *The Life of Margaret Laurence*. Toronto: Alfred A. Knopf, 1997.

Kingston, Anne. "Macleans Interview: Lynn Johnston." 27 August 2008. www.macleans.ca/canada/national/article.jsp?content=20080827_106252_106252___.

Klinck, Carl F., gen. ed. *Literary History of Canada: Canadian Literature in English*. Second edition. 3 vols. Toronto: University of Toronto Press, 1976.

Knowles, Ric, ed. *Judith Thompson: Critical Perspectives on Canadian Theatre in English, Volume Three*. Toronto: Playwrights Canada, 2005.

– *The Masks of Judith Thompson*. Toronto: Playwrights Canada Press, 2006.

– *The Theatre of Form and the Production of Meaning: Contemporary Canadian Dramaturgies*. Toronto: ECW Press, 1999.

Korinek, Valerie. *Roughing It in the Suburbs: Reading Chatelaine Magazine in the Fifties and Sixties*. Toronto: University of Toronto Press, 2000.

Kramer, Lawrence. *Music and Poetry: The Nineteenth Century and After*. Berkeley: University of California Press, 1984.

Kroetsch, Robert. "Circle the Wagons, Girls, Here the Bastards Come." In Verduyn, ed., *Aritha van Herk: Essays on Her Works*, 60–72.

Kröller, Eva-Marie, and Carol Howells, eds. *The Cambridge Companion to Canadian Literature*. Cambridge: Cambridge University Press, 2004.

Lai, Larissa. *Slanting I, Imagining We: Asian Canadian Literary Production in the 1980s and 1990s*. Waterloo, ON: Wilfrid Laurier University Press, 2014.
Lane, Anthony. "Warring Fictions." *The New Yorker*, 26 June 1995: 60–6.
Leach, Jim. *Film in Canada*. Second edition. Toronto: Oxford University Press, 2011.
Lecker, Robert, ed. *Canadian Canons: Essays in Literary Value*. Toronto: University of Toronto Press, 1991.
– *Making It Real: The Canonization of English-Canadian Literature*. Toronto: Anansi, 1995.
– "Where Is Here Now?" *Essays on Canadian Writing* 71–2 (2000): 6–13.
Lejeune, Philippe. *Le pacte autobiographique*. Paris: Seuil, 1975.
Lellis, George. "*La raison avant la passion*." In Elder, ed., *The Films of Joyce Wieland*, 56–63.
LePan, Douglas. "The Dilemma of the Canadian Author." In *Atlantic Monthly*, Supplement on Canada, November 1964, 160–3.
Létourneau, Jocelyn. "S'il te plaît, dessine-moi une passé! La forme de l'expérience historique canadienne." Delivered at the Royal Society of Canada symposium, "Rethinking Identities in Contemporary Canada / Repenser les identités dans le Canada contemporain," at Carleton University, 27 May 2009.
Levene, Mark. "Alice Munro's *The Progress of Love*: Free (and) Radical." In May, ed., *Critical Insights*, 143–59.
Levin, Laura. "Environmental Affinities: Naturalism and the Porous Body." *Theatre Research in Canada* 24.1–2 (2003): 171–86.
Levitin, Jacqueline, Judith Plessis, and Valerie Raoul, eds. *Women Filmmakers: Refocusing*. Vancouver: University of British Columbia Press, 2003.
Linteau, Paul-André, René Durocher, Jean-Claude Robert, and François Ricard. *Quebec since 1930*. Translated by Robert Chodos and Ellen Garmaise. Toronto: James Lorimer and Company, 1991.
Litt, Paul. *The Muses, the Masses, and the Massey Commission*. Toronto: University of Toronto Press, 1992.
– *Trudeaumania*. Vancouver: University of British Columbia Press, 2016.
Lynch, Gerald. *The One and the Many: English-Canadian Short Story Cycles*. Toronto: University of Toronto Press, 2001.
Lynch, Gerald, and Janice Fiamengo, eds. *Alice Munro's Miraculous Art: Critical Essays*. Ottawa: University of Ottawa Press, 2017.
MacDonald, R.D. "Time in Ethel Wilson's *The Innocent Traveller* and *Swamp Angel*." *Studies in Canadian Literature* 13 (1988): 64–79.
MacDonald, Tanis. *The Daughter's Way: Canadian Women's Paternal Elegies*. Waterloo, ON: Wilfrid Laurier University Press, 2012.

Mack, Marcia. "*The Sacrifice* and *Crackpot*: What a Woman Can Learn by Rewriting a Fairy Tale and Clarifying Its Meaning." *Essays in Canadian Writing* 67–8 (1999): 134–58.
MacKendrick, Louis K., ed. *Probable Fictions: Alice Munro's Narrative Acts*. Toronto: ECW, 1983.
MacLulich, T.D. "Our Place on the Map: The Canadian Tradition in Fiction." *University of Toronto Quarterly* 51 (1982): 191–208.
MacSkimming, Roy. *The Perilous Trade: Book Publishing in Canada 1946–2006*. New updated edition. Toronto: McClelland and Stewart, 2007.
Manole, Diana. "From Seaton Village to Global Village: Metonymies of Exile and Globalization in Judith Thompson's *Sled*." *Theatre Research in Canada* 34 (2013): 74–96.
Marentette, Scott. "'How the Silent Energy Coursed between Us': A Review of Karen Solie's *The Road In Is Not the Same Road Out*." *The Puritan* 30 (Summer 2015): n.p. Web. 25 July 2016.
Markotic, Nicole. "Freedom's Just Another Word / For Nothin' Left to Close: Desire Constructing Desire Constructing in Gail Scott's *Heroine*." In Lianne Moyes, ed., *Gail Scott: Essays on Her Works*, 37–51. Toronto: Guernica, 2002.
Marlatt, Daphne. "Entering In: The Immigrant Imagination." *Canadian Literature* 100 (1984): 219–24.
Marshall, Tom. *Harsh and Lovely Land: The Major Canadian Poets and the Making of a Canadian Tradition*. Vancouver: University of British Columbia Press, 1979.
Massey, Doreen B. *Space, Place, and Gender*. Cambridge: Polity Press, 1994.
May, Charles E., ed. *Critical Insights: Alice Munro*. Ipswich, MA: Salem Press, 2013.
Mazur, Carol, and Cathy Moulder. *Alice Munro: An Annotated Bibliography of Works and Criticism*. Lanham, MD: The Scarecrow Press, 2007.
McCallum, Pamela. "They Cut Him Down: Race, Class, and Cultural Memory in Dorothy Livesay's 'Day and Night.'" In Brandt and Godard, eds, *Wider Boundaries of Daring*, 191–212.
McCarthy, Dermot. "The Woman Out Back: Alice Munro's 'Meneseteung.'" *Studies in Canadian Literature* 19.1 (1994): 1–19.
McGillis, Roderick. *The Nimble Reader: Literary Theory and Children's Literature*. New York: Twayne, 1996.
McLeod, Neal, ed. *Indigenous Poetics in Canada*. Waterloo, ON: Wilfrid Laurier University Press, 2014.
McNeilly, Kevin. "Poetry." In Howells and Kröller, *The Cambridge History of Canadian Literature*, 422–40.

McPherson, Hugo. "Fiction 1940–1960." In Klinck, ed., *The Literary History of Canada*, vol 2, 205–33.
– "The Garden and the Cage: The Achievement of Gabrielle Roy." *Canadian Literature* 1 (1959): 46–57.
Meadowcroft, Barbara. *Gwethalyn Graham: A Liberated Woman in a Conventional Age.* Toronto: Women's Press, 2008.
Metz, Christian. *Film Language: A Semiotics of the Cinema.* Translated by Michael Taylor. Chicago: University of Chicago Press, 1991.
Miller, James R. *Lethal Legacy: Current Native Controversies in Canada.* Toronto: University of Toronto Press, 2004.
Moretti, Franco. *The Way of the World: The Bildungsroman in European Culture.* London: Verso, 1987.
Morisco, Gabriela. "The Charms of an Unorthodox Feminism: An Interview with Adele Wiseman." In Green, ed., *We Who Can Fly*, 125–46.
Morra, Linda M. *Unarrested Archives: Case Studies in Twentieth-Century Canadian Women's Authorship.* Toronto: University of Toronto Press, 2014.
Morris, Marika. "New Federal Policies Affecting Women's Equality: Reality Check." *Canadian Research Institute for the Advancement of Women* 8 (2006): 1–8.
Morriss, Margaret. "The Elements Transcended." In Bowering, ed., *Sheila Watson and* The Double Hook, 83–97.
Moser, Marlene. "Identities of Ambivalence: Judith Thompson's *Perfect Pie.*" *Theatre Research in Canada* 27 (2006): 81–99.
Moses, Daniel David, ed. *The Exile Book of Native Canadian Fiction and Drama.* Holstein, ON: Exile Editions, 2010.
Moss, John. *The Paradox of Meaning: Cultural Poetics and Critical Fictions.* Winnipeg: Turnstone Press, 1999.
Moss, John, ed. *Future Indicative: Literary Theory and Canadian Literature.* Ottawa: University of Ottawa Press, 1987.
Moyes, Lianne, ed. *Gail Scott: Essays on Her Work.* Toronto: Guernica, 2002.
Naficy, Hamid. *An Accented Cinema: Exilic and Diasporic Filmmaking.* Princeton, NJ: Princeton University Press, 2002.
Neatby, Hilda. *So Little for the Mind.* Toronto: Clarke, Irwin, 1953.
Nelles, Henry Vivian. *A Little History of Canada.* Toronto: Oxford University Press, 2004.
Neuman, Shirley. "Life-Writing." In New, ed., *Literary History of Canada: Canadian Literature in English,* second edition, vol. 4: 333–70.
Neuman, Shirley, and Smaro Kamboureli, eds. *A Mazing Space: Writing Canadian Women Writing.* Edmonton: Longspoon Press, 1986.
New, W.H. *A History of Canadian Literature.* Second edition. Montreal: McGill-Queen's University Press, 2003.

New, W.H., gen. ed. *Literary History of Canada: Canadian Literature in English.* Second edition. Vol. 4. Toronto: University of Toronto Press, 1990.

Nichols, Miriam. "Jay Macpherson's Modernism." In Brandt and Godard, eds, *Wider Boundaries of Daring*, 325–46.

Nischik, Reingard M., ed. *Margaret Atwood: Works and Impact.* Rochester, NY: Camden House, 2000.

Nodelman, Perry. *The Pleasures of Children's Literature.* Second edition. New York: Longman, 1996.

Nothof, Anne. "Crossing Borders: Sharon Pollock's Revisitation of Canadian Frontiers." *Modern Drama* 38.4 (1995): 475–87.

Nothof, Anne, ed. *Sharon Pollock: Essays on Her Works.* Toronto: Guernica, 2000.

Nunn, Robert C. "Spatial Metaphor in the Plays of Judith Thompson." In Knowles, ed., *Judith Thompson*, 20–40.

– "Strangers to Ourselves: Judith Thompson's *Sled*." *Canadian Theatre Review* 89 (1996): 29–32.

Orange, John. *P.K. Page and Her Works.* Toronto: ECW Press, 1989.

Ormsby, Eric. "Introduction." *Planet Earth: Poems Selected and New,* by P.K. Page. Erin, ON: The Porcupine's Quill, 2002.

Pallister, Janis L., ed. *The Art and Genius of Anne Hébert: Essays on Her Work.* Madison and Teaneck, NJ: Fairleigh Dickinson University Press, 2001.

Panofsky, Ruth. *The Force of Vocation: The Literary Career of Adele Wiseman.* Winnipeg: University of Manitoba Press, 2006.

– "Success Well-Earned: Adele Wiseman's *The Sacrifice*." *English Studies in Canada* 27 (2001): 333–51.

Panofsky, Ruth, and Kathleen Kellett, eds. *Cultural Mapping and the Digital Sphere: Place and Space.* Edmonton: University of Alberta Press, 2015.

Parpart, Lee. "Feminist Ambiguity in the Film Adaptations of Lynne Stopkewich." In Austin-Smith and Melnyk, eds, *The Gendered Screen*, 43–66.

Parr, Joy. *Labouring Children: British Immigrant Apprentices to Canada, 1869–1924.* Montreal: McGill-Queen's University Press, 1980.

Payette, Lise. *Des femmes d'honneur.* 3 vols. Montreal: Libre Expression, 1997–9.

Pearlman, Mickey, ed. *Canadian Women Writing Fiction.* Jackson, MS: University Press of Mississippi, 1993.

Pelletier, Gérard. "The Trouble with Quebec." *The Atlantic*, 215 (1965): 30.

Pevere, Geoff, and Wyndham Wise. "Mermaids Don't Sing the Blues: The Films of Patricia Rozema." *Take One* special issue (Sept.–Nov. 2004): 3–5.

Pollock, James. "Karen Solie's Triple Vision." *You Are Here: Essays on the Arts of Poetry in Canada*, 85–106. Erin, ON: The Porcupine's Quill, 2012.

Pollock, Zailig. "Introduction." *Kaleidoscope: Selected Poems of P.K. Page*. Erin, ON: The Porcupine's Quill, 2010.

Powers, Lyall. *Alien Heart: The Life and Work of Margaret Laurence*. Winnipeg: University of Manitoba Press, 2003.

Prentice, Alison, et al. *Canadian Women: A History*. Second edition. Toronto: Harcourt Brace and Company, 1996.

Rabinovitz, Lauren. "*The Far Shore:* Feminist Family Melodrama." In Elder, ed., *The Films of Joyce Wieland*, 118–27.

Rackham-Hall, Michèle. "The Visual Arts and the Conflict of Modernist Aesthetics in P.K. Page's 'Ecce Homo' and *The Sun and the Moon*." *Canadian Poetry* 75 (2014): 25–41.

Rasporich, Beverly. *Dance of the Sexes: Art and Gender in the Fiction of Alice Munro*. Edmonton: University of Alberta Press, 1990.

Reaney, James. "The Third Eye: Jay Macpherson's *The Boatman*." *Canadian Literature* 1 (1959): 23–34.

Redekop, Magdalene. *Mothers and Other Clowns: The Stories of Alice Munro*. London: Routledge, 1992.

Report of the Royal Commission on Bilingualism and Biculturalism. 6 vols. Ottawa: Queen's Printer, 1967.

Report of the Royal Commission on National Development in the Arts, Letters and Sciences 1949–1951. Ottawa: Edmond Cloutier, 1951.

Report of the Royal Commission on the Status of Women in Canada. Ottawa: Information Canada, 1970.

Ricard, François. *Gabrielle Roy: A Life*. Translated by Patricia Claxton. Toronto: McClelland and Stewart, 1999.

Richter, Miriam Verena. *Creating the National Mosaic: Multiculturalism in Canadian Children's Literature from 1950 to 1994*. Amsterdam: Rodopi, 2011.

Ricou, Laurence R. "Into My Green World: The Poetry of Miriam Waddington." *Essays on Canadian Writing* 12 (1978): 144–61.

– "Patricia Blondal's Long Poem." In Sproxton, ed., *The Winnipeg Connection*, 291–6.

– "Twin Misunderstandings: The Structure of Patricia Blondal's *A Candle to Light the Sun*." *Canadian Literature* 84 (1980): 58–71.

Rifkind, Candida. *Comrades and Critics: Women, Literature, and the Left in 1930s Canada*. Toronto: University of Toronto Press, 2009.

Rimstead, Roxanne. *Remnants of Nation: On Poverty Narratives by Women*. Toronto: University of Toronto Press, 2001.

- "Working-Class Intruders: Female Domestics in *Kamouraska* and *Alias Grace*." *Canadian Literature* 175 (2002): 44–65.
Roberts, Soraya. "Vivek Shraya Lands Her New Academic Gig with a Whitney Houston Song." *University Affairs*, 5 January 2018 (online).
Robinson, Dylan, and Keavy Martin, eds. *Arts of Engagement: Taking Aesthetic Action in and beyond the Truth and Reconciliation Commission of Canada*. Waterloo, ON: Wilfrid Laurier University Press, 2016.
Roy, Wendy. "Anti-imperialism and Feminism in Margaret Laurence's African Writings." *Canadian Literature* 169 (2001): 33–57.
- "Autobiography as Critical Practice in *The Stone Diaries*." In Eden and Goertz, eds, *Carol Shields, Narrative Hunger, and the Possibilities of Fiction*, 113–46.
- "Visual Arts and the Political World in P.K. Page's *Brazilian Journal*." *Canadian Poetry* 75 (2014): 61–82.
Rudakoff, Judith. "Judith Thompson: Interview." In Knowles, ed., *The Masks of Judith Thompson*, 27–42.
Rudakoff, Judith, and Rita Much, eds. *Fair Play. Twelve Women Speak: Conversations with Canadian Playwrights*. Toronto: Simon and Pierre, 1990.
Ruffo, Armand Garnet, ed. *(Ad)dressing Our Words: Aboriginal Perspectives on Aboriginal Literatures*. Penticton, BC: Theytus Books, 2001.
Russell, Delbert W. *Anne Hébert*. Boston: Twayne, 1983.
Ryga, George. "Preface." *The Collected Plays of Gwen Pharis Ringwood*. Ottawa: Borealis, 1982.
Sacks, Oliver. "Speak, Memory." *The New York Review of Books*, 21 February 2013: 19–21.
Sangster, Joan. "Irene Baird's 'North and South' in *The Climate of Power*." *Journal of the Canadian Historical Association* 23.1 (2012): 283–318.
Saul, John Ralston. *A Fair Country: Telling Truths about Canada*. Toronto: Viking Canada, 2008.
Scharfstein, Ben-Ami. *Art without Borders: A Philosophical Exploration of Art and Humanity*. Chicago: University of Chicago Press, 2009.
Schaub, Danielle, ed. *Reading Writers Reading: Canadian Authors' Reflections*. Edmonton: University of Alberta Press, 2006.
Schine, Cathleen. "Blown Away by Alice Munro." *The New York Review of Books*, 10 January 2013: 24–6.
Schuster, Marilyn R. *Passionate Communities: Reading Lesbian Resistance in Jane Rule's Fiction*. New York: New York University Press, 1999.
Scott, A.O. "Sometimes Attraction Becomes a Slow Dance around the Subject." *New York Times*, 28 June 2012. Movies.nytimes.com/2012/06/29/movies/take-this-waltz-directed-by-sarah-polley.html?
Shannon, Kathleen. "'D' Is for Dilemma." *Horizons* 9 (1995): 24–9.

Sheckels, Theodore F. *The Political in Margaret Atwood's Fiction: The Writing on the Wall of The Tent.* Burlington, VT: Ashgate, 2012.

Shek, Ben-Zion. *Social Realism in the French-Canadian Novel.* Montreal: Harvest House, 1977.

Sibley, Carol Hanson. "The Images of Children as Daydreamers in Marie-Louise Gay's Picture Books." *Children's Literature* 18 (1991): 271–8.

Siemerling, Winfried. *The Black Atlantic Reconsidered: Black Canadian Writing, Cultural History, and the Presence of the Past.* Montreal: McGill-Queen's University Press, 2015.

Silverstone, Catherine. "Shakespeare, Cinema and Queer Adolescents: Unhappy Endings and Heartfelt Conclusions." *Shakespeare* 10.3 (2014): 309–27 (online).

Smart, Patricia. *Les femmes du* Refus global. Montreal: Boréal, 1998.

Smith, David. "Women Are Still a Closed Book to Men: Research Shows Men Mainly Read Works by Other Men." *The Guardian*, 29 May 2005: 6.

Sorfleet, John R. "The Nature of Canadian Children's Literature: A Commentary." In Hudson and Cooper, eds, *Windows and Words*, 219–25.

Sproxton, Birk, ed. *The Winnipeg Connection: Writing Lives at Mid-Century.* Winnipeg: Prairie Fire Press, Inc., 2006.

Squier, Susan Merrill, ed. *Women Writers and the City: Essays in Feminist Literary Criticism.* Knoxville: University of Tennessee Press, 1984.

Staines, David. "Poetry." In Kröller and Howells, eds, *The Cambridge Companion to Canadian Literature*, 135–54.

Starnino, Carmine. *Lazy Bastardism: Essays and Reviews on Contemporary Poetry.* Kentville, NS: Gaspereau Press, 2012.

A Statistical Profile of Artists and Cultural Workers in Canada Based on the 2011 National Household Survey and the Labour Force Survey. Prepared by Kelly Hill. Hamilton, ON: Hill Strategies Research, Inc., 2014.

Steele, Charles, ed. *Taking Stock: The Calgary Conference in the Canadian Novel.* Downsview, ON: ECW Press, 1982.

Stefanelli, Maria Anita. "Queering Spectatorship in Léa Pool's and Judith Thompson's *Lost and Delirious.*" In Dominique Marçais, ed., *Modes and Facets of the American Scene: Studies in Honour of Cristina Giorcelli*, 355–74. Palermo: Ila Palma, 2014.

Steinsky-Schwartz, Georgina, et al. *Equality for Women: Beyond the Illusion.* Ottawa: Status of Women Canada, 2005.

Stephenson, Jenn. "Kneading You: Performative Meta-Auto/biography in *Perfect Pie.*" *Theatre Research in Canada* 31 (2010): 58–75.

Stock, Brian C. "Why Young Men Leave." In *Atlantic Monthly*, Supplement on Canada, November 1964, 113–14.

Stouck, David. *Ethel Wilson: A Critical Biography*. Toronto: University of Toronto Press, 2003.
Stovel, Nora Foster. *Divining Margaret Laurence: A Study of Her Complete Writings*. Montreal: McGill-Queen's University Press, 2008.
Sturzer, Felicia B. "'It is that damned woman that has ruined me': The Fragmented Feminine in Anne Hébert's *Kamouraska*." In Pallister, ed., *The Art and Genius of Anne Hébert*, 31–9.
Sugars, Cynthia, and Laura Moss, eds. *Canadian Literature in English: Texts and Contexts*. Toronto: Pearson Longman, 2009.
Sullivan, Rosemary. *By Heart. Elizabeth Smart, A Life*. London: Lime Tree, 1991.
– *The Red Shoes: Margaret Atwood Starting Out*. Toronto: HarperCollins, 1998.
– *Shadow Maker: The Life of Gwendolyn MacEwen*. Toronto: HarperCollins, 1995.
Sullivan, Rosemary, ed. *More Stories by Canadian Women*. Toronto: Oxford University Press, 1987.
– *Poetry by Canadian Women*. Toronto: Oxford University Press, 1989.
Suzack, Cheryl. *Indigenous Women's Writing and the Cultural Study of Law*. Toronto: University of Toronto Press, 2017.
Thacker, Robert. *Alice Munro: Writing Her Lives*. 2005. Updated edition. Toronto: McClelland and Stewart, 2011.
– "Quartet: Atwood, Gallant, Munro, Shields." In Howells and Kröller, eds, *The Cambridge History of Canadian Literature*, 355–80.
The 2015 CWILA Count: https://cwila.com/2015-cwila-count-infographic/.
Thompson, Dawn. *Writing a Politics of Perception: Memory, Holography, and Women Writers in Canada*. Toronto: University of Toronto Press, 2000.
Tippett, Maria. *Making Culture: English-Canadian Institutions and the Arts before the Massey Commission*. Toronto: University of Toronto Press, 1990.
Tompkins, Joanne. "Canadian Theatre and Monuments." *Canadian Theatre Review* 115 (2003): 5–11.
Trofimenkoff, Susan Mann. *The Dream of Nation: A Social and Intellectual History of Quebec*. Toronto: Gage, 1983.
Ty, Eleanor. *Asian Canadian Writing beyond Autoethnography*. Waterloo, ON: Wilfrid Laurier University Press, 2008.
– *The Politics of the Visible in Asian North American Narratives*. Toronto: University of Toronto Press, 2004.
– *Unfastened: Globality and Asian North American Narratives*. Minneapolis, MN: University of Minnesota Press, 2010.
Ursel, Jane, et al. *What's Law Got to Do with It? The Law, Specialized Courts and Domestic Violence in Canada*. Toronto: Cormorant Books, 2008.

Vanstone, Gail. *D Is for Daring: The Women behind the Films of Studio D*. Toronto: Sumack Press, 2007.
Verduyn, Christl. *Lifelines: Marian Engel's Writings*. Montreal: McGill-Queen's University Press, 1995.
– "*Murder in the Dark*: Fiction/Theory by Margaret Atwood." *Tessera* 3 (1986): 124–31.
Verduyn, Christl, ed. *Aritha van Herk: Essays on Her Works*. Toronto: Guernica, 2001.
– *Literary Pluralities*. Peterborough, ON: Broadview, 1998.
Visser, Margaret. *The Rituals of Dinner: The Origins, Evolution, Eccentricities, and Meaning of Table Manners*. Toronto: Harper Collins, 1991.
Wachtel, Eleanor. "An Interview with Audrey Thomas." *Room of One's Own* 10 (1985/86): 7–61.
Walker, Craig Stewart. *The Buried Astrolabe: Canadian Dramatic Imagination and Western Tradition*. Montreal: McGill-Queen's University Press, 2001.
Warf, Barney, and Santa Arias, eds. *The Spatial Turn: Interdisciplinary Perspectives*. London: Routledge, 2008.
Wasserman, Jerry. "*Walsh* and the (De-) Construction of Canadian Myth." In Coates, ed., *Sharon Pollock*, 13–28.
Waterston, Elizabeth. "The Nature of Children's Literature: A Commentary." In Hudson and Cooper, eds, *Windows and Words*, 227–32.
Weir, Lorraine. *Jay Macpherson and Her Works*. Toronto: ECW Press, 1989.
Wheeler, Brad. "Joni Mitchell: An Appreciation of Her Classic 'Both Sides, Now.'" *The Globe and Mail*. 15 June 2013. Web 28 February 2017.
White, Jerry. "Alanis Obomsawin, Documentary Form, and the Canadian Nation(s)." In Beard and White, eds, *North of Everything*, 364–75.
Whitfield, Agnes. "Gabrielle Roy as Feminist." *Canadian Literature* 126 (1990): 20–31.
Wiesenthal, Christine, "Taking Pictures with Stephanie Bolster." *Canadian Literature* 166 (2000): 44–60.
Wilson, Ann. "Canadian Grotesque: The Reception of Judith Thompson's Plays in London." *Canadian Theatre Review* 89 (1996): 25–8.
Wilson, Edmund. *O Canada: An American's Notes on Canadian Culture*. New York: Farrar, Straus and Giroux, 1965.
Wilson, Jean. "Introduction: Travelling Lives." *The Dorothy Livesay Issue. A Room of One's Own* 5 (1979): 5–12.
Wilson, Sharon Rose, ed. *Margaret Atwood's Textual Assassinations: Recent Poetry and Fiction*. Columbus, OH: Ohio State University Press, 2003.

"Women Fail to Seduce Male Readers (2000)." *Orange Prize for Fiction Website.* http://www.orangeprize.co.uk/show/feature/orange-faq-research.

Woodcock, George. "Sun, Wind, and Snow: The Poems of Dorothy Livesay." *Room of One's Own* 5 (1979–80): 46–62.

Wunker, Erin. "Timing 'I': An Investigation of the Autofictional 'I' in Gail Scott's *Heroine*." *English Studies in Canada* 33.1–2 (2007): 147–64.

Wyile, Herb. *Speculative Fictions: Contemporary Canadian Novelists and the Writing of History.* Montreal: McGill-Queen's University Press, 2002.

Xiques, Donez. *Margaret Laurence: The Making of a Writer.* Toronto: Dundurn Press, 2005.

York, Lorraine M. "The Habits of Language: Uniform(ity), Transgression and Margaret Atwood." *Canadian Literature* 126 (1990): 6–19.

– *Margaret Atwood and the Labour of Literary Celebrity.* Toronto: University of Toronto Press, 2013.

Young, Claire. *What's Sex Got to Do with It? Tax and the Family.* Ottawa: Law Commission of Canada, 2000.

Zichy, Francis. "The Lurianic Background: Myths of Fragmentation and Wholeness in Adele Wiseman's *Crackpot*." *Essays on Canadian Writing* 50 (1993): 264–79.

Zimmerman, Cynthia. "A Conversation with Judith Thompson." In Knowles, ed., *The Masks of Judith Thompson*, 14–22.

Zwicker, Heather. "The Limits of Sisterhood." In Suzack, ed., *In Search of April Raintree*, 323–37

Credits

Acknowledgments are due to the following publishers and individuals who have kindly granted permission for the inclusion of material in this book:
Bruce Peel Special Collections Library, University of Alberta, for all excerpts from the poetry of Dorothy Livesay, Dorothy J. Livesay Fonds;
Marilyn Dumont, for excerpts from *That Tongued Belonging, Green Girl Dreams Mountains,* and *The Pemmican Eaters*;
Éditions du Seuil, for Anne Hébert's "Mystère de la parole" from *Poèmes*;
House of Anansi, for the excerpt from Erin Moure's "Eleventh *Impermeable* of the Carthage of Harms," *O Cidadán*;
NeWest Press and the Lowther family, for the excerpt from Pat Lowther's "In Praise of Youth," *The Collected Works of Pat Lowther*, edited by Christine Wiesenthal;
Penguin Random House Canada, for the epigraph taken from Ethel Wilson's *Hetty Dorval* and for the excerpt from Dionne Brand's *Land to Light On*;
The Porcupine's Quill, for excerpts from Margaret Avison's "Four Words" and "On a Maundy Thursday Walk" from *Concrete and Wild Carrot*; and for the excerpt from P.K. Page's *Kaleidoscope*;
University of Ottawa Press, for excerpts from Miriam Waddington, *The Collected Poetry of Miriam Waddington*, edited by Ruth Panofsky.

Index

abandonment, 59, 117, 204, 229, 263
abortion: in fiction, 80, 90
abuse, 102, 105, 110–11, 117, 129, 208, 210, 244, 247
accented cinema, 128
activism, 15–16, 62, 78, 107, 141, 178, 191, 240, 251
adaptation (film), 49, 99, 128, 131–4
addictions, 110, 201, 240
Afghanistan, 121, 249, 251–4, 263
Afsaruddin, Asma, 279n2
aging, 86, 146, 167
Aglukark, Susan, 180; "Never Be the Same," 180; *Unsung Heroes*, 180
Agócs, Kati, 177
Aitken, Kate, 256; *Kate Aitken's Canadian Cook Book*, 256–7; *Making Your Living Is Fun*, 256; *Never a Day So Bright*, 256
Alderson, Sue Ann, 233; *Pond Seasons*, 233. *See also* Blades, Ann
alienation, 58, 72, 81, 117, 133, 147, 205, 228. *See also* outsiders
allusions: historical, 175; literary, 62, 115, 152; personal, 68; religious, 60, 168

Alvvays, 183; *Antisocialites*, 183; "Dreams Tonite," 183
Amelia Frances Howard-Gibbon Illustrator's Award, 219
Anderson, Marjorie, 9
Anderson-Dargatz, Gail, 110; *The Cure for Death by Lightning*, 110
Anglican. *See* religion
Annick Press, 219
anti-Semitism, 15, 34, 38
Appleford, Rob, 101
Aquash, Annie Mae Pictou, 213–14
Arbour, Madeleine, 20
Archer, Violet, 152, 177
Arden, Jann, 182; "Insensitive," 182; *Living under June*, 182; "Not Your Little Girl," 182; *These Are the Days*, 182
Arias, Santa, 12
Armatage, Kay, 124, 126; *Gendering the Nation*, 125
Armstrong, Jeanette, 164
Armstrong, Sally: *Ascent of Women*, 249, 251–2; *Veiled Threat*, 249, 251
Arnott, Joanne, 164
arranged marriage, 116, 128, 129

As It Happens (radio program), 245, 253
assimilation, 5, 6, 19, 103. *See also* residential schools
Atlantic Monthly: writing prize, 15; Supplement on Canada (1964), 27
Atwood, Margaret, 62, 78–89, 219, 262; *Alias Grace* (2017 television series), 85, 133; awards and prizes, 78, 84; biographical study of, 10; friendship with Gwendolyn MacEwen, 155–8; *The Handmaid's Tale* (1990 film), 83; *The Handmaid's Tale* (2003 opera), 83; *The Handmaid's Tale* (2017 television series), 83; Margaret Atwood Society, 78; motivation, 79; non-fiction, 9, 87–8; on Alice Munro, 68, 70, 71, 77, 78; on the north, 88; style, 78–9
Atwood, Margaret, works of: *Alias Grace*, 79, 84–5, 97, 114; *The Blind Assassin*, 84, 85; *The CanLit Foodbook*, 88; *Cat's Eye*, 81; *The Circle Game*, 157; *The Door*, 157; *Edible Woman*, 62, 79–81; *Good Bones*, 85–7; *The Handmaid's Tale*, 83–4, 96; *The Journals of Susanna Moodie*, 79, 157; *Lady Oracle*, 81; "Let Us Now Praise Stupid Women," 87; *Life before Man*, 81; "Linoleum Caves" (Clarendon Lecture), 87; *MaddAddam*, 83, 84; *Murder in the Dark*, 85, 86; *Negotiating with the Dead* (Empson Lectures), 79; *Oryx and Crake*, 83, 84; "Owl and Pussycat, Some Years Later," 157; *Payback* (Massey Lectures), 88; *The Penelopiad*, 87; *Procedures for Underground*, 88; *The Robber Bride*, 82–3; *Surfacing*, 80–1; *The Tent*, 85–6; *The Year of the Flood*, 83–4

autobiographical writing (fictionalized), 54; drama, 197–8, 209, 213; fiction, 64, 66, 100, 108, 237; film, 129
autobiography, 62, 139, 236–48. *See also* life writing
Avison, Margaret, 138, 151, 153; "A Child: Marginalia on an Epigraph," 154; *Concrete and Wild Carrot*, 154; *The Dumbfounding*, 154; "First," 154; "Jael's Part," 154; "On a Maundy Thursday Walk," 154; *Winter Sun*, 153; "Words," 154
Ayalik, Tiffany, 181

Baird, Irene, 33, 35, 36, 262; *Waste Heritage*, 15, 35; *The Climate of Power*, 36
Baker, Marie Annharte, 164
Bambrick, Winifred, 33, 40, 262; *(Keller's) Continental Revue*, 15, 40–1
Banff Centre, 135, 192; Writing Studio, 172
Banff School of Fine Arts, 16
Barber, Jill, 184; "Tell Me," 184; *Mischievous Moon*, 184
Barber, Lesley, 177; *Manchester by the Sea* (movie score), 177; *Mansfield Park* (movie score), 177
Barnardo children, 223–4
Barnett, Claudia: *Judith Thompson's Ghosts*, 205
Basran, Gurjinder, 115, 116, 123; *Everything Was Good-bye*, 116; *Someone You Love Is Gone*, 116
Bayard Bird, Florence, 17
BBC Radio, 40
Beecroft, Alexander, 5

Bellow, Saul, 180
Benoit, Jehane, 256, 257; *Madame Benoit's Library of Canadian Cooking*, 257–8
Bentley, David, 9
Beresford-Howe, Constance, 15; *The Unreasoning Heart*, 33; *The Invisible Gate*, 33
Berger, Thomas, 23
Berger Report. See *Northern Frontier, Northern Homeland*
Bessai, Diane, 186
Bethany House, 98
Bidwell, Norma, 255; *The Best of Stoveline*, 255; *Lifelines and Deadlines*, 255; *The Norma Bidwell Cookbook*, 255
Bildungsroman, 70, 110
Bishop, Elizabeth: "Sandpiper," 151
Bissoondath, Neil, 18
Blades, Ann, 232; *Mary of Mile 18*, 232; *Pond Seasons*, 233; *A Salmon for Simon* (illustrator), 232. See also Waterton, Betty
Blais, Marie-Claire: *La belle bête*, 14, 57, 58; *Mad Shadows*, 57, 58; and reading, 7–8; *Une saison dans la vie d'Emmanuel*, 59; *A Season in the Life of Emmanuel*, 59
Blake, William, 61
Blatchford, Christie, 252; *Fifteen Days: Stories of Bravery, Friendship, Life and Death from inside the New Canadian Army*, 252; *Helpless*, 249, 252
Blodgett, E.D., 28, 67
Blondal, Patricia, 60, 61, 262; *A Candle to Light the Sun*, 57, 60, 61–2; *From Heaven with a Shout*, 61
body: imagery of, 86, 90, 118, 132, 167–8, 211

Bolster, Stephanie, 166, 171, 263; *A Page from the Wonders of Life on Earth*, 171, 263; *Two Bowls of Milk*, 171; *White Stone: The Alice Poems*, 171
Bolt, Carol, 192; *Buffalo Jump*, 193; *One Night Stand*, 193; *Red Emma, Queen of the Anarchists*, 193; on Sharon Pollock, 192–3
Borduas, Paul-Émile, 20
Bouchard, Gérard, 26
Brand, Dionne, 107, 162, 264; *At the Full and Change of the Moon*, 107; *Land to Light On*, 163; *Ossuaries*, 162
Brandt, Di, 139, 142, 160; *Wild Mother Dancing*, 160
Brewster, Elizabeth, 151–3; "To the Male Muse," 153
Bringhurst, Robert, 177
British Columbia Lieutenant Governor's Award for Literary Excellence, 225
Brossard, Nicole, 108, 158, 161, 262; *Après les mots*, 161; *Aube à la saison*, 161; *La Barre du Jour*, 161; *Le désert mauve*, 108; *Mauve Desert*, 108; *Mécanique jongleuse*, suivi de *masculin grammaticale*, 161; *La Nouvelle Barre du Jour*, 108; on reading, 7
Brown, E.K., 140
Brown, Susan, x
Brun, Monica, 255; *Cooking with Mona: The Original Woodward's Cookbook*, 255–6
Brydon, Diana, 99
Bunyan, John, 62, 154; *Pilgrim's Progress*, 62

Buss, Helen, 236, 243; *Memoirs from Away: A New Found Land Girlhood*, 243
Butler, Edith, 178, 179, 182; *Asteur qu'on est là*, 179; *Chansons d'Acadie*, 179; *Un million de fois je t'aime*, 179; *De Paquetville à Paris*, 179
Butling, Pauline, 9, 158
Byatt, A.S.: on Alice Munro, 76

Calder, Alison, 9
Cambridge Companion to Canadian Literature, The (Kröller), 9
Cameron, Elspeth, 92
Campbell, Kim, 246; *Time and Chance: The Political Memoirs of Canada's First Woman Prime Minister*, 246
Campbell, Maria, 98, 219, 240; *Halfbreed*, 240
campus novel, 92, 119
Canada Act (1982), 18
Canada Council Children's Literature Prize, 219, 223
Canada Council for the Arts, 16
Canada Council for the Encouragement of the Arts, Letters, Humanities, and Social Sciences, 14
Canada Council Molson Prize, 65
Canadian Association of Children's Librarians, 232
Canadian Authors Association, 34, 35, 192
Canadian Broadcasting Corporation (CBC), 19, 247, 252; CBC Radio, 158, 187, 245, 256
Canadian Children's Literature, 220. See also *Jeunesse: Young People, Texts, Culture*

Canadian Literature in English: Texts and Contexts (Sugars and Moss), 5
Canadian National Exhibition (CNE), 255, 256
Canadian Opera Company, 193
Canadian Poetry, 150
Canadian Theatre Today conference, 191
Canadian Women: A History (Prentice), 10
Canadian Women in the Literary Arts (CWILA), 8
Canadian Writing Research Collaboratory (CWRC), x, 264
Cape, Judith, 147, 148. See also Page, P.K.
Carol Bolt Award, 192
Carrière, Marie, 168
Carscallen, James, 67
Carson, Anne, 166, 169; *Autobiography of Red: A Novel in Verse*, 169; *Decreation: Poetry, Essays, Opera*, 169; *Men in the Off Hours*, 169; *Nox*, 170
Carstairs, Catherine, 222
Catholic Church in Quebec, 22
Catholicism. See religion
Catullus, 170
Chalmer's Award, 215
Charles Scribner (publisher), 36
Charter of Rights and Freedoms, 18
Chateaugai, Quebec. See Oka crisis
Chatelaine, 61, 168, 251, 258
Chatterton, Anna, 215, 217, 264; *Quiver*, 217; *Within the Glass*, 215, 217–18
Cheechoo, Shirley, 209, 213–14; *Path with No Moccasins*, 213
Chile, 29
Chivers, Sally, 9

Chong, Denise, 242; *The Concubine's Children*, 242
Chowdry, Ranjit, 128
Chung, Kathy, 199
City of Vancouver Book Award, 242
Clark, Sally, 200; *The Trial of Judith K.*, 200, 201
Clarke, Margaret. *See* Buss, Helen
Clarkson, Adrienne, 245; *Heart Matters*, 245, 247
Cleaver, Elizabeth, 232; *The Wind Has Wings: Poems from Canada* (illustrator), 232
Clements, Marie, 209, 213, 214, 263; *Burning Vision*, 263; *Tombs of the Vanishing Indian*, 263; *The Unnatural and Accidental Women*, 214
Coady, Lynn, 110; *The Antagonist*, 111; *Hellgoing*, 111; *Strange Heaven*, 111; "Take This and Eat It," 111
Coleridge, Samuel Taylor, 29
colonialism, 5, 136, 198, 257,
comics, 259–60
composers, 177
Constitution Act (1982), 23
Consultation Commission on Accommodation Practices Related to Cultural Differences, 26
Contemporary Poets series, 141
Contemporary Verse, 142
Conway, Jill Ker, 244; *The Road from Coorain*, 244; *True North*, 244; *When Memory Speaks: Reflections on Autobiography*, 244; *A Woman's Education: The Road from Coorain Leads to Smith College*, 244
Conway, John, 27

Cook, Lyn, 220–1; *The Bells on Finland Street*, 220; *The Little Magic Fiddler*, 221
Cook, Sharon, 9
cookbooks, 254–9
Cooke, Nathalie, 89
Coulthard, Jean, 177
Coyote, Ivan, 245, 248; *One in Every Crowd*, 248; *Tomboy Survival Guide*, 245, 248
Crate, Joan, 110, 113; *Black Apple*, 113–14
Crawley, Alan, 142
Cree: culture, 136, 164, 207, 241; language, 12, 164–5, 240, 241
Cross, James, 22
Crozier, Lorna, 166; *Inventing the Hawk*, 166; "The New Poem," 166–7; *What the Soul Doesn't Want*, 167
cultural evolution, 3, 18, 261
cultural identity, ix, 12, 26, 97
Curie, Marie, 166, 170

Dahab, Elizabeth, 9
Daley, Eleanor, 177
Dallaire, Roméo, 25; *Shake Hands with the Devil*, 25
Damm, Katerii Akiwenzie, 164
Damrosch, David, 4–5
Danielson, Janet, 177
Davey, Frank, 9
Davies, Robertson, 27
DeFalco, Amelia, 67
Deitch, Donna, 62
de la Roche, Mazo: *Jalna*, 15; Whiteoaks saga, 32
Del Jordan (character in Munro's *Lives of Girls and Women*), 68–9

demographics: changing patterns, xi, 11–12, 22, 261
Deneau Publishers, 40
de Papp Carrington, Ildiko, 77
Department of Indian Affairs and Northern Development, 36
Depression era, 34, 49, 61, 116, 118, 142, 223
Dickinson, Peter, 131–2
discrimination, 18, 103, 194. *See also* racism
Djwa, Sandra, 147, 148
documentaries, 134–7
Doiron, Julie, 182; *I Can Wonder What You Did with Your Day*, 182
Dolan, Jill, 215
domesticity, x, 11, 87–97, 104. *See also* marriage and family
Dominion Drama Festival, 187
Donald Windham-Sandy M. Campbell Literary Prize, 216
Donne, John, 45
Dorothy Livesay Poetry Prize, 172
Doucet, Julie, 259–60; *365 Days*, 260; *Dirty Plotte*, 260; *My Most Secret Desire*, 260
Downie, Mary Alice, 231
Drawn and Quarterly publishers, 259
Driver, Elizabeth: *Culinary Landmarks: A Bibliography of Canadian Cookbooks, 1825–1949*, 255
du Maurier National Playwriting Competition, 210
Dumont, Marilyn, 98, 162, 163, 164, 264; *Green Girl Dreams Mountains*, 165; *The Pemmican Eaters*, 165; *A Really Good Brown Girl*, 164–5; *That Tongued Belonging*, 165

Duncan, Isla, 68
Dunham, Mabel, 15; *The Trail of the Conestoga*, 33; *Kristli's Trees*, 33
Dunning, Norma, 241
Duplessis, Maurice (Premier of Quebec), 14, 20–1
dystopian fiction, 83

Eaton, Evelyn, 15, 32–3
Edna Staebler Award for Creative Non-fiction, 242, 249
Edugyan, Esi, 261–2; *Half-Blood Blues*, 262; *The Second Life of Samuel Tyne*, 262
Edwards, Eileen Regina. *See* Twain, Shania
Edwards, Justin D., 4
Egoff, Sheila, 220, 221,
Eichhorn, Kate, 6
Elizabeth Mrazik-Cleaver Canadian Picture Book Award, 219
Ellis, Sarah, 227; *The Baby Project*, 227; *Next-Door Neighbours*, 227; *Out of the Blue*, 227; *Pick-Up Sticks*, 227
Elm Street (magazine), 249
Emblem Books, 152
Enchantment and Sorrow (Roy), 10
Endicott, Marina, 110, 112; *Close to Hugh*, 113; *Good to a Fault*, 112–13
Engel, Marian, 89, 91, 219; *Bear*, 92; biographical study of, 10; *The Glassy Sea*, 92; *The Honeyman Festival*, 92; *Lunatic Villas*, 93; *Sarah's Bastard Notebook*, 92, 119
Equality for Women (Status of Women Canada), 17
Erichsen-Brown, Gwethalyn. *See* Graham, Gwethalyn
Ethel Wilson Fiction Award, 116

Ethics and Affects in the Fiction of Alice Munro (DeFalco and York), 67
ethnicity, 48, 98, 128, 239
Euripides, 188

Faber and Faber, 41
family dynamics, 215–16, 233. *See also* marriage and family
fantasy writing, 228–31
Farfan, Penny, 207
Federation of Women's Clubs, 140
Feist, Leslie, 183; "1, 2, 3, 4," 183; *The Reminder*, 183
feminism: feminist waves, x, 11, 56; feminist fiction, 6; in fiction, 82; in film, 127, 134; post-feminism, 11; women's rights, 17
Ferne, Doris, 142
Ferris, Shawna, 109
Ferron, Marcelle, 20
Fiamengo, Janice, 67
fiction, 31–123; perceptions of, 31
Fiddlehead, 152
Fife, Connie, 9
Fifth House Publishers, 219
filmmakers, xi, 124
filmmaking, 124
Findlay, Len, 5
First Statement (magazine), 141
Fitzhenry and Whiteside (publisher), 221
Flahiff, Fred, 57
folk singers, 178–81
food writing. *See* cookbooks
Ford, Frazey, 183; "Done," 183; *Indian Ocean*, 183
Ford, Richard, 67
Foroughi, Sadaf, 126, 131; *Ava*, 131
Francis, Anne. *See* Bayard Bird, Florence

Franklin Expedition: in fiction, 156–7
Fraser, Sylvia, 244; *My Father's House: A Memoir of Incest and of Healing*, 244
Freake, Douglas, 147
Freeman, Mini Aodla, 241; *Life among the Qallunaat*, 241
French, Alice Masak, 241; *My Name Is Masak*, 241
Friedman, Sharon, 205
Friedrich, Caspar David, 175
Front de Libération du Québec (FLQ), 22
Frum, Barbara, 245, 253; *As It Happened*, 245
Frum, Linda: *Barbara Frum*, 245–6
Frye, Northrop, 138, 140, 154; *The Bush Garden*, 138
Fuller, Danielle, 9

Gale, Lorena, 209, 210, 264; *Angélique*, 210; *Je me souviens*, 210
Gallant, Mavis: on reading, 7; on Anne Hébert, 49; "By the Sea," 50; *Green Water, Green Sky*, 50
Gallus, Maya: *Derby Crazy Love*, 137; *Elizabeth Smart: On the Side of the Angels*, 40, 136–7; *The Mystery of Mazo de la Roche*, 137
Garcia Zarranz, Libe, 6, 9
Garneau, David, 6
Garnett, Angelica, 120
Garry Theatre, 192
Gay, Marie Louise, 234; *Rainy Day Magic* (translated from *Magie d'un jour de pluie*), 234; Stella and Sam series, 234
Gelfant, Blanche, 46
gender, 104, 124, 205, 248, 263

Genie Award, 134
geografictione, 242
Gerson, Carole, 35, 140
Gibb, Camilla, 104, 264; *Sweetness in the Belly*, 106–7, 248; *This Is Happy*, 10, 107, 245, 248
Gidney, Catherine, 11; "Feminist Ideals and Everyday Life," 11
Gilbert, Pamela, 12
Gilman, Phoebe, 233; *Jillian Jiggs*, 233; *Something from Nothing*, 233–4
Glass, Joanna, 200; *Play Memory*, 200, 201
globalization, 4, 7
Globe and Mail, 252
Godard, Barbara, 109
Goertz, Dee, 97
Goldman, Emma, 193
Gordon, Alison: on reading, 7
Goto, Hiromi, 102, 103; *Chorus of Mushrooms*, 103
Governor General's Award, 15, 25, 33, 35, 36, 37, 40, 41, 49, 54, 55, 63, 65, 78, 79, 83, 92, 96, 104, 112, 115, 143, 147, 153, 154, 157, 163, 166, 168, 171, 194, 198, 202, 203, 212, 215, 219, 222, 225, 227, 230, 232, 234, 242; for Children's Literature, 219; for Fiction, 15, 49, 54; for Non-fiction, 253; Literary Award for Juvenile Literature, 219
Gowdy, Barbara, 116, 121, 123, 263; *Little Sister*, 122, 263; *We So Seldom Look on Love*, 121; "We So Seldom Look on Love," 121, 132; *The White Bone*, 121–2
Grace, Sherrill, 9, 194, 207
Graham, Gwethalyn, 15, 33, 36–8, 262; biographical study of, 10; *Earth and High Heaven*, 15, 37–8, 277n2; *Swiss Sonata*, 36–7, 40

Grahame, Kenneth, *The Golden Age*, 46
grande noirceur, 21
Grant, Agnes, 9
graphic novels, 235, 259
Graphic Publishers, 34
Gray, Charlotte, 249; *Canada: A Portrait in Letters, 1800–2000*, 250; *Gold Diggers*, 249; *Mrs King*, 249–50; *The Museum Called Canada: 25 Rooms of Wonder*, 250; *The Promise of Canada: 150 Years – People and Ideas That Have Shaped Our Country*, 28, 250; *Reluctant Genius: The Passionate Life and Inventive Mind of Alexander Graham Bell*, 250; *Sisters in the Wilderness: The Lives of Susanna Moodie and Catharine Parr Traill*, 249, 250
Greek tragedy, 187
Green, Mary Jean, 48
Grey, Deborah, 245, 246; *Never Retreat, Never Explain, Never Apologize: My Life, My Politics*, 245
Gritt, Grey (of Quantum Tangle), 181
Groulx, Lionel (l'Abbé), 21, 22
Groundwood Books, 219
Guèvremont, Germaine, 33; *Le Survenant*, 33; *Marie-Didace*, 33; *The Outlander*, 33
Guilbault, Muriel, 20
Gunew, Sneja, 9

Halfe, Louise, 98, 162, 163, 164, 264; *Bear Bones and Feathers*, 164; *The Crooked Good*, 164
Hamilton, Mary, 223; *The Tin-Lined Trunk*, 223–4
Hamilton Spectator, 255
Hammill, Faye, 9

Hanrahan, Catherine, 109; *Lost Girls and Love Hotels*, 109
Harper, Elijah, 24
Harper, Stephen: and the national apology for residential schools, 19
Hawley, Alix, 114; *All True Not a Lie in It*, 114–15
Hay, Elizabeth: *Late Nights on Air*, 23
Haynes, Elizabeth Sterling, 186
healing circle, 25, 216
Hébert, Anne, 3, 46–9, 123, 262; on reading, 8; *Les chambres de bois*, 47; *Les songes en équilibre*, 15; *Le torrent*, 15, 47; *Kamouraska*, 48; *Les enfants du sabbat*, 49; *Children of the Black Sabbath*, 48; *Héloïse*, 49; *Les fous de bassan*, 49; *Collected Later Novels*, 49; *In the Shadow of the Wind*, 49
Hélier, fils des bois (le Franc), 33
Heller, Deborah, 72
Hémon, Louis, 32
Henderson, Ruth Watson, 177
Henderson the Rain King (Bellow), 180
Henry, Ann, 190, 191; *Lulu Street*, 190, 191
Henry Kreisel Memorial Lecture, 117, 261
Here and Now, 152
historical fiction, 91, 114
historical plays, 195–200, 202, 213–14
Hodgkinson, Will, 184
Hodgson, Heather, 9
Hofmann, Michael, 172
Hofsess, John, 194
Homemakers (magazine), 251
homophobia: in film, 127
homosexuality: in film, 132–3

Honouring the Truth, Reconciling for the Future (Truth and Reconciliation Commission), 19
Horizon (magazine), 40
Hornyansky, Michael, 155
Houghton Mifflin (publisher), 41
Howells, Coral Ann, 9, 98
Hoy, Helen, 9, 67
Hughes, Monica, 224; *My Name Is Paula Popowich!*, 224, 225
Hulan, Renée, 9
Hunter, Aislinn, 114; *The World before Us*, 114
Hunter, Lynette, 9
Hutcheon, Linda, 9, 134

Ideas (CBC Radio program), 159
Ignatieff, Michael, 28
Ignatz Award for Outstanding Graphic Novel, 235
illustrated books, 231–5
immigrants: portrayal of, 220
immigration: into Canada, 11–12; into Quebec, 26
inclusion, 8, 28, 221
independent adventures: in fiction, 89, 92–5, 119
Indian Act (1876), 18, 19
Indigenous and Northern Affairs Canada, 19
Indigenous Arts program, 135
Indigenous culture and language, 163, 180, 193, 230–1, 241. *See also* Cree
Indigenous lands, 23–4, 136, 165, 210, 264. *See also* Oka crisis
Indigenous-White relations, 98, 99, 127, 195–6, 200, 201, 240–1
infertility, 50, 83, 215, 217
infidelity, 34, 57, 64, 71, 76, 101, 129, 130, 132, 184, 259

Iraq war, 205
Irvine, Dean, 7, 10
Irwin, Arthur, 148
Irwin, Grace, 56, 262; *Andrew Connington*, 56; *Connington Saga*, 278n10; *In Little Place*, 56; *Least of All Saints*, 56
Irwin, P.K., 147. *See also* Page, P.K.

J.B. Lippincott (publisher), 37
Jacobs, Jane, 249, 251; *Dark Age Ahead*, 249, 251–2
"Jacques the Woodcutter," 232. *See also* Blades, Ann
Jane Jacobs Lifetime Achievement Award, 251
Jane Jacobs Medal, 251
Japanese internment camps: in fiction, 102–3
Jaques, Edna, 139, 262; "At a Tea," 140; *Drifting Soil*, 140; "In Flanders Now," 139; "Prairie Born," 139; *Uphill All the Way*, 139; *Verses for You*, 140
Jardine, Lisa, 8
Jenkins, Tom, 28
Jeunesse: Young People, Texts, Culture, 220
Joe, Rita, 164
Johnston, David (Governor General of Canada), 28
Johnston, Lynn, 259; *For Better or For Worse*, 259
Jonathan Cape, 36, 38
Jones, Evan, 174
Jones, Raymond, 220
Josephson, Hannah, 277n4
Joudry, Patricia, 190–1; *Teach Me How to Cry*, 190; *A Very Modest Orgy*, 191

Judaism. *See* religion
Judt, Tony, 4
Juno Awards, 177
Justice, Daniel Heath, 6
Jutra, Claude, 48, 131

Kamboureli, Smaro, 9, 10, 27
Kane, Margo, 210; *Confessions of an Indian Cowboy*, 210
Kant, Immanuel, 169
Kashyap, Anurag, 128
Katz, Welwyn Wilson, 230; *False Face*, 230–1
Keahey, Deborah, 9
Keith, W.J., 155
Kellett, Kathleen, 12
Kenney, Mo, 184; *In My Dreams*, 185; "Telephones," 185
Kerr, Rosalind, 194
Kertzer, Jonathan, 9, 28, 55–6
Kids Can Press, 219
King, James, 64
Klein, Bonnie Sherr, 136; *Not a Love Story: A Film about Pornography*, 136; *Shameless: The Art of Disability*, 136
Klein, Naomi, 137; *This Changes Everything*, 137
Knowles, Ric, 209
Knox, Elsie, 33; *By Paddle and Saddle*, 33; *Red River Shadows*, 33
Kogawa, Joy, 102, 219; *Obasan*, 102
Kostash, Myrna, 239; *All of Baba's Children*, 239; *Prodigal Daughter*, 240
Kreviazuk, Chantal, 183; "In This Life," 184; *What if It All Means Something*, 184
Kroetsch, Robert, 93

Kröller, Eva-Marie, 9
Kruth, Sydney, 222
Künstlerroman, 81, 90, 147

l'Action française, 21
Lai, Larissa, 9, 18, 102, 103–4; *Salt Fish Girl*, 104; *When Fox Is a Thousand*, 103–4
LaMarsh, Judy (Julia Verlyn), 246; *Memoirs of a Bird in a Gilded Cage*, 246
land rights, 264. See also Indigenous lands
Lang, K.D., 181; "Constant Craving," 182; *Ingénue*, 182
LaPorte, Pierre, 22
LaRoque, Emma, 164
Lau, Evelyn, 109; *Runaway: The Diary of a Street Kid*, 109
Laurence, Margaret, 60–1, 62, 89, 219; autobiographical fiction, 64; biographical study of, 10; *A Bird in the House*, 54, 64; *Dance on the Earth*, 10, 241–2; *The Diviners*, 65, 96, 189; *The Fire Dwellers*, 64; *A Jest of God*, 63–4, 79; Manawaka novels, 62–5; on Gwen Pharis Ringwood, 186, 187; *This Side Jordan*, 57, 60; *The Stone Angel*, 63–4
Laurendeau-Dunton Bilingualism and Biculturalism Commission. See Royal Commission on Bilingualism and Biculturalism
Lavigne, Avril, 182; *Complicated*, 182; "Let Go," 182
le Franc, Marie, 15, 33; *Hélier, fils des bois*, 33; *Le fils de la forêt*, 33
Lejeune, Philippe: *Le pacte autobiographique*, 236

LePan, Douglas, 27
Lesage, Jean, 22
Létourneau, Jocelyn, 28
Levene, Mark, 68
Levesque, Georges-Henri, 13, 14, 276n9
Levin, Laura, 206
Liberal government (Quebec), 22
life writing, 232, 243–4. See also autobiography
Lightfoot, Terra, 184; "Emerald Eyes," 184; *Every Time My Mind Runs Wild*, 184
Lill, Wendy, 40, 200; *Memories of You*, 40; *The Occupation of Heather Rose*, 200, 201
Lindberg, Tracy, 98, 102; *Birdie*, 102
"Lines Composed a Few Miles above Tintern Abbey" (Wordsworth), 173–4
L'Intégrale, 108
Literary Guild of America, 41
Litt, Paul, 4, 16
Littérature canadienne pour la jeunesse. See *Canadian Children's Literature*
Little, Jean, 221; *Goodbye, My Crutch* (Japanese translation of *Mine for Keeps*), 222; *Mama's Going to Buy You a Mockingbird*, 222; *Mine for Keeps*, 221–2
Littlechild, Wilton (Chief), 19
Livesay, Dorothy, 3, 15, 141–5, 152, 262; Communist party affiliation, 142; *Day and Night*, 16, 143–4; *Green Pitcher*, 142; "The Enchanted Isle: A Dialogue," 141; *Poems for the People*, 16, 143; *Signpost*, 142; *The Unquiet Bed*, 144

Longfellow, Brenda, 134; *Offshore*, 137; *Shadow Maker*, 134; *Weather Report*, 137
Loranger, Françoise: *Mathieu*, 33
loss, 222, 226
Lowther, Pat, 158, 159; *Collected Works*, 159; "Kitchen Murder," 160; "Losing My Head," 160; *Milk Stone*, 159, 160; on Dorothy Livesay, 159; *A Stone Diary*, 159; *This Difficult Flowring*, 159; "To a Woman Who Died of 34 Stab Wounds," 160
Lunn, Janet, 229; *Hollow Tree*, 229, 230; *The Root Cellar*, 229–30
Lynch, Gerald, 9, 67
lyrics as poetry, 178

Macbeth, Madge, 15, 33–4, 262; *Shackles*, 34, 262
MacDonald, Ann-Marie, 104, 105, 202, 264; *Adult Onset*, 106; *Belle Moral (A Natural History)*, 202–3; *Fall on Your Knees*, 105; *Goodnight Desdemona (Good Morning Juliet)*, 202; *The Way the Crow Flies*, 105
Macdonald, John A. (Sir), 165
MacDonald, Tanis, 9
MacEwen, Gwendolyn, 155, 219; biographical study of, 10; *A Breakfast for Barbarians*, 156; documentary, 134; friendship with Margaret Atwood, 155; *Shadow-Maker*, 157; *Terror and Erebus: A Verse Play*, 156–7
MacKendrick, Louis, 67
MacKenzie, Norman, 13
Mackenzie King, Isabel Grace, 249–50
Mackenzie King, William Lyon, 250
Macklem, Michael, 232; "Jacques the Woodcutter," 232. *See also* Blades, Ann
Maclean's (magazine), 251, 258
MacLeod, Alison, 115, 116, 119, 123; *All the Beloved Ghosts*, 119; *The Changeling*, 119; "Sylvia Wears Pink in the Underworld," 120, 167; "The Thaw," 119; *Unexploded*, 119
MacLeod, Joan, 215, 263; *Amigo's Blue Guitar*, 215; *The Valley*, 215, 216, 263
MacMillan, Margaret, 250; *History's People*, 250; *Nixon in China*, 250; *Paris 1919*, 249, 250; *The War That Ended Peace*, 250
Macmillan (publisher), 35, 45
MacPherson, Jay, 151, 153, 154; *The Boatman*, 154–5; *Welcoming Disaster*, 155
magic realism, 119
Making Canada New (Irvine, Lent, and Vautour), 7
Man Booker International Prize for Lifetime Achievement, 65
Man Booker prize, 78, 84
Manji, Irshad, 249, 251; *The Trouble with Islam*, 249, 251
Manley, Rachel, 242–3; *Drumblair: Memories of a Jamaican Childhood*, 242–3
Manole, Diana, 205
Maracle, Lee, 164, 241; *Bobbi Lee: Indian Rebel*, 241
Margaret Atwood Society, 78
marginalization, 98–9, 103–4, 109, 168, 202
Markotic, Nicole, 109

Marlatt, Daphne, 102, 103, 108, 123, 158, 160; *Ana Historic*, 104; *The Given*, 158, 160; *How Hug a Stone*, 160; *Steveston*, 160–1
marriage and family, x, 34–5, 46–53, 59, 63, 89–92, 98, 112, 119, 121, 127, 130, 187, 191, 203, 227
Marriott, Anne, 141, 142
Marshall, Tom, 145
Martin, Catherine, 213; *The Spirit of Annie Mae*, 213–14
Martin, Claire, 54, 62; *Dans un gant de fer*, 54, 79; *In an Iron Glove*, 54, 237; *La joue gauche / The Left Cheek*, 237; *La joue droite / The Right Cheek*, 237
Martin, Keavy, 9, 241
Martin, Stephanie, 177
Massey, Vincent, 13, 14, 276n8. *See also* Massey Commission
Massey Commission, ix, 13–16, 20–1
Massey Lectures, 78, 88
Mathieu (Loranger), 33
Maynard, Fredelle Bruser, 238; *Raisins and Almonds*, 238; *The Tree of Life*, 238
Maynard, Joyce, 239; *At Home in the World*, 239
Mayr, Suzette, 115, 116, 117, 123, 262; *Dr Edith Vane and the Hares of Crawley Hall*, 118–19; *Monoceros*, 118; *Venous Hum*, 118
McCallum, Pamela, 144
McCarthy, Dermot: on Alice Munro, 76
McGarrigle, Kate, and Anna McGarrigle, 178, 179, 180; "Dancer with Bruised Knees," 180; "Heart Like a Wheel," 180; *Kate and Anna McGarrigle*, 180

McGarrigle, Kate: marriage to Loudon Wainwright III, 180, 184
McGillis, Roderick, 220
McLachlan, Sarah, 183–4; *Fumbling towards Ecstasy*, 183–4
McLaren, Floris, 142
McLeod, Neal, 5, 9
McLuhan, Marshall, 57
Meadowcroft, Barbara, 38
Medea, 189
Meech Lake Accord, 23–4
Mehta, Deepa, 126, 128; *Beeba Boys*, 129; *Elements* trilogy (*Fire*; *Earth*; *Water*), 128; *Heaven on Earth*, 128–9; *The Republic of Love*, 128; *Sam & Me*, 128
Meigs, Mary, 108; *Lily Briscoe: A Self-Portrait*, 108; *In the Company of Strangers*, 108
memorybank movies, 65, 96
Mennonite. *See* religion
Metz, Christian, 124
Mezei, Kathy, 109
Michaels, Anne, 166, 170; *Miner's Pond*, 170; on Adele Wiseman, 170; on reading, 7; *Skin Divers*, 170; *Weight of Oranges*, 170
Miki, Roy, 27
Millar, Margaret: *The Iron Gates*, 33
Milne, Heather, 6
Minden, Robert, 160–1
Ministry of Indian and Northern Affairs. *See* Indigenous and Northern Affairs Canada
misogyny, 75–6, 82, 204
missing and murdered Indigenous women and girls, 136, 180
Mistral, Gabriela, 29
Mitchell, Joni, 178, 179, 263; "Both Sides, Now," 179; *Clouds*, 179–80

Mohawks: of Kahnawake, 24–5; of Kahnesatake, 24–5; occupation of Douglas Creek Estates, 252. *See also* Oka crisis
Mojica, Monica, 209, 212; *Princess Pocahontas and the Blue Spots*, 212–13
monoculture, 32
Montreal Automatist Movement, 20
Montreal Standard, 256
Moore, Mary Allen, 255; *The Mary Moore Cookbook*, 255
Moose Jaw Times Herald, 139
Moose Jaw Writer's Club, 140
Mootoo, Shani, 107; *He Drown She in the Sea*, 107–8; *Moving Forward Sideways Like a Crab*, 263
Morawetz, Oscar, 152
Moretti, Franco, 110
Morissette, Alanis, 181; "All I Want," 181–2; *Jagged Little Pill*, 181
Morlock, Jocelyn, 177; *My Name Is Amanda Todd* (movie score), 177
Morra, Linda, 57–8, 62
Moscovitch, Hannah, 215, 216; *East of Berlin*, 216; *Infinity*, 215, 216–17
Mosionier, Beatrice Culleton, 100; *In Search of April Raintree*, 100
Moss, John, 9
Moss, Laura, 5, 9
motherhood, 11, 39, 43–4, 89, 91, 264; and pregnancy, 43, 44, 63, 80, 91, 92, 111, 207, 227
Moure, Erin, 166, 167–8; *Empire, York Street*, 167–8; *Domestic Fuel*, 168; *A Frame of the Book*, 168; *Furious*, 167; *O Cidadán*, 168–9; *Search Procedures*, 168; *Songs for Relinquishing the Earth*, 169
Multiculturalism Act (1988), 18

Munro, Alice, 62, 65–78, 262; awards and prizes, 65; biographical study of, 10; "Baptizing," 74; "The Bear Came over the Mountain," 132, 133; "Boys and Girls," 72; "Chance," 76; "Changes and Ceremonies," 75; *Dance of the Happy Shades*, 68, 72; "Dance of the Happy Shades," 75; "Deep Holes," 72; "Family Furnishings," 71; "Fiction," 71; *Friend of My Youth*, 69; *Hateship, Friendship, Courtship, Loveship, Marriage*, 71, 133; "Lichen," 75–6; *Lives of Girls and Women*, 54, 69, 70, 87; "Lives of Girls and Women," 73, 75; "Material," 70; "Meneseteung," 76–7; "Miles City, Montana," 71; "The Moon in the Orange Street Skating Rink," 73; "The Peace of Utrecht," 68, 69; personal life, 66; "Princess Ida," 69; *The Progress of Love*, 67, 73, 75; *Runaway*, 76; "Silence," 76; *Something I've Been Meaning to Tell You*, 70; "Soon," 76; *Too Much Happiness*, 71, 74; "Too Much Happiness," 76; *The View from Castle Rock*, 66, 69; "Wenlock Edge," 74; *White Dump*, 71; *Who Do You Think You Are?*, 70; studies of, 67
Muslim. *See* religion
mythology: Christian, 154; Greek, 87, 160; Sumerian and Babylonian, 155

Naficy, Hamid, 128
National Book Critics Circle Award, 65

National Film Board (NFB), 17, 108, 126, 127,
National Gallery of Canada, 171
national identity, 4, 16
national imaginary, 240. *See also* national identity
national library: lack of, 14; plans for, 16
National Post, 252
National Research Council, 28
national space, x
National Theatre School, 205, 217
nationhood, 4, 21, 28. *See also* national identity
Neatby, Hilda, 13, 14, 276n10; *So Little for the Mind*, 276n10
Nelles, Vivian, 28
Neuman, Shirley, 236
New, William: *A History of Canadian Literature*, 9
new media, 7
New Republic of Childhood, The (Egoff and Saltman), 231
New Wind Has Wings, The, 232
New York Times Book Review Best Illustrated Children's Book, 235
New York Times bestseller list, 15
New Yorker, 49, 50, 66
Nichol, Barbara, 234; *Biscuits in the Cupboard*, 234; "The Tale of Canadian Jim," 234–5
Nichols, Ruth, 228–9; *The Marrow of the World*, 228, 229; *A Walk Out of the World*, 228–9
Nightwood Theatre, 217
Nobel Prize for Literature, 29, 65–6, 278n14
Nodelman, Perry, 220
Nolan, Yvette, 209, 213; *Annie Mae's Movement*, 213

Northern Frontier, Northern Homeland (Berger), 23
Northern Review: New Writing in Canada, 142
Nothof, Anne, 195, 198
Nunn, Robert, 205, 207

Obamsawin, Alanis, 135, 264; *Hi-Ho Mistahey!*, 136; *Kanehsatake: 270 Years of Resistance*, 136; *Our People Will Be Healed*, 136; *The People of the Kattiwapiskak River*, 136; *Rocks at Whiskey Trench*, 24, 136
October Crisis, 22, 109
Off, Carol, 249, 252, 263; *All We Leave Behind*, 249, 252–3, 263
Official Languages Act (1969), 22
oil and gas industry, 23, 137, 175, 180–1
Oka crisis, 24–5, 136
Oke, Janette, 98; *Drums of Change: The Story of Running Fawn*, 99; *Love Comes Softly*, 98; *When Calls the Heart*, 99
Oliver, Margo, 256
Ondaatje, Michael, 40; *In the Skin of a Lion*, 40; on P.K. Page, 149–50
O'Neill, Heather, 109, 115–16, 123, 124, 263; Kreisel Lecture, 117; *Lonely Hearts Hotel*, 117–18, 263; *Lullabies for Little Criminals*, 109, 117
Orange Prize for Fiction, 8
Order of Canada, 147
Organization for Economic Co-operation and Development (OECD), 26
Ormsby, Eric, 147
outsiders, 56, 57, 58, 133, 235, 239

Pacific Coast Transformation Mask, 28
Page, P.K., 141, 142, 146–51, 152, 219, 263; "After Rain," 148; *As Ten as Twenty*, 149; *Brazilian Journal*, 149–50; *Collected Works*, 147; "Could I Write a Poem Now?," 148; *Cry Ararat*, 150; "The Filled Pen," 149; "Hand Luggage," 149; *The Hidden Room: Collected Poems*, 151; *Hologram*, 151; *Kaleidoscope*, 147; *The Metal and the Flower*, 147; "The Permanent Tourists," 149; "Poor Bird," 150; "The Stenographers," 149; *The Sun and the Moon* (writing as Judith Cape), 147
Panofsky, Ruth, 12
Paperny, Myra, 223; *As Ever, Booky*, 223; *That Scatterbrain Booky*, 223; *The Greenies*, 223; *With Love from Booky*, 223; *The Wooden People*, 223
Paré, Jean, 256; Company's Coming Publishing, 256; *150 Delicious Squares*, 256
parody, 32, 81, 153,
Parr, Joy, 224
Parti Québécois, 23, 43
Pat Lowther prize, 166
patriarchy, xi, 14, 38, 55, 59, 80, 83–5, 92
Payette, Lise, 43; *Des femmes d'honneur*, 10
Pearlman, Mickey, 9
Pearson, Kit, 225; *Awake and Dreaming*, 225, 226; *The Guests of War*, 226; *A Handful of Time*, 225; "Jacques the Woodcutter," 232; *The Sky Is Falling*, 226–7
pedophilia: in fiction, 59, 117; in film, 127; in life writing, 243–4

Pemmican Publications, 219
PEN/Malamud Award, 65
Pentland, Barbara, 152, 177
Perreault, Jeanne, 9
Petrone, Penny, 9
Philip, Marlene Nourbese, 107; *Harriet's Daughter*, 107
philosophy, 169, 172
Pickton, Robert, 136
Pierce, Lorne, 141
Pierre Berton Award, 250
place, 12–13, 125
Plath, Sylvia, 120, 167
Playwright's Co-op. *See* Playwrights Canada Press
Playwright's Unit of Theatre Aquarius, 217
Playwrights Canada Press, 192, 206
Playwrights Guild of Canada, 200, 271; conference, 194
poetic prose, 39
poetics: Indigenous, 5
Polaris Prize, 179, 180
Polley, Sarah, 10, 126, 130, 263, 264; *Alias Grace* (adapted from Margaret Atwood's novel of the same name), 133; *Away from Her* (film adaptation of Alice Munro's "The Bear Came over the Mountain"), 132, 134; *Take This Waltz*, 130; *Stories We Tell*, 10, 245, 248
Pollock, James, 172–3
Pollock, Sharon, 192, 194, 264; biographical study of, 10; historical plays, 195–200
Pollock, Sharon, works of: *Angel's Trumpets*, 199–200; *Blood Relations*, 194, 197–8; *Collected*

Works, 193; *Doc*, 194, 196, 197–8; *Fair Liberty's Call*, 194, 198–9; *The Komagata Maru Incident*, 194, 196; *Moving Pictures*, 199–200; *One Tiger to a Hill*, 196; *Saucy Jack*, 198; *Walsh*, 194, 195–6; *Whiskey Six Cadenza*, 198
Pollock, Zailig, 147
Pool, Léa, 132, 264; *Lost and Delirious* (film adaptation of Susan Swan's *The Wives of Bath*), 132–3
Popular Library (publisher), 40
postmodernity, 12, 29
poverty, 35, 42, 43–4, 237
prairie regionalism, 186
pregnancy. *See* motherhood
Prentice, Alison, 10
Preview (magazine), 141, 149
Prix David, 15, 33
Prix Duvernay, 33
Prix Femina, 15
prohibition, 198
prostitution, 55, 60, 100, 109–10, 128, 240
psychological thriller, 32
publishers. *See individual publisher names*

Quan, Elyne, 211; *Surface Tension*, 211–12
Quantum Tangle, 181; *Shelter as We Go*, 181; "Tiny Hands," 181
Quebec Referendum on Sovereignty: 1980, 25; 1995, 25
Queen's Quarterly, 57
Quiet Revolution, 22, 26, 59, 238
Quin, Tegan, and Sara Quin, 183; *The Business of Art*, 183; "Frozen," 183

race, 4, 107–8, 237
racism, 4, 60, 101, 103, 113, 164, 196, 209, 218, 264
Rak, Julie, 241
Random House (publisher), 35
Reader's Digest, 258
readers, 7
reading, 5, 7–8
realist fiction, 42
Redekop, Magdalene, 67, 75, 77
refus global, Le, 10, 20–1, 276n16, 276–7n17, 277n18
religion, 116, 240; Anglican, 92, 113, 152, 241; Catholic, 92–3, 111, 113, 117, 174, 202, 240; Judaism, 55, 152, 238; Mennonite, 33, 112, 223, 232, 263; Muslim, 106–7, 249, 252
Renaud, Jeanne, 20
Renaud, Thérèse, 20
Report of the Royal Commission on Bilingualism and Biculturalism, 16–17
Report of the Royal Commission on National Development in the Arts, Letters, and Sciences. See Massey Commission
Republic of Childhood, The (Egoff), 222
residential schools, 18, 19, 101, 113, 135, 213, 241
Revolution Tranquille. *See* Quiet Revolution
Richter, Miriam, 221
Riel, Louis, 27, 165
Rifkind, Candida, 36
Riis, Sharon, 127
Rimstead, Roxanne, 48
Ringwood, Gwen Pharis, 16, 186, 262; *Collected Plays*, 187; *Dark Harvest*, 188; *Pasque Flower*, 188; *A Remembrance of Miracles*, 189;

Still Stands the House, 187; *The Stranger*, 189
Riopelle, Françoise, 20
Ritter, Erika, 200; *Automatic Pilot*, 200, 201
Robertson, Barbara, 231
Robinson, Dylan, 9
Robinson, Eden, 98, 101; *Monkey Beach*, 101; *Son of a Trickster*, 101–2
rock music, 181
roman de la terre, 32
romance, 32, 38, 126
Roy, Gabrielle, 33, 41, 42, 51, 59, 262; *Alexandre Chenevert, caissier*, 42, 53, 54; *Bonheur d'occasion*, 15, 41–3; *The Cashier*, 53; *La détresse et l'enchantement*, 10, 42; *Enchantment and Sorrow*, 42; *La petite poule d'eau*, 42, 53; *The Road Past Altamont*, 54; *La route d'Altamont*, 54; *Rue Deschambault*, 42, 54; *Street of Riches*, 53; *The Tin Flute*, 41, 44; *Where Nests the Water Hen*, 52
Royal Commission on Bilingualism and Biculturalism, 22
Royal Commission on the Status of Women, 17, 246
Royal Society of Canada, 277n19
royalties, 38
Rozema, Patricia, 126, 127; *I've Heard the Mermaids Singing*, 127; *Mansfield Park*, 128; *When Night Is Falling*, 127–8
Rudy, Susan, 9
Rule, Jane, 62, 108; *The Desert of the Heart*, 62; *Taking My Life*, 63
Rwandan genocide, 25
Ryerson Press, 141

Saint-Henri (quartier), 10, 15, 42–3, 277n5
Sainte-Marie, Buffy, 178–9; "Bury My Heart at Wounded Knee," 178; *Coincidence and Likely Stories*, 178; "He's an Indian Cowboy in the Rodeo," 178; *Indian Girl*, 178; "No, No Keshagesh," 179; "Now That the Buffalo's Gone," 178; *Native North-American Child: An Odyssey*, 178; *Running for the Drum*, 179; *You Got to Run (Spirit of the Wind)*, 179
Sakomoto, Kerri, 102; *The Electrical Field*, 103
Salinger, J.D., 239
Saltman, Judith, 220, 221
Samuel Johnson Prize, 250
Sangster, Joan, 36
satire, 36, 81, 83, 156
Saturday Night (magazine), 249
Saul, John Ralston, 28
Scholastic (publisher), 221
Scotiabank Giller Prize, 23, 65, 78, 84, 111, 115, 262
Scott, A.O., 131
Scott, Gail, 108–9; *Heroine*, 109
Sears, Djanet, 209; *Afrika, Solo*, 209, 211; *Harlem Duet*, 212; *Testifyin': Contemporary African Canadian Drama*, 211
self-discovery, 225, 230
separation: from family, 91, 223, 226–7, 230
separatism, 23, 25
sesquicentennial, ix, 4, 262
sexual assault: in drama, 205, 210; in fiction, 47, 59, 101, 105, 111, 117; in film, 125; in life writing, 243–4
sexuality, 34, 98, 108–11, 121, 144, 165, 235, 247

Shakespeare, William, 202, 212
Shannon, Kathleen, 17
Sheckels, Theodore, 89
Sheppard, Mary C., 227, 274; *Seven for a Secret*, 227
Shields, Carol, 89, 95; *A Fairly Conventional Woman*, 95; *Happenstance*, 95–6; *Larry's Party*, 97; *The Republic of Love*, 96; *Small Ceremonies*, 95–6; *The Stone Diaries*, 96–7; *Swann*, 96; *Unless*, 97
Shraya, Vivek, 166, 171–2, 263–4; *Even This Page Is White*, 171
Shum, Mina, 126, 263; *Double Happiness*, 129, 211; *Meditation Park*, 129
Siberry, Jane, 181; "Calling All Angels," 181; *When I Was a Boy*, 181
Sidhwa, Bapsi, 128
Simoneau, Yves, 49
Simonovitch Prize, 215
Simons, Beverley, 190, 191; *Crabdance*, 190, 191
Simpson, Leanne Betasamosake, 181, 263; "How to Steal a Canoe," 181; *f(l)ight*, 181
Sinclair, Murray (Justice), 19
singer-songwriters, xi
singer-songwriting, 178–85
Sky Dancer. *See* Halfe, Louise
Smart, Elizabeth, 33, 123; biographical study of, 10; *By Grand Central Station I Sat Down and Wept*, 16, 38–41; *The Assumption of Rogues and Rascals*, 40; writing about, 40
Smart, Patricia, 20
Smith, Ashley, 203

Smucker, Barbara, 223; *Underground to Canada*, 223
social media, ix, 88, 261
social realism (in fiction), 35
Social Sciences and Humanities Research Council: establishment of, 16
Solie, Karen, 172–6, 264; "All That Is Certain Is That Night Lasts Longer Than the Day," 175; "Bitumen," 175; "Cardio Room, Young Women's Christian Association," 173; "Cave Bear," 174; "Lines Composed a Few Miles above Duncairn Dam," 173–4; *The Living Option*, 172; "Medicine Hat Calgary One-Way," 174; *Modern and Normal*, 172, 173–4; "Montana," 173; *The Road In Is Not the Same Road Out*, 172, 174–6; "The Road In Is Not the Same Road Out," 176; "Roof Repair and Squirrel Removal," 175; *Pigeon*, 172, 174; "Prayers for the Sick," 174; *The Shooter's Bible*, 172; *Short Haul Engine*, 172, 173
Sorfleet, John, 220, 223
Southam, Ann, 177
space, 12–13, 125
speculative fiction, 83. *See also* dystopian fiction
Staebler, Edna, 256, 258–9; *Food That Really Schmecks: Mennonite Country Cooking*, 258
Star Weekly, 258
Statistical Profile of Artists and Cultural Workers in Canada, 6
Status of Women Canada, 17
Status of Women Report, 17
Stephenson, Jenn, 208

Stock, Brian, 27
Stopkewich, Lynn, 132, 264; *Kissed* (film adaptation of Barbara Gowdy's "We So Seldom Look on Love"), 132
Stott, Jon, 220
Stouck, David, 45
Stratford Festival, 198
strikes, 14, 21, 35, 190–1, 193
Studio D, 17
Sugars, Cynthia, 5, 9
suicide, 47, 158, 203, 207, 229
Sullivan, Françoise, 20
Sullivan, Rosemary: non-fiction, 9; on Elizabeth Smart, 40; on P.K. Page, 149; on Gwendolyn MacEwen, 156
Surveyor, Arthur, 13
Sutherland, John, 141
Suzack, Cheryl, 6, 9, 100–1
Swan, Susan, 132; *The Wives of Bath*, 132. *See also* Pool, Léa

Taché, Joséphine, 48
Tagaq, Tanya, 179, 180–1, 263; *Animism*, 180; *Retribution*, 180
Tamaki, Jillian, 235; *Skim* (illustrator), 235
Tamaki, Mariko, 235, 264; *Skim*, 235
Tamarack Review, 57, 152
Taylor, Charles, 26
Taylor, Simon Wilson, 21
Telfer, Nancy, 177
Tessera (journal), 108
Têtes de Pioche, Les, 108
Thacker, Robert, 66, 78; *Alice Munro: Writing Her Lives*, 66
Theatre Calgary, 192
Theatre New Brunswick, 192
Theatre Passe Muraille, 193

Théoret, France, 237; *Une belle education*, 237; *Such a Good Education*, 237
Theytus Books, 219
Thien, Madeleine, 114; *Certainty*, 115; *Do Not Say We Have Nothing*, 114, 115
Thomas, Audrey, 89, 229, 262; *Blown Figures*, 89; *Intertidal Life*, 90; *Isobel Gunn*, 91, 114; *Mrs Blood*, 90; *Real Mothers*, 90; "Ted's Wife," 90
Thomas, Dylan, 153; "In June and Gentle Oven," 153
Thomas Allen (publisher), 140
Thompson, Dawn, 9
Thompson, Judith, 167, 202–9, 217; *The Crackwalker*, 203, 204, 205–6 209; *Habitat*, 200; *Late 20th Century Plays*, 206; *Lion in the Streets*, 204; *Nail Biter*, 204; *Perfect Pie*, 167, 204, 207–8; *Sled*, 204, 205, 207; *Such Creatures*, 204; *The Other Side of the Dark*, 206; *Watching Glory Die*, 203; *White Biting Dog*, 204
Tippett, Maria, 16
Todd, Loretta, 135, 264; *Forgotten Warriors*, 135–6; *Kainayssini Imanistaisiwa: The People Go On*, 136; *The Learning Path*, 135
Toews, Miriam, 98, 110, 263; *All My Puny Sorrows*, 263; *A Complicated Kindness*, 112
Toronto Free Theatre, 193
Toronto International Film Festival (TIFF), 131
Toronto Star, 252
Toronto Sun, 252
Tostevin, Lola Lemire, 162; *Cartouches*, 162; *Color of Her*

Speech, 162; *Site-Specific Poems*, 162–3
Total Refusal. See *Le refus global*
TransCanLit, 27
travel writing, 240
Travers, P.L.: *Mary Poppins*, 46
Treaty 6 territory, 19
Tree Frog Press, 219
Trudeau, Pierre Elliott, 135
Truscott, Stephen, 105
Truss, Jan, 224; *Isis Trilogy*, 225; *Jasmin*, 224–5
Truth and Reconciliation Commission: criticism of, 6; artistic responses to, 9; establishment, 19; meaning for Canada, 28; report, 19. See *Honouring the Truth, Reconciling for the Future*
Tundra Books, 219
Twain, Shania: *From This Moment On*, 10, 245, 247–8; "Shoes," 182–3; *The Will of a Woman*, 182
Ty, Eleanor, 9, 211
Tyson, Sylvia, 178, 179; "River Road," 179; *River Road and Other Stories*, 179

Underground Railroad, 223
unemployment: in fiction, 35
United Empire Loyalists, 199, 230
United Nations: Peacekeeping Force in Rwanda, 25
University of Ottawa Press, 35
Urquhart, Jane, 104; *The Stone Carvers*, 105; *The Underpainter*, 104–5

Vallières, Pierre, 22; *Nègres blancs d'Amérique (White Niggers of America)*, 22

Vance, Jonathan, 38
van Herk, Aritha, 89, 93, 241; *Judith*, 93–4; *No Fixed Address*, 93, 94; *Places Far from Ellesmere*, 242; *Restlessness*, 93, 94–5; *The Tent Peg*, 93, 94
Verduyn, Christl, 85, 91
Vintage International, 40
violence: in fiction, 47, 101, 110, 160, 164, 202, 204, 205
Visser, Margaret, 254; *The Rituals of Dinner*, 254
Vollendungsroman, 63

Waddington, Miriam, 141, 145–6; "The Bond," 146; "Erosion," 146; *The Glass Trumpet*, 145; *Green World*, 145–6
Wainwright III, Loudon, 180, 184
Wainwright, Martha, 183, 184; "Bloody Motherfucking Asshole," 184
Walcott, Rinaldo, 261
Walker, Craig, 194, 208
War Measures Act, 22
Wardaugh, Robert, 9
Warf, Barney, 12
Waterson (publisher), 34
Waterston, Elizabeth, 220
Waterton, Betty, 232; *A Salmon for Simon*, 232. See also Blades, Ann
Watkins, Annie, 8
Watson, Sheila; biographical study of, 10; *Deep Hollow Creek*, 57; *The Double Hook*, 57–8; journals, 57
Weaver, Carol Ann, 152
Webb, Phyllis, 158–9; "Lear on the Beach at Break of Day," 158; "Letters to Margaret Atwood," 159; *Wilson's Bowl*, 158

Weekend Magazine, 256
Welsh, Christine, 136; *Finding Dawn*, 136
Wheeler, Anne, 126; *Augusta*, 126; *Better Than Chocolate*, 126; *Bye Bye Blues*, 126; *The Diviners*, 126; *Great Grandmother*, 126; *Living Out Loud*, 126; *Loyalties*, 126; *Mail Order Bride*, 126
White, Jerry, 135
Why Indigenous Literatures Matter (Justice), 6
Wieland, Joyce, 125, 137, 263; *The Far Shore*, 125–6; *Reason over Passion / La raison avant la passion*, 135
Wiesenthal, Christine, 160, 171
Wilkinson, Anne, 151, 219; "Carol," 153; *Counterpoint to Sleep*, 152; "Dirge," 153; "Folk Tale, With a Warning to Lovers," 152; *The Hangman Ties the Holly*, 151, 152–3; "Three Poems about Poets," 151; "The Up and Down of It," 152
Willis, Jane, 241; *Geneish: An Indian Girlhood*, 241
Wilson, Ann, 205
Wilson, Edmund, 26
Wilson, Ethel, 3, 16, 29, 33, 44–6, 51, 58, 262; *The Equations of Love*, 51; *Hetty Dorval*, 44, 45; *The Innocent Traveller*, 44, 45–6; *Love and Salt Water*, 52; *Mrs Golightly and Other Stories*, 52; *Swamp Angel*, 51–2, 58
Wilson, Ethel; biographical study of, 10
Wilson, Marie, 19
Wind Has Wings: Poems from Canada, The, 231
Winter, Kathleen, 116, 120, 123, 263; *Annabel*, 120; *Boundless: Tracing Land and Dream in a New Northwest Passage*, 120–1; *Lost in September*, 263
Wiseman, Adele, 54, 170, 219; *Crackpot*, 54, 55, 146; *The Sacrifice*, 54, 55
Wittgenstein, Ludwig, 169, 172
Women's Press, 219
women's writing: perceptions of, 8; studies of, 9
Woodcock, George, 143–4
Wordsworth, William, 173–4
workforce: women entering the, 11
World War I: in fiction, 117
World War II: in fiction, 117, 226; in film, 127, 136
Wunker, Erin, 108

York, Lorraine, 67; on Margaret Atwood, 88–9
Young, Phyllis Brett: novels, 278n11; *The Torontonians*, 56
young adult (YA) fiction, 228

Zeresenay, Mehari, 106
Zimmerman, Cynthia, 194, 205–6
Zwicker, Heather, 100
Zwicky, Jan, 166, 169, 262–3; *Alkibiades' Love*, 263; *Wittgenstein Elegies*, 169

www.ingramcontent.com/pod-product-compliance
Lightning Source LLC
Chambersburg PA
CBHW031405290426
44110CB00011B/263